Comics as a
Nexus of Cultures

CRITICAL EXPLORATIONS IN SCIENCE FICTION AND FANTASY
(a series edited by Donald E. Palumbo and C.W. Sullivan III)

1. *Worlds Apart? Dualism and Transgression in Contemporary Female Dystopias* (Dunja M. Mohr, 2005)

2. *Tolkien and Shakespeare: Essays on Shared Themes and Language* (ed. Janet Brennan Croft, 2007)

3. *Culture, Identities and Technology in the Star Wars Films: Essays on the Two Trilogies* (ed. Carl Silvio and Tony M. Vinci, 2007)

4. *The Influence of Star Trek on Television, Film and Culture* (ed. Lincoln Geraghty, 2008)

5. *Hugo Gernsback and the Century of Science Fiction* (Gary Westfahl, 2007)

6. *One Earth, One People: The Mythopoeic Fantasy Series of Ursula K. Le Guin, Lloyd Alexander, Madeleine L'Engle and Orson Scott Card* (Marek Oziewicz, 2008)

7. *The Evolution of Tolkien's Mythology: A Study of the History of Middle-earth* (Elizabeth A. Whittingham, 2008)

8. *H. Beam Piper: A Biography* (John F. Carr, 2008)

9. *Dreams and Nightmares: Science and Technology in Myth and Fiction* (Mordecai Roshwald, 2008)

10. *Lilith in a New Light: Essays on the George MacDonald Fantasy Novel* (ed. Lucas H. Harriman, 2008)

11. *Feminist Narrative and the Supernatural: The Function of Fantastic Devices in Seven Recent Novels* (Katherine J. Weese, 2008)

12. *The Science of Fiction and the Fiction of Science: Collected Essays on SF Storytelling and the Gnostic Imagination* (Frank McConnell, ed. Gary Westfahl, 2009)

13. *Kim Stanley Robinson Maps the Unimaginable: Critical Essays* (ed. William J. Burling, 2009)

14. *The Inter-Galactic Playground: A Critical Study of Children's and Teens' Science Fiction* (Farah Mendlesohn, 2009)

15. *Science Fiction from Québec: A Postcolonial Study* (Amy J. Ransom, 2009)

16. *Science Fiction and the Two Cultures: Essays on Bridging the Gap Between the Sciences and the Humanities* (ed. Gary Westfahl and George Slusser, 2009)

17. *Stephen R. Donaldson and the Modern Epic Vision: A Critical Study of the "Chronicles of Thomas Covenant" Novels* (Christine Barkley, 2009)

18. *Ursula K. Le Guin's Journey to Post-Feminism* (Amy M. Clarke, 2010)

19. *Portals of Power: Magical Agency and Transformation in Literary Fantasy* (Lori M. Campbell, 2010)

20. *The Animal Fable in Science Fiction and Fantasy* (Bruce Shaw, 2010)

21. *Illuminating Torchwood: Essays on Narrative, Character and Sexuality in the BBC Series* (ed. Andrew Ireland, 2010)

22. *Comics as a Nexus of Cultures: Essays on the Interplay of Media, Disciplines and International Perspectives* (ed. Mark Berninger, Jochen Ecke and Gideon Haberkorn, 2010)

23. *The Anatomy of Utopia: Narration, Estrangement and Ambiguity in More, Wells, Huxley and Clarke* (Károly Pintér, 2010)

# Comics as a Nexus of Cultures

*Essays on the Interplay of Media, Disciplines and International Perspectives*

*Edited by* MARK BERNINGER, JOCHEN ECKE *and* GIDEON HABERKORN

CRITICAL EXPLORATIONS IN
SCIENCE FICTION AND FANTASY, 22
Donald E. Palumbo *and* C.W. Sullivan III, *series editors*

McFarland & Company, Inc., Publishers
*Jefferson, North Carolina, and London*

LIBRARY OF CONGRESS CATALOGUING-IN-PUBLICATION DATA

Comics as a nexus of cultures : essays on the interplay of media,
 disciplines and international perspectives / edited by Mark Berninger,
Jochen Ecke, and Gideon Haberkorn.
  [Donald Palumbo and C.W. Sullivan III, series editors]
     p.    cm. — (Critical explorations in science fiction
  and fantasy ; 22)
  Includes bibliographical references and index.

  ISBN 978-0-7864-3987-4
  softcover : 50# alkaline paper ∞

  1. Comic books, strips, etc.— History and criticism.
  2. Animated films — History and criticism.   I. Berninger, Mark.
  II. Ecke, Jochen, 1979– .   III. Haberkorn, Gideon, 1976– .
  PN6714.C6515    2010
  741.5'9 — dc22                                              2009051817

  British Library cataloguing data are available

  ©2010 Mark Berninger, Jochen Ecke and Gideon Haberkorn.
  All rights reserved

  *No part of this book may be reproduced or transmitted in any form
  or by any means, electronic or mechanical, including photocopying
  or recording, or by any information storage and retrieval system,
  without permission in writing from the publisher.*

  On the cover: (clockwise from top) superhero (©2010 DigitalVision);
  single frame from *My New York Diary* (©2004, Julie Doucet); superhero turtle (©2010 Verena Reinhardt); manga girl (©2010 ATOMix)

  Manufactured in the United States of America

  *McFarland & Company, Inc., Publishers
   Box 611, Jefferson, North Carolina 28640
   www.mcfarlandpub.com*

# Table of Contents

*Introduction* . . . . . . . . . . . . . . . . . . . . . . . 1

### INTERMEDIAL

1. Spatializing the Movie Screen: How Mainstream Cinema Is Catching Up on the Formal Potentialities of the Comic Book Page . . . . . . . . . . . . . . . . . . . . . . 7
   *Jochen Ecke*
2. The Marvel Universe on Screen: A New Wave of Superhero Movies? . . . . . . . . . . . . . . . . . . . . 21
   *Andreas Rauscher*
3. From Trauma Victim to Terrorist: Redefining Superheroes in Post–9/11 Hollywood . . . . . . . . . . . . . . . . . 33
   *Dan A. Hassler-Forest*
4. "Picture This": Disease and Autobiographic Narration in the Graphic Novels of David B and Julie Doucet . . . . . . . 45
   *Jonas Engelmann*
5. Novel-Based Comics . . . . . . . . . . . . . . . . . . 60
   *Paul Ferstl*
6. In the Art of the Beholder: Comics as Political Journalism . . . 70
   *Dirk Vanderbeke*

### INTERNATIONAL

7. The Carrefour of Practice: Québec BD in Transition . . . . . . 85
   *Michel Hardy-Vallée*
8. The Use of Allusion in Apitz and Kunkel's *Karl* Comics . . . . . 99
   *Sandra Martina Schwab*

9. Cultural Specifics of a Scottish Comic: *Oor Wullie* ...... 108
   *Anne Hoyer*

10. Memento Mori: A Portuguese Style of Melancholy ...... 116
    *Mario Gomes and Jan Peuckert*

11. Otherness and the European as Villain and Antihero
    in American Comics .................... 127
    *Georg Drennig*

12. *2000AD*: Understanding the "British Invasion" of
    American Comics ..................... 140
    *Ben Little*

13. Whatever Happened to All the Heroes? British
    Perspectives on Superheroes ................ 153
    *Karin Kukkonen and Anja Müller-Wood*

14. A Cornerstone of Turkish Fantastic Films:
    From *Flash Gordon* to *Baytekin* ............. 164
    *Meral Özçınar*

15. From Capes to Snakes: The Indianization of the
    American Superhero .................... 175
    *Suchitra Mathur*

16. The Roving Eye Meets Traveling Pictures: The Field
    of Vision and the Global Rise of Adult Manga ...... 187
    *Holger Briel*

17. *Kawaii* vs. *Rorikon*: The Reinvention of the Term *Lolita*
    in Modern Japanese Manga ................ 211
    *Dinah Zank*

18. Mangascape Germany: Comics as Intercultural
    Neutral Ground ...................... 223
    *Paul M. Malone*

### INTERDISCIPLINARY

19. Workshop I: Toward a Toolbox of Comics Studies ...... 237
    *Karin Kukkonen and Gideon Haberkorn*

20. Workshop II: Comics in School ................ 245
    *Mark Berninger*

21. Workshop III: Teaching Comics and Literary Studies —
    Neil Gaiman and Charles Vess' "A Midsummer
    Night's Dream" . . . . . . . . . . . . . . . . . . . . . . 253
    *Mark Berninger*

22. Workshop IV: Teaching Comics and Film Studies —
    Ang Lee's *The Hulk* (USA 2003) . . . . . . . . . . . . . . 265
    *Andreas Rauscher*

23. Comic Linguistics: Comics and Cartoons in
    Academic Teaching . . . . . . . . . . . . . . . . . . . . . 274
    *Christina Sanchez*

*About the Contributors* . . . . . . . . . . . . . . . . . . . . 283
*Index* . . . . . . . . . . . . . . . . . . . . . . . . . . . . 287

# Introduction

Comics are arguably younger than literature, certainly older than moving pictures. Nevertheless, they have received less critical attention than either, and more importantly, they are the only one of the three media not to have an academic discipline devoted to it: The nineteenth century saw the rise of literary studies, the twentieth century the birth of film studies, but as yet no university has a department of comics studies. An obvious reason seems to be that comics are much more strongly rooted in popular culture than either film or literature, and thus often not taken as seriously. A second reason is that comics are not as distinct from the subject matter of the existing disciplines as these are from each other. It is difficult to argue that a film is a kind of novel or painting, but it is tempting for scholars of literature to regard comics as novels with pictures — a trend helped by labeling them *graphic novels*— just as it is tempting for art scholars to view them as pictures with text, or for film scholars to treat them as frozen film. Comics manifest at the intersection of text, image, and sequence. Because they are a hybrid form, it is deceptively easy to focus on their similarities to other media, and ignore their uniqueness. Yet, while comics are similar to the subject matter of many disciplines, they are also markedly different.

Literature, both written and oral, is an exercise in sequential linearity. Texts are like a river, flowing on in a line, just like this one, from left to right, or from right to left, usually top to bottom, page to page to page. Pictures, on the other hand, are like lakes, not flowing at all, just lying there — meaningful surfaces, abstractions, reductions of three-dimensional events into two-dimensional circumstances. When reading pictures, our eyes scan the surface, constructing temporal and meaningful sequences. As the picture remains static while the text flows past, our eyes are more or less* free to roam, and thus

---

*The eye does have preferred lines of movement across a picture, the so-called saccadic lines. However, they are not nearly as strictly imposed upon the eye as the reading order of written text.

the picture exists in a magical world in which time is not a line but a complex loop, and in which everything can acquire a temporal and causal connection to everything else: In a textual world, the sun rises and causes the cock to crow; in a pictorial world, the rising sun means the crowing cock, and vice versa. Thus, pictures are not simply frozen events, but rather complex circumstances.* A comic combines text and pictures into something quite unlike either. While there are comics which feature no words at all, most of them present a sequence of pictures featuring some form of text. The most obvious uses of writing in comics are dialogue, usually enclosed in a bubble, and narrative summary, usually separated from the picture and enclosed in a clean frame of its own. Writing also frequently represents sounds, usually through more or less onomatopoeic word creations, and sometimes even smells, emotions, and movements. All of these can alternatively be represented through graphic symbols (in the case of smells, for example, these are conventionally vertical wavy lines).

The comic's use of pictorial sequence has led many scholars to compare it to film, which — just like a comparison to literature or art — unfortunately causes them to ignore many unique features of the comic. Unlike most film, for example, the comic routinely displays a high degree of abstraction. Thus any details that are presented are automatically emphasized, simply because they are not left out. This abstraction may well make the comic visually more simple — though not more simplistic — and thus more accessible. The comic is also extremely flexible when it comes to the form of its pictures: Frames can vary in size and shape; the lines of the frame can be omitted altogether; the picture can even expand to fill the whole page. However, the most noteworthy aspect of the comic may well be its idiosyncratic treatment of time: One frame in any comic can include sounds, smells, and dialogue, as well as several consecutive actions. This means that the frames of a comic have an even more complex temporal nature than ordinary pictures, quite simply because several events are depicted, all of which take time and not all of which happen simultaneously. By including more or less events, by repeating single frames, by varying their shape and size, the comic can stretch or compress time.

Despite its sequential nature, the comic may also be best suited to illustrate the fragmentary nature of time. By breaking the flow of their stories into panels, comics draw attention to the fragmentary nature of narrative, and indeed of experience. They have, despite their name, been used to tell very serious stories about the fragmented experience of revolution, war, and ter-

---

*Cf. Vilém Flusser. Für eine Philosophie der Fotographie *(Göttingen: European Photography, 1983, 8–9)*.

rorism, but have also been employed to capture the very mundane fragmentation of autobiographical memory. In an essay in the present work, Jonas Engelmann explores the ability of comics to tell very personal and individual stories, while Dan Hassler-Forest discusses the way they can serve as public trauma narratives (with an eye on 9/11 but also with potential other uses). They can also adopt the more detached stance of political journalism, as Dirk Vanderbeke argues. Comics are thus a potential nexus of the public and the private, the social and the personal, and they may be uniquely suited to describe the multiple fragments of human experience.

As there is as yet no tradition of comics studies, it is illuminating to analyze adaptations, both from other media into comics and from comics into other media, and note which aspects and elements are retained and which are changed — and in the process explore which tools can be imported from literary studies, film studies, art theory, or any other field. Thus, Paul Ferstl discusses comic versions of novels, while Andreas Rauscher and Jochen Ecke take a look at film versions of comics. Comics emerge as a nexus between various art forms as they share characteristics with many of them but are ultimately distinct from all of them. Comics have proven to be eminently flexible in adopting material and techniques of other art forms and have at the same time themselves fuelled film (comic adaptations, comic-style action cinema), literature and pictorial art with their unique stories, medial quality and their direct recourse to pop culture.

Another kind of adaptation is that from one country to another, which helps illuminate the idiosyncrasies of both cultures concerned and their interconnectedness. There are essays in this collection focusing on the transplantation of specific comics, as well as whole movements and national styles. There are also discussions of the depiction of other cultures, specifically of Europeans as villains in American comics (Drennig). The other side of the coin is of course the use of the hero or even superhero as a more or less nationalistic identification figure, a crystallization of a culture's views and values (Hoyer). The essay by Karin Kukkonen and Anja Müller-Wood and those by Ben Little, Meral Özçınar, and Suchitra Mathur explore what happens if such heroes are suddenly created, or recreated, by artists from other cultures. Comics have developed several distinctive national "schools" — some better known, such as the Franco-Belgian *Bande Dessinée* or the Japanese *Manga*, some less well known, such as the Portuguese (Gomes and Peuckert) or German (Schwab) — but they also display a strong inherent potential for international reception, which allows them to transcend cultural boundaries easily. In some cases, like in francophone Canada, two national comics styles come into direct contact and thus create a fascinating hybrid (Hardy-Vallée). Another special and highly illuminating case is the global rise and spread of manga (Briel, Zank, Malone). Comics thus often form a very complex nexus between cultures, and this collection is unique in featuring academic voices from a variety of cultural backgrounds, discussing a truly international collection of works.

It seems only natural that the place of comics in academia should also be discussed — both where they can be used in teaching (as discussed by Christina Sanchez and in the workshop reports by Berninger and Rauscher), and also where they can be the central object of study.

This collection is the result of a conference that took place in May 2007. Academic conferences, if they are any good, are an opportunity to see the rather abstract academic discourse manifest as conversation between scholars — in the corridors between sessions, over dinner, in the evenings at the bar. If you will, such conversations are the nexus of academia. While this collection cannot capture the lively exchange of ideas that took place between the scheduled paper sessions, it does include reports from the two workshops held on the second day. While these exchanges were slightly more formalized and focused than the casual exchanges over dinner, they happened in the presence of a recording device, or a notepad. Thus, the reports by Berninger, Haberkorn and Kukkonen, and Rauscher can at least provide a snapshot of a limited section of the academic discourse on comics.

Comics have long been marginalized by critics and academics. They have been described as a fringe phenomenon, or, all too often, they have been ignored altogether. Yet, as this essay collection shows, comics are in fact central in many ways — they do not exist on the edges, but rather form a nexus between various areas and aspects of culture and cultures. While the 19th century saw the rise of the study of literature, and the 20th century saw the development of film studies as an academic discipline, comic studies have so far failed to materialize. It may be one of the new and exciting areas of the 21st century, and this collection offers a wide selection of perspectives and directions that may serve as starting points for future exploration.

#  INTERMEDIAL

# 1

# Spatializing the Movie Screen: How Mainstream Cinema Is Catching Up on the Formal Potentialities of the Comic Book Page

*Jochen Ecke*

In March of 2007 I got to sit down and talk with David Lloyd, the British artist most famous for his work with writer Alan Moore on *V for Vendetta*. The reason for the interview was the impending German publication of his graphic novel *Kickback*. When I told him that the structure and style of his latest work appeared to have a lot in common with the way Hitchcock had laid out his 1964 film *Marnie*, the cinematic comparison seemed to strike a chord. "The thing is," Lloyd said, "I'm more into movies. What I'm trying to do is to tell a story that is very much like a movie, using the same techniques as in the cinema" (Lloyd). This declaration of intent, coming from one of Anglo-American comics' master artists, struck me as somewhat odd. Why was he so eager to declare his medium* of choice a mere variant of another, presumably of the same nature and making use of the same basic techniques? His remark made me think of something Federico Fellini, himself a great admirer of the medium, had once said about what the Italians call *fumetti*:

> Comics and the ghostly fascination of those paper people, paralysed in time, marionettes without strings, unmoving, cannot be transposed to film, whose

---

*When I speak of comics as a "medium" in this essay, I use the term, following Wolf, "not in the restricted sense of a technical or institutional channel of communication [...] but as a conventionally distinct means of communication or expression" (qtd. in Rajewsky 7). By the term "convention," I understand, along David Bordwell's lines, "a piece of artifice that must be learned" in order to be understood (Bordwell 1996, 88).

allure is motion, rhythm, dynamic. It is a radically different means of addressing the eye, a different mode of expression [Fellini 122].

The statements could not be any more contradictory: here was Lloyd saying that, to him at least, comics should be "paper movies," and on the other hand, there was Fellini stressing that the two forms had little if anything in common.

From an academic point of view, the question — which is basically that of the "essential quality (or qualities)" of the comics medium — is of course a lot more complex than the polar opposite attitudes expressed by Lloyd and Fellini.* Certainly if one takes a look at a page from Lloyd's *Kickback*, it would be difficult to deny that the work has a cinematic quality to it. Many of the techniques used by the British artist — anthropocentric scaled framing methods, angle/reverse angle shots, etc. — have been appropriated from the cinema. But are they used to the same effect? And have they indeed been transported to the comics medium without any modifications? Upon closer inspection, one will find that there are many techniques at work on any given page of the graphic novel that necessitate a consideration of the page as a whole, not just as a sequence of shots. From a narrative point of view, most of these techniques depend on the human eye's anarchic tendency to roam and to sometimes disregard conventional sequence entirely. In this sense, Lloyd would probably agree that the translation of cinematic conventions into the comics medium always makes necessary or — as in the case of the point-of-view shot in panel seven — makes possible changes, both of which owe to the fundamental differences in the nature of the two mediums to be explored in this essay.

*Kickback* is certainly not the only instance one may cite to demonstrate that comics have always been substantially influenced by the cinema. The film industry, however, has largely ignored the vast formal potential of comics — until recently, that is. This essay will argue that, with the recent new wave of comic book adaptations, film directors have started to engage with comics on a much more intricate level, clearly identifying those properties of the medium that are entirely unique to it and using them in a cinematic context, not just as a mere formal experiment, but to greatly enrich the work on a thematic level as well. In order to substantiate and illustrate this claim, however, it will first of all be necessary to demonstrate on a theoretical level just what some of the unique properties of the comics medium might be.

*Asking for the "essential quality or qualities" of a given medium is, of course, in itself a highly problematic, but also a necessary step in an intermedial study such as this essay. In this respect, I wholly agree with Irina Rajewsky, who argues that any analysis of intermedial phenomena will always have to take into account that the perceived "essential qualities" of a given medium are, in fact, in no way truly "essential," but entirely based on historical circumstance (cf. Rajewsky 36). My identification and discussion of the spatial properties of the comics medium in this essay is founded on the medium's current conventional incarnation in printed, material form. The perception of comics might change radically, for example, with the move to the digital media.*

## The "Spatio-Topia" of the Comic Book Page(s)

Many contemporary scholars identify the features to be discussed here by way of the parameters of space and time, which will also help to demonstrate one of the most significant differences between the two media. Comics are an art form that exists fixed and unchanging in *space*, on the page or on a different carrier medium, as well as representing diegetic space visually; on the other hand, a comic book also unfolds in *time*, meaning both the time that elapses in the reading process and the story time established by the narration. In the cinematic medium, said time elapses all by itself. Many different accounts of this specific quality of the film image have been given. In David Bordwell's neo-formalist terminology, the phenomenon is called "screen duration" or "projection time" (Bordwell 1985, 81) and refers to the absolutely fixed amount of time the projection of any given film will take. In short, the representation of time is inevitably part of the cinematic image.

No such claim can be made for the comic book page. As a matter of fact, it can be considered particularly difficult to represent the passage of time in the visual arts. Earlier generations of scholars even went so far as to declare the ambition of establishing any sophisticated narration in the visual arts nigh-on impossible, or at least undesirable. The founder of said "school" of scholarship was Gotthold Ephraim Lessing, who in his *Laocoön* study examines what to him are the "narrow confines" of the visual arts as opposed to the "wide sphere" of the verbal (Lessing 114). To define the critical difference, Lessing introduces two concepts that would inform art historical debates for centuries — even to this day — namely the distinction between *spatial* and *temporal* arts. He posits that painting, in its quest for Aristotelian mimesis, makes use of "ganz andere Mittel, oder Zeichen [...] als die Poesie; jene nämlich Figuren und Farben in dem Raume, diese aber artikulierte Töne in der Zeit" (Lessing 114). To paraphrase, the painter composes figures and forms on the space of the canvas, thus creating, in cooperation with the beholder, the illusion of "real" space. Represented on the canvas by various material means, we can thus identify objects that "exist" in a spatial relation to each other, "next to each other" in an illusory space.

Consequently, at least for Lessing, painting's range of expression is, or rather should be,* severely limited. In Lessing's words, "nebeneinander geordnete Zeichen," that is, the signs in a painting, whose relation to each other is purely spatial, can only express "Gegenstände, die nebeneinander, oder deren Teile nebeneinander existieren," whereas poetry, because of the tem-

---

*As it turns out, Lessing is not really trying to demonstrate the "essential qualities" of the visual and the verbal arts. Rather, he is trying to establish representational norms for both media. Cf. Breithaupt for a modern-day, less dogmatic reading of the Laocoön study.

poral sequence of the reading or listening process, can only express "Gegenstände [...] die aufeinander, oder deren Teile aufeinander folgen" (Lessing 114). In short, according to Lessing, the fine arts should concentrate on the representation of bodies (both natural and material), which in visual representation supposedly stand in a purely spatial relationship to each other, whereas poetry should focus on the representation of actions, that is, on narrative.

This is, of course, a rather dogmatic view, disproved by countless works of visual art that are clearly both "temporal" as well as "spatial" in nature (in fact, the Laocoon statue Lessing studies provides a fairly good example of visual narration). W.J.T. Mitchell offers a contemporary and far more balanced conclusion to what has, since the days of Lessing, come to be called the "Laocoon debate":

> Painting presents bodies indirectly, through pictorial signs, but it does so less indirectly than its presentation of actions. The representation of bodies is easy or "convenient" for painting. The representation of actions is not impossible, just more difficult or inconvenient [Mitchell 102].

It is this particular inconvenience that the comics medium has been struggling with ever since its creation. Comics artists thus strove to temporalize the space of the page with the use of a plethora of devices and the clever transformation of the visual arts themselves: among many developments that have been crucial in the development of the comics medium as we know it, one may cite the use of what E.H. Gombrich calls the "abbreviated style" (Gombrich 288) of caricature, that is, the reduction of noncommunicative "noise" in visual representation, which partially eliminates the problem that "[t]he image is syntactically and semantically dense in that no mark may be isolated as a unique, distinctive character (like a letter of an alphabet)" (Mitchell 67). The cartoonish or at the very least reductionist approach to visual representation in most comic books can therefore be regarded as a move away from the ideology of mimesis, "from the idea of imitation and observation of the visible world to that of an exploration of our own imitative faculty" (Gombrich 288). Or, as Benoît Peeters puts it, in the comics medium,

> la référence à un modèle réel disparaît. Le dessin ne renvoie plus à l'intériorité d'un sujet, mais à une identité de papier, née pour les besoins du récit; il laisse triompher le signe pur, l'invention plutôt que l'observation [Peeters 10].

Apart from this struggle to turn visual representation itself into a clearly legible system of signs — as comics pioneer Rodolphe Töpffer put it, "signes connus de tous, familiers à tous" (Töpffer 148) — one may also cite such inventions as the word *balloon*, the numerous uses of the frame or panel, or the

## 1. Spatializing the Movie Screen *(Ecke)* 11

various possible relationships between the different frames of the comic book, which Thierry Groensteen subsumes under the heading of "arthrology" (cf. Groensteen 22ff.). All of these techniques and devices were introduced to further what one may call "orthodox comics narration." Will Eisner, certainly one of the masters of this mode of comic book storytelling, sums up the intention of the classical comics raconteur as follows:

> The most important obstacle to surmount is the tendency of the reader's eye to wander. On any given page, for example, there is absolutely no way in which the artist can prevent the reading of the last panel before the first [...]. Without [the] technical advantages [of film] there is left to the sequential artist only the tacit cooperation of the reader. This is limited to the convention of reading (left to right, top to bottom, etc.) and the common cognitive disciplines. Indeed, it is this very voluntary cooperation, so unique to comics, that underlies the contract between artist and audience [Eisner 40].

In short, what the classical storyteller tries to prevent at all cost is that "the eye wanders" in disregard of conventional sequence. To achieve this aim, comics creators have overwritten the dominant spatial aspects of the page with narrative cues in a long and difficult process of the temporalization of the image, to the point where the continuity and linearity of narration has become so absolute a value that comic book creators even appear to be afraid of foregrounded spatiality, which is seen as the equivalent of chaos.

And yet, as Eisner indirectly points out here, it is precisely the *spatial* nature of the page and the simultaneity of vision and perception (and consequently, the absolute control of the reader) that is central to the experience of the comics medium — the fact that one *cannot escape* disregarding conventional sequence in the reading process, at the very least subconsciously. Thierry Groensteen describes the process of reading a comic book page in the following way:

> A page of comics is offered at first to a synthetic global vision, but that cannot be satisfactory. It demands to be traversed, crossed, glanced at, and analytically deciphered. This moment-to-moment reading does not take a lesser account of the totality of the panoptic field that constitutes the page (or the double page), since the focal vision never ceases to be enriched by peripheral vision [19].

Groensteen's view can be substantiated by way of the findings of modern-day science. When we are reading a comic book page, our perception is made possible by a physiological phenomenon called the *saccades*, which are

> conjunctive, consciously or unconsciously evoked eye movements that orientate the fovea towards a point of special interest. Normally, when we explore our environment or read a text, we perform 2–4 saccades per second. Saccades are very fast, up to 900°/s, and ballistic, i.e. once evoked a correction or modification can only be made by the second, corrective saccade [Awater 4].

About the process of reading a comic book page, this scientific account tells us that, even though we can make a conscious effort to direct our gaze, to read "just the text" or "just look at the images," the organism's unconscious operations are far more complicated. We are always reading the text *and* the images at the same time, in a manner that, again, does not necessarily follow the linear cues given by the conventional signs on the page.

To sum up and draw conclusions from these findings, then, one can say along Groensteen's lines that "[c]omics panels, situated relationally, are, necessarily, placed in relation to space and operate on a share of space" (21), the distribution of which he sums up under "spatio-topia," "a term created by gathering, while maintaining distinct, the concept of space (*espace*) and that of place (*lieu*)" (Groensteen 21). Groensteen holds the view that said spatio-topia is what centrally governs both the artists' and the readers' operations, in that it is *not* the story that will "create or dictate, relative to its development, the number, the dimension, and the disposition of panels," but rather the "spatio-topical apparatus" comics has developed, which he calls the "system" of comics (Groensteen 21). To him,

> [t]he taking into account of the form and the preconception of the mode of spatial organization that will be adopted are [...] the preliminary conditions to every beginning, and the constraints that never cease to inform each phase of creation [Groensteen 21].

If one assumes the spatio-topia to be the basic condition of the comic book page, several conclusions follow. Most importantly, in the form of *mise-en-page* or page layout, the artist has at his or her disposal a tool unlike anything found in the cinema. The page layout, the very use of space itself, can carry meaning, not just the individual panel in relation to its siblings.

Johann Schmidt only hints at one of the numerous possibilities the spatio-topia harbors for storytelling on the comics page: "Anders als im Film wird ein Verhältnis von Gleichzeitigkeit vorausgesetzt, das erst vom Rezipienten produktiv in das Nacheinander einer Geschichte aufgelöst werden kann" (25). Comics writers and artists such as Alan Moore use this condition of spatial simultaneity quite frequently in their work; one might even say that Moore's *Watchmen*, *A Small Killing* or *From Hell* depend centrally on the comic page's unique capability to represent past, present and future as entirely simultaneous, united on the forever-unchanging space of the page.

To give an example: in their collaborative work *A Small Killing*, Moore and artist Oscar Zarate seem to propagate a "comic book perspective" on the formation of identity by these very same spatial means. Practically every page of the graphic novel foregrounds its own spatiality and short-circuits the linear progression of narration in some way or the other. Flashbacks and "contemporary" events occupy the same space (*and* diegetic place, most often) and form chains of causal connections, thus furthering the theme of the presence of the protagonist Timothy's past in whatever he does in the present, and often simultaneously creating the agonizing impression of an "eternal present" that is just as static as the comic book page on which it is represented. In the final chapter of *A Small Killing*, Timothy's recovery of agency and of control over a meaningful construction of identity is then explicitly associated with his becoming "aware" of the structures of simultaneity the comic book has hitherto presented us with by foregrounding the spatial properties of the page.

## Bringing the "Spatio-Topia" to the Movie Screen: Three Examples

In the following three brief analyses I will present examples of how film directors have engaged with the "spatio-topia" of the comic book page, and the notion of simultaneity in particular. My first demonstration will be based on Italian director Mario Bava's 1968 *Danger: Diabolik*, a much-overlooked metafictional treatise of the Italian tradition of serialized *fumetti* from a filmmaker who is often unjustly frowned upon by academia. To my mind, until the recent new wave of American comic book adaptations, no director ever quite matched the standards Bava set with *Danger: Diabolik* as far as intermedial negotiations between comics and the silver screen are concerned. I will subsequently venture a look at Zack Snyder's adaptation of Frank Miller and Lynn Varley's graphic novel *300*, a film that has been much scrutinized from an ideological point of view but that has received hardly any commentary as to its engagement with the comic book medium (except for superficial remarks as to Snyder's faithful rendering of whole swaths of pages from the comic book, of course). Finally, I will examine Ang Lee's 2003 adaptation of Marvel Comics' *The Hulk*, and demonstrate how Lee transports precisely those properties of the spatio-topia to the screen that comics creators like Alan Moore use to achieve the impression of the "presence of the past."

### Mario Bava's *Danger: Diabolik* (1968)

Bava's *Danger: Diabolik*— unlike Ang Lee's *The Hulk* or the work of Alan Moore — is entirely unconcerned with notions of the past. In fact, like much of the filmography of the Italian director of B and C genre pictures, *Diabolik*'s disinterest for any notion of "realism" or relevance to the everyday world of its viewers could hardly be any more pronounced. For the greater part of his career, Bava instead proved himself an early postmodernist, recklessly plundering the archives of popular culture and reveling in camp, irony and artificiality. His interest in *Diabolik*, a modestly budgeted adaptation of the Italian comics serial of the same name, is rooted in the same attitude. The character of Diabolik, an immoral thief who recklessly steals from the rich for his own hedonistic ends and who is also quite eager to constantly ridicule and subvert the establishment, could easily have been used to explore leftist politics; but Bava does no such thing. Instead, he seems fascinated by the character's flatness, by the amused suspicion that the most characteristic trait of Diabolik might be his physicality — the way he moves and rolls his eyes melodramatically. In short, four years before Umberto Eco's famous 1972 essay on the static character of superhero stories ("The Superman Myth"), Bava and his team of writers had realized that the very appeal of the popular comics serial lay in its constant return to a forever-unchanging status quo.

Bava's discovery or interpretation of the *Diabolik* comic books as a static, entirely fictional construction is clearly mirrored in the film's structure: eschewing a classical three-act model, the film instead presents itself as a series of very loosely connected, seemingly arbitrary episodes that do not even pretend to be working toward a common climax. Instead, each vignette deals with some kind of robbery perpetrated by Diabolik, who then proceeds to skillfully evade the government's moronic attempts at apprehension, only to reap the fruits of his wicked labors in his stylish pop art lair.

Even when Diabolik is finally caught at the end of the film, Bava finds a highly fitting visual metaphor to encapsulate the whole of his approach to the character in one image that clearly foreground's the shot's spatiality: Diabolik, clad in a protective suit, is caught in a stream of liquefied gold. As the metal settles down and solidifies, we find Diabolik in a suspended pose, frozen in place by the very object of desire that is at the root of the character's stasis. This is not simply a reproduction of any particular comic book panel, and neither is the shot intended to merely emulate a hypothetical comic book page. Bava makes this abundantly clear by having the camera slowly push in on Diabolik, ending on a close-up of the character, who proceeds to wink at the camera. The film thus signals that the circular structures it had hitherto hinged on will be reproduced *ad infinitum*. Importantly, the gist of this moment is transported by cinematic means — camera and character movement — and by cinematic means only. We might say that Bava spatializes the shot here not to simply *imitate* the medium he is negotiating with, that is, comics, but also to demonstrate the constitutive difference between the two media that can be located in the representation of time. In other words, the slow movement of the camera and the actor's subtle gesture are the cinema's means of commenting on *Diabolik*, the comic book: the frozen moments of the comic's panels become, from Bava's point of view, the very metaphor for the serial's eternal return to the status quo, and genre cinema winks at the serialized comic book in amused recognition of their similar-but-different nature.

This is not the only instance where Bava recognizably aims at the spatialization of the movie screen. In fact, *Danger: Diabolik* abounds with shots that make use of frames-within-the-frame in order to fragment and foreground the space of the screen. This is a common enough cinematic technique that is used, by European directors especially, to a great variety of ends. At times, Bava's adoption of additional frames in the film is indeed rather conventional, if not even clichéd. But for the most part, the use of up to ten (!) additional frames that partition a given shot is clearly meant to draw attention to the screen's spatiality and imitate the paneling of a comic book page. Bava only ever employs this kind of framing method in scenes with multiple characters, and he skillfully commands the *mise-en-scène* to place his actors fairly precisely within the space of these *faux*-panels. When his actors move about the room, they will always take up a position that will reframe them in a new panel. Bava refrains from having the dialogue spoken in what would be the conventional reading order on a comic book page, though. He only aims to reproduce the experience of reading a comic book page as, to again quote Groensteen, a "synthetic global vision," a space representing numerous simultaneous actions that the viewer can roam at will. Again, Bava's negotiations with the comic medium's formal properties end up as a demonstration of difference: the very fact that each scene has a particular duration, that the characters move about the diegetic space and that the viewer's "synthetic global vision" is actually *not* in total control of the reading process proves that the comic book's "spatio-topia" can only be partly reproduced on the space of the movie screen.

### Zack Snyder's Adaptation of Frank Miller's *300* (2007)

Zack Snyder's engagement with the spatio-topia of Frank Miller and Lynn Varley's graphic novel *300* partially takes an approach similar to Mario Bava's. However, Snyder does not have to come up with any metafictional commentary on the medium he is working from since his source material is in itself already a heavily intermedial image-text — a fact that becomes immediately clear when considering the book version of *300* as a material object. For his highly stylized interpretation of the Battle of the Thermopylae, Miller has chosen a format of 12.9 × 9.9 inches, much wider than the usual American comic book measurements of 10 × 6.1 inches. The book therefore foregrounds the spatiality of the page already by the choice of an unusual format. If one subsequently examines the actual page layouts or *mise-en-page*, the suspicion that Miller's intent is to allude to and imitate the spatiality of the fine arts is further substantiated. Most pages present vast panoramas, emphasizing the representation of space and objects/bodies in spatial relation to each other over temporal sequence. Individual actions driving the plot are mostly relegated to a number of much smaller panels that are often purely functional or diagrammatic in nature — in short, narration is an afterthought in *300*.

Instead, Miller seems intent on stressing the fictitious nature of the propaganda story of the 300 Spartans defending Greece at the Hot Gates. *300* self-reflexively marks the narrative as yet another artistic and therefore explicitly artificial variation on a tale that has been tackled by countless artists before — an intention that makes itself clear already in the choice of a narrative frame. The story of the 300 Spartans is told by a military leader aiming to rouse his troops to battle; by way of focalizing the events through an unreliable narrator, all the events at the Thermopylae are relegated to the status of rhetorical artifice serving the ends of propaganda. Miller's artistic choices fit the rhetorical thrust: his panoramas of battles and well-exercised male bodies harken back to artistic models of the past as well as to actual ancient Greek representations of history — equally steeped in ideology, and equally unreliable.

Snyder chooses to faithfully reproduce many of the pivotal scenes of the graphic novel down to the most minute detail: the moment in which the Spartans witness part of the Persian fleet being crushed in a storm, for example, or the end of the first day of defending the Thermopylae, when the Spartans drive part of Xerxes' forces off a cliff. Most of these moments are taken from sequences of the graphic novel that stress spatiality, thus aiming for a painterly effect and eschewing the temporal progression of narration for, at best, the representation of numerous events and actions taking place simultaneously (e.g., the Spartans watching the Persian fleet being partially destroyed while on the ships soldiers are being crushed by toppling masts or hurled into the sea). In emulating Miller's *faux-*"canvasses," Snyder points out the essential difference between the two media in much the same way Bava did, that is, he adds the factor of movement and duration to the panoramas, albeit in slow motion — which can be regarded as a uniquely cinematic means of calling attention to the shot's spatiality. In this sense, almost forty years after Bava's negotiations with the formal properties of the comics medium, Snyder seems to have little to add to the ongoing experiment of adapting comics' spatio-topia for the movie screen.

*300* is much more interesting in its interpretation of the comic book reading process for the cinema. Snyder and his crew shot several of the movie's big action sequences with three cameras of different focal lengths, all simultaneously running film from approximately the same position.\* One camera

---

\**Cf. Snyder's audio commentary on the DVD version of 300 for a thorough discussion of this particular cinematic technique.*

would thus record a long shot of the action, a second camera a medium shot, and a third camera a tight medium shot. Via sophisticated computer-generated zooms, it was then possible to seamlessly connect all three shots as though they had been caught by a single, impossibly agile camera. In other words, Snyder and his crew of technicians have found a means by way of which the technical apparatus of the cinema can imitate the way the human eye roams the space of the comic book page: taking everything in synthetically or cumulatively at first, but then — to quote Groensteen for a third and final time — "travers[ing], cross[ing], glanc[ing] at, and decipher[ing]" (19). Again, this imaginative and visually exciting negotiation with the comics medium can only serve to point out another fundamental difference between the media: what Snyder offers us is the *simulation* of the spatio-topian freedom of the reader, not the thing itself. In fact, it might be argued that the thrill of these sequences is generated precisely by their coercing the spectator into a specific rollercoaster-like way of witnessing the action, not by granting the audience the freedom to roam at leisure.

### Ang Lee's *The Hulk* (2003)

Zack Snyder may claim the honor of having perfected the cinematic simulation of the spatio-topia by way of computer-generated zooms, but the film that actually came up with the technique was Ang Lee's *The Hulk* (2003). For a big-budget blockbuster production, Lee's film is an immensely experimental endeavor. Apart from the above-mentioned zooms, the director and his collaborators make use of complex digital dissolves, multiple exposures uniting a number of different shots in one frame, three-dimensional cubes onto which the cinematographic image is pasted digitally, and time and time again extensive passages of split-screen. In other words, from this evidence alone one can draw the conclusion that the filmmakers are intent on spatializing the screen in imitation of the spatio-topia or *mise-en-page* of the comic book. Lee says so explicitly on the DVD's audio commentary:

> So the scientists [in the film scene Lee is commenting on] experiment with a frog and we experiment on the cutting. This is a very interesting cinematic language to explore, because you not only line up in time the pictures [sic], *you design spaces and you choreograph different images* [my emphasis].

Most of these techniques are put to thematic use, furthering the over-the-top notion of psychology that the film has adopted. Lee employs the split-screen technique, for example, to convey emotions by the synthetic impression of the simulated spatio-topia. Entirely abstract images of biological structures, textures and patterns combined with images of actual narrative content thus come to express feelings such as anger or rage as well as the violent repression of memory. Again, this can be likened to the way comics artists make use of *mise-en-page* to transport the emotional content of the story. Comics creator Steve Lieber describes the process in the following way in an interview:

> I'll look at the panel and if the moment isn't angry enough, my approach in drawing will switch to try to make it angrier. At a certain point, it becomes a lot like music, where a purely abstract arrangement of marks is communicating one emotion or another [Lieber].

For the most part, though, Lee's use of the split-screen is connected to the idea of subverting the usual temporal order of narration in the cinematographic medium. This particular fascination with the spatio-topia may take the form of a mere dynamic compression of time and action: in one particular instance of simulated *mise-en-page*, for example, Lee shows a helicopter flying over the desert in one split-screen, while the very same helicopter can already be seen landing in the desert in another frame. Present and future are both *present* in this particular arrangement, united in the simultaneity of the spatio-topia. Time is effectively spatialized to the point where all actions shown in the different split-screens become part of an all-encompassing present.

Most importantly, though, the split-screen and various complex digital dissolves are used to develop the theme of the presence of the past in Bruce Banner's life. In making repression the central concern of their film, Ang Lee and writing partner Gareb Schamus's adaptation of the Marvel serial is just as hugely Freudian as it is shamelessly operatic: as in the comic books, the Hulk is interpreted as a Mr. Hyde figure, the very embodiment of sublimation. Unlike the comic book version, though, the film is much more specific as to which traumatic events are actually being repressed by Bruce Banner. The young scientist does not simply have anger management issues; rather, he has had to witness as a child the murder of his mother at the hands of his own father. The central conflict of the film can therefore be interpreted as a sort of bizarre reversal of the œdipal confrontation: in the end, Bruce Banner will kill his father for his various transgressions against the "natural" order, of which the killing of his wife is only a small part. Before this generational conflict can be openly waged, though, Banner has to go on a sort of therapeutic odyssey, during which he will become aware of the presence of the past in his life — a traumatic personal history of which the Hulk is but the physical manifestation.

It is this repressed past (which nevertheless greatly informs and devastates Banner's present) that Lee chooses to represent by way of a number of simulated spatio-topias. In the scene working toward Banner's first transformation into the Hulk, for example, Lee spatializes the screen in such a way as to show his protagonist surrounded by symbols of his troubled past: computer screens show data from Banner's blood samples, which attest to the experiments his father has conducted on him. Flashbacks are superimposed on close-ups of Bruce in which we are presented with fragmentary bits and pieces of repressed memories — for example, Banner's father taking a blood sample of his son or the explosion Banner senior provokes when his research project is cancelled by the authorities. Later shots show the father's cleaning gear* in the hall of Bruce Banner's laboratory as further proof of the very real presence of the protagonist's personal history, not just in a figurative sense. Past and present are thus again united on the space of the screen and shown as simultaneous to each other — the past even has the power to cause Banner's transformation in the present.

The conflict is partly resolved and agency is regained for Banner when — in a figurative sense — he learns to recognize the presence of the past and starts to interpret the spatio-topia, much like Timothy, the protagonist of Alan Moore's *A Small Killing*, does. The moment of partial spatio-topian epiphany arrives when Banner returns to the house in which the murder of his mother took place. Production designer Rick Heinrichs fashions the bungalow as though it were a gigantic, three-dimensional comic book to be roamed at will: the structure seems to consist of nothing but frames or panels, all of which culminate in a highly symbolic empty panel, the door behind which Banner's mother was murdered. As Banner starts to "read" the space/place — a process indicated by Lee by an unusual number of point-of-view shots — memory returns, and Bruce becomes aware of his repressed past. Significantly, this turning point in the film is connected to the notions of space and place — except that now, the space to be read and interpreted is discernible for the protagonist as well, not just for the audience.

## Conclusions

In the course of this essay, I hope to have demonstrated that the comics medium also functions as a "nexus of cultures" on a formal level: the thorough intermedial negotiations that the film industry has entered into with comics in recent years have greatly helped to enrich the cinematic language. Film directors and their collaborators have learned to integrate the possibilities of *mise-en-page* and the spatio-topia into their cinematic adaptations — not just as merely ornamental accessories, but as incentives to reconsider the advantages that foregrounding the movie screen's very own spatiality might yield. The formal experiments of films like *300* or *The Hulk* can be regarded as the avant-garde products of this new, serious interest in comics as a medium,

---

*Banner's father has infiltrated his son's research facility in the disguise of a caretaker.*

not just as a supplier of character and story materials, as was most often the case in the past. Further developments in this new dialogue between the two media should yield fertile grounds for academic study.

BIBLIOGRAPHY

Awater, Holger. *Perception of Visual Space at the Time of Saccadic Eye Movements*. Diss. Ruhr-Universität Bochum, 2002.
Bordwell, David. "Convention, Construction and Cinematic Vision." *Post-Theory. Reconstructing Film Studies*, edited by David Bordwell and Noel Carroll. Madison: University of Wisconsin Press, 1996, 87–107.
_____. *Narration in the Fiction Film*. London: Routledge, 1985.
Breithaupt, Fritz. "Das Indiz. Lessings und Goethes Laokoon-Texte und die Narrativität der Bilder." *Ästhetik des Comic*, edited by Michael Hein, Michael Hüners and Torsen Michaelsen. Berlin: Erich Schmidt Verlag, 2002, 37–50.
Eco, Umberto. "Der Mythos von Superman." *Apokalyptiker und Integrierte*, by Umberto Eco. Frankfurt am Main: Fischer, 1992, 187–222.
Eisner, Will. *Comics and Sequential Art*. Expanded Edition. Tamarac, FL: Poorhouse Press, 2005.
Fellini, Federico, and Milo Manara. *Trip to Tulum. From a Script for a Film Idea*. Catalonia: Catalan Communications, 1990.
Gombrich, E.H. *Art and Illusion*. Third Edition. London: Phaidon, 1968.
Groensteen, Thierry. *The System of Comics*. Jackson: University of Mississippi Press, 2007.
Lessing, Gotthold Ephraim. *Laokoon oder Über die Grenzen der Malerei und Poesie. Mit beiläufigen Erläuterungen verschiedener Punkte der alten Kunstgeschichte*, edited by Julius Petersen and Waldemar von Olshausen. Stuttgart: Reclam, 1964.
Lieber, Steve. "Interview with Steve Lieber." *G-wie-gorilla.de*. http://www.g-wie-gorilla.de/content/view/835/5/ (7 July 2007).
Lloyd, David. "Interview with David Lloyd." *G-wie-gorilla.de*. http://www.g-wie-gorilla.de/content/view/321/18/ (5 July 2007).
_____. *Kickback*. Milwaukie: Dark Horse, 2007.
Miller, Frank, and Lynn Varley. *300*. Milwaukie: Dark Horse, 2006.
Mitchell, W.J.T. *Iconology. Image, Text, Ideology*. Chicago and London: University of Chicago Press, 1986.
Moore, Alan, and Oscar Zarate. *A Small Killing*. Urbana, IL: Avatar Press, 2004 [1991].
Peeters, Benoît. "Le visage et la ligne: zigzags töpfferiens." *Töpffer. L'invention de la bande dessinée*, edited by Benoît Peeters and Thierry Groensteen. Paris: Hermann, 1994, 1–64.
Rajewsky, Irina. *Intermedialität*. Tübingen and Basel: A. Francke, 2002.
Schmidt, Johann N. "Schwierige Verwandtschaften." Schnitt.de. http://www.schnitt.de/211, 1015,01 (7 July 2007).
Töpffer, Rodolphe. "Réflexions à propos d'un programme." *Töpffer. L'invention de la bande dessinée*, edited by Benoît Peeters and Thierry Groensteen. Paris: Hermann, 1994, 144–60.

FILMOGRAPHY

*300*. Dir. Zack Snyder. Gerard Butler, Lena Headey, Dominic West. Warner Bros, 2007.
*Danger: Diabolik*. Dir. Mario Bava. John Phillip Law, Marisa Mell, Michel Piccoli. Dino de Laurentiis Cinematografica, 1968.
*The Hulk*. Dir. Ang Lee. Eric Bana, Jennifer Connelly, Nick Nolte. Universal, 2004.

# 2

# The Marvel Universe on Screen: A New Wave of Superhero Movies?

*Andreas Rauscher*

The Silver Age of American comic books began in the 1950s with the first publications of DC Comics, later well known for iconographic superheroes such as Superman, Wonder Woman, the Flash, and Batman (who was, in regard to his childhood trauma and the darker and more ambivalent mood of the early comic books, almost a predecessor of the Marvel heroes). But it was not until the Marvel heroes of the 1960s that the superhero genre came of age and turned toward more down-to-earth characters who offered a variety of identification patterns. The Fantastic Four, who were launched as Marvel's answer to DC's Justice League in November 1961, were not able to return to their former civil identities after they gained superpowers in a cosmic storm. In contrast to Superman, who willingly accepted his job as a never-resting boy-scout, the Marvel heroes considered their supernatural skills to be both a blessing and a curse. The mutants of the heroic X-Men team are met with fear and prejudice by the public, and their only hideaway is a school established as a decoy for the secret mutant headquarters by Professor Charles X. Xavier. Even Peter Parker, aka Spider-Man, whose catchphrase, "with great power comes great responsibility," reminiscent of the classic "men in tights," complains repeatedly that his superhero job as "your friendly neighborhood Spider-Man" is ruining his private life.

The innovative writing of authors such as Stan Lee and Chris Claremont, and drawings by artists like Stan Kirby, Steve Ditko and John Romita introduced ambivalent heroes who had to cope with a difficult private life and a society prejudiced against them. In contrast to the shining (and in the long run superficial) larger-than-life role models from the heyday of early superhero comics, the Marvel protagonists were outcasts. The green colossus Hulk continued the tradition of the misunderstood monster made popular by classical Universal horror films such as James Whale's *Frankenstein* (USA 1931/ 1934). The X-Men reflected the struggles between integrationists and separatists within the civil rights movement of the 1960s. Spider-Man had to deal with teenage angst situations and a troublesome love life. He also had to accept underpaid occasional jobs in order to get through college and cope with being the target of denunciatory tabloid press campaigns.

The adventures of the Marvel characters play against the backdrop of the greater New York area. Instead of being located in fictitious cities like the clean, retro-futuristic Metropolis or the expressionistic boiling-pot Gotham, the Marvel comic books dealt with issues of everyday life in the Big Apple and included numerous references to pop culture phenomenon from music and fashion to film and television. In 2002, Stan Lee explained in his autobiography, "I've always tried to make our characters as realistic as possible, given the fact that they were living in a world of fantasy. In fact, I tried to inject reality into that world itself" (137). In present-day issues of the *X-Men* series, the mutant Kitty Pryde criticizes the anti-feminist backlash caused by shallow celebrities such as Paris Hilton. Similarly, in *The Amazing Spider-Man*, which has turned into one of the most successful ongoing Hollywood franchises, the hype surrounding superhero blockbusters is parodied by a campy fictitious film series starring the "Incredible Lobster Man."

In contrast to the self-contained episodes and circular narrative structure of traditional superhero comic books, Marvel used intertextual links between the different series and established a continuity that allowed for a new level of character development and constant conflicts. This strategy was subsequently picked up by rival publishing house DC, and prepared the ground for influential graphic novels of the 1980s with artists such as Frank Miller (*Daredevil, The Dark Knight Returns, Sin City*) writing so-called "runs," which focused on an elaborated story arc and were shaped by the individual style of the author. Today the links between cinema and comic books offer a variety of intersections and numerous forms of productive exchange. Screenwriter J. Michael Straczynski, who is well-known for creating the ambitious TV series *Babylon 5* (USA 1994–1998), has been writing *Spider-Man* for several years. Veteran independent director and actor Kevin Smith (*Clerks*, USA 1994; *Chasing Amy*, USA 1997) has not only included references to comics throughout his oeuvre, but he also contributed "runs" to *Daredevil* and *Green Arrow* that offer the same sophisticated and ironic approach toward pop culture that appears in his films. Joss Whedon, creator and producer of innovative TV series like *Buffy the Vampire Slayer* and *Firefly*, wrote a miniseries for *X-Men* that, in turn, provided several central plot elements for Brett Ratner's film *X-Men—The Last Stand* (USA 2006). With several ongoing film franchises based on comic books, and screenwriters participating in the development of superhero comics, the ties between the two media seem to be stronger than ever.

Nevertheless, it took almost 30 years before the approaches introduced by Marvel to the comic book world found their way to the big screen. Although TV feature series based upon *Spider-Man* and *The Hulk* had already been quite popular in the 1970s, and some trashy low-budget films featuring *Captain America* and *The Fantastic Four* were produced in the early 1990s, a process of continuing stylistic differentiation only became possible because of the success of Bryan Singer's *X-Men* and Sam Raimi's *Spider-Man*.

The new wave of comic book adaptations of the last ten years has been dependent on two key factors that do not appear in former major productions based upon super hero comics. The first factor was the introduction of digital effects in the 1990s that enabled feature film visuals to come closer to comic book art than matte paintings and model effect shots ever could. In his study *The Language of New Media* (2001), media theorist Lev Manovich observed:

> If digital compositing and digital painting can be thought of as an extension of cell animation techniques (since composited images are stacked in depth parallel to each other, as cells on an animation stand), the newer method of computer-based postproduction makes filmmaking a subset of animation. In this method, the live-action photographic stills and/or graphic elements are positioned in a 3-D virtual space, thus giving the director the ability to move the virtual camera freely through this space, dollying and panning [305].

The dynamic direction of photography found in the *Spider-Man* films (USA 2002/04/07), directed and co-written by Sam Raimi, relies on a combination of sequences shot on location, digital animation and virtual backgrounds. In the first film, Spider-Man (Tobey Maguire) and the Green Goblin (Willem Dafoe) fight each other in front of a digitally altered Times Square that was put together from shots recorded on a sound stage, CGI-graphics and footage from the real location. The second film opens with a visually stunning chase across the rooftops of Manhattan again combining real footage with a CGI-animated Spider-Man. Finally, *Spider-Man 3* features a fight in the New York subway that appears to have more in common with the digital flow of action-adventure video games than with the real thing. The virtual camera pans and tracks around as if it were on a real location. In this mode of production the two-dimensional drawings of comic panels and traditional matte paintings have turned into three-dimensional sets comparable to the digital architecture of the navigable worlds presented in comic/film–based video games such as *Ultimate Spider-Man* (2005) or *Marvel: Ultimate Alliance* (2006).

The second factor that has contributed significantly to the success of comic book adaptations is the influence of the individual styles of ambitious directors. This influence is missing in most Hollywood mainstream fare but is prominent in recent comic book adaptations like *Spider-Man*, *X-Men* (USA 2000/03/06), *Hellboy* (USA 2004) and *Hulk* (USA 2003). As noted above, a closer look at the *Spider-Man* film series indicates that Manovich's thesis fits certain sequences featuring spectacular fights and dynamic web-slinging through New York. Sam Raimi, however, a passionate fan of the Marvel comic books, also integrated two other trademark elements from the comics that do not rely on heavy use of CGI, but on the actors and an elaborate *mise-en-scène*: There are interludes presenting precisely timed situation comedy dealing with the troublesome everyday life. Raimi also establishes several melodramatic subplots developing over the course of three films that focus on the complicated love triangle between Peter Parker (Tobey Maguire), his long-time love, Mary Jane Watson (Kirsten Dunst), and his former best friend turned enemy, Harry Osborne (James Franco).

The most convincing mainstream comic book adaptations of recent years avoid the repetitive formulas typical for Hollywood franchises. The serial narrative is an essential aspect of the comic books and the films consequently do not make any attempts to continue an already finished story. They do however include open ends for future narratives. In the case of Tim Burton, Bryan Singer, Sam Raimi, Guillermo Del Toro, and Ang Lee these open-ended features may even be considered to be stylistically coherent entries into the director's oeuvre. The filmography of the versatile director, Raimi, includes the horror slapstick trilogy *The Evil Dead* (USA 1981–1993), the comic book homage *Darkman* (USA 1990), as well as serious drama such as *A Simple Plan* (USA 1998). But, instead of strictly separating his more underground-orientated work from his mainstream dramas, Raimi has integrated stylistic devices and motives from all these efforts into the *Spider-Man* series.

Even though the third *Spider-Man* film (released in 2007) did not live up to most expectations, its predecessor from 2004 demonstrates Raimi's subtle play of visual effects and the absurdity of everyday life in an exemplary way. The opening sequence, in which Peter Parker (Tobey Maguire) does not manage to successfully deliver a box of pizzas even though he switches to his Spider-Man outfit in order to get through the rush hour in Manhattan, employs CGI effects to create a traditional slapstick narrative. Other comical scenes serve as a stylistic counterbalance to the elaborated fight sequences. When Peter Parker ruins his white shirts by absent-mindedly washing his Spider-Man costume with his ordinary laundry, and in the scenes in which Peter Parker is merely a nerdy student, the film does not employ any visual effects at all. In contrast to the rapid editing and ever-changing camera angles used in contemporary Hollywood action films, Raimi even leaves the camera for several minutes in one position to highlight a bizarre encounter between Spider-Man and a passer-by who has no idea that he is confronted with the real superhero but thinks that someone has put a lot of effort in creating a fan-made Spidey outfit.

The prolific dialectic between blockbuster CGI extravaganza and personal directorial vision is a result of the changes brought about by the success of the Marvel films. Comic book adaptations in the mainstream as well as in the independent sector are no longer only directed by reliable realisateurs, such as Brett Ratner or Rob Bowman, but by passionate auteurs who try to find a synthesis between their individual style and the trademarks established by the comic books. Comparable to the comic book "runs" authored by individual artists within the fixed mythology of a continuing series, the directors contribute their own interpretations to an ongoing franchise. Richard Donner's and Richard Lester's *Superman* films from the late 1970s and early 1980s proved that superhero adaptations could be true to the comic book as well as be attractive to a larger commercial audience. But it was Tim Burton's dark and psychologically complex character study of Bruce Wayne in *Batman* (USA 1989) and *Batman Returns* (USA 1992), which portray the Dark Knight as almost similar to the nemesis he created himself, that allowed the director to keep his artistic integrity even while delivering a high-budget event movie. The first two *Batman* films were inspired by the work of Frank Miller and Alan Moore, who presented a more adult-orientated and ambivalent version of the (anti-)hero. It is due to their efforts that changes initiated by mature graphic novels in the 1980s made their way to the screen, and it took only a few more years before Hollywood finally began to avoid the shallow spectacle of lack-luster, unintentionally funny, badly staged and badly scripted releases like *Judge Dredd* (GB 1995) and *Spawn* (USA 1997).

Although they were similar in their stylistic coherence, there is still one important difference remaining between most of the Marvel films and Tim Burton's noncamp reimagination of *Batman*. Burton's films were conceived as self-contained entries to a franchise that drastically changed its tone when Joel Schumacher took over the director's chair for the third and fourth installment. The Marvel films, even if they went from auteur to realisateur as in the case of *X-Men 3*, rely in the sequels on the continuation of plot arcs established in earlier films. This concept helps to avoid the mistakes of former adaptations that tried to put all characteristic plot points into one single film instead of paying tribute to the wide variety of characters and stories developed over the course of several decades in the comic books. Even though mainstream superheroes are only allowed a certain amount of character development, many Marvel series at least tried to suggest the passing of time. Spider-Man's high school love, Gwen Stacy, dies in the early 1970s, so traumatizing the hero for many years. Peter Parker turns from a naïve high school student into a socially conscious part-time teacher in his former neighborhood. In the crossover event *Civil War* (2006/2007), he is caught between rivaling groups of Marvel protagonists. In the struggle over a registration act concerning superheroes he chooses to reveal his secret identity. This too leads to changes that will affect the series for many years.

Stephen Norrington's vampire action adventure *Blade* (USA 1998) marked the beginning of Marvel's cinematic new wave, but this cycle of ambitious comic book adaptations was only noticed by most critics and the general audience after the artistic and commercial success of Bryan Singer's *X-Men* in the summer of 2000. It became one of the first films based on a comic book series that not only left the door open for further installments like Richard Donner's *Superman* had done, but it also explicitly developed the set-up for a future conflict by hinting at a mutant registration act that would be dealt with in the sequels. A darker and more serious tone differentiates *X-Men* from most superhero adaptations of the late 1990s. The films are based on the popular 1970s version of the team, when the more conventional (and firmly American) mutants of the 1960s were replaced by a more international team of heroes. Fan favorite and declared loner Wolverine, a Canadian with adamantium claws and skilled in various martial arts, joined forces with the African weather goddess Storm, the German demon-like Nightcrawler, and the Russian hero Colossus.

The first sequences of *X-Men* are characteristic for the film's versatile and serious approach. Singer's direction consequently avoids cartoonish ingredients. The absence of over-the-top elements is even ironically commented on within a scene in which Wolverine (Hugh Jackman) teases the other X-Men about their black leather suits and is asked in return by Cyclops (James Marsden) if he would rather prefer yellow spandex. According to the original comic books such a yellow spandex outfit would have been Wolverine's dress of choice. But Singer and his art department stay away consciously from bright colors and tights. In this, they continue the trend initiated by the Marvel comic books to create a more believable and realistic style within the limits of the super hero genre. In retrospect, Singer explained to film journalist James Mottram: "Since Richard Donner did the first *Superman*, we've seen that comic book adaptations can be taken seriously. And we've seen with a lot of good science fiction and fantasy that, when it's taken seriously, we can learn a lot about ourselves" (Mottram 308).

Instead of restricting the plot to the emotional journey of one character, *X-Men* features an ensemble of protagonists establishing a diversity of possible metaphorical readings. Wolverine continues the long tradition of classical rebel heroes in popular culture, not unlike many of the roles played by Clint Eastwood, a character type which is attractive for an older part of the audience. The insecurity of puberty, which is experienced by the younger X-Men Rogue (Anna Paquin), Iceman (Shawn Ashmore), and Pyro (Aaron Stanford), corresponds on the other hand to the standards of teenage coming-of-age dramas. The topic of being an outsider and threatened by (in some cases even lethal) bigotry is introduced on a personal as well as on a political and more historical level. The first *X-Men* film opens with young Magneto helplessly witnessing the murder of his parents in a Nazi concentration camp. This flashback gives insight into the motivation behind the later mutant separatist Magneto (played by Ian McKellen) and provides a differentiated explanation of his militant position that transcends the rather one-dimensional frontline drawn between good and evil in traditional superhero stories. The experience of discovering mutant powers is explored in the following introduction of teenage girl Rogue. During a romantic moment with her boyfriend, she learns that she drains energy from everyone she touches. Teenage angst is articulated in this scene in terms of otherness caused by supernatural incidents. Similar motives can be found in *Carrie* (1976), based on a novel by Stephen King, or in slasher series' like *A Nightmare on Elm Street* (USA since 1984). In contrast to the visceral horror cinema of the 1970s and 1980s, the *X-Men* stories are told from the outsider's point of view and favor a coming to terms with otherness instead of adjusting to prevalent conventions. Those who try to restore the status quo and ignore that society itself demands a change toward more tolerance, are portrayed as narrow-minded populists like Senator Kelly (Bruce Davidson) in the first film or as hateful fanatics like Colonel Stryker (Brian Cox) in the second film.

The political story framework of *X-Men 2* is introduced in two sequences during the hearing of a Senate Committee in Washington. In the first sequence, scientist Jean Grey (Famke Janssen) is seen attempting to convince the attending politicians that the restriction of personal freedom imposed by the mutant registration act could result in a dangerous conflict. The public does not know that she is a mutant herself and works as a researcher at Professor Xavier's school. The fierce response she gets from Senator Kelly evokes associations of Senator McCarthy's House Committee on Un-American Activities. This sequence indicates how easily history could be repeating itself. The second sequence is a meeting between former friends Magneto and Charles Xavier after the hearing that develops the political references by echoing the differences between Martin Luther King and Malcolm X. Xavier, cast with Patrick Stewart, who created Captain Picard as the iconographic personification of *Star Trek*'s humanist message, demands a better understanding between mutants and men in order to find a peaceful solution. In contrast to him the embittered Magneto promotes militant separatism and violence as self-defense. Xavier and the X-Men decide to help mankind even if they are not accepted by the majority of them. Magneto and his Brotherhood of Mutants fight human supremacy without considering the results of their actions on neutral parties.

The allegorical elements of the film are further strengthened by the cast. Hugh Jackman, Halle Berry, Ian McKellen (who has drawn parallels between his own position as a gay activist and the mutant metaphor on several occasions), Patrick Stewart, and Famke Janssen avoid any of the cartoonish overacting, a characterization that is often wrongly associated with comic book adaptations in general. Instead of a continuous presentation of set pieces the *X-Men* films rely on the precisely timed interplay between action sequences, staged by experienced martial arts choreographers such as Hong Kong director Corey Yuen, and memorable character-driven scenes like the imprisoned Magneto playing chess against Xavier while discussing the threat of a war between mutants and humans. In one of the film's key scenes, Magneto looks at the Statue of Liberty, the setting of the showdown between the Brotherhood and the X-Men, and articulates his disappointment: "America was to be the land of tolerance, peace." Scenes like this indicate that the differences between fictional cities like Superman's Metropolis and the New York of the Marvel comics is not only motivated by references to real-life locations and pop-cultural phenomena, but also from a political perspective. Bryan Singer described *X-Men* as a comic book version of Arthur Miller's *The Crucible*.*

One of the central recurring themes of the comic series is the confrontation with bigotry and prejudices, especially in the stories written by the renowned author Chris Claremont. Originally related to the political backlash of the Reagan era, Claremont's graphic novel *God Loves, Man Kills* still provided the appropriate background story for Singer's second *X-Men* film in 2003. *X-Men 2* elaborates on the political content of the first film. Bryan Singer explained that he wanted to integrate certain subtext within a mainstream cinema format: "There's a lot of subversive things happening in X2 [...]. Some of them are not so under the surface. You have socio-political issues happening, you have analogies to 'coming out'" (Mottram 311). Political and private conflicts overlap in many cases. The state of emergency brought about by Colonel Stryker's intrigues affects many of the X-Men on a personal level. The openly gay Singer directed a scene in which Rogue's boyfriend Iceman confesses to his parents that he is a mutant. As Singer indicated in the interview quoted above, this confession is comparable to a "com-

---

*Interview with Bryan Singer included on the X-Men DVD Special Edition. Twentieth Century Fox, 2003.

ing-out." In contrast to the easy solutions offered by conventional blockbuster cinema his relatives do not show any kind of understanding. Iceman and his companions, Wolverine, Pyro and Rogue, have to escape from suburbia when his little brother calls the police. The law enforcers, who do not recognize the situation at all, suppose that Iceman's family has been taken hostage by the mutants. These misunderstandings are the result of a campaign orchestrated by Colonel Stryker and his forces, who intentionally made up allegations of a connection between an assassination attempt on the president and mutant activism. The opinionated media coverage dealing with the case is presented as television soundbytes that appear in the background in several scenes. With this, Singer not only comments on the one-sidedness of news reports, but also successfully employs a stylistic device also seen in many graphic novels like Frank Miller's *The Dark Knight Returns*.

The message of tolerance and not trusting first impressions is again articulated with the introduction of a new character. Teleporting mutant Nightcrawler is assumed to be a radical assassin. After the X-Men discover that he has been manipulated, he turns out to be a German circus artist from Munich who looks like a blue-skinned devil but is deeply pious. His personal faith offers an alternative to the bigotry of the Moral Majority represented by Stryker and his henchmen. The process of moving beyond a deceiving outer appearance captures the attitude of the comic book series accurately.

Some plot details from Chris Claremont's *God Loves, Man Kills* have been updated to suit the political situation of today. The televangelist Stryker from the graphic novel is turned into a fanatical Colonel who stages an assassination attempt on the President of the United States in order to stir up the conflict between men and mutants. He also knows about Wolverine's mysterious past as part of a secret military project. Scenes of the implantation of the adamantium skeleton that are only alluded to in short flashback sequences in the first film are developed in more detail in X2. Subsequently, Wolverine realizes that Stryker and his troops regard him as a monstrous by-product of their research for creating efficient human weapons.

The function of the X-Men crew as a substitute family that gives the social outsiders dignity and provides them with a sense of unity develops into one of the central themes of the second and the third film. This includes a short-time reconsideration of certain uneasy ties within the mutant community. The state of emergency results in a temporary alliance between Magneto and the X-Men and blurs, at least for a short time, the dividing line between good and evil before they go separate ways again after the showdown. The conflict between the Brotherhood and the X-Men comes to a head in *X-Men 3—The Last Stand*, which is directed by Brett Ratner (*Rush Hour, Red Dragon*) in a solid way that does not quite live up to Singer's more innovative *mise-en-scène*. A new serum, euphemistically called the "cure," permits reversion of the mutant gene. The political subtext of the first two films becomes more explicit, but at the same time discoursive aspects are reduced in favor of impressive action sequences.

Although both *X-Men 3* and *Spider-Man 3* are quite superior to the average blockbuster fare produced by Hollywood studios, they are representative of a more commercial approach recently taken by the studios. The studios became more averse to risks when the rather art-house adaptation *Hulk* (USA 2003) by the internationally acclaimed director Ang Lee did not turn out to be as successful as Universal Pictures expected. *Hulk* included experimental features such as split-screen compositions emulating panels from a page within a comic book. The sometimes rapid change between different points of view from one panel to the next is imitated by unusual camera angles and abrupt editing. Ang Lee followed the tradition of psychologically complex Marvel characters and stayed true to his own fascination with difficult family structures. He added a traumatic conflict with a highly problematic father (Nick Nolte) to the *Dr. Jekyll and Mr. Hyde*-inspired story of scientist Bruce Banner (Eric Bana), who after an accident in a laboratory turned into the monstrous green giant Hulk. Nolte's mad scientist father, who used his own son as a guinea pig in his experiments, is mirrored by the authoritarian General Ross (Sam Elliott). The father of Bruce's long-time love interest, Betty (Jennifer Connelly), tries to keep his daughter away from the tragic hero. Supported by the government, Betty's father declares open season on the Hulk and hunts Banner and his alter ego in much the same way FBI agents from the 1960s cult TV series *The Fugitive* pursued the innocent Dr. Kimble. Although *Hulk* features state-of-the-art special effects, Ang Lee takes his time to include a radically reduced and intense confrontation between Bruce Banner and his estranged father. The focus on the actors reminds more of a stage drama than a blockbuster with a budget of over a hundred million dollars.

Ang Lee's *Hulk*, with its challenging visual concept and its psychologically detailed character development, even took the risk of not introducing the monster until 40 minutes into the film. All this in combination with Lee's explicit critique of narrow-minded military demonstrate the creative potential of the Marvel adaptations. More commercially orientated efforts such as *The Punisher* (USA 2004) and *The Fantastic Four* (USA 2005/2007) nevertheless indicate that the studios are only willing to take moderate risks to ensure that the productions continue to be at least moderately successful at the box office. Renewed departures from conventional standards of comic book adaptation are only tolerated if the film in question still promises to be accepted by a larger audience. Where Ang Lee could indulge an openly experimental approach, the ambitious ideas of other directors involved with Marvel adaptations now rather tend to manifest themselves in the subtext or as Bryan Singer puts it: "I feel whenever there's unrest in the world, it does breed creative revolution of sorts [...]. If on the surface merely to give someone distraction from the day to day terror of the news, on the inside it gives artists the chance to express their own point of view" (qtd. in Mottram XXVI). The *X-Men* films developed the subversive political potential of the Marvel adaptations in the same way the *Spider-Man* films demonstrated visual creativity in combining superhero adventures with serious drama and an ironic depiction of everyday life.

Even if films like *Hulk 2* (USA 2008), produced by a newly founded Marvel film production company, should return to a more conventional form than their precursors by Singer, Raimi, and Lee, the new wave of serious comic book adaptations initiated by *X-Men* and *Spider-Man* seems to have had a lasting effect on the genre. Studios are willing to accept more director-influenced comic book adaptations such as Christopher Nolan's *Batman Begins* (USA 2005/2008) or *Sin City* (USA 2005) by Robert Rodriguez and Frank Miller. In contrast to the mediocre output of ten years ago, producers are now ready to finance a new variety of comic book adaptations from the modernized, family-orientated high camp of Tim Story's *Fantastic Four* to politically committed graphic novels like *V for Vendetta* (USA/GB 2006) and sophisticated indie adaptation *Hellboy*. The involvement of the comic book artists in the film adaptations has increased to the point that they are no longer restricted to short cameo roles in the films but actively participate as executive producers. So, for example, Stan Lee acts as executive producer in almost every Marvel adaptation, Mike Mignola as creative consultant for the *Hellboy* films. A few artists like Frank Miller (*Sin City*, *The Spirit*, USA 2008), Enki Bilal (*Tykho Moon*, France 1996, *Immortal*, France 2005) and Dave McKean (*Mirror Mask*, GB 2005) have even become directors themselves. The technological advances in the field of computer-generated imagery herald an increasing convergence between designing graphic art and creating cinematic scenarios for the big screen.

In the same way in which Marvel changed the mainstream of American superhero comics 40 years ago by merging serial storytelling with the creative handwriting of individual artists, the Marvel productions initiated a more complex and differentiated approach toward comic book adaptations for the big screen. In their best moments they correspond to the demands of a box-office hit and to the criteria of a personal, director-driven film at the same time. That this does not always work is shown by films like Rob Bowman's *Elektra* (USA 2005), which brightly illuminated all the dark corners that provided Frank Miller's comic book with the characteristic shades of noir, or by Mark Steven Johnson's *Ghost Rider* (USA 2007), which left unfinished some promising ideas of a Faustian pact between a motorcross driver and the devil and favored cheap visual effects instead. Yet, even in these worst cases, the results are at least an indicator for the new diversity in comic book adaptations.

BIBLIOGRAPHY

Howe, Sean (ed.). *Give Our Regards to the Atomsmashers*. New York: Pantheon, 2004.
Lee, Stan, and George Mair. *Excelsior—The Amazing Life of Stan Lee*. New York: Fireside, 2002.
Manovich, Lev. *The Language of New Media*. Cambridge, MA: MIT Press, 2001.
Mottram, James. *The Sundance Kids—How the Mavericks Took Back Hollywood*. London: Faber & Faber, 2006.
Wein, Len (ed.). *The Unauthorized X-Men—SF and Comic Writers on Mutants, Prejudice and Adamantium*. Dallas: Benbella, 2006.

# 3

## From Trauma Victim to Terrorist: Redefining Superheroes in Post–9/11 Hollywood

*Dan A. Hassler-Forest*

*Remember Pearl Harbor* (dir. Joseph Stanley, 1942) was the first feature film to offer a fictionalized depiction of the attack on Pearl Harbor, and it appeared within a year of this "day of infamy." Although the crowds may not have rushed to see this low-budget B-movie, cinema screens were soon awash with propaganda films meant to encourage American audiences to support the war effort. At this time in history, American popular culture was universally aligned to a single cause, which was reflected not just in feature films and cartoons, but also in comic books, which "never wavered in their support for the war effort" (Wright 54). World War II marked that "rare convergence of interests between publishers, creators, readers, and government policy" (Wright 54) that would not only provide that burgeoning medium with many of its most enduring characters, but that would help to define the ways in which comic books would develop an ongoing relationship with political and social conflicts in the following decades.

But Hollywood has proved much more reluctant to fictionalize the events of 9/11 in commercial feature films. Unlike the American comic book industry, which was quick to publish issues in which superheroes like Spider-Man and Captain America make appearances at Ground Zero and subsequently play a role in the Bush administration's War on Terror, none of the major Hollywood film studios released a film about the attacks until 2006.* Even

---

*\*Before 2006, the only Hollywood film to make specific reference to the 9/11 attacks was* 25th Hour *(dir. Spike Lee, 2002), which incorporated footage of Ground Zero as part of a backdrop to a story that—although it can easily be read as a metaphoric treatise on guilt, responsibility and punishment— does not deal directly with the events of 9/11. Other films such as* 09'11"01— *(continued on page 34)*

then, the premieres of *United 93* (dir. Paul Greengrass, 2006) and *World Trade Center* (dir. Oliver Stone, 2006) were surrounded by controversy. The ensuing public debate centered on the question whether it was appropriate for a fictionalized film to recreate events that had caused such an intense national trauma. The common perception is that any Hollywood film, which is an inherently commercial product, would trivialize the experience by turning it into a commercial commodity, or as Adorno would claim: "making it too accessible by turning it into yet another saleable commodity" (qtd. after Storey 51).

Although one might raise the obvious Frankfurt School objections to commodifying "authentic" experience, it is more likely that the American film industry has been hesitant to address the events of 9/11 head-on. Psychoanalytic film theory, and more specifically trauma theory, offers a viable explanation for the fact that popular cinema has only made cloaked references to these events until very recently. As defined by trauma theorist Cathy Caruth, the term *trauma* should be understood as a mental wound that "is experienced too soon, too unexpectedly to be fully known and is therefore not available to consciousness until it imposes itself again, repeatedly, in the nightmare and repetitive actions of the survivor" (Caruth 3/4). Therefore, by watching films that offer an indirect representation of the 9/11 attacks, it becomes possible for viewers to give meaning to events that were too sudden and traumatic to be understood as they occurred.

In this chapter, I will demonstrate how two recent Hollywood films featuring superhero narratives, both of which were adapted from highly influential and well-known graphic novels, can be read first and foremost as texts that engage directly with debates surrounding the American national trauma of 9/11. To varying degrees, both films actually encourage a reading that runs counter to the current American administration's policies, and which has been dubbed subversive and even irresponsible by the American press. By comparing and contrasting the films *Batman Begins* (dir. Christopher Nolan, 2005) and *V for Vendetta* (dir. James McTeigue, 2006) with each other as well as with the graphic novels upon which they were based, I aim to illustrate how both films refer explicitly to cultural discourse post–9/11, and how they encourage viewers to relate the moral choices presented in these narratives to real-life contemporary social and political discourse. Both films feature protagonists who are portrayed from within the superhero tradition, and both address the problem of redefining the relevance of superheroes in a post–9/11 environment. I will argue firstly that these films present a new kind of superhero narrative that is a direct adaptation of the "revisionary" graphic novels

September 11 *(dir. Youssef Chahine et al., 2002) were aimed exclusively at (predominantly European) arthouse cinema audiences, and had no impact on American popular culture.*

that appeared in the late 1980s, presenting a break with previous superhero films. Secondly, by pointing out key differences between the films and the graphic novels on which they were based, I will demonstrate how the films refer explicitly to 9/11, and can therefore be identified as trauma narratives. And thirdly, by providing a close analysis of key sequences in both films, I will show how the films engage in a political debate on the nature and causes of terrorism.

## THE REVISIONARY SUPERHERO NARRATIVE

*Batman Begins* and *V for Vendetta* were based on graphic novels that were published in the late 1980s, when comic books came of age in a bid for cultural and literary legitimacy. Controversy surrounds both films' relationship to their source material: while *V for Vendetta* was clearly based on the collected comic book series that was published as a single-volume graphic novel in 1989, author Alan Moore had his name removed from the credits, stating that in his opinion the story had been "turned into a Bush-era parable by people too timid to set a political satire in their own country" (Moore 2006). The plot of *Batman Begins* on the other hand is not drawn from any single work, but the film features a large number of similarities with characters, props and events from Frank Miller's graphic novels *Batman: The Dark Knight Returns* and *Batman: Year One*. Although Frank Miller has no screen credit in the film, *Batman Begins* clearly "us[es] his work without invoking his name" (Newman 21).

Geoff Klock has described those works as "revisionary" superhero narratives.\* The key texts identified by Klock as revisionary superhero narratives are both Batman books by Frank Miller, as well as Alan Moore's and Dave Gibbons' *Watchmen* and his collaboration with artist Brian Bolland, *Batman: The Killing Joke*. Klock convincingly argues that these works constitute a movement (in which we could easily include *V for Vendetta* as well, since it appeared in the same period and has a similarly deconstructionist approach to superhero narratives) that marks the point at which comic books make the transition from "mere" popular culture artifacts to literature. Central to his theory is the idea that these authors successfully deconstructed the superhero narrative in multi-layered texts that problematize the extensive narrative history that has come to define the American comic book tradition.

*Batman Begins* and *V for Vendetta*, both highly successful blockbuster

---

*\*Klock's work is based largely on Harold Bloom's literary theory on the poetic tradition as driven by the anxiety of influence.*

action films produced and distributed by a major Hollywood studio, achieve a similar effect for the figure of the superhero in cinema. As Klock writes, "central to understanding the revisionary superhero narrative is the re-imagining of origins" (50), which is at the very core of both these films: *Batman Begins*— as its very title suggests — deals entirely with the creation of a new origin story that connects the character's childhood trauma to the ensuing danger of recruitment by a terrorist organization, while *V for Vendetta* goes even further in its depiction of a superhero character as an advocate of terrorism as a legitimate means toward political change. Since the superhero movie franchise became a powerful commercial force in the Hollywood blockbuster marketplace following the release of *Superman* (dir. Richard Donner, 1978), superhero movies have followed the example of mainstream comic books by including a "political dimension, usually supporting whatever hegemonic discourse (most often conservative) the decade at hand had to offer" (Klock 39). I will argue that *Batman Begins* and *V for Vendetta* distinguish themselves from more traditional mainstream superhero film franchises like *Spider-Man*, *X-Men* and *Blade* by including an ideological slant that runs counter to the direction of U.S. policy in the 2000s.

## *BATMAN BEGINS*—THE "OTHERING" OF AN AMERICAN HERO

In the previous four Batman films, which appeared between 1989 and 1997, Batman was portrayed as a figure that fought crime in league with the police force as a masked vigilante, his dual identity the direct result of the trauma suffered by the murder of his parents. The first and third films in the cycle, *Batman* (dir. Tim Burton, 1989) and *Batman Forever* (dir. Joel Schumacher, 1995), included flashbacks to this trauma and the hero's resultant dual nature. But Batman's motivations and his commitment to justice were never questioned, neither by himself nor by others. His status is raised in these films from violent, proto-fascist vigilante to unquestioned agent of morality by means of the "Bat-Signal," the beacon used by the police whenever the superhero's aid is required. Rather than the "brooding psychopath" of the revisionary graphic novels *The Dark Knight Returns* and *Year One*, Batman was portrayed as the "square-jawed law-enforcer of earlier comics," and in *Batman & Robin* (Joel Schumacher, 1997) even as a character resembling "the camp, pop-art figure of the classic 1960s TV series" (Sabin 87). These films, like almost every other superhero movie to emerge from Hollywood in the past 25 years, certainly benefited from the fact that the revisionary work of Moore and Miller brought with it a renewed public interest in superhero narratives. But their narratives — without exception — fall within the realm of the "Silver Age" in the history of American comics that presented straightforward, nonironic superhero narratives.

*Batman Begins* digs much more deeply into the issues of childhood trauma and morality, firstly by making it clear how thin the line is that separates Batman's vigilantism from the ideology of a terrorist organization. The first part of the film consists of flashbacks to Bruce Wayne's childhood trauma, followed by a sequence about his self-imposed exile in an unidentified mountainous region in Asia. While there, seeking an outlet for his trauma-induced grief by beating up fellow inmates in a Chinese prison, Wayne is approached by Henri Ducard, who entices him to join a secret society called the League of Shadows. Ducard has little trouble convincing Wayne to join his organization:

> BRUCE WAYNE: What makes you think I need a path?
> HENRI DUCARD: A vigilante is just a man lost in the scramble for his own gratification. He can be destroyed, or locked up; but if you make yourself more than just a man, if you devote yourself to an ideal, and if they can't stop you, you become something else entirely.

Once he joins the League, Wayne is trained in martial arts and various other fighting techniques. This makes him an effective unit in a terrorist organization bent on maintaining order in the world by punishing societies it deems overly decadent and/or corrupt. What makes this training sequence remarkable and what sets it apart from other superhero film narratives is the fact that a clear process of "othering" takes place. As Edward Said argued in his seminal work *Orientalism*, the West has tended to identify itself as separate from the East by using simplistic dichotomies (e.g., scientific vs. religious thought, rational vs. irrational thinking) that justify viewing entire populations as inherently "other" from a Western "us." This kind of thinking has allowed for reductive statements about the nature of terrorism that cast perpetrators of the 9/11 attacks as "an irrational 'Other' bent on destroying the West" (Norlund 3).

This reinvention of Batman as a character who learned his skills in the Far East also presents a first strong departure from Miller's graphic novels: *Batman: Year One* includes panels that show Bruce Wayne in training to become Batman, all of which takes place on the grounds of Wayne Manor. This is significant for the fact that as much as Miller's graphic novel represents a revisionary approach to the character's roots, Batman/Bruce Wayne remains firmly anchored within Gotham City (and therefore within the United States), as are the threats from which he must defend the city. *Year One* begins with Wayne's return from abroad (a 12-year absence is specified, but his activities during this period are not), while the film *Batman Begins* frames the character's beginning from a very specific foreign context.

The League of Shadows' headquarters, where Wayne undergoes his combat training in *Batman Begins*, are set in a temple in a remote Asian mountain range, recalling the headquarters of terrorist organization Cobra in *GI Joe* comics, which are described as "designed architecturally to resemble a temple hidden in a Himalaya-like region" (Norlund 8). Like Cobra's leader, the head of the League of Shadows, Ra's Al Ghul, is also "a terrorist personality [portrayed] as a disingenuous religious leader, suggest[ing] that no terrorist or religious leader is authentically devout" (Norlund 8). This connection between terrorism and Eastern mystical religion is made explicit in the film by the League's headquarters' resemblance to a temple. It is further solidified by the presence of signifiers such as Buddha figurines on prominent display in the first interior shot. Bruce Wayne is successfully recruited, trained and indoctrinated by the League of Shadows, but later rejects the organization when he is assigned the task of executing a criminal as a required rite of passage. Wayne decides to reject the League's absolutist ideology, defining a subtle but crucial difference between revenge and justice, terror and fear. He immediately thereafter makes his separation complete by blowing up the temple where he has undergone the training that will later make him a superhero.

Wayne's rejection of the League of Shadows and its ideology becomes even more evident when he exchanges his Eastern ninja garb for high-tech American military armor, which he re-appropriates and transforms into his superhero costume. Thus, by portraying Bruce Wayne as someone whose childhood trauma has made him vulnerable to recruitment and indoctrination by a foreign and therefore "Other" terrorist organization, this revisionary superhero narrative and its re-imagining of Batman's origins breaks explicitly with Batman's established tradition of facing "a different and independent villain each issue, since a variety of them reside in Gotham City" (Norlund 2). This break with tradition, relocating the main threat from inside Gotham to a sectarian rebel militia in the Far East, is the first element that connects *Batman Begins* with 9/11 discourse, a connection that is further developed in the narrative once Ra's Al Ghul's scheme becomes clear.

Later on in the narrative, when Batman has established his role as a vigilante who fights criminals by using their own fear as a weapon against them, Bruce Wayne is again confronted by his former mentor, Henri Ducard, who reveals himself as the true Ra's Al Ghul, and reiterates his plan to destroy Gotham City:

> RA'S AL GHUL: Gotham's time has come. Like Constantinople or Rome before it the city has become a breeding ground for suffering and injustice. It is beyond saving and must be allowed to die. This is the most important function of the League of Shadows. It is one we've performed for centuries. Gotham [...] must be destroyed.

The League's plot to destroy Gotham City, Batman's fictitious city of residence since 1941 that "for all intents and purposes is still New York, and more specifically Manhattan" (Brooker 48), ultimately involves an attack that is to culminate in the destruction of Wayne Tower, Gotham's skyline-defining skyscraper and the symbolic and infrastructural heart of the city. The similarity to recent real-world events could hardly be more obvious. As Kim Newman has described it in his article "Cape Fear," Gotham City is attacked "by a fanatic eastern sect with a charismatic but impossible-to-catch figurehead which is bent on crashing a mode of transport into a skyscraper to trigger an explosion of panic that will destroy society" (21). Again, this climactic attack represents a departure from both primary sources, neither of which includes any reference to a skyscraper as a target singled out for destruction by the villain.

Rather than offering a literal allegory that restages the events of 9/11 to which *Batman Begins* refers, the film casts its hero as the city's (partial) savior. In a fevered frenzy of wish fulfillment, the attack is averted at the last possible moment by Batman, who succeeds in stopping the train with the help of future police commissioner Gordon, once again reinforcing Batman's alignment with the police force. But unlike previous Batman films and most other superhero movies, Batman's victory over the villain is not complete: part of the city has fallen victim to the terrorist attack, and crime is still rampant throughout the city. Wayne Manor has been burnt to the ground, and the last shot we see of Bruce Wayne (without his Batman costume) is of him and butler Alfred walking through the smoking ruins.

In the film's final scene, Batman meets Gordon on a rooftop, and their exchange emphasizes the ambiguous mixture of hope and loss that summarizes the film's narrative:

BATMAN: We can bring Gotham back.
GORDON: What about escalation?
BATMAN: Escalation?
GORDON: We start carrying semi-automatics, they buy automatics. We start wearing Kevlar, they buy armor-piercing rounds.
BATMAN: And?
GORDON: And you're wearing a mask and jumping off rooftops.

Instead of the usual signature shot of the superhero's silhouette atop a skyscraper, watching over the city's well-being like a gargoyle, *Batman Begins* ends with one of the film's key villains, Scarecrow, on the loose, and with the introduction of Batman's best-known nemesis, The Joker, as the next case for the Dark Knight to pursue. This lack of formal closure can be read to reflect the current situation of American post–9/11 trauma, which the film addresses without offering a resolution. Rather than engaging in the usual reductionist answers prevalent in American popular culture and political speeches about how terrorists simply "hate 'freedom and democracy,' they irrationally want to 'kill Americans'" (Norlund 4), *Batman Begins* actually presents an ideological debate with Wayne's mentor that establishes the difference between fear, employed by Batman, and the League's world of terror that sets them apart from each other (Newman 21).

## *V FOR VENDETTA*—THE TERRORIST SUPERHERO

Many of the same issues recur in *V for Vendetta*, in which one trauma victim teaches another a terrorist ideology, but this film offers an entirely different kind of resolution. In the film, which was based on the graphic novel by writer Alan Moore and artist David Lloyd, masked superhero figure V introduces himself to Evey, the film's other main character and the primary focus for audience identification. The introduction is made through an act of terrorism: he proudly orchestrates the blowing up of a public building in London. As the film progresses, Evey is educated by V, ultimately leading to her embracing his view that terrorist acts can be a legitimate form of protest:

> V: The building is a symbol, as is the act of destroying it. Symbols are given power by people. Alone, a symbol is meaningless, but with enough people, blowing up a building can change the world.

Throughout the film, the media are portrayed as government-controlled propaganda tools that help maintain control over the population through fear. Every act of resistance to the regime is reported as a terrorist act against a government that purports to keep the population safe from perpetual danger by maintaining a regime of fear that includes measures like an evening curfew and a quarantine zone that apparently makes all areas outside the city off-limits for regular citizens. This creates a binary opposition in which the government is established as unambiguously evil (a first departure from the far more complex graphic novel), and V's resistance to this government as therefore implicitly good. Evey, who initially does not question the status quo and who holds a job at the government-owned TV station, is abducted and imprisoned by V after saving his life. During her imprisonment, she grows increasingly intimate with V, who becomes a father figure to her who will instruct her, whose life she will save, and who will ultimately give his own life for his cause. Like Bruce Wayne, who is also surrounded by "a superfluity of Fathers" in *Batman Begins*, Evey is indoctrinated by this "hyperstitional mentor-guru" to change her perception of the world around her and to undergo a form of conditioning that will allow her to follow in this mentor's footsteps (Fisher 3). Both films therefore offer as their primary targets for audience identification characters that are defined by the authorities within the film as terrorists, thereby redefining this highly demonized term from a more nuanced perspective.

Another similarity between the two is the presence of a sympathetic police detective investigating the case: James Gordon has been Batman's loyal ally throughout most of the character's history within a police force that has been portrayed as corrupt and incompetent. In *Batman Begins*, Gordon (Gary Oldman) is specifically presented as a lone man of integrity, unwilling to accept bribes in a department fraught with corruption. Similarly, in *V for Vendetta*, Finch (Stephen Rea) realizes that the police force he works for is irredeemably corrupt, ultimately leading him to condone Evey's destruction of the Houses of Parliament. Also like Wayne, Evey has another father figure who functions as a "maternal carer": Deitrich (Stephen Fry) mirrors V in the way he is portrayed visually within the film frame and in his caring for Evey following a moment of crisis. Both men, in fact, serve her the same dish for breakfast, framed in a sequence of near-identical shots, while Deitrich jokingly identifies himself as the masked V.

However, unlike Bruce Wayne, who rejects his mentor Ra's Al Ghul as a father figure and who embraces the unconditional love offered by maternal father figure Alfred instead, Evey witnesses her maternal father figure Deitrich falling victim to the regime in a way that directly mirrors the childhood trauma of the loss of her parents. This is where the politics of *V for Vendetta* move far beyond the moral middle ground of *Batman Begins*. For whereas Bruce Wayne rebels against his conditioning, re-appropriating his training and costume in order to press "Gothic Fear into the service of heroic Justice" (Fisher 4), Evey comes to an entirely different conclusion: she moves from skepticism to self-discovery and enlightenment thanks to the tutelage of father figure V, clearly motivated in part by her witnessing of Deitrich's grisly fate. In a scene that serves as a re-enactment of her memory of losing her mother, Evey witnesses Deitrich being beaten, bound and hooded as she hides under the bed.

Evey's re-living of this severe childhood trauma is followed by her capture and torture, for which the government first appears to be responsible, but which later is revealed to be masterminded by V. During her solitary confinement, Evey receives a journal through a hole in the wall from another prisoner who shares her experiences with her. Not until she is willing to die rather than submit to her captors does V release her and teach her his final lesson. This experience, which is a re-enactment of V's own trauma, has a transformative effect on Evey, who now metaphorically becomes "V": the new embodiment of the idea he has stood for. Her transformation is visualized when she walks onto the rooftop in the rain, her arms spread toward the sky. The shots in the film recreate the panels in the graphic novel, albeit with one major difference: they are intercut with flashback shots of V as he emerges through fire out of his own prison, his arms similarly raised upwards. In the book, no such connection is made within the panels. By creating these graphic matches in the edit, underscored by the complementary backgrounds of fire and water, the viewer is made to understand that Evey has now become the same as her captor, and can fulfill her destiny by stepping into his shoes.

This notion of becoming the superhero/terrorist informs the film's climax, which is not only the point where it veers off most dramatically from *Batman Begins*, but also from the graphic novel upon which it was based. Similarly to Bruce Wayne in *Batman Begins*, Evey was traumatized at a young age by the death of her parents, who were arrested and killed by the government. She too requires the guidance of a father figure/mentor to transform her grief and anger into a form of power that will allow her to become an agent of justice, or even a kind of superhero. She is first introduced to her mentor in a familiar superhero trope: when Evey is assaulted in a dark alley by a group of nefarious hoodlums (identified here as government agents), the masked and cloaked V, who is seemingly invincible, dispatches her attackers and leads her to safety. He also invites her along as a spectator to his first terrorist act in the film: he blows up London's Old Bailey to Tchaikovsky's *1812 Overture*, an act visualized in the film as a spectacular — and victimless — fireworks display. This act is in fact a conflation of two separate scenes from the book, in which V — with Evey as his witness — first blows up the Houses of Parliament and later targets the Old Bailey.

The graphic novel ends with the eruption of citywide anarchy, triggered by Evey's appearance on a rooftop clad in the martyred V's costume and mask. During this outbreak of violence, the prime minister's residence is blown up by the underground train carrying V's corpse, but this is entirely unlike the climactic explosion that destroys the Houses of Parliament at the end of the film. For while the film depicts a peaceful conclusion in which a mob of spectators, all clad in V's Guy Fawkes mask and hat, march peacefully to witness the spectacular explosion of Big Ben and the Houses of Parliament, the blowing up of Downing Street that ends the book is witnessed from afar by two individuals, alone within the comic book frame, while the mob that marches through the city is portrayed as violent and anarchic.

In the same way that the endings of the two films differ, so does their message veer from the nuanced revisionary framing of Batman as a former terrorist who turns against his own organization to Evey's acceptance of an ideology that condones terrorist acts as legitimate forms of protest against a fascist government.

## Conclusion

What I hope to have demonstrated in this chapter is how both films offer readings of American culture and politics post–9/11 that run counter to the war rhetoric that has fuelled most American popular discourse on the subject. The Bush administration rhetoric draws on the age-old dichotomy that simplifies differences between East and West in order to legitimize "they hate our freedom" as the terrorists' only motive. As a counterexample, the recent film *World Trade Center* (dir. Oliver Stone, 2006), which was the second Hollywood film to fictionalize 9/11, again reinforces the interpretation of the attacks as an act of war by explicitly connecting them to the war in Iraq. Apparently, it is up to superheroes like Batman and V, heroes of fantasy worlds, to make clear to global audiences that this conflict is more complicated than the American administration's war rhetoric would have us believe, and that in today's world, even they can no longer afford to indulge in absolute ideas about right and wrong.

### Filmography

*Batman*. Dir. Tim Burton. Michael Keaton, Jack Nicholson. Warner Bros. Pictures, 1989.
*Batman & Robin*. Dir. Joel Schumacher. George Clooney, Arnold Schwarzenegger, Alicia Silverstone. Warner Bros. Pictures, 1997.
*Batman Begins*. Dir. Christopher Nolan. Christian Bale, Michael Caine, Liam Neeson. Warner Bros. Pictures, 2005.
*Batman Forever*. Dir. Joel Schumacher. Val Kilmer, Jim Carrey, Nicole Kidman. Warner Bros. Pictures, 1995.
*Batman Returns*. Dir. Tim Burton. Michael Keaton, Michelle Pfeiffer, Danny De Vito. Warner Bros. Pictures, 1992.
*Remember Pearl Harbor*. Dir. Joseph Stanley. Don Barry, Alan Curtis. Republic Pictures, 1942.
*Superman*. Dir. Richard Donner. Christopher Reeve, Margot Kidder. Warner Bros. Pictures, 1978.
*United 93*. Dir. Paul Greengrass. J.J. Johnson, Polly Adams. Universal Pictures, 2006.
*V for Vendetta*. Dir. James McTeigue. Hugo Weaving, Natalie Portman. Silver Pictures, 2006.
*World Trade Center*. Dir. Oliver Stone. Nicolas Cage, Maria Bello. Paramount Pictures, 2006.

### Bibliography

Brooker, Will. *Batman Unmasked: Analyzing a Cultural Icon*. London: Continuum, 2000.
Caruth, Cathy. *Unclaimed Experience: Trauma, Narrative and History*. Baltimore: Johns Hopkins University Press, 1996.
Dittmer, Jason. "Captain America's Empire: Reflections on Identity, Popular Culture, and Post–9/11 Geopolitics." *Annals of the Association of American Geographers* 95.3 (2005): 626–43.
Fisher, Mark. "Gothic Oedipus: Subjectivity and Capitalism in Christopher Nolan's Batman Begins." *ImageText* 2.2 (2006). http://www.english.ufl.edu/imagetext/archives/v2_2/fisher/ (14 July 2008).
Klock, Geoff. *How to Read Superhero Comics and Why*. New York: Continuum, 2002.
Miller, Frank, and David Mazzucchelli. *Batman: Year One*. New York: DC Comics, 1987.
\_\_\_\_\_, Klaus Janson and Lynn Varley. *Batman: The Dark Knight Returns*. New York: DC Comics, 1986.

Moore, Alan. Interview with Jennifer Vineyard. "Alan Moore: The Last Angry Man." *MTV Online*. 30 August 2006. http://www.mtv.com/shared/movies/interviews/m/moore_alan_060315 (7 July 2007).
\_\_\_\_\_ and David Gibbons. *Watchmen*. New York: DC Comics, 1987.
Moore, Alan, and David Lloyd. *V for Vendetta*. New York: Vertigo, 1989.
Newman, Kim. "Cape Fear." *Sight and Sound* 15.7 (2005): 19–21.
Norlund, Christopher. "Imagining Terrorists Before September 11: Marvel's GI Joe Comic Books, 1982–1994." *ImageText* 3.1 (2007). http://www.english.ufl.edu/imagetext/archives/v3_1/norlund/ (14 July 2008).
Orr, Philip. "The Anoedipal Mythos of Batman and Catwoman." *Journal of Popular Culture* 27.4 (1994): 169–84.
Sabin, Roger. *Adult Comics: An Introduction*. London: Routledge, 1993.
Said, Edward. *Orientalism*. New York: Vintage Books, 1979.
Spiegelman, Art. *Maus: A Survivor's Tale*. London: Penguin, 1987.
Storey, John. *Cultural Theory and Popular Culture*. Fourth edition. Harlow: Pearson Education, 2006.
Wright, Branford W. *Comic Book Nation: The Transformation of Youth Culture in America*. Baltimore and London: Johns Hopkins University Press, 2001.
Xenakis, Nicholas J. "T for Terrorist." *The National Interest* (Summer 2006): 134–38.

# 4

## "Picture This": Disease and Autobiographic Narration in the Graphic Novels of David B and Julie Doucet

*Jonas Engelmann*

The contemporary independent comic scene has produced a veritable wave of autobiographical comics and has thus created a new mainstream trend in black and white. Two of the most successful comics of the past decade, *Persepolis* (2000–2003) by Marjane Satrapi and Craig Thompson's *Blankets* (2003–2005), were, like many other recent publications, primarily autobiographic. A tradition of autobiographic comics can, of course, be traced back to the American comic underground of the 1960s, Keiji Nakazawa's *Barefoot Gen* (1973–1975), and Will Eisner's *To the Heart of the Storm* (1991).* The current boom, however, invites a closer look at structural parallels between these newly emerging works. Charles Hatfield writes: "Autobiography has become a distinct, indeed crucial, genre in today's comic books—despite the troublesome fact that comics, with their hybrid, visual-verbal nature, pose an immediate and obvious challenge to the idea of 'nonfiction'" (112). It appears that the comic as a medium provokes an examination of the self. Thus the following chapter will inquire into the cause of this phenomenon, as well as into the aesthetic possibilities of the recent trend toward the autobiographical in comics.

A look at literary criticism in the field of autobiography, like Philippe Lejeune's seminal description of the autobiographical mode in *Le pacte auto-*

---

*Andreas Platthaus even identifies Frank King's* Gasoline Alley *(1918–1959) as an important precursor (cf. Platthaus 201–6).*

*biographique* (1975) shows that what Lejeune calls the "autobiographical pact" cannot easily be transferred to comics. In his examination, Lejeune claims to establish objective rules to define "the autobiographical" but comics are not discussed in his analysis, because they are not autobiographical (cf. Lejeune 14). Even if some aspects of Lejeune's theory (like the unity of author, narrator, and protagonist) are important for the graphic novel, his all-too-narrow definition proves too schematic to serve as a proper basis for the analysis of comics. Lejeune's analysis can also hardly be squared with the tendency of many comics to consider the unreal and the world of dreams as of equal importance as reality.

Where literary criticism has failed, comic studies themselves have developed a number of different approaches toward autobiography as a comics genre. Jan Baetens locate this phenomenon within the more general context of the cult of authenticity. He puts its popularity down to postmodernism, to the often-described disappearance of the "master narratives," which makes the small narratives of the autobiographical subject gain greater importance (cf. Baetens n.p.). In contrast to this, Andreas Platthaus argues that a graphic novel claims no objectivity because, in its visual representation, "reality" is always visibly transformed, and authenticity can thus hardly be pinpointed in comics (cf. Platthaus 197). The central and notoriously controversial issue therefore seems to be the question of "authenticity." The potentially endless discussion arising from this* can perhaps be avoided by a concentration on questions of aesthetics deriving from the materiality of comics.

Georg Seeßlen considers comics a graphic medium whose intensity even surpasses that of films, since nothing—apart from drawing instruments—resides between the subject and the world. "The drawing is the (auto-)biographic as such: writing life on paper" (Seeßlen 51). Hence comics are often characterized by an extreme subjectivity that is combined with the possibility of reflection through a combination of text and image. One result of this tension is an ongoing fascination of artists with comics as a tool for the examination of the self. Bourdieu's criticism of established concepts of identity, especially his famous assumption that the attempt to describe life as a singular sequence of incidents is pointless (cf. Bourdieu 88), is thus transformed by comics artists into comic-specific aesthetics based on self-reflexivity.

In the following, two examples will show how artists working on similar themes can develop different graphic realizations. In their work, both David B and Julie Doucet discuss the topic of epilepsy against an autobiographical background and they develop aesthetic representations of the topic that are vastly different but make perfect sense in their own particular con-

---

*For a discussion of the issue "authenticity" in autobiographical comics, see Hatfield 108–27.

text. The wide aesthetic spectrum that is visible in the work of these two artists demonstrates the vast aesthetic possibilities of the graphic novel in the autobiographical mode. We have to ask to which extent the aesthetics of the examined comics are connected to the disease and if there is a conjunction between the configuration of the single panels (the text body) and the bodies of the protagonists, that is, if there is a relation between form and content.

It should be clear from this, that the following chapter does not intend to finalize the discussion on autobiographical comics but rather aims at asking some specific questions that touch on comic aesthetics and thus might, in turn, illuminate that field in general. Where, for example, can we trace the origin of the tendency in comics to consider the unreal, fantasy, and dreams as equal in importance to reality? Can it be seen as a relic of or rather as a link to the tradition of superhero comics? A comparison with film, a medium that also operates with pictures, shows the extent of the "surreal" in comics. The chances of an autobiographical film introducing a mammoth to enable the protagonist to discuss inner conflicts, as Frederik Peeters does in *Pilules bleues* (Peeters 161ff),* or place God at the dining table, as can be seen in Satrapi's *Persepolis* (Satrapi n.p.), are slim indeed. What would seem at least rather curious in films does not surprise much in comics. It is interesting that, by introducing an element of the surreal, the objective "reality" of an autobiography is usually challenged in other media, yet in comics the opposite seems to be the case.

## DAVID B

David B's *L'Ascension du haut mal* employs this surrealist method, the integration of dream fragments into an alleged reality, in a more intensive way than most other graphic novels. Pierre-François (David B) describes his brother's epilepsy as a history of struggles: the struggle against the disease, the struggle against the consequences of his parents' shock after the diagnosis, and the struggle against his own exposure to Jean-Christophe's epileptic fits. At the same time, it is a story of alienation: The graphic novel, narrated

---

*Pilules bleues *is also a very interesting comic in the context of disease and autobiography: it deals with AIDS and how the knowledge about the disease overshadows the relationship between the HIV-positive Cati and Fred. The graphic novel concentrates on the characters while the reduced drawings focus on the questioning, troubled faces. The more liberated Fred and Cati feel, the less the reader gets distracted from them; when their self-doubt is growing, the pictures get darker and darker and begin to swallow up the two protagonists. The connection between the level of content and the image level remains a cautious and intimate one. The disease is completely superimposed with fears and smattering. The blue pills, life-prolonging medication on the one hand but connected with severe side effects on the other, become a symbol that contains everything that characterizes the disease.*

Pierre-François hardly recognizes his brother (David B: *L'Ascension du haut mal.* ©1996 L'Association).

in retrospect, starts in the present in the parental bathroom, where Pierre-François is at first not able to recognize his brother: "He's got abrasions all over his body. His eyebrows are scarred. He doesn't have any hair at the back of his head, because of the collapses. He is corpulent because of the medication and the lack of exercise." This experience is transferred to the reader, who has probably obtained a first impression of the siblings from the image on the cover.* This prelude anticipates the general development of the tale: The physical nonidentification and the unfamiliarity that accompanies the disease prevent Pierre-François from getting into contact with his brother; his childhood companion becomes more and more of a stranger, with whom — as the bathroom scene shows — communication is hardly possible.

This alienation from his brother is transferred by the narrator into a general renunciation of reality, a phenomenon that becomes visible in the appearance of the phantoms. In literary studies as well as in trauma research, the image of the phantom marks the void that represents an incident that detracts from a structural subsumption (cf. Weigel 65). The brother's disease as a non-

---

*The six volumes of the series accompany the growth of the two brothers. The cover of the first volume portrays them as children and while Pierre-François can easily be recognized, his brother, Jean-Christophe, has changed beyond recognition over the years in the way described in the first panel.

4. "Picture This" *(Engelmann)*

The brother's disease as a phantom (David B: *L'Ascension du haut mal.* ©1996 L'Association).

comprehensible fact — neither from the child's perspective, nor in retrospect from the adult's point of view — can be read as an incident that detracts from subsumption.

However, it would be a reduction to see the phantoms only as symbols or metaphors for the disease: They rather have to be read in a metonymical way. All aspects connected with the disease, on a personal as well as on a social level, culminate in the phantoms. Not only do the brothers live through a process of alienation, but also a similar progressive marginalization takes place on a social level: The uncontrollability of the epileptic fits largely excludes them from central domains of social life. Jean-Christophe's identity is reduced to his disease; his body is fragmented by medical examinations, a process that is directly visualized by David B.

Foucault has thought along similar lines when he defined the powers that permeate, characterize, and constitute the social body and at the same

Jean-Christophe's fragmentation (David B: *L'Ascension du haut mal.* ©1996 L'Association).

time discipline it through that process: "The human body was entering a machinery of power that explores it, breaks it down, and rearranges it. A 'political anatomy' which was also a 'mechanics of power' was being born" (Foucault, *Discipline and Punish* 138). The ineffective medical treatment Jean-Christophe receives also functions as a disciplinary force and causes other modes of regulation that finally result in his exclusion from society: He is eventually placed in a center for disabled people after he had to leave a Rudolf-Steiner School because of his seizures.

In analogy to Foucault's depiction of the genealogy of social definitions of "madness" in *Madness and Civilization,* one could trace the social view on epilepsy back through the centuries, as one can see via the different versions of its name. Epilepsy was considered a "sacred disease" in some cultures because the persons concerned seemed to transform into a state of trance easily and even involuntarily.* In ancient Greece this seizure was reckoned a "penetration by the power of the Gods" and it attracted the attention of Hippocrates, who became the first researcher into epilepsy. In contrast to the positive aura it carried in antiquity, it was seen as a "Haut Mal" or "great evil" in the Middle Ages, a divine punishment or demonic possession that had to be exorcized.† This negative public perception and stigmatization influenced early modern medical research, which, in turn, created new prejudices. As most scientific research in this field in the 19th and early 20th century was conducted only psychiatrically, the public regarded epilepsy as a mental illness well into the 20th century. This only changed in the 1960s when new medical findings unveiled epilepsy as a neurological cerebral disease.‡

One of the main concerns of David B is to show that these new findings however did not change much about the actual social exclusion of epileptics and their families. He illustrates this for example by stressing the similar mechanisms of social exclusion of foreigners and ill people, which derives from hearsay, fear, and a lack of knowledge about the other. Some children in the neighborhood warn the siblings about the Algerians: "Be careful, Jean-Christophe! They kill people with knifes. My father has been there, he told me so" (*L'Ascension du haut mal* 12). Finally the brothers are convinced that an Algerian building worker has actually committed murder. A few pages later, this situation is mirrored when the same children accuse Jean-Christophe of having similar intentions because of his disease: "He is dangerous. When

---

*This is reflected for example in the title of the German translation of David B's graphic novel, which is called* Heilige Krankheit *[Sacred Disease].*

†*David B alludes to this with the title of his graphic novel but he combines the "great evil" of the disease with the Christian term "ascension," which conjures up the image of sainthood and martyrdom.*

‡*For a more detailed history of epilepsy, see Owsei 1971 and Schneble 2003.*

he goes bad, he wants to kill everyone! He keeps his hands as if he wanted to strangle someone! He tries to grab our throats" (*L'Ascension du haut mal* 34). The underlying social conditions — in this case the consequences of the Algerian War but also the antipsychiatry movement and the trauma of two World Wars — become interlinked with the disease although they, on the surface, seem to have nothing to do with epilepsy.

In this context, the use of the surreal — in the case of *L'Ascension du haut mal* the depiction of the phantoms — serves a specific purpose. It supports the theme of the graphic novel in two ways: on a personal as well as a social level. If *L'Ascension du haut mal* is seen against the background of the complete oeuvre of David B, an ongoing reflection on autobiographic elements in the use of the surreal can be identified. In *Le Cheval blême* (1995), which contains a visualization of David B's nightmares, one of the phantoms of *L'Ascension du haut mal* has its first appearance: the ghost of the dead grandfather. Here, the motif is clearly assigned to a dream world but later in David B's work it becomes part of the "real" autobiography.

This inclusion of already-established motifs in new work becomes central when autobiographic key scenes of David B's oeuvre are depicted, for example Jean-Christophe's first epileptic fit. *Babel*, drawn and published after finishing *L'Ascension du haut mal*, contains an episode in which David B returns to the place where the first fit took place (*Babel* 11). The scene is similar to its rendering in *L'Ascension du haut mal* but in the latter case David B's mother is on the spot to absorb his confusion, whereas in *Babel* he is left alone. The narration in *L'Ascension du haut mal* is thus marked as just one of many possible variations, as just one special piece of memory. The two versions of the same scene consequently reflect the limits and possibilities of autobiography in general.

Epilepsy is the limit against which the narration in David B's work constantly struggles. The phantoms, however, do not cover the whole dimension of the disease. It is simultaneously represented as a transgression, which gives the graphic novel much of its tension. Jean-Christophe's unattainability as a person is contrasted with the unreal, childish imagination of epilepsy as a monster that takes possession of his body. The suspension of the usual rules of realism on the aesthetic level here serves the purpose of reflecting the difficulties of understanding epilepsy on the content level. According to Manfred Weinberg, a phantom represents a complex structure of memory that puts unconscious *reenactment* of trauma and conscious remembrance into an indubitable context (185). A similar link is made by David B's graphic novel: It presents the experience of having a brother with a disease and one's own ensuing social marginalization as a traumatic childhood experience that cannot be approached in a direct way. Simultaneously, the act of trying to con-

Jean-Christophe's first epileptic fit (David B: *L'Ascension du haut mal.* ©1996 L'Association).

sciously remember these experiences brings to light the voids in memory that are often filled with phantoms.

## JULIE DOUCET

The Canadian artist Julie Doucet visualized one year she spent in New York as a comic diary in *My New York Diary* (2004), in which her subjective perception of the city takes center stage. She obviously felt overawed by life in the metropolis and this fact takes possession of every single panel. Walter Benjamin characterized a similar experience at the beginning of the 20th century in the continuous presence of letters in the form of advertisements in the street, which necessitated a constant alteration of perception (*Einbahnstraße* 103). The passer-by has to adapt his perception to the simultaneity of conflicting sensual impressions and has to correlate all these various influences. According to Benjamin, these multifaceted impressions have to be perceived in an uncentered and distracted way, and this new kind of perception is introduced as an antagonism to the paradigm of contemplative immersion, which

An overflow of graphic detail (Julie Doucet: *My New York Diary.* ©1999, 2004, Julie Doucet).

characterizes the traditional concept of the artist. This modified perception is compared with the impact of the then-new and visually challenging medium of film in Benjamin's famous *Kunstwerk* essay (381).

Doucet depicts this change of perception in her personal situation of shock and uses the overwhelming impressions as an aesthetic instrument. She draws panels that are essentially unmanageable due to the immense number of detail and thus leaves the reader little chance to read continuously, just as the protagonist experiences no moment of peace and quiet. As the protagonist experiences New York as a confusing challenge, this impression is transferred to the reader as an aesthetic shock. The gap between text and image and the incongruity between the time levels is kept as vast as possible. Aesthetically, Doucet paints and writes in the tradition of American underground artists like Robert Crumb or Art Spiegelman, whose work is also characterized by the rejection of contemplative immersion in the artwork or the panel (cf. Packard 214f). Their aesthetic approach has its roots in the aggressive modernist challenge, which Walter Benjamin characterized in the description of Dada art as a ballistic instrument that hits the spectator like a bullet (see "Das Kunstwerk im Zeitalter seiner technischen Reproduzierbarkeit" 379).

In Doucet's work this aggressive and offensive aesthetic has a corresponding element on the content level. As in David B's *L'Ascension du haut mal*, epilepsy plays an important part in Doucet's graphic novel even if the disease is only mentioned in passing. Unlike David B, however, Doucet is epileptic herself and transforms her disease into different pictures than David B. While David B tries to approximate something alien to him, Doucet tries to render

Julie's fits start to appear more and more regularly (Julie Doucet: *My New York Diary*. ©1999, 2004, Julie Doucet).

her own feelings. The permanent situation of stress and excessive demands of her surroundings are catalysts for the fits that start to appear more and more regularly. As already described above in the discussion of *L'Ascension du haut mal*, epilepsy is primarily inscribed into the body and not focused to the outside world. The violent consequences of the disease for the real body cannot be communicated, and therefore they are transferred in the comic to a formal level. As a consequence, the text body itself becomes the location of the literary and visual memory. Similar to David B, the formal level of Doucet's graphic novel becomes a tool for the examination of the disease while it is largely marginalized on the content level.

One of the aesthetic instruments Doucet uses to visualize the transformation of the text body are the claustrophobic drawings that leave little to no free space and are very difficult to penetrate at a glance. The treatment of the text adds to the impression of claustrophobia. The speech bubbles seem to take up what little space is left, and seem to try to crush the protagonist. When the reader concentrates on graphic details in the various panels, the overall impression of aggressive intrusion is strengthened by the symbolic and visual impact of the objects mapped: knives, scissors, broken bottles, and waste. While ostensibly remaining on a realist level, Doucet fills each panel with so much concentrated information that the limited space of the images nearly bursts. The claustrophobic visual presentation connects various levels of *My New York Diary*: the limitedness of the flat the protagonist lives in, the increasing problems with her boyfriend, the stress of living in a foreign city, her drug usage, and finally physical weakness. Apart from frequent epileptic

Visual calmness is regained (Julie Doucet: *My New York Diary.* ©1999, 2004, Julie Doucet).

fits, the protagonist also has a miscarriage. A visual calmness appears only in the last few panels, after she has decided to leave the city.

On the whole, the graphic novel is characterized by a sharp discrepancy between image and text. Doucet lets the images tell a different story than the one suggested in the dialogues. While she creates the illusion of normality in the diary entries, the images are threatening from the beginning. This distinguishes *My New York Diary* in its drastic visuality from other works by Doucet. Though her early work like *Lève ta jambe mon poisson est mort* (1993) seems visually similar at first glance, the protagonists quite literally receive more space in it and the speech bubbles don't crush them. Later works, for example, *The Madame Paul Affair* (2000), on the whole appear much tidier in the true sense of the word. Hence I read *My New York Diary* as an effort to transform the precarious living conditions Doucet experienced, and of which epilepsy was an important part, into images. The tension between image and text, which are partly in conflict with each other, reflects the autobiographical condition. Though epilepsy is only part of the whole narrative, it affects the protagonist's entire life in New York and ultimately leads to a paradoxical fear of leaving the restricting flat because of the danger of being seized by an epileptic fit in the streets while alone. This fear of being exposed to a dangerous solitude among the multitude of people in the city is contrasted with the self-imposed solitude within her flat in the last panels.

This self-imposed solitude in Doucet's comic can also be read as a feminist statement. Similar to David B's treatment of epilepsy, Doucet also links fundamental social structures with the representation of the disease. In this case the disease mirrors questions of feminism, sexuality, and gender. The relationship of the protagonist and her boyfriend develops from a balanced partnership to a suppressive system of control that he establishes over her when Julie becomes more and more successful as a comic artist. The epileptic fits increase parallel to this development and in the end the boyfriend, who remains nameless, even blames the disease for the problems the couple encounters: "You know Julie, I think something is wrong with your new dose of medication! Haven't you noticed, you're acting different since you're on it ... you're treating me so coldly" (*My New York Diary* 45). While the disease increasingly dominates Julie's body, her boyfriend wields social control. He tries to preserve the territorial borders of his masculinity and the protagonist's female body is thus captured under a double pressure. She can only free herself by turning away from her New York life. Ann Miller and Murray Pratt consequently see Doucet's text as an example of a reterritorialization of the female body (n.p.).

The crucial question is, however, in which way and by whom the female body gets reterritorialized.* Miller and Pratt understand the reterritorialization as an alternative "cultural mapping" of the female body whereby, according to Mary Douglas, "social taboos institute and maintain the boundaries of the body as such" (see Butler 131) But how does Julie Doucet transgress these borders of her body, and how does she redefine the cultural mapping she is subjected to? At this point the autobiographical aspect kicks in: By drawing herself and thereby creating a distance to herself or staging herself at a distance from herself, she discusses the comic in general, and the autobiographical comic specifically, as a constructed medium that is far from displaying absolute authenticity.† By disclosing the comic as something constructed, she unmasks the constructed character of the social implications connected with epilepsy. The restriction of the individual's free space as a result of the disease is similar to the restrictions of the protagonist by her partner by means of social control. In the last panel of the comic Doucet disengages from the strict constructedness of the rest of the comic. She dissolves the limiting borders of the panels and of the social framework, which allows her protagonist, Julie, to transgress the constructedness of her disease, her female body, and her life in the city. A New York brass band, which stands metonymically for the determining forces she has experienced in the city, virtually blows her out of the metropolis.

In a similar way as David B, Doucet uses the motif of epilepsy as a start-

---

*As Leigh Gilmore observes, even "women's self-representation describes a territory that is largely unmapped, indeed unrecognizable" (5). The field of autobiographical writing and the academic criticism dealing with it are largely dominated by men.*

†*This does not mean that the content of an autobiographical comic is necessarily "untrue." The problem of authenticity concerns all kinds of autobiography. Graphic novels are as "true" as any other autobiographical text.*

A brass band sees Julie out of NYC (Julie Doucet: *My New York Diary.* ©1999, 2004, Julie Doucet).

ing point for an examination of her personal environment and society as a whole. The disease's effects on the body are mirrored in the aesthetical configuration of both graphic novels, yet in two quite different ways. Precisely this similarity of theme and difference in aesthetical realization reveals the wide range of possibilities inherent in the graphic novel, which proves a flexible medium for the development of an independent aesthetic strategy for an approximation of one's own biography. Both David B and Doucet use the specific elements of comics and operate — in different ways — with the contrast between the overabundance of what is drawn in the panels and the empty space. This connects their work and divides their graphic novels at the same time. Where David B fills the panels with surreal images, they get loaded with threatening objects in Doucet's case. In the work of both artists, a conventional attribute of the comic — the limitation of the panels — is employed to represent an absence, something that is not directly pictured in the panel. The inclusion of surreal elements and dream-like artwork in *L'Ascension du haut mal* does not so much refer to something beyond reality but primarily communicates social facts of exclusion and social stigmatization. Doucet uses the limitation of the panels to express the restriction caused by the disease. The phrase "picture this" strikingly encapsulates both attempts to show something beyond mere illustration. This can also be seen as a call on the reader to use his own imagination, as Andreas Platthaus has noticed (195). The reader should not stop short at a passive reception of an illustration but understand the image as an offering, as an open system that, along the lines of Umberto

Eco's understanding of this term, becomes a receptory field for one's own experience and which is more open to questions than to delivering answers (cf. Eco 162ff). This questions, for example, the social implications connected with epilepsy and invites to reflect on the possibilities of autobiographic graphic novels in general.

This self-reflexivity unites the two approaches of David B and Doucet and shows that they don't envision their individual, autobiographical rendition of the disease as the only one possible approximation of epilepsy. Their work illustrates that a working definition of autobiographical comics should not derive from a claim of authenticity but from a search for an intense narrative and graphic rendition of the subjective perception of one's own life.

BIBLIOGRAPHY

Baetens, January "Autobiographies et Bandes Dessinées." *Belphégor* IV.1 (2004). http://etc.dal.ca/belphegor/vol4_no1/articles/04_01_Baeten_autobd_fr.html (10 September 2007).
Benjamin, Walter. "Das Kunstwerk im Zeitalter seiner Technischen Reproduzierbarkeit. Zweite Fassung." *Gesammelte Schriften. Band VII.1,* edited by Rolf Tiedemann and Hermann Schweppenhäuser. Frankfurt am Main: Suhrkamp, 1991, 350–84.
———. "Einbahnstraße." *Gesammelte Schriften. Band IV.1,* edited by Rolf Tiedemann and Hermann Schweppenhäuser. Frankfurt am Main: Suhrkamp, 1972, 83–148.
Bourdieu, Pierre. *Raisons Pratiques. Sur la Théorie de l'Action.* Paris: Seuil, 1994.
Butler, Judith. *Gender Trouble. Feminism and the Subversion of Identity.* London: Routledge, 1990.
David B. *Babel.* Paris: Vertige Graphic, 2004.
———. *L'Ascension du haut mal.* Paris: L'Association, 1996–2001.
———. *Le Cheval Blême.* Paris: L'Association, 1992.
Doucet, Julie. *Lève ta Jambe mon Poisson est Mort!* Montreal: Drawn & Quarterly, 1993.
———. *My New York Diary.* Montreal: Drawn & Quarterly, 2004.
———. *The Madame Paul Affair.* Montreal: Drawn & Quarterly, 2000.
Eco, Umberto. *Einführung in die Semiotik.* München: Fink, 1994.
Foucault, Michel. *Discipline and Punish. The Birth of the Prison.* Harmondsworth: Penguin, 1991.
———. *Madness and Civilization.* London: Routledge, 2001.
Gilmore, Leigh. *Autobiographics: A Feminist Theory of Women's Self-Representation.* New York: Cornell University, 1995.
Hatfield, James. *Alternative Comics: An Emerging Literature.* Jackson: University Press of Mississippi, 2005.
Lejeune, Philippe. *Le Pacte Autobiographique. Nouvelle Édition Augmentée.* Paris: Seuil, 1996.
Miller, Ann and Murray Pratt. "Transgressive Bodies in the Work of Julie Doucet, Fabrice Neaud and Jean-Christophe Menu: Towards a Theory of the AutobioBD." *Belphégor* IV.1 (2004). http://etc.dal.ca/belphegor/vol4_no1/articles/04_01_Miller_trnsgr_fr.html (10 September 2007).
Packard, Stephan. *Anatomie des Comics. Psychosemiotische Medienanalyse.* Göttingen: Wallstein, 2006.
Peeters, Frederik. *Pilules Bleues.* Genève: Atrabile, 2001.
Platthaus, Andreas. "Sprechen Wir Über Mich. Die Rückkehr des Autobiografischen Elements in den Comic." *Szenarien des Comic. Helden und Historien im Medium der Schriftbildlichkeit,* edited by Stefanie Diekmann and Matthias Schneider. Berlin: Sukultur, 2005, 193–208.
Satrapi, Marjane. *Persepolis 1–4.* Paris: L'Association, 2000–2003.

Schneeble: Hansjoerg. *Heillos, Heilig, Heilbar: Die Geschichte der Epilepsie von den Anfängen bis Heute*. Berlin: de Gruyter, 2003.
Seeßlen, Georg. "Geschichte als Trauma. Der Französische Zeichner Jacques Tardi Arbeitet an einer Chronik des Apokalypse des Bürgertums." *Konkret* July 2006: 51–53.
Temkin, Owsei. *The Falling Sickness. A History of Epilepsy From the Greeks to the Beginnings of Modern Neurology*. 2nd edition. Baltimore: Johns Hopkins Press, 1971.
Thompson, Craig. *Blankets*, Marietta, GA: Top Shelf, 2003–2005.
Weigel, Sigrid. "Télescopage im Unbewußten. Zum Verhältnis von Trauma, Geschichtsbegriff und Literatur." *Trauma. Zwischen Psychoanalyse und Kulturellem Deutungsmuster*, edited by Elisabeth Bronfen, Birgit R. Erdle and Sigrid Weigel. Cologne, Weimar and Vienna: Böhlau, 1999, 51–76.
Weinberg, Manfred. "Trauma — Geschichte, Gespenst, Literatur — und Gedächtnis." *Trauma. Zwischen Psychoanalyse und Kulturellem Deutungsmuster*, edited by Elisabeth Bronfen, Birgit R. Erdle and Sigrid Weigel. Cologne, Weimar and Vienna: Böhlau, 1999, 173–206.

# 5

# Novel-Based Comics

## *Paul Ferstl*

The comic adaptation of literary classics has already formed its own tradition. It started to rouse general interest with the success of Albert Kanter Lewis' series *Classics Illustrated*, which published 167 titles of world literature from 1941 to 1969 (cf. Horn 204). The series was designed to improve the image of comics, which suffered more and more from the assertion that young comic readers would more likely be drawn toward crime and even violence as a result of the "atrocities" depicted in particular in horror magazines (cf. Horn 859–913). *Classics Illustrated* sought the approval of education experts and parents alike by using established literary works as a basis for the series; it presented comics as a way of introducing children and teenagers to the world of literature while retaining the concept of action- and suspense-driven storylines to attract the young readers' interest.

With copies selling by the million and several reprints from different publishers until the end of the 20th century, the concept proved successful. Comics were even used as teaching material in literature classes which led to several publishers' specializing in producing comics designed for use in schools, along with teachers manuals to optimize the medium's potential in education (e.g., the Hodder & Stoughton series *Livewire Graphics*).

The concept of incorporating familiar storylines, motives and protagonists of the literary pool was widely used in other popular series as well — in the Disney universe alone hundreds of literature adaptations were published, especially by Italian artists whose works were also frequently translated for circulation in the German-speaking market. This development coincided with the rise of the comic artists' lobbying for greater acceptance of the medium as a form of art, and teaming up comic art with literature seemed a promising way to gain further respect.

In recent years artists have often been striving to reach an adult audience by adapting literature and consequently have distanced themselves from the concept used in *Classics Illustrated*. That series, while it relied on the status of canonized works, offered artwork of variable quality and was designed to convey the greatest amount of information possible at a rapid pace while reducing the storyline to a simple thread that could be followed easily. Thus comics were created whose famous titles were sometimes not more than vessels containing horror stories quite similar to those that were the reason for so much concern in the United States of the 1950s. The 89th issue of *Classics Illustrated*, an adaptation of Dostoyevsky's *Crime and Punishment*, offered nothing more than the story of an axe-murderer trying to avoid discovery. A central element of the novel, the sudden bouts of regret which lead to the murderer giving himself up to the police, are only shown in two quite unexpected pages at the end of the story. In the essay accompanying the comic in the 1997 version, Andrew J. Hoffman points out that the murderer does not do justice to Dostoevsky's Raskolnikow; the essay therefore tries to supply the information on *Crime and Punishment* the comic version does not offer (*Crime and Punishment* 55). Considering this and other daring enterprises of the series, for example, summing up Goethe's *Faust II* in merely ten pages (*Classics Illustrated* Nr. 167), it is understandable that comic artists yearning for critical acclaim showed little interest in being connected to this series, choosing instead to display open criticism.

With the rise of what has been termed the "graphic novel" which backed the development of book-length comics dealing with "serious" matters, the interest in collaboration with literature increased once more. The main reasons for adapting literature in comics were similar to those that had led to *Classics Illustrated*: improving the perception of the medium by visualizing literature and thus profiting from the esteem paid to the latter. This could be combined with the greater probability of commercial success of the comics due to their connection to already widely known titles. But—in contrast to previous projects like *Classics Illustrated*—these new adaptations of literature presented content and artwork worthwhile for an adult audience and thus aimed at demonstrating the comics' potential for telling complex stories in a unique style—as an independent form of narrative visual art.

In the early 1990s, the comic artist Art Spiegelman convinced his editors to try to collaborate with "some serious novelists to provide scenarios for skilled graphic artists" (Spiegelman, *City of Glass*, "Preface"). This resulted in the adaptation of Paul Auster's *City of Glass* by Paul Karasik and David Mazzucchelli in 1994. In the adaptation's introduction Spiegelman stated "that the goal here was not to create some dumbed-down 'Classics Illustrated' versions, but visual 'translations' actually worthy of adult attention" (Spiegelman, *City of Glass*, "Preface"). Similar views were expressed by Jules Feiffer in his introduction to Peter Kuper's adaptations of a collection of Kafka's short stories. Feiffer calls this project a good idea "(e)specially for those of us who detest the *Classics Illustrated* concept, which is to upgrade the image of comic art by cross-dressing it with culturally significant heavyweights" (*Give it up!* 3).

Together with other interesting adaptations of literature since the early 1990s (especially the series of Stéphane Heuet based upon Marcel Proust's *À la recherche du temps perdu*, Posy Simmonds' *Gemma Bovery*, Martin Rowson's *The Life and Opinions of Tristram Shandy, Gentleman* and Will Eisner's discussion of Charles Dickens' *Oliver Twist* in *Fagin the Jew*), the comics by Kuper and Karasik/Mazzucchelli will serve as examples for the following analysis of general techniques used in comic adaptation. This will be followed by the discussion of a probably less well-known comic from the German-speaking market, Isabel Kreitz's version of Uwe Timm's *Die Entdeckung der Currywurst* (The Discovery of Curried Sausage).

## Techniques of Adaptation

The techniques used in comic adaptation are similar to those used in other media crossovers and may be compared to preparing a drama for the stage. Decisions must be made considering the general plot, especially if dealing with complex structures involving different narrative levels; storylines have to be connected, abridged or omitted; a pool of characters has to be established and maybe characters have to be merged to reduce the dramatis personae.

Deciding on the incorporation of original text into the comic version is another crucial step, as it plays an important role in defining the comic's style. Using large portions of original text may automatically lead to employing a narrative strategy similar to the original, for example by establishing a narrator's point of view. A narrator's voice may be inserted using text-only panels, creating a similar but arguably less convincing effect than voice-overs used in film. But, generally speaking, a text narrated in the first person is inevitably drawn toward a third person point of view in the adaptation, even if parts from the original are prominently featured in the comic. This is due to the almost unavoidable graphic depiction of protagonists referred to as "I," which widens the gap between reader and narrator and makes identification and the classical perception through the eyes of the first person narrator more difficult.

Text used in speech balloons is usually derived from dialogue in the original, from free indirect speech or context. The artist's task of conveying the original's information is often met by manipulating the available space and employing the tools of the trade: panel-management, cuts, changes of perspective, timing, and imagery in the chosen style.

A rather obvious difference between adaptations and other comics lies in product presentation. The adaptations make frequent use of paratexts (forewords, introductions and afterwords) explaining the choice to adapt literature by discussing motivation and/or methods. A section offering information on the adapted text is often included for educational purposes especially in the *Classics Illustrated* series. Other adaptations may contain further information on the comic's topic.

The various reasons for adapting literature in comics are closely related. If the interest lies in content, the original is chosen because it offers a good and sound story and/or addresses a topic of special interest. This is of course combined with the obvious marketing advantages of being linked to a well-known title and thus hopefully appealing to a greater audience. Adaptations range from detailed retelling to being "loosely based on" or just "inspired by" the original. They may use all or only some storylines of the original, or they might even concentrate on a single character (not necessarily the protagonist of the original). The adaptations can transport events to another setting or present sequels of the original. The possibilities of manipulating the original material are indeed numerous. If the artist wants to influence public opinion on sensitive issues not addressed in the original, they may be shown in new light in the comic version by changing the point of view and expanding or rewriting the original storyline.

An interesting example of this strategy is Will Eisner's *Fagin the Jew* (2003), which sets out to tell the life story of Moses Fagin, the infamous villain of Dickens' *Oliver Twist*. As Eisner states in his foreword: "I was examining folktales and literary classics for possible graphic adaptation, [and] I became aware of the origins of the ethnic stereotypes we accept without question. Upon examining the illustrations of the Original editions of *Oliver Twist*, I found an unquestionable example of visual defamation in classic literature" (4).

Eisner's comic builds on the rich tradition of Dickens-related reception. It deliberately cites the works of George Cruikshank, the original illustrator of Oliver Twist (see *Fagin the Jew* 125), and sheds new light on the reception of the cultural influence of Dickens' work by fleshing out Fagin's character by constructing a backstory for him that bears obvious similarities to Oliver Twist's fate. Eisner thus changes the novel's content to fit his ends by simplifying the plot related to the original protagonist, Oliver Twist, and by omitting some of the negative characteristics of Fagin, but he retains the main events and shows them in the context of Jewish life and anti–Semitism in 19th-century Britain.

Another creative example of a somewhat similar strategy is Posy Simmonds' *Gemma Bovery* (1999). This comic relates the story of a young English woman who tries to start a new life in rural France in the 1990s. Unfortunately, her life seems to be constantly influenced by her name that bears a striking resemblance to that of Gustave Flaubert's heroine Emma Bovary. The parallels and differences between the stories of these two women form an intriguing pattern of links as *Gemma Bovery* tries to break away from the inevitable fate set by the original.

As a part of the reception of a major oeuvre, comic adaptations may contribute to the reception of a known work of literature by illustrating certain parts or even a complete series of novels in order to introduce new readers to the original novel or add further interest for those already familiar with the book. Starting out close to the original text (often featuring many direct citations), such a comic offers a complementary "view" on the events by illustration. Paintings, cities, buildings and landscapes featured in the original may be "cited" by graphic reproduction, a method frequently employed in Stéphane Heuet's adaptation of Marcel Proust's *À la recherche du temps perdu*.\* Starting in 1998, Heuet has so far published four albums that are based on parts of the first two novels, *Du côté de chez Swann* and *À l'ombre des jeunes filles en fleurs*. So far roughly 350 pages of text have been adapted, filling 216 comic pages — in his last album almost reaching the unusual rate of one comic page per page adapted.

Heuet has adopted the narrative structure of the original text and is closely following the sequence of events, using special panels for inserted original text. It is easy to trace Proust's text in Heuet's comic as he does not merge different scenes. Considerable gaps in the citation of sentences from the original occur only in long passages describing the scenery whose function is largely taken over by the images provided by Heuet. All the text in the comic is taken straight from the original; minor changes occur only in form of abridgements (especially in the case of extended metaphors, comparisons, digressions and off-topic reflections) or altered pronouns and conjunctions. Speech balloons are filled with text from dialogue in the novels, from free indirect speech, or with sentences from the context given in the original. In album I (*Combray*) Heuet omits only two scenes from the original text: Ms. Swann's father is not portrayed and the dialogue between the narrator's mother and Ms. Swann is not given but it figures in the comic nonetheless as they are seen talking in the background of a picture (page 9, panel 3) until their conversation is interrupted by the same sentence that interrupts it in the original text (page 9, panel 4; cf. Proust 29).

---

\**See, for example, the use of* La Charité de Giotto, *which features prominently in Proust's novel (72) and also appears in Heuet's first album (page 34, panel 7).*

In addition to the manifold ways that famous literary plots are manipulated to create innovative graphic novels, literature is sometimes used in comics to provide a basis for rather experimental visual expression. An experimental graphic vocabulary is then used to interpret the text while relying on its familiarity to the reader. Graphic associations and the visualization of metaphors and comparisons offer the reader additional information as well as the possibility of re-reading a familiar text while at the same time presenting the medium's potential. The use of a well-known text also strengthens the comic artist's control of the narrative as he is able to manipulate likely expectations. Examples of such graphically innovative, novel-based comics are Peter Kuper's Kafka adaptations, Martin Rowson's *The Life and Opinions of Tristram Shandy, Gentleman* (1996), or Karasik/Mazzucchelli's *City of Glass*, which all make extensive use of flexible panel management and hard contrasts in black and white to illustrate abstract concepts with creative imagery. Karasik and Mazzucchelli highlight the different narrative and emotional levels of the original in a compact and effective way by using different graphical styles as their characteristics and interlink those levels, side by side, on a single comic page. Rowson's stylized incorporation of 18th-century paratexts (such as erratum plates or dedications) links the comic with the original while it establishes an intriguing alienation effect.

## A CLOSER LOOK: *DIE ENTDECKUNG DER CURRYWURST*

Isabel Kreitz's comic version of Uwe Timm's novella *Die Entdeckung der Currywurst* was published in 1996 under the title *Die Entdeckung der Currywurst. Nach einem Roman von Uwe Timm.* The novella relates the story of 43-year-old Lena Brücker who hides the deserted German Navy soldier Bremer in her apartment during the last days of World War II. All of this is told by Lena years later, as an old woman, to the narrator of the novella. The main interest of Timm's text is that Bremer — who meets Lena Brücker by chance while being transferred to Hamburg to serve in the already lost battle in eastern Germany, spends the night at her apartment and subsequently accepts her offer to hide him — is kept unaware of the capitulation of the German forces, as Brücker, 19 years his senior, does not want to lose her young lover. When Bremer finally leaves, Brücker starts a successful take-away as a result of her "discovery" of the now famous curried sausage.

The comic version by Isabel Kreitz, which transforms the 220 pages of the original into 45 pages, is true to the text as far as the overall narrative structure is concerned. The frame narrative, which relates the narrator's search for Lena Brücker and their subsequent interviews, is retained but considerably abridged. It figures only briefly at the beginning and the end of the comic and in four short inserted scenes. The narrator is visualized, but fulfills his narrative function only in the opening and closing scenes of the comic. In the frame and main narrative, the pool of characters is reduced to those absolutely necessary; the storyline is condensed accordingly and often combines similar scenes from different sections of the original text into a single event on a comic page.

With the exception of the frame narrative, all written information is conveyed through speech balloons. The text is taken directly from dialogue or free indirect speech of the original and occasionally combined with text derived from the general context. Again, abridgements seem inevitable. The language of the comic is slightly less formal than the novella's. Northern German dialect is more often employed and the dialogue between the main characters is more casual and implicates a first-name basis right from the start.

Each page in the comic consists of four regular rows of panels with one notable exception: the opening scene of the main narrative that shows a street of war-time Hamburg covering half the page. The number of panels per page generally ranges from six to eight, except for three pages where the narrative flow is changed by increasing the number of panels per page to ten to create suspense or illustrate turning points (see Kreitz 24; 33; 43).

The realistic style drawn in black and white employed by Kreitz recalls war-time photographs. The absence of visual metaphors such as sweat drops indicating fear or excitement and the reserved use of speed lines add to the impression of calm realism. Lena Brücker's piercing gaze creates an impression of suspicion and exhaustion held in check by stern determination, occasionally softened by fleeting moments of happiness (see Kreitz 25; 44; 45). One unusual formal device stands out against the straight realism of Kreitz's comic: The adoption of a passage of the novella in which the events that lead directly to the discovery of the "Currywurst" are presented in a condensed way as opposites juxtaposed: Despair and hope, regret and joy, loss of hard-to-come-by goods and the discovery of a recipe; failure and new beginning (see Kreitz 42 in comparison to Timm 211). Other scenes that could have led to surrealistic images — such as Bremer's account of his dream after first having eaten curry, when he dreamt he was a tree being tickled to fits of laughter by the wind (see Timm 98) — were not included in Kreitz' version.

This seemingly simple realism of the comic version is somewhat deceptive. For a clearer understanding of the potential of the adaptation in question, a closer look at the text is necessary. Pages 30 and 31 of the comic version of *Die Entdeckung der Currywurst* skillfully condense several passages of the novella and use the material to prepare one of the story's turning points. In panel 1 (Kreitz 30), Bremer is seen smoking one of the cigarettes Lena Brücker has brought him. His comment on its quality is a direct citation, "Meine Güte! Wer solche Zigaretten macht, gewinnt auch Kriege!" ("Good Lord! People who produce such cigarettes will win wars!" Timm 138). This is unwittingly ironic as he is unaware, due to Lena's deception, that he is not smoking a German cigarette but a British brand.

Panel 2 refers to Bremer's habit of following the war's "progress" on a map after he has been led to believe by Brücker that Germany has joined forces with the western Allies against Russia.* The ironic potential of this situation, which is referred to in the novella as the "Great War Council of the Admiral's" ("Große Lagebesprechung beim Admiral," Timm 138), is omitted. Panel 4 once again features a direct citation ("Die Wende," Timm 114).

Panels 5, 6, and 7 show Bremer's surprise at discovering that black-market business is conducted rather openly in the streets, an unusual occurrence for times of war (cf. Timm 149). This leads to his suspecting that something is amiss with the information he gets from Brücker. The following nine panels then illustrate the violent struggle following Brücker's refusal to obtain a radio for Bremer. The dialogue used here is constructed from the original's free indirect speech and reduced to a minimum. Bremer starts cursing, knocks everything off the table and confronts Brücker, who is driven against the wall with outstretched hands and open, empty palms. While he is speaking of execution, he is shown in a menacing pose, his body nearly crushing the panel's frame, his right hand pointed at Brücker as if he were about to shoot her. The cut from this panel to the next is difficult to follow as Brücker is suddenly behind him, forcing him to the floor.

In the novella, Bremer's fear for his life is confronted with Brücker's nonchalant soothing, which is based on her knowledge that there are no more Nazi execution squads in the streets. Unable to understand her cool reaction, Bremer enters into a screaming fit, throws the dishes off the table and tries unsuccessfully to leave the apartment. The door is always kept locked by Brücker. Venting his aggression against the closed door, Bremer is overpowered by Brücker until he calms down (cf. Timm 153).

This example clearly shows the strategy used by Kreitz. Wartime experience is emphasized in the comic. The unavoidable condensation of material in a relatively short adaptation made it necessary to simplify the story of

---

*The text Kreitz uses here is mostly derived from information given indirectly in the novella. There are, however, a few significant deviations from the original. In the novella, Brücker offers the information that she has heard that Montgomery was advancing toward the East ("Sie hatte in der Kantine gehört, daß Montgomery weiter nach Osten vorrückte" Timm 138). Kreitz transfers this honor to Winston Churchill. It is possible that this was a deliberate choice, supposedly because the British field marshal, Montgomery, would be less well known to a broader audience than the prime minister. Yet in panel 3 Montgomery is referred to, taking the place of General Eisenhower in the original (Timm 138), which leads to the assumption that the change is probably due to a genuine mistake on Kreitz' part.

a complex woman in times of war who, after finally having a fulfilling relationship, quite understandably tries to make it last a little longer. In the comic, the relationship as a whole is kept as unproblematic as possible. Complications are omitted or understated. The heavy sexual allusions of the original are significantly reduced and the age difference between the protagonists is not noticeable visually.*

The comic's focus is certainly on Germany at the end of World War II, showing life in a bombed city in 1945. The struggle for survival in the aftermath of the war is combined with a love entanglement. Accordingly, the comic offers an additional 12-page documentation by the journalist Frank Giese about Hamburg in this period, underlining the book's inherent claim of being serious and informative (see Kreitz 50–61). The parallels between the concept used by Kreitz and *Classics Illustrated* are obvious.

The comic version of *Die Entdeckung der Currywurst* is what one could call a "straight war-time story" set in Nazi Germany and in the weeks immediately after the war. The Nazis are the evil Nazis. The finer shades of the original's wide range between open support of and resistance to the Nazi regime are largely omitted. The heroine is an independent, resourceful, strong woman, who is critical of the regime, courageous and passionate, but not larger than life. From the ashes of war rises new life, and Lena Brücker's struggle for survival and her eventual success mirror that of her country.

The war is over. Its result: curried sausage.

## Conclusion

The comic adaptation of literature has formed a rich tradition offering numerous titles. The connection with "culturally significant heavyweights" has its dangers, of course — staying too close to the original may lead to results that do not improve the status of comics. The reductive concept of *Classics Illustrated* is still a tempting one, as it has proven its commercial potential, but the cooperation of comic art and literature has far more to offer than mere illustration, even if, unfortunately, comic adaptations are still frequently presented as such. The original's title and its author are usually emphasized while the work of the comic artist is mentioned only in a by-line. Notable exceptions are the comics by Eisner, Kreitz, Rowson and Simmonds.

At their best, comics adaptations transform the chosen text into a new

---

*The pictoral rendition makes Brücker look younger and Bremer older than they are in the novella. The age difference is only once spoken of directly in the comic and then even incorrectly as the comic's Lena Brücker states in retrospect that Bremer was nearly 15 years her junior (Kreitz 27) instead of the 19 years that divide them in the novella.

independent piece of art that gains its own momentum when the links to the original are skillfully manipulated in order to form a pattern of intricately woven ties. A novel may be an auspicious starting point — but only if the journey leads to the creation of a comic that makes full use of the graphic medium's potential.

BIBLIOGRAPHY

Auster, Paul. *City of Glass*. Adaptation by Paul Karasik and David Mazzucchelli. New Introduction by Art Spiegelman. New York: Picador, 2004.
Dickens, Charles. *Oliver Twist*. Edited by Kathleen Tillotson. Oxford: Clarendon Press, 1974 [1837].
\_\_\_\_\_. *Oliver Twist & Notes*. Art by Arnold Hicks. Adaptation by Georgina Campbell. New York: Acclaim, 1997. (*Classics Illustrated* 23.)
Dostoyevsky, Fyodor. *Crime & Punishment & Notes*. Art by Rudolph Palais. New York: Acclaim, 1997. (*Classics Illustrated* 89.)
Eisner, Will. *Fagin the Jew*. New York: Doubleday, 2003.
Goethe, Johann Wolfgang von. *Faust & Notes*. Art by Norman Nodel. New York: Acclaim, 1997. (*Classics Illustrated* 167.)
Horn, Maurice (ed.). *The World Encyclopedia of Comics*. Philadelphia: Chelsea House, 1999.
Kafka, Franz. *Give it up! And Other Short Stories*. Illustrated by Peter Kuper. New York: NBM, 1995.
\_\_\_\_\_. *The Metamorphosis*. Adapted by Peter Kuper. New York: Crown, 2003.
Kreitz, Isabel. *Die Entdeckung der Currywurst*. Adapted from the novel by Uwe Timm. Hamburg: Carlsen, 2005.
Proust, Marcel. *À la recherché du temps perdu*. Texte établi sous la direction de Jean-Yves Tadié. Quarto Gallimard. Paris: Éditions Gallimard, 1999 [1913–1927].
\_\_\_\_\_. *À la recherche du temps perdu. Combray*. Adaptation et dessins de Stéphane Heuet. Paris: Editions DelCourt, 1998.
\_\_\_\_\_. *À la recherche du temps perdu. À l'ombre des jeunes filles en fleurs. Volume I*. Dessins de Stéphane Heuet. Paris: Editions DelCourt, 2000.
\_\_\_\_\_. *À la recherche du temps perdu. À l'ombre des jeunes filles en fleurs. Volume II*. Dessins de Stéphane Heuet. Paris: Editions DelCourt, 2002.
\_\_\_\_\_. *À la recherche du temps perdu. Un amour de Swann*. Adaptation et dessins de Stéphane Heuet. Paris: Editions DelCourt, 2006.
Rowson, Martin. *The Life and Opinions of Tristram Shandy, Gentleman*. London: Picador, 1996.
Simmonds, Posy. *Gemma Bovery*. London: Jonathan Cape, 1999.
Timm, Uwe. *Die Entdeckung der Currywurst*. Köln: Kiepenheuer & Witsch, 1993.

# 6

# In the Art of the Beholder: Comics as Political Journalism

## *Dirk Vanderbeke*

Over the last decades, comics and graphic novels have accumulated quite a number of ancestors from high culture, chiefly in the attempt to boost the medium's respectability in the face of the traditional accusations of mediocrity, if not outright degeneracy. Among the worthy forefathers we can find Frans Masareel, Wilhelm Busch, Rudolphe Töpffer, and if we look further into the past there is William Hogarth with his sequential works. Then there are the pictorial narratives to be found in medieval frescoes, illuminations, stained glass windows or the Bayeux Tapestry. Even earlier are pre–Columbian art or Egyptian narrative paintings (cf, for example, McCloud 10–19 and Zimmermann 250–51), and ultimately we can reach back to the very first works of art, that is, prehistoric cave painting, in our quest for the first parents of the comic strip (cf. Burgdorf 9 and Zimmermann 250).

Other ancestors are not quite as often linked to the comic in the quest for an honorable pedigree, as, for example, erotic or pornographic series of pictures — the Tijuana Bibles also have a long history.

Then there are popular religious series like the *Danse Macabre*, and, to jump just a little into a later part of my paper, the most famous comics journalist, Joe Sacco, has pointed out that Brueghel's *The Triumph of Death* has been an inspiration for his work (cf. Sacco "Presentation from 2002 UF Comics Conference"), and that picture shares many of its characteristics with the *danse macabre*.

However, the genre that is most interesting here comprises the broadside, catchpenny or similar popular publications, and specifically their relevance as an early form of journalism. In his introduction to a selection of texts from the Newgate Calendar, Clive Emsley writes:

6. In the Art of the Beholder *(Vanderbeke)* 71

A broadside depicting a horrible murder (Johann Schubert: *A Musician Kills Pregnant Wife and Child*. Broadside with Woodcut, Neisse 1653 ©Staatsbibliothek Bamberg VI G 111). For the broadside with text see Cheesman, xviii.

> Most people get their knowledge of crime from different forms of media representations; and it has been thus for centuries. The print medium has had a long affair with crime, especially lurid, sensational, violent crime. From at least the seventeenth century, broadsides were printed and sold at public executions, detailing the crimes, and the last dying speeches, of offenders [Emsley IX].

And as a major part of the audiences at such public events was illiterate, the written accounts were frequently accompanied by woodcuts presenting the reader with the fascinating and shocking details of the hideous deeds.

According to Tom Cheesman,*

> The performance of the "news singers," "bench singers" ("cantabancs") and "picture singers," as they were variously known, constituted the most accessible, mobile and all-round popular form of public multi-media spectacle through the period of the early growth of the culture industry: between the first emergence of a market in vernacular print publications, and the development of the electrical technologies of mass communication — colour magazines, cinema, radio, gramophones — which finally made picture-balladeers redundant [Cheesman 2].

The shocking ballads presented in these spectacles are usually categorized as part of the cheapest and lowest forms of literature.

Shocking balladry has long been castigated for failing both by the standards of literary, musical, dramatic and visual aesthetics, and by those of journalistic and historiographical ethics (Cheesman 5).

---

*I should like to thank Sigrid Rieuwerts, who brought the book by Tom Cheesman to my attention and directed me to this woodcut.*

However, the very assaults on this medium as recorded in this quote evoke the recognition of a similarity rather than an incompatibility, and the critique resembles very much the more recent complaints about the tabloids. The term "news singer" indicates a transmission of information commonly associated with journalism:

> It is obviously a forerunner of the tabloid press, of the commercial cinema, indeed of the "actuality" shows and "true crime" and "disaster and rescue" series currently popular on television and their equivalents in magazines and books [Cheesman 8].
>
> *Zeitung* came to mean "newspaper" in the 18th century, but before that it meant "piece of news" or "report," *Neue Zeitung* ("new tiding/report") was the generic early modern term for ballad news-sheets [Cheesman 2, fn].

The shocking ballad made it into the early 20th century, but the journalistic aspect of the crude and roughly made images did not survive the rise of photography and film as the new appropriate media for the representation of reality. Instead, the various forms of crime comics rather appear to be the true descendants of the broadsides, while a faint echo of the claim to authenticity can still be heard in the occasional bold assertion that the ghastly story is based in truth and nothing but the truth.

The comic as a medium has for most of its history been generally associated with distortions of reality, and, famously, it lends itself to the vision of imaginary worlds, supernatural events or, alternatively, to abstractions that can be not only funny but also useful in manuals or for educational purposes. In addition, for most of its history the comic has been categorized as a primarily juvenile medium, even if it has always been read by adults as well.* And finally comics have been predominantly regarded as a form of entertainment — and when utilized in the educational sector they have often been regarded as a kind of didactic deceit, a sugar coating for the bitter pill of learning. However, this traditional perspective has been increasingly challenged and comics have gradually gained acceptance and status. When Silbermann in 1986 offered a list of examples from different cultural contexts (comics in schoolbooks, Third World Comics for educational purposes, a biography of Pope John Paul II in comic form, a political comic "Marx for Beginners" etc., cf. Silbermann 23) it may not yet have convincingly re-evaluated the medium as a mature form for an educated readership but rather as a means to approach audiences that cannot be successfully — and commercially — reached by the

---

*According to research done by Alphons Silbermann, adults "form a big, if not the biggest part of comic consumers" (Silbermann 23). However, the subsequent analysis of the reader's actual interest in the medium shows aspects that indicate a "juvenile" approach, that is, identification with a hero who has an energetic personality, thinks and acts independently and ultimately conforms to some ideal (cf. Silbermann 23).*

more usual channels. However, it did indicate a trend with increasing momentum toward a visual culture in which comics could reclaim positions the sequential arts had lost to other media, among them the ability to address social and political reality in nontrivial and mature works of journalism.

I want to suggest that at least two important developments contributed to this trend. On the one hand the photographic claim to authenticity came under attack with the postmodern challenge to each and every form of representation. The reproduction of reality on film and photo has been retheorized as a construction involving the usual "ways of world-making" like composition and decomposition, selection and combination, etc., and thus it has become more difficult to maintain unqualified claims to truthfulness. On the other hand and within a less theoretical context, the audiences' trust in photographic and cinematographic authenticity has decreased with the advance of digital media and the new possibilities of postproduction. Once the impossible and the fantastic become commonplace in film and photo, indistinguishable from the real, the aura of authenticity is lost and Godard's claim that "film is truth, 24 times per second" rings hollow. In contrast to traditional responses, it is no longer the perfect illusion created by a movie that evokes an aura of authenticity but the very imperfection of the visual material. *The Blair Witch Project* now seems far more realistic than any of the other recent blockbusters that rely on extensive digital postproduction. The jump cut or the slightly unstable handheld camera of the Dogma movies have become the hallmark of a new "redemption of physical reality"; the real requires the visual traces of constructedness to appear as real.

Journalism has not been exempt from these developments, and one might even argue that some subgenres of journalism carried the torch for a re-evaluation of authenticity. In particular the New Journalism that flourished in the 1960s and 1970s employed previously unacceptable methods of fiction and a departure from the various codes of verification for its own ends. An important aspect was a turn toward a subjective perspective and the emphasis on experience rather than accuracy and factuality. John Hollowell suggested that "the events reported daily by newspapers and magazines [...] often strained our imaginations to the point of disbelief. Increasingly, everyday 'reality' became more fantastic than the fictional visions of even our best novelists" (Hollowell 3). In particular the experience of war and extreme violence seems to have required a revision of the traditional modes of realism — "the inability of the imagination and language to grasp and express what is happening characterizes reality as fantastic" (Hegerfeldt 218). The departure from the realistic mode is then a way to deal with a world that resists representation not only for the well-rehearsed theoretical reasons but also because its horrors have become ineffable. This is, of course, also a phenomenon in Holocaust literature, that is, authors struggling with the trauma of the Holocaust have argued that the events were so far beyond the thinkable and imaginable that they can only be accessed by a rejection of the strictly realistic mode and by a turn to the fantastic (cf. Hegerfeldt 212–15). Returning finally to the comic, this is quite obviously one of the most important aspects of Art Spiegelman's famed *Maus*. The displacement of the inexpressible terrors of the Holocaust by the transformation into a genre usually associated with commercial entertainment and the disneyfication of the world results in an incompatibility of content and form that in turn emphasizes the impossibility of coming to narrative terms with the unreal realities of the Holocaust. A similar approach can be found in Spiegelman's *In the Shadow of No Towers* in which he tries to work through the trauma of his experience of 9/11. I want to argue that this is a work of political journalism in the tradition of New Journalism rather than a satirical account.* Of course, the work is primarily based in the subjective experience of its author; however, this perspective offers a necessary counterbalance to the official appropriation of 9/11 by the Bush administration for its own political agenda and to the increasingly nationalistic and bellicose response by the media, which did not allow for any dissenting view — after all, *In the Shadows of No Towers* was rejected by various American newspapers and journals that had regularly published Spiegelman in the past, for example, *The New Yorker*, *The New York Review of Books* and the *New York Times*.

As Kristian Williams has pointed out, comics journalism's "inherent subjectivity contrasts sharply with the newsroom's dispassionate prose" (Williams) and it thus adopts a perspective previously explored by New Journalism. Moreover, the use of fantastic elements may now serve as a new form of realism, and Williams writes about Alan Moore and Bill Sienkiewicz's contribution to *Brought to Light*, that is, a comic book version of the history of the CIA:

> [T]he facts are there, and the nightmarish surrealism seems to fit the subject matter. Indeed, the reader is forced to question the propriety of the standard journalistic conceits — the calm recitation of facts, the carefully hedged allegations, the measured tone. A drunken eagle swimming in blood may actually come closer to the point [Williams].

While such an image is, of course, hardly compatible with traditional journalism, it is also a powerful metaphor — and as such it makes use of the cognitive potentials that have over the last decades been recognized as part and parcel of the epistemology of metaphor. It is the very tension between the

---

*The similarity between the methods of comics journalists and New Journalism has also been addressed by David J. Pett.

metaphorical and the factual that turns the image into an alternative path to cognition.* To return to Spiegelman, *In the Shadow of No Towers* has a wonderful panel with a miniscule plane crashing into a TV set with an interference pattern resembling a distorted American flag. The image not only reflects on the potentials of comics — and logos — but also presents a very precise metaphor for the way the media were hijacked into patriotic frenzy in the aftermath of 9/11 (cf. Spiegelman 1).

In contrast to the official images as distributed by the media, Spiegelman's work then attempts to recapture the personal visual experience on that day in Manhattan — there is one recurring image "that didn't get photographed or videotaped into public memory but still remains burned onto the inside of my eyelids several months later [...] the image of the north tower's glowing bones just before it vaporised" (Introduction to Spiegelman).

There is an account of the search for his daughter who went to school in the vicinity of the World Trade Center. There are political cartoons. And finally there are a multitude of intertextual quotes from comics of the late 19th and early 20th centuries. Of course, these pictures are highly subjective, but then Art Spiegelman argues that

> [t]he phoney objectivity that comes with a camera is a convention and a lie in the same way as writing in the third person rather than the first person. To write a comics journalism report you're already making an acknowledgment of biases and an urgency that communicates another level of information [qtd. after Williams].

The turn from the assumed truth of the photographic image and also from the detached perspective and bland rhetoric of traditional journalism toward an emphasis of personal experience and artistic metaphorization challenges the notions of accurate representation. It suggests that the reader cannot simply rely on the journalistic voice but has to recreate the truth behind the narrative on his or her own. Moreover, when the photographic recordings of traditional journalism are usurped and turned into logos for political agendas — and this is what happened to the image of the burning towers in America — the resistance against these pictures and their replacement by alternative images becomes a strong statement for a truth that will not succumb to the hegemony created by the coalition between the media and the political elite.

Art Spiegelman is at present probably the most famous of the serious

---

*Don Swanson writes about a psychology of metaphor that "a metaphor, because it is an erroneous statement, conflicts with our expectations. It releases, triggers, and stimulates our predisposition to detect error and to take corrective action. [...] It preempts our attention and propels us on a quest for the underlying truth" (Swanson 162).

comic artists, but in the field of comics journalism Joe Sacco is best known as the author of the books *Palestine, Safe Area Goražde* and *The Fixer*.

*Palestine* deals with the experiences of his visit during the first Intifada, *Safe Area Goražde* with his stay in that city while it was an enclave in the Bosnian War and *The Fixer* with one of his informants and translators in Sarajevo. And while Spiegelman is highly imaginative in the creation of an alternative reality that serves as a metaphor for political despair and his frustration over the present state of the American nation, Sacco's work sticks closer to the realistic mode, even though his pictures are of course artistic and frequently, as he calls it, cartoony. An important aspect of his works is once more the rejection of the detached and seemingly unbiased journalistic voice and photographic view. Joe Sacco has freely admitted that he is not an objective journalist (cf. Sacco "Presentation from 2002 UF Comics Conference"), and a lecture he gave in 2006 was titled "To Hell with Objectivity: How Comics Journalism Redefines Reporting." However, that does not indicate that he does not strive for some essential truth in his work, and Inara Versemnieks argues that "Sacco's work seems to come a bit closer to the truth than an account told from a detached, omniscient point of view, one that washes out all sense of the storyteller" (Versemnieks).

The comic format offers several advantages to Sacco's version of journalism. As he is interested in daily life under the most terrible circumstances, he can visually transmit the living conditions as background without having to use excessive descriptions. A photo of the not particularly exciting street scene as represented on page 77 would probably never get printed, but as a panel in a visual narrative it serves its purpose and certainly saves the proverbial thousand words.

This level of general personal observation is nevertheless still in accordance with usual journalistic reports or documentaries. A different approach to the visualization of Sacco's experiences in an unfamiliar environment can be found when his own face recurs over and over again and the thoughts are fragmented into isolated banners adding to the sense of alienation and also fear.

Then there are the encounters and meetings with the people Sacco talks to or interviews. Hospitality is a recurring topic even though the hosts are destitute and have little to offer. But the personal observation of the journalist, who for some time lived in Palestine and Bosnia, are only part of this approach, and Sacco also offers visual accounts of the stories and experiences of the people he interviews. The artistic form of the comic now no longer replaces other readily available forms of visualization — after all, his own observations and the meetings could easily have been presented in the form of a photo novel. But the stories he is told — stories of daily oppression, of cru-

6. In the Art of the Beholder *(Vanderbeke)* 77

*Left:* A street scene in Palestine (Joe Sacco, *Palestine.* ©2007 Fantagraphics Books). *Right:* Joe Sacco's face recurs over and over again (Joe Sacco, *Palestine.* ©2007 Fantagraphics Books).

elty, torture, war crimes, massacres and the suffering endured in consequence — have, of course, not been recorded or filmed, as documentation is hardly in the interest of those who commit atrocities. (At least so we thought before we learned from the pictures of Abu Ghraib that the torturers love their work so much that they take their own pictures and exchange these tokens of fond memories with like-minded colleagues or send them home to their loved ones.) Be that as it may, Sacco tries not only to give a voice to the unheard, but also to provide images of the unseen, based on the narrations of those who have lived through the experience. In an increasingly visual culture he tells stories that would otherwise be lost like the tale told by a Bosnian girl.

Moreover, in Bosnia Sacco also talked to the men who took part in the fighting and who witnessed or even committed atrocities, and these stories are also presented in visual form. The stories themselves are shocking and once more the visual impact plays an important role. In addition they occasion-

Part of a tale told by a Bosnian girl (Joe Sacco, *Safe Area Goražde*. ©2007 Fantagraphics Books).

ally clash with the image of the specific narrators — men Sacco met and talked to in bars and cafés — and thus the tales become slightly unreal while their terrifying reality is not in question. This was one important aspect in New Journalism and it is certainly also artfully employed here.

Another important aspect is the actual portrayal of the people Sacco talks to, but also those he just encounters on the streets or even in massscenes. Sacco himself points out that: "each face is individualized and that was important to me. I didn't want to show a mass of people in the sense that they all look like a bunch of ants or something. To me, they're all individuals who have suffered enormously, and even though none of those faces might be true to any particular individual, the point, I think, is coming across. The essential truth, as I said, comes across" (Sacco "Presentation from 2002 UF Comics Conference").

However, there is, as you may have already noticed, an exception: his own face is exempt from this rule, as he is almost always strongly cartoon-

A visual representation of atrocities in the Bosnian war (Joe Sacco, *The Fixer*. ©2007 Drawn and Quarterly).

*Left:* A photograph of Joe Sacco (Joe Sacco, *Palestine*. ©2007 Fantagraphics Books). *Right:* Joe Sacco as a comic figure (Joe Sacco, *Palestine* ©2007 Fantagraphics Books).

ized and thus in stark contrast with the other faces in the panels. This difference probably serves various purposes. On the one hand he is the stranger in the environment he depicts and certainly feels to be an outsider who has not suffered with the people he encounters and interviews. This displacement is emphasized, but the hierarchy often noticeable in documentaries and reports — that is, the journalist is better dressed, controls the situation by asking the questions, directs the gaze and is thus coded as empowered — is turned on its head. Sacco appears frequently as a little ridiculous; he misunderstands situations and occasionally does not get a joke that others share, and the cartoonish image stresses this aspect. Moreover, it is his perspective that is presented, and as Scott McCloud has pointed out, a cartoonish iconicity increases the potential for audience identification (cf. McCloud 42–43).

And then there is possibly one more aspect to his self-portrayal, but this is chiefly speculation. There is another comics figure that the drawn Sacco resembles: Monsieur Acquefacques, the prisoner of dreams in the claustrophobic works of Marc-Antoine Mathieu (cf. Mathieu, passim). This resemblance possibly emphasizes the dystopian character of the world Sacco depicts; reality matches or surpasses the horrors we can imagine in our darkest dreams and nightmares.

To sum up: comics journalism offers possibilities that traditional journalism cannot pursue. It makes use of subjective perspectives, visual metaphorization, fictionalization and artistic distortions of reality in its quest for

An individualized face (Joe Sacco, *Palestine*. ©2007 Fantagraphics Books).

an essential truth that cannot always be successfully transmitted by a neutral and seemingly detached form. In doing this, comics journalism questions the claim of authenticity and truthfulness of photographic representation and thus suggests a necessary reconceptualization that also plays a role in postmodern theory of representation. In addition, it visually addresses aspects of reality that are not accessible to traditional journalism. An important aspect is the inherent subjectivity of the artistic form, and here comics journalism ties in with recent theories about the relevance of first-person narratives even in scientific contexts — trauma research, psychiatry, neurophysiology, etc.

However, in its focus on the visual form, comics journalism also has its problems. It is less capable of complex argument and thus tends to reduce the complexity of the world it depicts. In consequence, it ultimately cannot replace the written word — and we might want to keep in mind that one of the first statements about comics journalism stems from a time before comics journalism was invented: In the movie *Fahrenheit 451*, the protagonist, Montag, is reading a comic-newspaper in bed. In the dystopian society, all newspapers and journals are published in comics form, as each and every form of written text is banned. The rapid advancement of visual culture may well bring its own brand of problems, and there can be just too much of a good thing.

BIBLIOGRAPHY

Burgdorf, Paul. *Comics im Unterricht*. Weinheim and Basel: Beltz, 1976.
Cheesman, Tom. *The Shocking Ballad Picture Show: German Popular Literature and Cultural History*. Oxford and Providence: Berg, 1994.
Emsley, Clive. "Introduction." *The Newgate Calendar*. Ware, Herfordshire: Wordsworth Editions, 1997, IX–XVI.

Hegerfeldt, Anne. *Lies That Tell the Truth. Magic Realism Seen Through Contemporary Fiction from Britain.* Amsterdam: Rodopi, 2005.
Hollowell, John. *Fact and Fiction: The New Journalism and the Non-Fiction Novel.* Chapel Hill: The University of North Carolina Press. 1977.
Mathieu, Marc-Antoine. *Der Ursprung (L'origine* [1991]). Berlin: Reprodukt, 2003.
McCloud, Scott, *Understanding Comics.* New York: HarperPerennial, 1994.
Pett, David J. "Drawn in." *Ryerson Review of Journalism.* 23 October 2005. http://www.rrj.ca/online/585 (27 April 2007).
Sacco, Joe. *The Fixer.* Quebec: Drawn and Quarterly, 2003.
_____. *Palestine.* Seattle, WA: Fantagraphics Books, 2001.
_____. "Presentation from 2002 UF Comics Conference." *ImageTexT: Interdisciplinary Comics Studies* 1.1 (2004). Dept of English, University of Florida. *http://www.english.ufl.edu/imagetext/archives/v1_1/sacco* (17 April 2007).
_____. *Safe Area Goražde.* Seattle, WA: Fantagraphics Books, 2000.
Silbermann, Alphons. "The Way Toward Visual Culture: Comics and Comic Films." *Comics and Visual Culture*, edited by Alphons Silbermann and H.-D. Dyroff. München et al.: K.G. Saur, 1986, 11–17.
Skeaping, Lucy, "The English Broadside Ballad. Street songs of the 17th century." http://www.lucieskeaping.co.uk/lecture.htm (27 April 2007).
Spiegelman, Art. *In The Shadow of No Towers.* New York: Pantheon, 2004.
Swanson, Don. R. "Toward a Psychology of Metaphor," *On Metaphor*, edited by Sheldon Sacks. Chicago: Chicago University Press, 1978, 161–64.
Versemnieks, Inara. "Drawn to the Truth." *The Oregonian*, 23 October 2005. http://www.drawnandquarterly.com/newsList.php?item=a435e77e531eb5 (17 April 2007).
Williams, Kristian. "The Case for Comics Journalism." *Columbia Journalism Review* March/April 2005. http://www.cjr.org/issues/2005/2/ideas-essay-williams.asp (27 April 2007).
Zimmermann, Hans-Dieter. "Comic strips, ihre Geschichte und ihre Kritik." *Comics im ästhetischen Unterricht*, edited by Dietger Pforte. Frankfurt/M.: Fischer Athenäum, 1974, 248–76.

# INTERNATIONAL

# 7

## The Carrefour of Practice: Québec BD in Transition

*Michel Hardy-Vallée*

In the pantheon of annoying questions, besides the crowned champion "What is art?" we should probably consider "What is literature?" as the Second Most Annoying Question (SMAQ). But being annoying does not necessarily render it worthless. We live in an age where the pronouncement that comics can be a form of literature surprises few, but solid arguments to this effect are rare. Perhaps that is because the concept of literature itself is a slippery one, yet difficulty cannot be an excuse for not addressing a question. I propose here to look at the work of a Québec author whose graphic novels are gaining solid recognition as literary works, and explain *how* they are literature first by taking a position on *what* literature is, and second by showing *why* they are considered literature, and not as something else.

For the last 20 years, both academic and popular publications have repeated in chorus that comics can deal with so-called "serious" issues and topics: history instead of fantasy; intimacy instead of adventure; real war instead of intergalactic super-conflicts between the imperial armies of trans-dimensional eternal beings. It is a starting assumption of Joseph Witek's *Comic Books as History*, for example:

> A critical analysis of the comic-book form is especially necessary now, when a growing number of contemporary American comic books are being written *as* literature aimed at a general readership of adults and concerned, not with the traditionally escapist themes of comics, but with issues such as the clash of cultures in American history, the burdens of guilt and suffering passed on within families, and the trials and small triumphs of the daily workaday world [Witek 3].

What Witek refers to as "theme," I would rather call "topic": the clash of cultures in American history is a topic that can be treated to embody the various themes of betrayal, religious uncertainty, or filial love. Witek's position that content determines, in a certain manner, literariness is cognate to the one developed here, but I must stress that Witek's argument implies that the recurring "topoi" of superhero comics cannot be part of a literary work. Moreover, his position also implies that an adult audience is a necessary condition for literary comics. The mere existence of literary works dedicated to an audience of children, like *Alice in Wonderland* or *Huckleberry Finn*, should be proof enough that literature need not be essentially "aimed at a general readership of adults." As to the question of what constitutes a literary topic, my position is broader, and does not prevent a priori the story of the rise and fall of the Zurglub Empire to be a candidate for literariness.

Turning away from the content of the work and focusing on cultural circumstances, Charles Hatfield argues in *Alternative Comics: An Emerging Literature* that the Pulitzer prize given to *Maus* "served to ratify comic art as a literary form; the reception of *Maus* suddenly made serious comics culturally *legible*, recognizable in a way they had not been before" (xi). Hatfield does not imply that winning a special Pulitzer suddenly transformed *Maus* from nonliterary to literary work, but this institutional recognition *underlines* a literary aspect, without *explaining* it.

Hatfield leaves unanswered the Second Most Annoying Question and creates the following question-begging logic: literary prizes can only be given, by definition, to literary work. If *Maus* has won a literary prize, then it must have been a literary work in the first place. Clearly, a little work on the SMAQ is necessary. However, he does argue why comics can be literature and not something else by presenting them as an art of reading and writing: "These are images that *stay*, unlike the successive moments in a film or video as it is being viewed. In that sense, the images in comics read more like printed words or characters" (Hatfield 33). At best, Hatfield suggests that the medium of comics functions like the medium of literature, taken to be printed text, and that this similarity in medium is enough to understand *Maus* through a literary lens, as evidenced by its institutional recognition.

Regrettably, although it gestures toward the social norm of defining literature, Hatfield's position brings us back to a definition of literature as a property of texts, a special mode of using a medium — language — like the Formalists and the Structuralists did. The basic problem with a definition of literature as a special mode of language is that it fails to account for the moments at which so-called literary language is indistinguishable from ordinary language, and forces us to consider pictures as linguistic tokens in order for comics to be literary. The alternative way I want to consider now is to understand literature first as a human activity, not as a property of texts. In contradistinction to Hatfield's argument, this human activity is constitutive rather than indicative of literature.

In *Truth, Fiction, and Literature*, Peter Lamarque and Stein Haugom Olsen argue that literature is a practice of production and appreciation of texts shared between writers and readers, and that no textual features a priori distinguish literary works from nonliterary ones.

> A text is identified as a literary work by recognizing the author's intention that the text is produced and meant to be read within the framework of conventions defining the practice (constituting the institution) of literature[...]. Adopting the literary stance towards a text is to identify it as a literary work and apprehend it in accordance with the conventions of the literary practice. The mode of apprehension which the practice defines is one of *appreciation*. The literary stance is defined by the expectation of (and consequently the attempt to identify) a certain type of value, i.e. literary aesthetic value, in the text in question [256].

This definition shifts the locus of literariness from the "text" to the "work." The notion of "work" is here derived from the one developed by Gregory Currie: the text is a sequence of words in a natural language (cf. Currie 335), but the work is the actual act of its composition (cf. Currie 336). Without the notion of work, it would be impossible to account for certain aesthetic features like irony, for instance. A sequence of words can be understood literally or ironically, but only if we interpret it in conjunction with some awareness of the way in which it was produced.

The concepts that identify the literary features of a work exist at three levels for Lamarque and Olsen: form, content, and theme. At the formal level, understanding a literary work demands an ability to decode its internal organization (cf. Lamarque and Olsen 258). To understand *Paradise Lost*, it is necessary that I have a basic grasp of the epic form, and of blank verse meter. At the content level, one must be able to identify the subject of a work. Describing the subject of a work essentially taps into the reader's ability to apply everyday life concepts to the world of the novel, such as characters, actions, objects, or settings (cf. Lamarque and Olsen 259). Baudelaire's poem "Spleen" is about a psychological state, not about the various items of spiders, coffins, and craniums, which serve as metaphors. Finally, the literary signature of a work and what makes it valuable is our construction of the subject under a perspective as the bearer of a theme. A theme is "an organizing principle that seeks coherence both among diffuse elements of a work's subject and in the imaginative interest aroused by the work" (Lamarque 370). *Dubliners* shows us how an intellectually sclerosed society thwarts its individual members' ambitions, and how the minutest actions can in fact perpetuate this sclerosis. The internal organization of a work along the lines of form, content, and theme make it suitable for literature, as a practice of production and appreciation.

The logic of literary evaluation relies on two contracts between author and reader. First is the creative-imaginative convention: the expectation that a work of literature is a product of imagination, of invention (cf. Lamarque and Olsen 262). This is not to say that literature must be fictional: the retelling of a true story satisfies the creative-imaginative convention for example through the imposition of a form over subject, in the treatment the author gives to it. The creative-imaginative convention is an expectation of subject and form in a literary work, one that results from the work of an author. In this sense, we expect the author to perform a work in a medium, to metaphorically carve something beautiful or interesting out of a block of stone. Second, literature carries the expectation that a work is relevant to a human being, instead of fulfilling a purpose better suited to the study of arctic seals or the construction of a Martian spaceship. This expectation is the mimetic convention, that is, the presentation of concerns of interest to humans through either theme or subject choice (cf. Lamarque and Olsen 266). It is thus not by virtue of being "good" that a work is considered literary: it is by functioning within a specific logic of valuation that it is. Comics may be candidates for literariness not because they have abandoned the stigmatized genres, but because they can function within the practice of literature.

But why should comics be literature and not simply another form of art like painting, sculpting, or music? Precisely because they were devalued as literature since their earliest days, especially in the United States, but also in Europe, though with less venom against the publishing industry. Around the turn of the 20th century, traditionalist literary critics in the United States dismissed illustrations in general as a hindrance to the acquisition of a genteel, literate culture. For instance, in the June 1895 edition of *Lippincott's Monthly Magazine*, Sidney Fairfield opposed strongly the illustration of novels: "The written word is the first and the highest expression of thought, and it ever will be. To illustrate the perfect literary production does not necessarily improve it artistically[...]. [I]s not the literary art of a master amply sufficient to portray to the appreciative, intelligent reader all in his book that is charming or thrilling or pathetic or humorous?" (5–6). In the *Dial* of November 1, 1903, Annie Russell Marble warned readers: "To cultivate individual ideas, to educe subjective interpretations of life and letters, is the desideratum of all education; such results are often hindered by excess of scenic material" (8). And the most infamous of comics critics, Fredric Wertham himself, stressed the idea that "the comic-book format is an invitation to illiteracy" (118). The irony of this devaluation is that literature was then identified with literacy in the minds of the critics. The proper response against the above criticisms should not have been to create more literary comics, but more literate comics. Such an equation between literature and literacy persists to this day, for instance in Charles Hatfield's argument for comics as a different type of literacy.

Literary devaluation of comics as it was practiced in the United States did not happen to the same extent in Québec, yet this province has contributed some major milestones to the history of literary comics in the recent years. For the history of comics, Québec represents a certain singularity. Unlike English-language comics in Canada, French-language comics have had some opportunities to avoid the summersault of the American comics industry. This culture of independence eventually benefited to, and from, their English-language counterparts, creating in the current times a small but influential haven for comics outside the mainstreams.

Since the 19th century, there had been many locally created illustrated stories, wordless pantomimes and similar works in the style of Wilhelm Busch in Canadian newspapers. However, the arrival of the syndicated comic strips coming from the United States between 1910 and 1940 eventually flooded the pages of local newspapers at rates more advantageous for the editors than the local production (cf. Falardeau 32). During the World War II years, trade barriers and protectionist legislation helped the francophone and anglophone local markets to thrive independently of foreign competition for a while (cf. Canada n.p.), but the rebooted economy of the 1950s erased many of these trade barriers, and the Canadian market was once again flooded with American productions.

All of Canada is occupied by American comics.

All? Not quite!

A province inhabited by indomitable Gauls is holding out....

In fact, the strong Catholic Church in the province of Québec spurred after World War II the creation of *bande dessinée* (BD) periodicals targeted at the youth market (cf. Canada n.p.). Whereas Anglophone Canada then lost many of its creators like Joe Shuster (Superman), Harold Foster (Prince Valiant), or Edmond Good (Red Ryder) to the American industry, the American hegemony has had the reverse effect to strengthen the local Québec production. Eventually, the European hegemony of *Spirou* and *Tintin* periodicals also displaced many local comics, but stories of Québec exiles to Belgium or France are actually rare, while European authors have been at times very keen on gesturing toward their trans–Atlantic fellow authors. Nevertheless, the remaining independent productions suffer from lack of long-term stability.

Equally unstable, but ultimately influential, the underground movement provided the seeds of daring production, and sprouted across Canada in both languages. If most publications of the 1970s did not flourish past a dozen issues

(Falardeau 61), one succeeded tremendously in the 1980s: *Croc* ("fangs"). Propelled by the creators of the 1970s, renewed constantly by the influx of new authors, *Croc* is perhaps as close to an institution of BD that Québec ever had. A satirical magazine in the vein of *Mad, Hara-Kiri, National Lampoon*, and countless others, *Croc* supported and established more BD writers than any other magazine (Falardeau 70). It was also a laboratory of writers, many of which are still prominent in varieties, theatre, cinema, television, and media. Yet in a pathetic recurrence of history, *Croc* blipped off the radar screen in 1995, after publishing their 189th issue, ironically a special anniversary issue celebrating their 15 years of existence.

In parallel to the Québec underground movement, a new scene based in Toronto sprouted during the early 1980s, and artists like Chester Brown or Seth started to consolidate an alternative market of idiosyncratic, innovative comics, in explicit rupture from the Marvel/DC superhero productions from the United States. This movement converged eventually toward Montréal in the 1990s, creating a new bilingual scene in cities like Montréal, and fostered artists like Julie Doucet, Rick Trembles, Henriette Valium, Richard Suicide, but also publishing houses like Drawn+Quarterly or La Pastèque, who are now the two epicenters of anglophone and francophone graphic novel publication in Canada, with authors like Michel Rabagliati, Chris Ware, Chester Brown, Joe Matt, Seth, Julie Doucet, Adrian Tomine, Charles Burns, Guy Delisle, Dylan Horrocks, Jason Lutes, Joe Sacco, and *Croc* authors such as Pierre Fournier and Réal Godbout. Together, these two publishing houses integrate 30 years of alternative production across the cultural landscape of North America (some authors are published in translation at the two houses).

Of all the movements to influence Québec comics, the literary status-laden graphic novel is one the francophone authors little considered until recently. In a large francophone chain library the BD section is still occupied in majority by the franco-belgian *albums*— self-contained stories of recurring realistic heroes— punctuated by translations of mangas and Marvel/DC comic books. Yet it is also in this medium that Michel Rabagliati achieved literary ambitions, got published in book form right away, and is gathering recognition as a prominent author.

Rabagliati is a relative newcomer in the world of comics. His first book, *Paul à la campagne*, was created on a whim, and published in 1999 by La Pastèque. Prior to this book, he was a professional illustrator, and has had little to no involvement in the world of comics. He never created a fanzine, inked for Marvel, lettered for DC, nor did he run a periodical like Daniel Clowes's *Eightball* or Adrian Tomine's *Optic Nerve*. Equally singular is the fact that his work is culturally bivalent: for an anglophone, *Paul* reads as a graphic novel, but for a francophone it reads as a European *album*.

Paul's imitation of Belgian *bandes dessinée* characters Gaston Lagaffe and Spirou (Michel Rabagliati, *Paul in the Metro*. ©2003 Drawn & Quarterly).

If Michel Rabagliati reads as a heir to the graphic novel movement for many in the English translation, it is in part because his contact with authors like Chester Brown, Seth, Joe Matt, or Chris Ware. They spurred the interest of this graphic designer to revisit the medium he had so far only associated with the Franco-Belgian BD of his youth, and to write in the autobiographical mode. In the *Edmonton Journal* of 29 December 2005, reviewer Gilbert Bouchard writes: "Michel Rabagliati continues to produce work that does great justice to Canada's rich graphic novel tradition of sensitive autobiographical work produced in a Europeanesque clean-line cartooning style" (C2). If he reads for a francophone audience as heir to Hergé or Franquin, it is not only because of his explicit reference to these authors, but also because he uses, so far, the format of a recurring character across self-contained works, like the European *albums* do. However, unlike the serials of *Spirou* and *Tintin* magazines, the *Paul* series saw no pre-publication in magazine form before its book publication. The direct-to-book approach is also coherent with the *auteur* approach of the graphic novel movement, which tends to emphasize a continuous approach to story reading, by the creation of thematically united works (Sabin 238).

The irony of graphic novels in Québec is that this most trans–Atlantic of form — the product of a back-and-forth exchange of attitudes toward the comics medium between the Europeans and the Americans — never sprouted natively in the province whose comics market was flooded by these very same superpowers. The appearance of this form in Québec comes again from external influence, mostly the result of Toronto-based artists moving toward Montréal. The graphic novel is a borrowed form in Québec, but one that now flowers, because it integrates the cultural background of the two major linguistic groups, and thereby resolves perhaps certain cultural tensions. Rabagliati could be a symptom that the debate over the value of comics has settled enough in Québec to open a market for creators who already take for granted the idea that comics can be literary, and who did not take part earlier on in the debate itself.

In Rabagliati's graphic novels, broad concerns about artistic value embedded in the story help to understand the literary approach sub-tending the production and intended appreciation of his works. *Paul Has a Summer Job?* tells in the autobiographical mode the story of Paul, the author's alter ego, who has a job in a holiday camp in the Laurentians during the summer of 1979, after he dropped out of high school. A quiet and somewhat disgruntled suburban kid, Paul confronts for the first time autonomy and responsibilities, the classic *Bildungsroman* trajectory leading the teenager toward adulthood. In one scene, Paul plays before his work buddies the music of Georges Brassens, a popular French singer-songwriter, known for his clever and saucy compositions. He excuses himself from being out of fashion with the "yéyés," the British Invasion–inspired French light pop in vogue after the mid–1960s, but after a few chords, he hooks his audience, and engages them in chorus singing. His closing remarks about the scene express his initial doubts regarding Brassens's value but also comment on the unexpected success he reaps, which he grants to the artist's timeless and universal quality.

These words echo the notion of literary value as a value shared by the people who participate in the practice of production and appreciation. Although the audience is confronted with a work they are unfamiliar with, they ultimately identify its value because they understand how it functions, how to appreciate it, and how it is meant to be understood. A similar process operates with Rabagliati's work, written in a medium that many people still

An impromptu campfire song from Georges Brassens (Michel Rabagliati, *Paul Has a Summer Job*. ©2003 Drawn & Quarterly).

associate with whimsy or light topics (in the same manner that saucy songs are not expected to engage with important themes), but which participates in the wider concerns of humanity (as Brassens's songs do).

More than a simple nod to a great artist, this scene is understandable at the formal level through the agency of characters, plot events, narrator, and the fourth panel functions as a synecdoche for the whole process of singing accompanied by music. At the topical level, this scene mingles artistic value, social standing, self-discovery, and friendship. Thematically, it shows through the device of art how we break out of our sense of solitude to form emotional bonds with others, as evidenced by the final, collective word-balloon. Emblematic of a generation of francophone Quebecers, this scene also shows how foreign artistic production serves as a focus of identity, a buoy for communication between the young.

Beyond the fact that this scene functions in a literary manner, it depends on formal devices that are not part of literature's heritage: the first and last panel answer to each other by showing visually confusion and union. The superimposed harangues of the eager audience in the first panel become the harmonized chorus singing of the last panel, and whereas it is possible to explain this transformation in purely linguistic terms, it is here made *visible*. But does it detract from literary appreciation? My answer is no: if literature functions as an institution, as a contract between artists and audiences, it can be extended by new formal devices when the latter function in tandem with the existing practice. The emotional, or cognitive impact of a picture differs widely from that of the word, but it can nevertheless be made to serve theme, character development, or a synecdoche.

The process of discovery and influence is a recurring theme between the different *Paul* stories. In an equally poignant and graphic scene of *Paul Moves Out*, after a passionate evening of discussion, wine drinking, smoking and music with friends, Paul returns home with his girlfriend, Lucie, to learn that his aunt has just died. The ecstasy of discovery clashes with the emotional maturation of life experience, and the parallelism of the two processes suggests that they are perhaps both faces of the same coin. The final close-up on the face of Paul is brought toward another close-up on the Congolese mask his aunt gave him at his last visit to her, creating a similar parallelism. In the end emotional maturation leaves the strongest impression; the imaginative vision provides a sense of meaning and appeasement to Paul. Here, the formal devices come from both the comics and cinematic traditions, but they function as well within the orb of literary value, of theme and topic.

If Michel Rabagliati's work insists so strongly on the importance of perennial themes, and of storytelling, it is probably because he only came to the world of comics with the intention of telling stories first. From his own admission, in an interview with him I am hoping to publish this year, he read comics abundantly as a kid and a young man, but never had any interest in working in the industry, nor does he care much for its history and conflicts. As a commercial illustrator, he saw instead both the opportunity to return to pen and paper, away from the computer, and the opportunity to create in a

## 7. The Carrefour of Practice *(Hardy-Vallée)*

*Left:* Paul and Lucie, after an entertaining evening... *Right:* ...learn about the death of Paul's aunt (both by Michel Rabagliati, *Paul Moves Out.* ©2005 Drawn & Quarterly).

literary manner out of his own graphic skills. His work pays nods here and there to authors that he admires, or borrowed from, but these concerns are not fundamental to the stories themselves. Case in point are the two versions, French and English, of his first encounter with Lucie. In the original French, she drops a running gag from Marcel Gotlib's *Rubrique-à-brac*, which piques his curiosity. Later in the day, Paul re-reads Gotlib's work and wonders if he can further the connection with Lucie. In the translated English version, Lucie borrows lines from Harvey Kurtzman's *Krazy Kat*, to the same effect on Paul. However, when he later wonders if Lucie knows about Gotlib, his gesture now takes the meaning of crossing a cultural line: does the American comics fan girl know about this great French comics author?

Once the old cultural barriers have been crossed in Canada, once it does not matter whether you like Krazy Kat or Gotlib, your art is not weighed down by tradition, established formats, and you can make what you want of a rich medium. Literature is not the final destination of comics, nor should it be. Graphic novels stretch the existing canvas of literature, but they do not have to be a department of it either. This is not a bad thing: the graphic novel can

A few final words of wisdom from the aunt (Michel Rabagliati, *Paul Moves Out* ©2005 Drawn & Quarterly).

have a literary value, and as academics we do not have to pull our hair wondering about an either/or situation because of the visual medium. We do not have to invent "visual literacy," stick to a universal theory of signs, or regress to an ideographic myth to understand why comics can be literary. If literature is a way of appreciating and creating, it demands from those who wish to participate in it a certain distance from their previous agendas; crossing cultural lines is thus perhaps one important step to take to foster literary comics.

## 7. The Carrefour of Practice *(Hardy-Vallée)*

*Left:* **Bandes dessinées** as a pickup line. *Right:* Comics as a pickup line. *Below:* Plans to follow up on a pickup line, and to cross cultural boundaries (all by Michel Rabagliati, *Paul Moves Out.* ©2005 Drawn & Quarterly).

### Bibliography

Canada, Library and Archives. "Beyond the Funnies: The History of Comics in English Canada and Quebec." Website created 24 June 2002. http://www.collectionscanada.ca/comics/index-e.html (30 March 2007).
Currie, Gregory. "Work and Text." *Mind* 100.3 (1991): 325–40.
Fairfield, Sidney. "The Tyranny of the Pictorial." *Arguing Comics: Literary Masters on a Popular Medium*, edited by Jeet Heer and Kent Worcester. Jackson: University Press of Mississippi, 2004, 4–6.
Falardeau, Mira. *La bande dessinée au Québec.* Collection Boréal Express 9. Montréal: Boréal, 1994.
Hatfield, Charles. *Alternative Comics: An Emerging Literature.* Jackson: University Press of Mississippi, 2005.

Lamarque, Peter. "Cognitive Values in the Arts: Marking the Boundaries." *Contemporary Debates in Aesthetics and the Philosophy of Art*, edited by Matthew Kieran. Malden, MA: Blackwell, 2006, 370.

\_\_\_\_\_ and Stein Haugom Olsen. *Truth, Fiction, and Literature: A Philosophical Perspective.* Oxford and New York: Oxford University Press, 1994.

Marble, Annie Russell. "The Reign of the Spectacular." *Arguing Comics: Literary Masters on a Popular Medium*, edited by Jeet Heer and Kent Worcester. Jackson: University Press of Mississippi, 2004, 7–8.

Rabagliati, Michel. *Paul en appartement*. Montréal: Les éditions de la Pastèque, 2004.

\_\_\_\_\_. *Paul has a Summer Job*. Trans. Helge Dascher. Montreal: Drawn & Quarterly, 2003.

\_\_\_\_\_. "Paul in the Metro." Trans. Helge Dascher. *Drawn & Quarterly*, edited by Chris Oliveros. Vol. 5. Montreal: Drawn & Quarterly, 2003, 76–90.

\_\_\_\_\_. *Paul Moves Out*. Trans. Helge Dascher. Montreal: Drawn & Quarterly, 2005.

Sabin, Roger. *Adult Comics: An Introduction*. London and New York: Routledge, 1993.

Wertham, Fredric. *Seduction of the Innocent*. New York: Rinehart, 1954.

Witek, Joseph. *Comic Books as History: The Narrative Art of Jack Jackson, Art Spiegelman, and Harvey Pekar*. Jackson: University Press of Mississippi, 1989.

# 8

# The Use of Allusion in Apitz and Kunkel's *Karl* Comics

*Sandra Martina Schwab*

In 1985/86, the publishing house Apitz and Kunkel was founded as a small private venture by two enthusiastic young men, Michael Apitz and Patrick Kunkel. The first publication, a collection of satirical poems by Kunkel's father, Eberhard Kunkel, followed in spring 1986 (Apitz and Kunkel, *Alles Karl!* 13). But what Michael Apitz and Patrick Kunkel actually wanted to publish was comics. Furthermore, they wanted to prove that, contrary to what is still common belief in Germany, comic books are not publications only for children or people who cannot read properly (42). What Michael Apitz and Patrick Kunkel were still missing, though, was a story, and so they asked Eberhard Kunkel to write something for them that could be turned into a comic (16–17). The result of this collaboration was released in 1988 under the title *Karl: Der Spätlesereiter*. The book deals with the discovery of the qualities of late vintage wine in the Rheingau area in 1775. In that particular year, the grapes of Schloß Johannisberg were harvested late due to the delay of the courier bringing the permission of the Bishop of Fulda to start the harvest. So by the time he finally arrived, noble rot had already set in. Even though the monks thought the grapes must surely be ruined, they still picked them and pressed them, and much to their surprise, the resulting wine was of a quality unheard of before (Apitz and Kunkel, *Spätlesereiter* 47). Today, a statue in the courtyard of the abbey of Johannisberg commemorates this event, yet nothing is really known about the delayed messenger and why he was so late. Eberhard Kunkel decided to fill this historical void by inventing a tale about this man, whom he called Karl (Apitz and Kunkel, *Alles Karl!* 18–19).

Ever since the publication of *Der Spätlesereiter*, the stories about Karl —

all set in late-18th-century Germany — have enjoyed an immense success, which even resulted in spin-off wine books and mystery novels. The popularity of Apitz and Kunkel's comics might partly be explained by the local setting and themes, but their particular brand of humor also plays a decisive role. Much of this humor stems from the numerous allusions, many of them intertextual and intermedial references, that are woven into the text and the pictures. In the following, I will deal with the means the authors and the illustrator employ to establish these allusions and how they use them within the context of their stories.

Already in the choice of settings Apitz and Kunkel's style of humor becomes apparent. The *Karl* books have been called "regional comics" (Apitz and Kunkel, *Alles Karl!* 60) as large parts are set in the Rheingau area, where the authors and the illustrator hail from. However, the story also moves to other parts of Germany, to cities like Frankfurt or Karlsruhe, and also to other parts of Europe, such as England or France. To establish historical settings, Apitz, the illustrator, often models panels on old engravings (Apitz and Kunkel, *Alles Karl!* 25), for example, a view of Cologne in *Der Fall Loreley* (5) and one of Speyer in *Lord am Rhein* (23). Typically, Apitz depicts the characteristic "skyline" of churches in order to enable the reader to recognize a specific town or city and thus to identify the setting for a particular scene. Hence, when Karl and his sidekick, Oskar, arrive in Paris, the reader is presented with a view of Notre Dame (*Paris* 37). However, we find this particular panel only toward the end of the book in question, and this is not how the city is introduced at the beginning of the story. There, Apitz uses an image of Montmartre, complete with several windmills as well as a cabaret in a red mill — the Moulin Rouge. And thus we leave the historical reality behind and enter what I call "historicized modern reality," for the Moulin Rouge did not yet exist in 1794 and Montmartre was still a green hill outside the city with vineyards, gardens and a few windmills (see *Paris* 47). This blending of historical setting and modernity recurs in the characterizations of other towns and areas, for example in a picture of London (*Lord* 5), which does not only show the Tower, but, with the inclusion of caricatures of Boris Becker and Björn Borg, also contains an anachronistic reference to the famous tennis tournament in Wimbledon. To an even greater extent, Apitz employs this technique when it comes to German settings, especially to the cities of Mainz and Frankfurt.

Frankfurt is famous for its cathedral, in which the German Kaiser used to be crowned, for its town hall (the Römer), and for Goethe. All this correctly belong to the late-18th-century setting of the *Karl* comics. Yet the books also feature historicized transformations of modern Frankfurt. The international airport is represented by the take-off and arrival of different birds (*Spätlesereiter* 15 and *Krönung* 26). This includes a "big American" (Apitz and

Kunkel, *Krönung* 26), a bald eagle that serves as a reference to Boing's Jumbo Jets and Frankfurt's role as a major hub for transatlantic flights. A wayside cross in the same panel alludes to the Frankfurt motorway intersection (the literal translation of the German term *Autobahnkreuz* is "motorway cross"). The skyscrapers that today dominate the skyline that has earned Franfurt am Main the nickname "Mainhattan" are depicted in the comic as multistory, half-timbered houses (*Spätlesereiter* 15). Squirrels busily exchanging nuts represent the stock exchange and (as the German words for "bench" and "bank" are homonyms) an assortment of benches allude to the numerous banking houses in Frankfurt (*Nibelungen* 16). In some instances only the combination of image and text makes the allusion work. For example, the badger balancing on a lantern in *Die Krönung* (32) is both a pictorial and a textual pun: the German stock market index, DAX, is pronounced like the German word for "badger" (*Dachs*).

Apitz and Kunkel use a similar mixture of historically correct and anachronistic icons to make the city of Mainz recognizable to the readers. The authors mix the historical cathedral with historicized elements of modern Mainz, such as the famous *Meenzer Fassenacht*, the carnival (*Italiänische Reise* 15), and especially with the large carnival parade on Shrove Monday (*Zisterzienser* 25).

Given the main setting of the series, the Rheingau area, the *Karl* comics also feature many panels depicting the famously scenic Upper Middle Rhine Valley, which the authors and illustrator use to introduce cultural satire by poking fun at the emerging tourism along that particular stretch of the river. In the late 18th century British tourists had just discovered the Romantic Rhine and started to flock to the Upper Middle Rhine Valley with its famous sights like the Loreley rock or the Mouse Tower of Bingen (see Plummer 28). During the Napoleonic Wars traveling came more or less to a halt, but immediately afterward the second wave of British tourists arrived on the banks of Father Rhine (see Kroener n.p.). They became so numerous that in 1839 the writer Thomas Hood remarked:

> It is a statistical fact that since 1814 an unknown number of persons, bearing an indefinite proportion to the gross total of the population of the British empire, have been more or less "abroad."[...] It resembled a geographical panic — and of all the country and branch banks in Christendom, never was there such a run as on the banks of the Rhine[...]. It was impossible to go into Society without meeting units, tens, hundreds, thousands of Rhenish tourists[...]. What a donkey they deemed him who had not been to Assmannshausen — what a cockney who had not seen a Rat's Castle besides the one in St. Giles's! [245–46].

In the depictions of the Rhine tourism in the *Karl* comics, Apitz and Kunkel once again blend historical reality and historicized modern reality.

Historically correct, a group of tourists travels along the Rhine on a traditional boat trailed by a horse but the travel business is given a typical modern name, "Treidel Tours." The company also offers package holidays, which include a tour guide wearing a (Bavarian) dirndl, thus alluding to today's clichés about Germans and Germany (*Das Boot* 6–7).

Apart from cultural satire, Apitz and Kunkel's puns also extend to the realm of politics, again either within the historical reality or as historicized modern reality. Thus both *Das Boot* and *Das Faß der Zisterzienser* feature panels showing the German Michel. This historical cartoon character stands for the ostrich-like behavior of the middle classes in the late 18th and especially in the 19th century, when the frightened burghers did not want to have anything to do with the social and political unrest of the times. That is why the German Michel is always depicted wearing his nightcap as a sign that he does not want to be disturbed and would prefer to sleep through times of upheaval. In *Das Boot* he thus sits dreaming in his neat front garden next to a garden gnome (both icons of the German petite-bourgeoisie). The gnome is holding a mop and a bucket as symbols for the proverbial German obsession with cleanliness. A sign on the picket fence reads "Please don't disturb" (25). However, the historical fact that Germans did indeed get involved in the various political revolutions of the late 18th and early 19th centuries is indicated in *Das Faß der Zisterzienser*, which is set against a revolutionary backdrop and where Michel in his nightcap finally gets out of bed in order to fight for his rights (28). As an anachronistic contrast, the band playing at a rural dance in *Der Spätlesereiter* consists of the leaders of the German political parties in 1988. In this panel the text adds significantly to the satire. One of the dancers wonders why the band always plays horribly out of tune (6).

The panel with the politicians' band highlights another feature of Apitz and Kunkel's series, the inclusion of caricatures, a technique borrowed from Goscinny and Uderzo's *Asterix*. As in the French series, much of the enjoyment of reading the *Karl* comics derives from spotting the caricatures of politicians and other local, national and international celebrities. They all make guest appearances in roles that, in one way or another, reflect on their role in real life, for example, in *Die Krönung*, where the person responsible for the organization and the budget of the imminent coronation of the new Kaiser has the features of Ludwig Ehrhard (5–6), Germany's first minister of trade and commerce after World War II and the man usually considered responsible for the so-called "Wirtschaftswunder." Later on in the story, international celebrities arrive for the coronation, among them Prince Charles and Mad King Ludwig of Bavaria (*Krönung* 34). In *Lord am Rhein*, the volume that deals most explicitly with British tourism along the Rhine, the members of the Travelers Club in London all look like famous Englishmen: Charlie Chaplin,

Alfred Hitchcock, Winston Churchill, Roger Moore, and Sir Peter Ustinov (6). Most of the time, the joke about familiar faces is only between the authors and the readers while the characters do not notice the anachronistic additions to their stories. A notable exception is Karl's dog Grandpatte in the very first volume; when he catches sight of Gutenberg and Kaiser Wilhelm II, who — although they both are firmly connected to the Rheingau area — do not belong in the late 18th century, the dog turns to the reader and comments on the stupidity of his author and illustrator (Apitz and Kunkel, *Spätlesereiter* 14–15).

In another nice metafictional turn, all three contributors to the *Karl* books appear in their own comics: As Eberhard Kunkel usually comes up with ideas for new stories and, as a historian, is responsible for the authenticity of the historical background, he takes on a role of responsibility in the comic, namely as Pater Anselm, the steward of the abbey of Johannisberg (Apitz and Kunkel, *Alles Karl!* 30). Michael Apitz and Patrick Kunkel, by contrast, appear as themselves in the comics, or rather as their younger reporter-selves, collecting stories for their student newspaper (see Apitz and Kunkel, *Loreley* 9–10). Their anachronistic appearance and inquisitive behavior frequently get them into trouble in the politically restrictive climate of the late 18th century.

Another group of people who are consistently featured in the comics as themselves are authors. The most prominently featured person in the *Karl* books is Johann Wolfgang von Goethe, whom Apitz and Kunkel regard as the literary patron of their series (Apitz and Kunkel, *Alles Karl!* 54), and who frequently "quotes from his own works" (Apitz and Kunkel, *Spätlesereiter* 2). Indeed, Apitz and Kunkel's Goethe loves citing famous passages from his own plays, poems, and prose texts, which becomes another ongoing joke of the series. When Goethe, for example, offers his arm to the female lead character, Maria, he uses a now-proverbial quote from Faust's first meeting with Gretchen: "Mein schönes Fräulein darf ich wagen, / meinen Arm und Geleit ihr anzutragen?" (My beautiful young lady, dare I / offer you my arm and company?). Naturally, Goethe receives the same shattering (and equally proverbial) reply as Faust: "Bin weder Fräulein weder schön, kann ungeleitet zur Tafel gehn." (I'm neither a lady nor beautiful, and can go alone to the table. *Spätlesereiter* 35).

The *Karl* comics also recount events from Goethe's life. For example, volume 9 is called *Italiänische Reise* ("The Italian Journey") and starts with descriptions from Goethe's travelogue of the same title (5–6). The accompanying pictures form an ironic contrast by showing these events in an exaggerated way and thus acting as a sometimes playful but mostly reverential parody. Goethe's original text and Apitz and Kunkel's parody are presented side by side, and an ironic tension is created between text and image.

*Der Fall Loreley* introduces the two authors who created the Loreley myth, Clemens Brentano and Heinrich Heine. Apitz and Kunkel use the meeting of these two for another metafictional comment: "Heine...? Aren't you a bit too early?" Brentano asks and alludes to the fact that, being born in 1797, Heine is not really a contemporary of Karl. But, "[t]he true poet is timeless," Heine answers (Apitz and Kunkel, *Loreley* 32). In the following, they both quote from their respective poems about the Loreley and even start an argument about whether it is her beauty or her singing that causes so many boating accidents on the Rhine, thus highlighting the difference between their respective poems. At the end of the comic, Brentano and Heine still have not resolved their quarrel. The last panel shows them swimming in the Rhine at the foot of the Loreley rock after their boat has crashed. Brentano insists it has all happened because of Loreley's beauty, while Heine blames her singing: "...das hat mit ihrem Singen die Lorelei getan!" (44). So the comic ends with the last line of Heine's poem.

In the most recent volume of the series, *Das Erbe*, the reader then meets Loreley herself, sitting on her rock and in turn quoting the beginning of Heine's poem. Not only do the lines from Heine's version fit the context of Apitz and Kunkel's story more neatly than Brentano's, but Heine's text is also the poem that readers are more likely to recognize. After Friedrich Silcher composed a tune for it in 1838, it has become far more famous than the older poem by Brentano.

Literary characters that appear in the Apitz and Kunkel comics include Hagen (the antagonist of Siegfried in *Das Nibelungenlied*), who here accidentally drops the Rhinegold onto the head of Father Rhine, who is not amused (Apitz and Kunkel, *Nibelungen* 5). Hauke Haien from Theodor Storm's novella *Der Schimmelreiter* also appears and takes part in a horse race, during which his horse first turns into a skeleton and then disappears (Apitz and Kunkel, *Spätlesereiter* 9–11). Conan Doyle's Sherlock Holmes plays a role in *Lord am Rhein* and alludes to "The Adventure of the Speckled Bands" (*Lord* 6). Finally, Heinrich Hoffmann's infamous Struwwelpeter also has a guest appearance (*Krönung* 5).

The reference to the characters from Hoffmann's children's book is not just an example of a literary character simply taking part in the *Karl* stories, but also an instance of pictorial quotation and parody. The naughty, unkempt boy standing on the rim of a fountain mimics the figure on the cover of Hoffmann's book. In addition, Apitz has included another character from *Der Struwwelpeter*, Flying Robert, in the same panel. Other examples of pictorial parody include two versions of Tischbein's famous portrait of Goethe in Italy, one with the historicized skyline of Frankfurt in the background instead of the Italian landscape of the Campagna (*Spätlesereiter* 15), and another with

8. The Use of Allusion in Apitz and Kunkel's *Karl* Comics *(Schwab)*   105

Karl as Goethe on the cover of *Italiänische Reise*. In *Das Faß der Zisterzienser* Karl meets a strangely pale, muscular young man in a fitness center: Michelangelo's *David*. "Boy, he's got muscles like marble!" Karl cannot help thinking and thus makes the joke complete (34).

Sometimes a whole panel parodies a work of art, for example, when an archivist looking up some information in his books becomes Spitzweg's *Bücherwurm* (*Zisterzienser* 24), and a showgirl in the anachronistic Moulin Rouge mimics the showgirl on Toulouse-Lautrec's famous poster *Moulin Rouge — La Goulue* (*Paris* 6). In contrast to this, the picture of the statue of the Spätlesereiter on the cover of the first *Karl* comic forms a reference to art as a work of art, similar to the parody of Caravaggio's *Bacchus* in *Das Erbe* (8, 9).

The series also contains allusions to film. On the one hand, there are caricatures of actors, which allude to specific roles they have played but there are also characters from animated films or puppet shows. The former group, though, is by far the largest, and several examples can be found in all of the *Karl* books, for example, in *Der Fall Loreley*, a mystery story, the villains steal the wine of a famous monastery in the Rheingau — Kloster Eberbach, where the interiors for the film version of Umberto Eco's *The Name of the Rose* were shot. In what was in itself a nice parodic turn on Eco's professed liking for the Bond movies, Sean Connery played the part of the monk turned sleuth in the film. Consequently, in Apitz and Kunkel's *Der Fall Loreley* the abbot of Kloster Eberbach is of course none other than Sean Connery (24).

In *Lord am Rhein* the reader meets another detective, namely Germany's most famous TV detective, Derrick, portrayed in the eponymous TV series by actor Horst Tappert (13). Yet while in the TV series he has a human partner called Harry, in the comic he is accompanied by a German shepherd dog called Harro. Why a German shepherd? This is an allusion to another German crime series called *Kommissar Rex*, in which the lead character, Rex, is a German shepherd. Furthermore, the lord who is abducted in *Lord am Rhein* is modeled on Sir Francis Bond Head, whose description of his journey to the Rhine was published in 1834 as *Bubbles from the Brunnens of Nassau* and became a bestseller in Great Britain. Because of his name, Apitz and Kunkel decided against using the features of Sir Francis for their lord and gave him a real "Bond head" instead: he looks like Roger Moore (*Lord* 47–48).

Other examples of actors in the *Karl* books include John Wayne in cowboy costume, taking part in the same horse race as Hauke Heine (*Spätlesereiter* 9–11) or Sylvester Stallone as the manager of a fitness center (*Zisterzienser* 14). Harrison Ford appears as Indiana Jones (*Nibelungen* 38) and Marlon Brando lends his features to a black market dealer in a reference to his role in *The Godfather* (*Krönung* 22–23). Yet he is not the only one doing shady business on this black market. There is also the hissing character from Sesame Street who tries to sell an E to Ernie (*Krönung* 22).

Naturally, Apitz and Kunkel also incorporate references to other comics in their work. A closer look at the organizers' team of the coronation in *Die Krönung* reveals a humanized version of Scrooge McDuck. Just like his cartoon counterpart, this character is very reluctant to part with the money he keeps in a money bin (Apitz and Kunkel, *Die Krönung* 5–6). When Karl crosses the Alps in *Italiänische Reise*, he meets a little girl and asks her whether this is the right way to Italy. But alas, she only knows the way to Frankfurt (34). Most readers will immediately identify the little girl as Heidi from the anime series of the same title.

This shows that, in order to make their allusions work, Apitz and Kunkel make use of what Terry Pratchett, talking about his own *Discworld* novels, has called "white knowledge": "If I put a reference in a book I try to pick one that a generally well-read (well-viewed, well-listened) person has a sporting chance of picking up; I call this 'white knowledge,' the sort of stuff that fills up your brain without you really knowing where it came from" ("Words from the Master"). Similar to Pratchett, who refers to the musical version of *The Wizard of Oz* rather than to the book version in *Witches Abroad* (see *Witches* 139–43), Apitz and Kunkel allude to the better-known anime version of *Heidi* instead of the literary character from the novels by Johanna Spyri, just as their Lorelei in *Das Erbe* quotes from Heine's poem and not from Brentano's.

Allusions in Apitz and Kunkel's *Karl* series are so manifold that only a small number of them could be discussed in this essay. The amount of intertextual and intermedial references, of political and cultural satire, can be regarded as an essential part of Apitz and Kunkel's effort to prove that comic books are not a medium only for children—a point that the authors of *Karl* have certainly proven.

BIBLIOGRAPHY

Apitz, Michael, Eberhard Kunkel, and Patrick Kunkel. *Alles Karl!* Walluf: Apitz & Kunkel, 1998.
\_\_\_\_\_. *Karl: Das Boot*. Vol. 11. Walluf: Apitz & Kunkel, 2002.
\_\_\_\_\_. *Karl: Das Erbe*. Vol. 12. Eltville-Martinsthal: Apitz & Kunkel, 2004.
\_\_\_\_\_. *Karl: Das Faß der Zisterzienser*. Vol. 2. Martinsthal im Rheingau: Apitz & Kunkel, 1989.
\_\_\_\_\_. *Karl: Das Gold der Nibelungen*. Vol. 5. Martinsthal im Rheingau: Apitz & Kunkel, 1994.
\_\_\_\_\_. *Karl: Der Fall Loreley*. Vol. 4. Martinsthal im Rheingau: Apitz & Kunkel, 1992.
\_\_\_\_\_. *Karl: Der Spätlesereiter*. Vol. 1. Walluf: Apitz & Kunkel, 1988.
\_\_\_\_\_. *Karl: Die Krönung*. Vol. 8. Walluf: Apitz & Kunkel, 1997.
\_\_\_\_\_. *Karl: Italiänische Reise*. Vol. 9. Walluf: Apitz & Kunkel, 1999.
\_\_\_\_\_. *Karl: Lord am Rhein*. Vol. 7. Walluf: Apitz & Kunkel, 1996.
\_\_\_\_\_. *Karl: Paris, 9. Thermidor*. Vol. 10. Walluf: Apitz & Kunkel, 2000.

Hood, Thomas. *Up the Rhine*. Vol. 2 of *The Works of Thomas Hood*, edited by Epes Sargent. New York: Putnam, 1862 [1839].
Kroener, Wolfgang. "Rhein-Romantik: 1: Vom Schauer der Ruinen ergriffen." *Rhein-Zeitung online*. 2002. http://rhein-zeitung.de/magazin/rhein_romantik/serie/serie1.html (1 October 2007).
Plummer, Patricia. "'...the loveliest paradise on earth': Englische Romantikerinnen am Rhein." *Romantik, Reisen, Realitäten: Frauenleben am Rhein*, edited by Helga Arendt. Bonn: Ed. Lempertz, 2002.
Pratchett, Terry. *Witches Abroad*. 1991. London: Corgi, 1992.
\_\_\_\_\_. "Words from the Master." *The Annotated Pratchett File, v. 9.0*, edited by Leo Breebart and Mike Kew. 2005. *L-Space*. www.us.lspace.org/books/apf/words-from-the-master.html (1 October 2007).

# 9

# Cultural Specifics of a Scottish Comic: *Oor Wullie*

## *Anne Hoyer*

*Oor Wullie*, a comic series about the adventures of a ten-year-old schoolboy, has been published since 1936 by Scotland's most popular Sunday paper in Dundee, the *Sunday Post*. Despite its long publication history, this series has attracted little critical attention. Early research on *The Beano*, *The Dandy* and other comics of the publishing company DC Thomson was conducted in 1973 by George Rosie, a former employee of the publisher. DC Thomson itself has released some background information (1996), and *Oor Wullie* and *The Broons*, the series that appears on a double page next to *Oor Wullie*, are mentioned in studies that focus on linguistic aspects of Scottish literature, for example, Corbett and Görlach in connection with language and stereotypes. The most recent analysis of *Oor Wullie's* publishing history can be found in Maureen Farrell's article, "The Lost Boys and Girls of Scottish Children's Fiction," in the *Edinburgh History of Scottish Literature*.

Elsewhere, I have investigated the dynamics of Scottish stereotypes on the level of content; the linguistic changes within the comic over the long period of its publication; and the mechanisms of *Oor Wullie*'s success (see *The Scottishness of Oor Wullie* and "Thematic and Linguistic Changes of *Oor Wullie*"). This chapter focuses in particular on the popularity of the comic.

### ORIGINS AND COMPOSITION

The figurehead of DC Thomson's newspapers and magazines is the Sunday paper, which was founded as the *Post Sunday Special* in 1914 in Glasgow and has been published as the *Sunday Post* since 1919. On 8 March 1936, *The Broons* and *Oor Wullie* came into being under the influence of the American newspaper "funnies." Robert Duncan Low, the chief editor of several children's publications, created the character "Oor Wullie" with artwork by the Nottingham-born artist Dudley Dexter Watkins (1907–1969).

During Watkins' era as the series' graphic artist, competing DC Thomson employees submitted written outlines for the strips every week, from which the best was printed in the *Sunday Post* as the weekly cartoon. In this way, Watkins and the authors continuously improved the comics' quality. In 1940, following the publication of highly popular double pages of *The Broons* and *Oor Wullie* in the *Sunday Post*, DC Thomson satisfied the still-rising demand for the series by publishing annual collections. Since then, an *Oor Wullie* annual and a *Broons* annual have been published alternately every autumn, in time for the Christmas season, and this release date has become an important event in the Scottish cultural calendar.

However, the path to success was by no means a smooth one. The steady rhythm of the publication of the annuals was interrupted by World War II until 1948 when the first postwar *Oor Wullie* annual was finally published to great acclaim. Watkins and the authors of the series improved the comic's quality further in the following years until *Oor Wullie* became a Scottish icon in the late 1940s and early 1950s with sales reaching record levels. This phase of the series is often referred to as the "Golden Age of Dudley Watkins." The artist was so famous that he was exempt from military service in World War II. Apparently, the nation's morale during the war profited so much from *The Broons* and *Oor Wullie* that the authorities did not wish to risk losing the series' unifying and supportive force.

After Watkins's death in 1969, for over seven years DC Thomson was unable to find a cartoonist who could satisfy the readers' demand for an authentic continuation of the series. Thus, the publisher kept the regular string of *Oor Wullie* and *The Broons* comics alive by reprinting old stories every Sunday in the paper, and each year in the annuals. This helped to keep the fame of the double comic page of the *Sunday Post* alive, which it did from the late 1970s with Ken H. Harrison, until a new cartoonist was finally found, Peter Davidson, in 1997. Both artists introduced some changes but kept the essence and visual character of the series alive. Consequently, *Oor Wullie* is still seen by most Scots as a living national icon.

Considering its fame within Scotland, its production team is rather small. There is no central editorial pool for comics within DC Thomson, but each title of the various series has its own small office. The present "Broons/Wullie-team" consists of no more than three members of staff, who pursue the various tasks connected with the series but also work on other projects. They compile the *Special Collections*,* design the *Broons* calendar and discuss the scripts the chief editor composes. From January 2005 until March 2006 all scripts were written by BBC broadcaster Tom Morton. From March 2006 onward Dave Donaldson has written the manuscripts, which are then sent to the cartoonist who draws the story panels.

## An Exemplar

A very illustrative example of an *Oor Wullie* strip appeared on 15 October 1944, when hunger had become a constant companion of many Scottish families. In the story, the protagonist, ten-year-old Wullie, envies his friend, Fat Bob, who has received a pie as a present from Jeannie, a girl who admires him. Wullie tries to find a way to attract the girl's attention so that she will give him a pie, too. He passes by a statue of Robert Burns, the Scottish national poet who, Wullie surmises, must obviously have known how to get about successfully in life. In imitation, Wullie decides to write a poem for the girl.

His first attempt is a failure. Jeannie chases Wullie away and throws an empty casserole after him which he, in turn, takes to a bramble bush and uses to pick blackberries with while he is thinking about an improved version of his poem. He then returns to Jeannie with a second piece of poetry. The poem and the additional gift of the pot of blackberries please Jeannie very much and, in return, she gives Wullie two pies, which he eats — enthroned in front of the statue of Robert Burns on his trademark bucket. In a way typical for *Oor Wullie*, a defeat has been turned into a marvelous success. Wullie very often manages to make something out of nothing by applying his natural cleverness. In this strip, if only for a short time, he has distanced himself from hunger and misery and he has gained recognition. Wullie has thus met the standards set by his Scottish role model, Robert Burns, who rose from an impoverished farmer to national fame through his poetry.

In much the same way that Burns captured the Scottish national imagination with his poems on rural life, love, and drink, *Oor Wullie* offered a figure of identification for the Scottish population with the short stories of a *wee lad* from a simple working-class family who does not know upper-class

---

*\*Since 1996, additional collectors' books have appeared, i.e. the Special Collections. The 60th anniversary volume* The Broons and Oor Wullie, 1936–1996 *was the first of nine collectors' books published so far. In these volumes the best stories of certain epochs are reprinted in chronological order. In addition, striking historical and cultural events of the time are illustrated with pictures as well as headlines and excerpts from newspaper articles. The many decades of* Oor Wullie *and* The Broons *publications have thus become a repository for an illustrated history of Scotland in the 20th century.*

manners but manages to get along due to his natural wit. He has become a figure of identification for Scottish society as a whole despite his lack of social graces, and probably exactly because of his "rough but hearty" approach.

## OOR WULLIE'S STATUS

With the topics it addresses and with its language, *Oor Wullie* strengthens Scottish identity. This has always been one of the secrets of the success of the series, which can be estimated when one considers the following facts: "Reading the *Broons* and *Oor Wullie*" was among the "100 Things to Do in Scotland before You Die" by the *Glasgow Herald*. Old annuals are sold at top prices rising up to £4,000. *Oor Wullie*'s and Watkins' iconic status was also underlined when a family moved into Watkins' former home in Dundee in 2002 and discovered murals on the walls, which the artist probably drew for his children. The murals have been officially recognized as a national treasure, and consequently the wall is now owned by the Scottish National Trust. Furthermore, as part of the *Tartan Day* festivities in April 2004, *Oor Wullie* was voted the most important Scottish icon.

At least four factors are responsible for the striking effect *Oor Wullie* has had on the Scottish readership. The first two hold true for many comics. Firstly, the structure and symbols of the comics are consistent. From time to time Wullie addresses the reader directly in a short prologue or epilogue. Several of the stories thus begin and end with Wullie sitting on his typical bucket, which has become the symbol of Wullie's cleverness and his ability to improvise. Similar symbols that support his main character traits are Wullie's rough but also practical dungarees, his self-made wooden cart and the shed where Wullie, "the inventor," creates new things to entertain and amuse people.

Secondly, the mechanism of what Konrad Lorenz has termed *Kindchenschema* leads to an intense identification with the protagonist. The character's round cheeks and big smile are an invitation to identify with him. The figures in comics have to be universal for readers to be able to identify with them.

Third, the character's attributes — as well as the topics — are typically Scottish, which means that they are easily recognizable for the readers. This is demonstrated by the frequent portrayal of Scottish inventiveness depicted in the main characters but it also frames the plotlines, which are often firmly linked to Scottish life and culture. The editorial board considers the Scottish setting to be an obligation, unlike other comic series, like the Belgian *Tintin*, which are mainly based on "foreign adventures," rather than being set in the home country of the protagonist.

Finally, the language of the strip is very convincingly Scottish for the readership in Scotland, not least because of the subtle orthographical transcription of the Scottish accent. Along the lines of what Allan Bell has termed *ingroup referee design* (187f), the authors of *Oor Wullie* use language as an expressive instrument for the declaration of identity and thus signal "you and I are an ingroup" to the audience.

## Stereotypes of Content

The topics in *Oor Wullie* constitute a corpus of recurring subjects. Considered chronologically, topics like "school," "money, work and jobs" are used less and less. In contrast, "growing up," and "cultural Scottishness" as well as "ingenuity," "food" and "authority" are very stable topics. "Sports" and "pets," on the other hand, increase in frequency. These changes mirror developments in Scottish society and culture as well as the decisions of the editorial teams as to which topics might be most interesting for the readers.

The topics revolve around four main stereotypes. First, the vital Highlander, the image of the strong and rebellious Scot, who often appears in 19th-century romantic views of the past, as, for instance, in Sir Walter Scott's novels *Waverley* (1814) and *Rob Roy* (1817). Second, the "Kailyard," a derogatory term that refers to a specific nostalgic genre of Scottish literature that was extremely popular from about 1880 to 1914. The name "kailyard" refers to the little "cabbage gardens" behind the modest Scottish tenement houses that have come to represent the petit-bourgeois ideology of "home sweet home," which is often seen as reaction against the evil forces of industrialization. This is best embodied by *The Broons*, the harmonious Scottish family often depicted in front of the fireplace. The third stereotype of significance to *Oor Wullie* is the "Hardman," the strong, sweaty Glaswegian worker with his cigarette and smoky voice. Finally, there is the "Improvising Scot" with his cleverness. Wullie demonstrates his skill at improvising for example when he fills his ubiquitous bucket with water and uses it variously as a shower, foot warmer, or cooler. Similarly, he employs his self-made wooden cart for various jobs, for example, for carrying tourist's luggage.

The Improvising Scot is a stereotype the Scottish can most easily identify with and can be regarded as the native equivalent of the "mean/stingy Scot" stereotype, which so dominates the foreign perception of Scotland. The latter occurs almost never in *Oor Wullie*. Both images originate at the same source, namely—and in decisive contrast to England's wealth—the scarcity of Scottish resources. In the foreign view, the Scottish response to the lack of resources represents niggardliness. From the Scottish perspective, it represents the skill to improvise.

## Linguistic Stereotypes

In 1977, Macaulay first described the "linguistic inferiority complex" that purportedly causes the Scots to hesitate before they speak. This is illustrated in the following quotation: "The accent of the lowest state of Glaswegians is the ugliest accent one can encounter" (University lecturer, in Macaulay 94). Problems can be observed in school and in job interviews, where dialect can precipitate discrimination. Epithets such as "slovenly," "vulgar" or "coarse" are commonly used to characterize Scottish English (Scots).

Scots rarely appears in newspapers, except in articles that deal mainly with the language itself or with gossipy topics. It is, however, more frequently used in novels and poetry, but if so mostly in experimental pieces. There has been an upsurge of Scots in literature since the mid–1980s in prose (e.g., in the novels of authors like Irvine Welsh and James Kelman) and — even more outspokenly — in poetry (e.g., in pieces by Tom Leonard and Robert Crawford). This has partly been influenced by the boost of Scottish self-confidence in 1990, when Glasgow was the European cultural capital.

With the exception of Oor Wullie, Scots is only rarely used even in Scottish comics. Oor Wullie's forerunner in the *Sunday Post*, *Wee Jimmy* from the early 1930s, used very little Scots. From 1971 until 1974 Vic Neill's *McTickles* ran in *The Beano* and in the 1990s *Angus Óg* ("Young Angus") was a comic that was set in Scotland and contained a few Scottish words. Since 2005, the weekly *Orcadian* has published the comic-strip *The Giddy Limit*, which makes use of the Orcadian dialect. None of these comics have been as successful in managing the "right measure" of Scottishness in language and content as *Oor Wullie*. This was investigated with the help of a text corpus that consisted of ten percent of all *Oor Wullie* stories.

There are some Scots-specific features which occur repeatedly. Some of these increase over the years, for example, the negative suffix *-nae* in words such as *cannae* (cannot). There are also very stable features, for example, *ye* (you) and words with the characteristic Scottish long monophthong, for example, *oot* (out). However, most features appear with decreasing frequency, for example, the negative suffix *-na* and Wullie's exclamation *jings* (gosh, golly, gee, goodness), which will be used here to illustrate the various reasons for linguistic change in the series over the years.

Many words display the negative suffix *-na* and *-nae* as in *doesna* and *doesnae* (doesn't). Words with the suffix *-nae* increase in comparison to those with *-na*. The diminishing use of *-na* is one of the most indicative features in *Oor Wullie*. The form *-na* is older in language history and has its origins in the Northeastern Scotland, that is, the area around Aberdeen, a region often described as sporting the most archaic rural Scots and hence referred to as "Doric." In contrast, *-nae* is associated with the densely populated, industrial Central Belt between Glasgow and Edinburgh, and consequently has strong working-class connotations.

The change from *-na* to *-nae* may reflect the sociocultural and economic development within Scotland as well as the orientation toward readers of the strip. Although the comics are still published in the northeastern town of Dundee, the northeast has lost much of its traditional economical weight to Glasgow, Edinburgh and the "Silicon Glen" in between. In the first decades of *Oor Wullie,* the northeastern variant *-na* was dominant because the northeastern dialects then best represented the image of an essentially rural country. In the second half of the 20th century, *-nae* has taken over reflecting a shift of the nation's self-perception from a nostalgic image of rural purity to an increasingly confident working-class urbanism. The trend toward *-nae* also reflects the tendency to adjust the language of the comic to a wider readership based mainly in the Central Belt, away from the local and toward the general. It is also likely that the Central Belt variant increases the metropolitan prestige of *Oor Wullie.*

There are yet other factors that influence the linguistic change: The dilution of the specifically nostalgic "Doric" toward the more central form also demonstrates the decrease of Scots-specific features in favor of English ones. A typical example is the very Scottish *jings* (gosh, golly, gee, goodness), which appeared frequently in the early years of *Oor Wullie* but then gradually decreased. In the 1980s, however, the frequency increased again when the editor wished to increase the Scottishness of the comics. Thus, the speech bubbles were full of *jings* again, and the language also was adorned with other antiquated words. This tendency toward nostalgia also influenced the content level. Suddenly, Wullie had a West Highland Terrier, and he went hiking in the Highlands and attended traditional Scottish festivities such as the Highland Games or traditional dances. The Tartan and Kailyard stereotypes also occurred with increasing frequency. This may reflect a trend toward a touristy "Tartan Industry" in the 1980s but changed again in the late 1990s when the editorial team regarded these alterations as too artificial and, in an attempt to attract younger readers, reduced the glaring Scotticisms. Somewhat less linguistic nostalgia was now regarded as more attractive. This also shows in the contents. More topics of today's concerns occurred, for example, sporting and cultural events. *Oor Wullie* is still as iconic as ever, demonstrated, for example, by the fact that the protagonist was voted a "Scottish icon" in 2006. The authors try, however, to adjust the language and the content to the preferences of modern readers. This still includes a little dose of nostalgia. As far as the key stereotypes are concerned, there are increasing occurrences of the Hardman stereotype, and the Improvising Scot has remained a stable feature of the series from its origin. Despite their deliberate use of stereotypes, the authors of *Oor Wullie* take great care not to produce too overtly stereotypical texts, which will easily appear nostalgic and artificial.

BIBLIOGRAPHY

Bain, Ewen. *Angus Óg from the Óg Logs*. Glasgow: Zipo, 1999.
Bell, Allan. "Language Style as Audience Design." *Language in Society* 13 (1984): 145–204.
Corbett, John. *Language and Scottish Literature*. Edinburgh: Edinburgh University Press, 1997.
Farrell, Maureen. "The Lost Boys and Girls of Scottish Children's Fiction." *The Edinburgh History of Scottish Literature*, edited by Ian Brown et al. Edinburgh: Edinburgh University Press, 2006, 198–206.
Görlach, Manfred. *A Textual History of Scots*. Heidelberg: Winter, 2002.
Hoyer, Anne. *The Scottishness of Oor Wullie*. Unpublished PhD Thesis, Ruprecht-Karls Universität, Heidelberg, 2007.
_____. "Thematic and Linguistic Changes of *Oor Wullie*: The Dynamics of a Popular Scottish Comic." *Scottish Archives* 13 (2007).
_____. "Thematische und sprachliche Veränderungen eines populären schottischen Zeitungscomics." 2006. Gesellschaft für Comicforschung. www.comicforschung.de/tagungen/06 nov/06nov_hoyer.pdf (1 October 2007).
_____. "Thematische und sprachliche Veränderungen eines populären schottischen Zeitungscomic." *Landauer Schriften zur Kommunikations- und Kulturwissenschaft* (15), edited by H.H. Lüger / H.E.H. Lenk. Landau: Verlag Empirische Pädagogik, 2008.
Leonard, Alex. "The Giddy Limit." *The Orcadian*. Kirkwall: The Orcadian, since 2005.
Lorenz, Konrad. "Die Angeborenen Formen Möglicher Erfahrung." *Zeitschrift für Tierpsychologie* 5 (1943): 235–49.
Macaulay, Ronald K. S. *Language, Social Class and Education: A Glasgow Study*. Edinburgh: Edinburgh University Press, 1977.
McClure, J. Derrick. "Language." Edited by Tom Crawford. *Scottish Literary Journal: The Year's Work in Scottish Literary and Linguistic Studies* (1990): 72–86.
"100 Things to Do in Scotland before You Die." *The Sunday Herald*, 28 March 2004. www.sundayherald.com/np/100things.-shtm (1 October 2007).
"Oor Wullie." *The Sunday Post*. Dundee: D.C. Thomson, since 1936.
*Oor Wullie Annuals*. Glasgow: D.C. Thomson, since 1940.
*Oor Wullie Special Collections*. Glasgow: D.C. Thomson, since 1996.
Rosie, George. "The Secret World of the Comic Kings. The Private Life of Lord Snooty: An Investigation by George Rosie." *The Sunday Times Magazine*, 29 July 1973.
*A Scottish Success Story*. London: D.C. Thomson, 1996.

# 10

# Memento Mori: A Portuguese Style of Melancholy

*Mario Gomes and Jan Peuckert*

### COMICS IN PORTUGAL (A SAD COMICAL FADO)

A discourse on anything concerning Portugal can but start with a set of clichés. For whenever the character of Portugal is to be expressed in concise terms, the common denominator usually comes in the shape of a well-known expression: "saudade." All the unnamable characteristics of that which is essentially Portuguese are believed to be condensed and archived in this untranslatable term which is probably best conveyed by the minor chords of Fado music. While the word "saudade" remains a somewhat cryptic signifier standing for a whole national culture, its transmediation into music seems more adequate than verbal explanations to bring the blue mood that "saudade" encompasses into terms.

Whatever saudade may be, it surfaces in Fado.

Such at least is the cliché.

But Fado does not only serve as a way of translating Portugality for the Englishman.* In the past it has also been used as a privileged means to convey the meaning of Portugal to the Portuguese themselves by nation builders and dictators engaged in defining a national identity. Especially during the regime of António de Oliveira Salazar, Fado was promoted as a signifier of national culture. Fado, Fátima, futebol, as the famous alliteration goes, were fostered to form the substratum of a whole way of life. In spite of all the changes the country underwent since the revolution in 1974, the structures

---

*The Portuguese expression "para inglês ver," "for the Englishman to see," is used to describe something that is made with the sole purpose of impressing.

of significance inherent to this triple-f devotion still seem to be deeply rooted in a country where melancholy self-pity, feverous mysticism and enthusiasm for talented dribblers of the ball are still cultivated as Lusitanian idiosyncrasies. Though the political program of the "Estado novo" may have become obsolete, the symbols of national identity it propagated for decades still subsist. The way in which such symbols are dealt with nowadays is not merely a political issue but also an aesthetic challenge.

For many, the reinvention of Portugality has thus become an artistic task. While experimental musicians draw on Fado harmonics or use guitar samples in electronic compositions, and while filmmakers and writers keep revising the country's colonial past over and over, visual artists, and particularly the comic artists we shall be dealing with, are often found trying to convert whatever connotations "saudade" may conjure up into a graphic style. The same mood that translates into the harmonics of Fado and into the somber semantics of its lyrics also governs the settings of many a Portuguese comic plot. If there actually were something like a Portuguese comic school, it would probably be best defined by the way this toned-down temper is rendered visually.

As things stand, however, there seems to be no such thing one could label a "Portuguese comic tradition." Whereas other European countries look back on a record of successful comic best-sellers, Portugal has neither brought up any popular comic figures nor recognized comic artists. Significantly enough there is not even a genuinely Portuguese term for the genre that has become known under the loanword "banda desenhada," adapted from the French "bande dessinée." While Spanish "tebeos" or Italian "fumetti" stand as signposts for a national tradition, the Portuguese have preferred to import French words and foreign comic books.

If during the "Estado-novo"-regime the comic strip was under sharp scrutiny by the censors and was most commonly used as a political instrument, the democratic changes after 1974 have not, however, encouraged the creation of national comics. They have, rather, facilitated the import of foreign books, mostly from overseas, from the United States and from the largest Portuguese-speaking nation: Brazil. Apparently the small Portuguese market was not big enough to allow the upsurge of national publications. Since the offer of pop products from abroad seemed to satisfy the demand of the larger comic-reading public, Portuguese comics were confined to a niche, somewhere down in the artistic underground. Even after the democratic revolution, Portuguese comic authors kept working clandestinely. And little seems to have changed since.

If the genre of comics is usually regarded as a product of mass popular culture, in Portugal the domain of comic publications has almost exclusively been taken over by fine arts scholars and so-called "intellectual artists." Rather than producing pulp for youth, Portuguese comic authors have tended to produce a peculiar sort of fanzine comic poetry, whose addressees have at all times been academics or well-read comic aficionados. In this sense it may not surprise that, for instance, even the best-selling comic author in Portugal, José Carlos Fernandes, has not produced an œuvre for a broad public, but rather for a small, cultivated audience. Comics produced in Portugal have never been products of pop culture but rather of the "fine arts."

## Fatality — Waiting for a Certain Death

One of the works most apt to illustrate what has been argued so far and which in the following shall be regarded as representative of a new generation of Portuguese comic authors is a joint production by the illustrator Miguel Rocha and the writer João Paulo Cotrim entitled *Salazar* (2006). The unusual impact on public opinion this book has had is not, as one might at first suppose, due only to the prominence of the subject it deals with, but mostly to its aesthetic achievement. The number of renowned prizes the book has been awarded makes the magnitude of its impact quantifiable and speaks for its quality — or at least for its recognition as a fine piece of "fine art."

The room for reflection *Salazar* opens up is immensely vast and its distinctive stylistic and compositional features are redolent of elemental aesthetic questions that regard the very boundaries of the comics genre. As the full title of the work, *Salazar. Now, in the Hour of His Death*, already suggests, the questions it brings up are literally questions of life and death. And indeed the motif of death holds a privileged position in Rocha and Cotrim's interpretation of António de Oliveira Salazar's biography.

The way it is traditionally delivered, Salazar supposedly died after falling from a chair. What the anecdote leaves out is that between Salazar's clumsy accident (that effectively caused severe injuries from which he would not recover again) and his actual decease almost two years elapsed. In the popular account of the facts this time span has been condensed to a single happening in which the moment of the fall is inextricably linked to the moment of the later death. It is the grotesque effect conveyed by the image of the despot dying after falling from his throne that actually makes it possible to treat Salazar's death as an anecdote.

In *Salazar* Rocha and Cotrim take this anecdotal compression of events literally, positioning the fall from the chair and the later death of the dictator as prologue and epilogue, respectively. Within the narrative frame that is thereby constituted, death ceases to be an event at a certain point in time and

Salazar's death as an anecdote (Miguel Rocha and João Paulo Cotrim, *Salazar. Agora, na Hora da Sua Morte*. ©2006, Parceria A. M. Pereira).

becomes a frozen eternal moment. Each depicted instant is set equal to the dictator's double death. But instead of adding up to a linear narrative, the fragmentary episodes that are shown between these two key moments acquire their significance chiefly by establishing a thematic nexus with the central motif of death. The homogeneity that the patchy narration is not able to produce is hence supplied by the numerous variations of the motif that are presented in the comic. Through the connotative load lent to each image death disseminates semiotically. It installs itself virtually everywhere.

When Salazar's childhood is depicted, for instance, the comic figure's body is given the face of the waning dictator. As the elderly man is shown as an intrinsic part of the child, a symbol is constructed that embodies the disintegration of time and gives human mortality a face. The differences between young and old are thus suspended and temporality is renounced as a category in which evolution occurs and biographies are written.

The hybrid figure of the aged infant is however only one out of a set of visual tropes that pervade the comic and symbolically expose its atemporality. Among these tropes the predominant role is, consequently enough, given to the figure of death whose trace is constantly at work in Rocha's compositions. In some occasions it is merely the distorted, skull-like physiognomy or the hollow eyes of the comic figures that hint at death; in others the allusion to traditional allegories, such as the grim reaper, which the shadow of a field worker holding a hoe resembles.

In a comic where there is no evolving plot scheme it is this imagery that establishes the cohesion between the abstract death theme and its concrete thematic variations issued in each panel. Rocha's drawings are hence linked back to the title of the book, "now in the hour of his death," at the same time illustrating and playing on its significance. By relating to this one central theme every symbol out of the set of symbols that is constituted in the book acquires its particular significance and at the same time assures the general consistency of the work.

Maria Emília, Salazar's housemaid, a keen expert in astrology, seems at least to hold the key to some of the secrets that constitute the analogue death code,* which is transmitted by the images of the book. The moment she notices the withering flowers that decorate the dictator's office, she is at once aware of the underlying significance and presages a "risk of an accident to be caused by the native." For the reader who has already seen the moment of the accident it becomes clear that the fatal fall from the chair is traced and that death is programmed beforehand.

In a world where future events lie inscribed in present symbols, every effort to challenge destiny is certainly useless. That is why Salazar and his maid may just as well sit back, resign, and give in to the melancholy mood of "Fado," which, apart from designating a musical genre, is also commonly used as a synonym for "fate." As a matter of fact, the etymology of "Fado" and "fate" can be traced back to a common root. Both words derive from the Latin past participle "fatum," meaning something that has been spoken by a divine authority. What is uttered as a "fatum" is part of a divine plan, sure to be materialized in the future.

This mood of waiting for the ineluctable fate is Fado, and Fado is the general mood governing life in Rocha and Cotrim's Salazarist Portugal. "Tudo isto existe, tudo isto é triste, tudo isto é Fado" ("All this exists, all this is sad, all this is Fado"), a shadow surrounded by a bunch of children is seen saying in one of the comic panels, quoting the famous lines of a well-known Fado song, which in this context certainly lends itself to a self-referential reading. Given that the deictic pronoun "isto" ("this") lacks a direct referent, the quo-

---

*In his essay "The Photographic Message," Roland Barthes introduces the idea of an "analogue code" or "message without code," as he prefers to formulate it. Like other "imitative arts" comics comprise (at least) two messages, "a denoted message, which is the analogon itself, and a connoted message [...]." Connotation and style convey a message that is not encoded digitally. Cf. Barthes, "The Photographic Message" 16ff.

tation may as well be read as referring to everything in *Salazar*'s Portugal or — going one step further — to the basic mood of the comic itself. Since the "fatum" of death, as *Salazar* shows, is unavoidable, life ends up being a mere execution of the plan written down by a divine entity, this writing being mirrored graphically by the comic artist. In their function as reminders of an announced, ever-present death, the panels in *Salazar* become a suite of *memento mori* representations. In these representations the dissolution of life is engendered by a hybrid linguistic and pictorial *écriture* in which the *stilus* both of the writer and of the designer engage in creating a space where these symbols of death become significant.*

## Bloodstained Diptychs

At a certain point the French journalist Christine Garnier, who is depicted strolling around with Salazar through his private grounds near his hometown, Santa Comba Dão, remarks that whenever she is together with him she feels so sheltered that time seems to stop. And right she is, indeed, for the time one spends with *Salazar* is frozen time, stopped forever on an ever-present "now" that is also "the hour of his death." What the journalist intends to be a flattering remark, is thus far more than that. For timelessness is there to be grasped on the page, held up graphically by the image of Salazar's and Mrs. Garnier's distorted reflection in a pond, an image that extends to the borders of the printed page, without the contours of a comic panel that would force it back into a chronological alignment.

As Scott McCloud explains in his popular meta-comic *Understanding Comics* the dissolution of the comic grid is a fairly common means to render, spatially, the disintegration of time:

> When "bleeds" are used — i.e., when a panel runs off the edge of the page [...] time is no longer contained by the familiar icon of the *closed panel*, but instead *hemorrhages* and escapes into *timeless space* [103].

Judging by the bleedings it causes, the elimination of the closed lines of the comic panel seems to be a somewhat violent act. As McCloud's metaphor suggests, bleeds hurt the comics at the core, interfering with the illusion of chronological sequence, which the juxtaposition of panels is to suggest. McCloud also maintains that the space between the panels, that is, the so-called "gutter," "plays host to much of the *magic* and *mystery* that are at the

---

*The etymology of "graphics" is of interest here as "graphein" in Greek means both "writing" and "drawing." Cf. Risthaus (226), who proposes the application of Derrida's notion of* écriture *to the study of comics.*

very *heart of comics*" (66). As the images swap over the boundaries of the comic panel, they thus are taken out of a diegetic sequence. The linearity of the narrative is quashed and brought to a halt, directing the concentration onto the visual perception of the motionless image. There is a switch from a predominantly syntagmatic reading to the aesthetic contemplation of the visual signs that lie side by side on the page. Bleeding pictures, as it were, cease to narrate, placing themselves on the threshold of the realm of painting.

While the progression of narration freezes and the comic panel extends to the borders of the printed page, the materiality of the medium comes into play. As Will Eisner points out, the page of the comic, which usually contains several other graphically delimitated panels, may itself be seen as an underlying macropanel, or "metapanel," as he calls it (cf. Eisner 63). Rocha and Cotrim's comic nevertheless shows that a restricted definition of the metapanel to the single comic page may not take full account of the particularities of the medium. The systematic usage these authors make of double-page compositions suggests that the actual macropanel in comic books is not the single folio but rather the double page lying open before the reader's eye.

Strictly speaking, all comic books are structured as diptychs.

As the composition extends so to fill the double page, the last scrap of dialectics between the single pages that lie side by side is annulled. Differences are no longer marked and no sequence is left running between the two open pages (which in *Salazar* quite significantly are not numbered). Without the "gutter" between the one-page macropanels, the suggestion of passing time is obliterated. The frozen image stands for itself, detached from a sequence, that is, from everything that precedes or follows the isolated moment.

In Rocha's diptychs, time bleeds to death.

*Salazar* does not, however, build solely on double-page dyptichs. But even when the traditional comic grid is employed in a conventional way, it does not set a flow of action running, but simply develops a short fragmentary motif until it is followed by the next episode out of the dictator's life or out of the everyday life of the Portuguese living under his regime. Each of these episodes is a particle cut out from a suggested whole that stands as a closed independent unit, nonetheless linked one way or another to the thematic nub of the book, that is to say, to the dictator and his death.

## Tableaux

The underlying compositional method according to which such isolated episodes are formed is laid open in a section of the work itself. Taking a series

Time bleeds to death (Miguel Rocha and João Paulo Cotrim, *Salazar. Agora, na Hora da Sua Morte*. ©2006, Parceria A. M. Pereira).

of Salazarist propaganda pictures as a starting point, short narrative sequences are developed in which the "real life" hidden beyond the still image is exposed. At the same time it deconstructs the propagandistic message that is encoded in the original placard. This aesthetic procedure, here made explicit, is employed in a similar way throughout the whole book where, consecutively, themes are set, developed and then displaced by what follows. Without being repetitive, each episode sheds a new light on one particular aspect of the life of Salazar and of the country he governs. Each fragment thus is rendered in the form of what — odd though it may sound — could be dubbed a "tableau vivant."

In his essay "Diderot, Brecht, Eisenstein," Barthes defined the theatrical or filmic tableau as an arranged scene cut out from a whole, *decoupée*, independent from what comes before and what comes after. Such tableaux do not represent scenes picked out randomly from a chain of events, but rather particular "pregnant moments" in which past, present and future are condensed. By transforming the epic work into a succession of aesthetically perfect "pregnant moments," the playwright or the film director can be said to operate in the same way as the painter. Touching on Diderot's reflection on painting, Barthes writes:

In order to tell a story, the painter has but one instant at his disposal, the instant he is going to immobilize on the canvas, and he must thus choose it well, assuring it in advance of the greatest possible yield of meaning and pleasure. Necessarily total, this instant will be artificial [...] a hieroglyph in which can be read at a single glance (at one grasp if we think in terms of theatre and cinema) the present, the past and the future; that is the historical meaning of the represented action. This crucial instant, totally concrete and totally abstract, is what Lessing subsequently calls (in Laocöon) the *pregnant moment* ["Diderot, Brecht, Eisenstein" 97].

Like Brecht's *Mother Courage* or Eisenstein's *Battleship Potëmkim*, which Barthes takes as examples to illustrate his idea, *Salazar* is organized as a succession of "pregnant moments" that all point to the crucial instant of death. What distinguishes the comic tableau from the dynamic theatrical tableau as well as from the static painting is that it is twofold.

Literally.

As a hybrid art form between the pictorial and the epic, comics may combine two categories of tableau arrangements, that is to say they may be displayed statically on the two-page dyptich, to be "read at a single glance," but also dynamically, as a "tableau vivant" that is not scattered with the turning of the page, but instead may extend over several comic book dyptichs, its unity being established mentally.

The still-standing image of the dictator lying prostrate on the floor with what seem like double book pages flying about serves as the perfect illustration for the way in which the alignment of dyptichs is laid out in Rocha and Cotrim's comic. *Mises en abîme*, the flattering pages on the paper canvas double the group of still tableaux that together form the Barthesian *tableau vivant*.\*

The possibility of combining both of these forms of tableaux is specific to the comic genre and results from its basic organizational features, which Stephan Packard calls primary and secondary hybridization (cf. Packard 97), that is to say on the one hand the macrostructural syntagmatic alignment of the panels and on the other the paradigmatic composition of each single panel.

In Rocha and Cotrim's arrangement of the comic, this specificity of the genre recurs as a structural support in rendering the main theme of the book and suggesting its underlying mood. The tensions between macrostructure and tableau, between suggested life and the frozen dead images that represent it, are made meaningful and used in order to sustain the central thematic

---

\**After turning the page, the way in which still pictorial tableaux are linked in the book becomes evident. The motif of the flattering pages extends to the next dyptich, where the shapes dissolve into abstract shades arranged in a manner that reminds one of Escher's well-known "day and night." Both dyptichs are hence suggested to be one unit, intact in spite of the turn of the page that separates them.*

*Top:* A combination of two forms of tableaux. *Bottom:* "¡Viva la muerte!"—the metapoetical slogan of the comic (both by Miguel Rocha and João Paulo Cotrim: *Salazar. Agora, na Hora da Sua Morte.* ©2006, Parceria A. M. Pereira).

motif of the dissolution of time in death. In *Salazar* the still images, constituents of each comic, are not imbued with the suggestion of life and of passing time. "¡Viva la muerte!"—printed in stout letters and highlighted in Spanish—is the metapoetical slogan of the book. By renouncing a mimesis of life, Rocha and Cotrim suggest that the dynamic suggested in comics is necessarily built on static corpses. As a genre constituted by dead images, comics are obviously a privileged means to represent a Portugal ruled by dictators and fatalistic beliefs.

BIBLIOGRAPHY

Barthes, Roland. "Diderot, Brecht, Eisenstein." *Image, Music, Text*, edited and translated by Stephen Heath. New York: Hill, 1977, 69–78.
_____. "The Photographic Message." *Image, Music, Text*, edited and translated by Stephen Heath. New York: Hill, 1977, 15–31.
Eisner, Will. *Comics & Sequential Art*. Tamarac: Poorhouse, 1985.
McCloud, Scott. *Understanding Comics. The Invisible Art*. New York: Paradox, 1993.
Packard, Stephan. *Anatomie des Comics. Psychosemiotische Medienanalyse*. Göttingen: Wallstein, 2006.
Risthaus, Peter. "Ent-sinnung. Die Unheimliche Comic-Theorie des Jacques Derrida." *Schreibheft* 51 (1998): 225–27.
Rocha, Miguel, and João Paulo Cotrim. *Salazar. Agora, na Hora da Sua Morte*. Lisbon: Parceria A. M. Pereira, 2006.

# 11

## Otherness and the European as Villain and Antihero in American Comics

*Georg Drennig*

> *In the universe of Batman artists, phrenology and allied "sciences" have never lost their explanatory power.*
> — Uricchio and Pearson 204

> *The network has told us we cannot put minorities in criminal or disparaging situations.*
> — Boyd Kirkland, qtd. in Garcia 97

The quotes above frame the central questions that guide this paper. How can the comics industry, which is still using physiognomy to represent character traits, encode Otherness through ethnicity without being seen as racist? Do the ways and means through which the characters' villainy is encoded resort to ethnic stereotyping, and if so, which stereotypes do they employ? In the following, I will argue that American comics frequently use anti–European discourse and the representation through stereotypes as a part of comics vocabulary. This is usually done in order to construct Otherness and thus mark characters as morally corrupt. In other words, although the villains may be Caucasian, they still occupy a cultural space that is traditionally allocated to ethnicities-as-criminals (cf. Ross 34). These characters thus represent a racist construction beyond the color paradigm (cf. Mac an Ghaill).

After a glance at the problems surrounding the study of ethnically stereotyped characters, I will first discuss two *Batman* characters who are loaded with American cultural anxieties about European Others: the Mad Hatter and Mr. Freeze. The analysis will then turn to the Irish Proinsias Cassidy and the

German Herr Starr from the series *Preacher*, who are both explicitly identified as non–American. The final example of a European Other in American comics will then be *Hellblazer*'s John Constantine, who proves to be a more complicated and ambiguous character than the other villains discussed here.

Two crucial factors complicate the proposed discussion: First, the textual (in)stability of character constructions in longer-running titles, and second, the fact that stereotypes are often amorphous and highly dependent on historical context. In what has become labeled the Golden Age of American comics, this issue of stereotyping was still rather simple and uncontroversial, as discourses "of unashamed hatred for the racial 'other'" (Brooker 91) were prevalent in the industry in the 1940s. Ironically enough, this tendency toward a racist portrayal of non–Caucasian ethnicity was also noticed and criticized by the much-reviled anti-comics crusader Frederic Wertham (cf. Brooker 112f). Since then, cultural values and the modes of representation, and therefore also the outline of comic characters, have changed, which complicates their analysis.

The first problem one encounters is that characters in longer-running series like *Batman* have developed a fragmented textual existence over the years, including changes in character history and physical appearance. Most of this is due to the industry's mode of production by teams of artists (cf. Brooker, Uricchio and Pearson). Statements about character construction in the case of *Batman* therefore generally apply to a specific iteration of that character. Yet, this also offers a special analytical opportunity since the recurring features of a character identify that character's core identity. That is, if this core identity reflects encodings of ethnicity, this ethnicity can then be understood as a key constituent of the villain's Otherness.

Ethnic encodings, however, are often only understood within a certain historical time frame. They lose their explanatory power to contemporary readers at some point and then either vanish or remain "encapsulated in media forms," becoming "dormant stereotypes" (Cinnirella 39). As the discussion of the Mad Hatter will show, they may remain bound to certain signifiers that are still understood as connected with ethnicity and can thus be "activated" by association (in contrast to fully "dormant" stereotypes). Another possibility is that they retain connotations of ethnic Otherness even if they have lost their specific associations. Although they are amorphous, such stereotypes still work as a clear code for non–American ethnicity or, even more diffuse, for "Europeanness" as a broad category of foreign "white ethnicity."

This is not to argue that a stereotype based on Europeanness is in any way equal to the racist representations of Blacks or East-Asians in the 1940s. The basic cultural process, however, is similar. Through the use of stereotypical representation, the Otherness of characters is highlighted, which establishes a link between their national or ethnic background and their behavior. The standard connection between being non–WASP and being morally corrupt, therefore, does not have to rest directly on stereotypes that may have long been dormant, but can be established as soon as a villain is recognized as being culturally different.

## THE MAD HATTER

One such collaboration of dormant, implicit, and still active stereotypes can be observed in the *Batman* villain Jarvis Tetch, better known as the Mad Hatter. In this character, the iconographic traditions of depicting Irishmen as subhuman* are still evident in the 1980s. In a more recent take on the character, the visual characteristics have become less pronounced but the presence of anti–Irish is still visible.

The inspiration for the Mad Hatter is taken from *Alice's Adventures in Wonderland*, as the villain in *Batman* repeatedly makes clear by quoting Lewis Carrol, and by dressing like John Tenniel — the illustrator of the first (1865) edition of the novel, who envisioned the character. It is however not only the stereotypically "Irish" clothes that mark the Mad Hatter as a cultural Other. The physiognomy of this *Batman* character was likewise based on Tenniel's design, which depicts the Mad Hatter as a simian subhuman. This is highly significant if one considers that John Tenniel was one of the most important cartoonists of the late Victorian era and one of the artists chiefly responsible for creating the visual stereotype of the simian-subhuman-Celt Irishman (cf. Curtis 36–45). Tenniel's Mad Hatter closely resembles what had become the negative image of a generic Irishman: he has an ape-like face and posture and thus embodies the notion of an ethnically inferior and even monstrous status in contrast to the more angelic and noble Anglo-Saxons.

In the postbellum United States, John Tenniel's fellow cartoonist and contemporary Thomas Nast created a similar mode of portraying the Irish as racially inferior and subhuman (cf. Curtis 58–67). Nast's Irish were violent, ape-like brutes unfit for participation in American democracy. A number of anti–Irish sentiments contributed to the creation of this stereotype: The perceived infiltration of police departments by Irish immigrants was one anxiety in this xenophobic atmosphere, while their Catholicism influenced the view of them being a danger to the fabric of American society (cf. Avin). In fact, not only did Catholicism mark the Irish as religiously different and

---

*See Curtis and Leerssen on the long English tradition of the stereotypical depiction of the Irish. This is a tradition that has been inherited by American culture.*

potentially disloyal, but it also bore the connotation of a predisposition to sexual deviancy (cf. Schultz). A mixture of anxieties on various levels thus informed the stereotypical representation of Irishness.

In a mid–1980s version of the Mad Hatter in *Batman* issues #378 and #379, the iconographic tradition of the simian-subhuman Irishman can be seen as still at work. Tetch's bent posture and his dangling limbs resemble movements usually associated with primates, and stand in stark contrast to the literally upright protagonists, Batman and Nocturna. His facial features are equally subhuman, and match those of Victorian caricature, including oversized lips and a receding forehead. Additionally, the Mad Hatter is repeatedly shown with a half-open mouth and vacant expression, and is given a monkey companion, which further highlights his association with the subhuman. This accumulation of signifiers marks the Mad Hatter clearly as less human than his superhero opponents or any other characters in the issues. It also ties in with a stereotype of Irishness employed in anti–IRA cartoons of the time (cf. Curtis). In addition to the usual graphic vocabulary, a special visual strategy is employed in the construction of the villain in the *Batman* series to further highlight his association with the Irish Other: The color scheme of his outfit reflects the flag of the Republic of Ireland — green, orange, and white.

A couple of years later, in Morrison and McKean's graphic novel *Arkham Asylum* (1989), the Mad Hatter's face has shed its apish features, yet it still retains visual associations with Irishness. This Mad Hatter appears like a malevolent Leprechaun with a reddened nose and bushy eyebrows and thus tunes in with a different tradition of stereotype of Irish physiognomy, which is only seemingly less subhumanizing due to its merry, folkloristic element. The Mad Hatter's monologue, however, triggers different associations: "That's why children ... *Interest* me. [...] To know them is to know myself. Little girls especially. Little *blonde* girls. Little shameless bitches! Oh God." This utterance allows for a number of different readings. It can be seen as an allusion to the protagonist of *Alice in Wonderland* or to Lewis Carrol's alleged pedophile tendencies. It can also be understood, however, as a reference to the widespread representations of child molesters in American culture. One of the prime personifications of this anxiety are Catholic, that is, Irish, priests. This must not be understood as a direct equation, but as yet another stereotype that is enmeshed into the fabric of representations of Irish ethnicity.

In 2001, in *Detective Comics* #758–60, the original character design is still recognizable, but his physiognomy is more human than his predecessor's. The only "animal" attribute that is still in place are the prominent teeth, which is the only trait that disturbs the Mad Hatter's otherwise inconspicuously human appearance. His modus operandi, however, still encodes ethnicity. Tetch infiltrates the Gotham City Police Department with nanotechnology mind control devices, and thus is able to control one-third of the police force. This points at a dormant stereotype that has already been named above, namely that of an Irish subversion of law and order through an infiltration of the police force. Yet, the Mad Hatter achieves this by disguising himself as a coffee vendor named Fez, a man of unidentified middle–Eastern origin. A different ethnic and religious Other now embodies anxieties of subversion from within. This can probably be read as an indicator of changing cultural roles for certain ethnicities and thus allows me to rephrase Ross (cf. 34), arguing that "Middle-Eastern" has now taken a cultural space once allocated to "Irishness." It comes as no surprise that the character's new disguise follows a similar naming pattern as his original identity. Instead of the iconic large hat, he is now named for an equally foreign and thus significant headdress, that is, the Fez.

## MISTER FREEZE

A different fear of subversion from within informs the character construction of a *Batman* villain best known from the 1997 film *Batman & Robin*: Mr. Freeze. Because of the manifold and vastly different screen and comic-book versions of the villain, the following discussion deals only with the few stable traits that govern the respective character constructions. In this core identity, anxieties of cold-war American culture about amoral scientists find clear expression in a dehumanized figure that has distinctly European traits. In contrast to the Mad Hatter, the stereotypes that denote the character's national background are much more explicit and far less based on dormant imagery.

Mr. Freeze's real name already makes the ethnic reference clear: Victor Fries is a name that puts him on a level with other characters that are considered prime representations of the amoral scientist stereotype. The list includes such obviously German names as Dr. Hoenikken, inventor of Ice Nine in Kurt's Vonnegut's *Cat's Cradle*—a book which was, however, published after Mr. Freeze had already become part of *Batman*'s repertoire of antagonists—or, maybe more famously, the former Nazi-scientist Dr. Strangelove in *Dr. Strangelove or: How I Learned to Stop Worrying and Love the Bomb*. In a culture saturated with fear of possible nuclear annihilation, the mad scientist was not only a powerful image for an antagonist, but was also almost automatically endowed with distinctly German traits, a tendency that stemmed from anxieties of post-war America in which former Nazi scientists played a key role in advanced sciences (cf. Haynes 261–63). The following quote referring to Stanley Kubrick's popularization of Dr. Strangelove can be applied to the broader cultural background, and thus to Victor Fries as well: "[F]rom the theme of 'German as Mad Scientist' Kubrick has progressed to the notion of 'Mad Scientist as German'" (Mahoney 429, see also Haynes 261–63).

Apart from his German name, Mr. Freeze's character configuration alludes to another tradition of stereotype: the "wheelchair-bound madman." This special variation of the mad scientist type is marked by his dehumanized body, which is "abnormal" and in constant need of technical support. Similar configurations of grotesque bodies as an aspect of the American iconography of Germans can be traced back to the 19th century (Zacharasiewicz 207), and in the depiction of Mr. Freeze this deformation is the most powerful marker of his Otherness. Although his body may be marked as a distinct Other, Mr. Freeze is rather de- and not subhumanized like the Mad Hatter. This becomes evident in *Batman & Robin* where Arnold Schwarzenegger's vivid impersonation of Victor Fries makes him rather superhuman, an Übermensch, literally more white-skinned and blue-eyed than any other character. Had the reading of Mr. Freeze as a "Mad Scientist as German" escaped anyone, the casting choice left little doubt.

## Proinsias Cassidy

Unlike the villains of the *Batman* universe, the characters of Garth Ennis' 1995 to 2000 comics series *Preacher* have a stable textual existence. In this series with its proud, American protagonist, Jesse Custer, the Northern Ireland–born writer Ennis uses characters with an explicitly non–American background in roles that range from the series' half-friendly rogue to absolute villain. For the purpose of this paper, the focus will lie on the Irish Proinsias Cassidy and the German Herr Starr, both of whom perform according to (still active) national stereotypes.

The character of Cassidy is Othered in several ways. First of all, his role in the series as a member of the trio of protagonists is ambiguous; he is a more bi-moral rogue than the hero's sidekick is. He also gleefully exhibits his Irish ethnicity and, finally, he is a vampire, a creature that does not only stress the de-human aspect of the character but also marks him fundamentally as an ethnic and ethical Other.

As mentioned above, Cassidy is an ambiguous figure. At times, his values conform with those of the series' main voice, the protagonist, Jesse Custer. His notions of masculinity, honor, and of taking the law into one's own hands basically mirror Jesse's mindset, for example in *Dixie Fried*, where Cassidy executes a fellow vampire for killing an innocent for her blood. As is explained by a character in the comic, Cassidy behaves according to a code of honor that is inscribed as deeply masculine: "Men respond to that rogueish [sic!] free spirit of his on some basic male level: A comrade, a good mate as he would say" (*Dixie Fried* 217). Yet throughout the series Cassidy is also revealed as betraying those who trust him, as beating women he has a relationships with, as cheating on his friends, and as generally leading a cursed existence: "Shit happens in his wake," one of his former friends states (*Dixie Fried* 217). His final act in the series mirrors his ambiguous morality: He delivers Jesse into the hands of his enemies, but in doing so saves Jesse's life and thus achieves a redemption of sorts.

Cassidy's gleeful performance of Irishness is fused with his overall performance of violent masculinity. This is remarkable, given that he relates to the story of his arrival in the United States as a new beginning. In fact, his first act toward beginning a "new life," that is, the creation of a new identity, is the denying of his Gaelic first name, "Proinsias," in favor of his more American last name, "Cassidy" (see #26). Yet, even after 80 years in the United States, he has neither lost his accent nor assimilated to the degree that he wouldn't remain instantly recognizable as an Irishman. From his point of view, Americans are also alien, especially when it comes to their judgment of his behavior: "Typical Yank attitude: if yeh've more'n two pints at a sittin',' everyone says yeh've a fuckin' drinks problem" (*Dixie Fried* 192). Before he dies at the end of the series, he nevertheless once more declares his love for America. As with morality, his approach to identity is thus marked by duality and by instability.

Another aspect of the character underscores this theme. Cassidy is a vampire. This status as a supernatural creature of myth in combination with his "doomed existence as an immortal wandering-jew" (Kitson) is not only an obvious marker of Otherness but can be interpreted as a specifically Catholic cultural aspect (cf. Kitson). The unhuman living dead are open to a number of possible interpretations, whether as an ethnic threat (cf. Arata) or as hybrid creatures that mark the return of a repressed Other (cf. Reichstein and Copjec). It would not be in line with the overall character of Cassidy, however, if his textual assignment as a vampire went unchallenged. In *Dixie Fried*, he makes a point of not adhering to the generic conventions of vampiric behavior, and issue #6 relates an anecdote of him having a lethal fight with a Hell's Angel who had insulted the pope, because he "always get[s] Catholic on Heroin" (9). Although Cassidy thus defies generic conventions, his vampirism is still a mirror of the aspects of his character that show him as a specifically Irish Other.

It transpires from the above how directly Proinsias Cassidy's Irishness is linked to his general Otherness. In contrast to the Mad Hatter, the later date of publication and the Northern Irish background of the author enable a differentiated use and variated meaning of the stereotypes. Yet the fact that Cassidy revels in the "dirtiness, drunkenness, laziness and violence of the alien Irish" (Mac an Ghaill 138), his Catholicism, his monstrousness and dehumanized status all are inextricably linked. The stereotypes may have changed and been subjected to a postmodern update, they might even have shifted from representing the Irish as subhuman, yet the allusion to stereotypes and their configuration in the case of Cassidy in *Preacher* show that they remain culturally powerful, and are fraught with meaning that can be used to construct villainy.

## Herr Starr

If stereotypical representations of Irish masculinity constitute one aspect in the complicated character of Cassidy, the *Preacher* series villain Herr Starr by comparison is reduced to little more than an anti–German caricature. The reader never gets to know his first name and the characters' sticking with the German "Herr" instead of "Mister" increases the impression that he is rather a caricature than a fully developed character. In contrast to the time-specific anxieties that informed Mr. Freeze's character construction, the features that inform Starr's "Germanness" are timeless and still highly recognizable. Both physically and in his actions, he is a monstrous villain who conforms almost exactly to all the main character traits political caricaturists have attributed, and still do attribute, to German subjects (cf. Böhme-Dürr).

As mentioned above, the grotesque body has long been a feature of the iconographical German seen from an American perspective. Herr Starr's initial disfiguration, his scarred face, however, has a more precise connotation in the iconography of German ethnicity — it refers to the dueling, nationalist student (Zacharasiewicz 220). In the course of events in *Preacher*, Starr acquires a set of further mutilations that make his body progressively more grotesque and less human: He loses an ear and then acquires a scar on the top of his bald head, which leads to the often-commented-on result that his "head looks like a great pecker" (*War in the Sun* 199). He then has one of his legs eaten by cannibals and is finally emasculated by a Rottweiler dog. Ennis' approach in dehumanizing his villain may enter the realm of dark humor, but it does also serve another purpose: Starr's losing control over his body mirrors his increasingly monstrous and uncontrolled behavior as his quest for order becomes a crusade for personal revenge.

Starr's intense sense of order, which to him takes the shape of a personal war against anarchy, is the initial driving force behind his actions. As he puts it, "I am at war. I have been all my life. And I would kill a million little girls to win" (*War in the Sun* 53). Karin Böhme-Dürr has identified such a "compulsive sense of order," coupled with "brutality, megalomania," and "militarism" in her survey of American editorial cartoons as a key character trait attributed to Germans. Each of these features is present in the figure of Starr, who takes each of them to excess. This results in an ethnic overperformance that associates him firmly with the worst stereotypes about Germans available. His background story as given in *War in the Sun* includes a monologue that makes these issues explicit in a telling misnomer:

> Our cities are filled with degenerate scum. We're ruled by fools whose only qualification is that a bunch of sheep found them more attractive than the other fools [...]. Democracy is for ancient Greeks [...] I joined the German Wehrmacht because I sought order. To live with it, to instill it, to impose it [19–20].

The timeline in the comic makes it clear that Herr Starr cannot have joined the Wehrmacht, as he was born after World War II. This leaves the question whether the wrong use of the term is Ennis' mistake, or that of his character.

This shows that Herr Starr is characterized by an overperformance of stereotypes of German ethnicity. Neither his quest for order nor his brutality know any constraints. Herr Starr thus becomes absurd just as his physical monstrousness is driven to an excessive point of absurd humor. It is through this drastic characterization and the ridicule Ennis employs — Starr is so militaristic that standing in front of a tank regiment under his command gives him an erection (*War in the Sun* 92) — that his use of highly problematic stereotypes becomes an exercise in dark humor. Ennis' comic here also borders on the realm of political caricature. Thus, the use of negative stereotypes is masked as politically legitimate — no matter how problematic the underlying prejudices are.

## John Constantine

*Hellblazer*'s protagonist represents a different use of Otherness as compared to the use of now-partially dormant stereotypes of *Batman* villains, and the exaggerated and grotesque characters of *Preacher*. The Englishman John Constantine is neither a simple villain nor is the series written from an exclusively American point of view. In Brian Azzarello's tales of Constantine's travels to the United States, however, the ambiguity of his character is evaluated from the point of view of American characters, and his Otherness is associated with his worst actions.

Azzarello's *Hellblazer* storyline (collected in *Hard Time*, *Good Intentions*,

*Freezes Over*, and *Highwater*) features John Constantine traveling around the United States in a tale that resembles a road movie. Even though the people he meets are, to a large extent, outcasts themselves — prison inmates, Appalachian porn producers, white supremacists, or Gatsbyesque sexual deviants — their point of view eventually becomes privileged over that of John Constantine. The role of the observer of Otherness is thus taken by the Americans, and not, as could be expected, by the traveler himself. Through this observation by Americans, the ambiguity and Otherness of Constantine's character is highlighted trough his Europeanness.

Like Cassidy in *Preacher*, Constantine revels in being different. He smokes nonstop, walks or hitchhikes instead of driving, takes deviant sexuality to an extreme, and speaks with a noticeable accent. All these are traits that are observed as exotic, and commented upon, by the comics' other characters. Only twice in the whole story, however, does the comic present Constantine's point of view on the experience of Otherness: Once when he is complaining about the taste of American cigarettes and coffee in the prologue to *Good Intentions* (6), and then when he enters a pub in an interlude in *Highwater* (123–25).

Constantine's Otherness is then associated in a further step with traits of villainy and infernality. In *Highwater*, Constantine enters the comic book page to the words of a white supremacist monologue, his face first appearing beneath the text block "meaning the seed of Satan had been planted" (9). While the monologue's point of view is not validated from within the comic itself, the infernality of Constantine's actions is stressed by the graphical arrangement. The remarkable issue regarding his use of witchcraft is that it is directly associated with some of the traits that mark him as European. In *Hard Time*, he uses cigarettes to do magic. These "fags" are either visible in the panel whenever characters are affected by his magic or become the subject of an individual panel connected with magic (e.g., pages 27, 36, 42, 48, 94, 98). As has already been mentioned, Constantine's accent and choice of words are something other characters repeatedly comment upon as irritatingly foreign, but language is also his magical tool of choice in *Highwater*, where he creates a golem by inscribing Hebrew letters on a corpse. In *Freezes Over* he manages to literally talk two characters to their deaths: "All I'm sayin,' is choose the right words [...] and you can talk a person into just about anything" (107).

His role as an English alien in the United States is best summed up in *Good Intentions*. He relates his perception of the situation in an anecdote about a friend of his: "An' I ask her, 'Why do I always end up in bad places?' An' without missing a beat she says, 'Don'cha see John ... it's you what makes 'em bad'" (29). This comment summarizes the position of Azzarello's series:

It's the visit by John Constantine that brings death and destruction to U.S. locales. He is the European infernal Other, and as he leaves the United States, he also leaves a pile of bodies behind. The last panel of *Highwater*, the series' final volume, shows detectives around a dead body lying in a pool of blood. One of them asks, "Is someone smoking?" (260). Constantine is gone, but the smell of his cigarette lingers and invites one last reading of his Europeanized smoking habit as the sulphurous smell of hell.

CONCLUSION

This paper has outlined different strategies of Othering and vilifying strategies employed in the American comics industry. By relying on stereotypes that are either seen as harmless or are dormant, and through the use of character ambiguity, these modes of representation constitute the continuation of a tradition of depicting Europeanized Otherness as villainy, which is rooted in 19th-century discourses. In the cases of the *Batman* universe's Mad Hatter and Mr. Freeze, now-dormant stereotypes make a distinct reading of the character's Otherness difficult within the context of the late 20th century. The depiction of these villains thus relies on a character update in the case of the Mad Hatter, and the signifying power of stardom concerning Mr. Freeze to revalorize notions of non–American background as a denotation of villainy. Garth Ennis' approach in *Preacher* is much less subtle. Two vastly different strategies are employed in this series. Cassidy is an ambiguous character whose villainous Europeanness sometimes is a matter of viewpoint. Herr Starr is more of an anti–German cartoon than a fully developed graphic novel character. John Constantine, finally, is a more complicated figure altogether. His European Otherness is, however, firmly bound up in the negative aspects of his character.

Ambiguous or not, villain or antihero, all these characters share one important trait: They bring death and destruction, anarchy and mayhem from without. They are also European and hence Others in a U.S. setting. Their core identity is based on these facts, and both aspects are inextricably linked. Without his German name and the notions of "Mad Scientist as German" (Mahoney 429), Mr. Freeze would not fully function as a villain, just as John Constantine would not be the ambiguous antihero he is without his smoking habit and ostentatious Englishness. Thus the comics analyzed here have not only established Europeans as villains and antiheroes, but they also have progressed to the notion of villains and antiheroes as Europeans.

FILMOGRAPHY

*Batman & Robin.* Dir Joel Schumacher. Prod. Peter MacGregor-Scott. 1997. DVD: Warner Bros., 1998.

BIBLIOGRAPHY

Arata, Stephen D. "The Occidental Tourist: *Dracula* and the Anxiety of Reverse Colonization." *Victorian Studies* 33 (1990). Rpt. in Gelder, 161–71.
Avin, Benjamin Herzl. *The Ku Klux Klan, 1915–1925: A Study in Religious Intolerance.* MA thesis. Georgetown University, 1952.
Azzarello, Brian (w), Marcelo Frusin (a). *Hellblazer: Freezes Over.* New York: Vertigo – DC Comics, 2001.
———. *Hellblazer: Good Intentions.* New York: Vertigo – DC Comics, 2001.
———. *Hellblazer: Highwater.* New York: Vertigo – DC Comics, 2002.
Azzarello, Brian (w), Richard Corben (a). *Hellblazer: Hard Time.* New York: Vertigo – DC Comics, 2001.
Böhme-Dürr, Karin. "Deutschland im amerikanischen Cartoon." *Medienlust und Mediennutz: Unterhaltung als öffentliche Kommunikation*, edited by Louis Bosshart and Wolfgang Hoffmann-Rien. [Schriftenreihe der Deutschen Gesellschaft für Publizistik und Kommunikationswissenschaft 20]. München: Ölschläger, 1994, 435–46.
Brooker, Will. *Batman Unmasked: Analyzing a Cultural Icon.* London: Continuum, 2000.
Cinnirella, Marco. "Ethnic and National Stereotypes: A Social Identity Perspective." *Beyond Pug's Tour: National and Ethnic Stereotyping in Theory and Literary Practice*, edited by Cedric C. Barfoot. [Studies in Lit. 20]. Amsterdam: Rodopi, 1997, 37–51.
Copjec, Joan. "Vampires, Breast-Feeding, and Anxiety." *October* 58 (1991). Rpt. in Gelder, 52–63.
Curtis, Perry L. *Apes and Angels: The Irishman in Victorian Caricature.* Washington, D.C.: Smithsonian Press, 1971.
Ennis, Garth (w), Steve Dillon (a). "Of the Irish in America." *Preacher* #57 (January 2000). New York: Vertigo – DC Comics.
———. *Preacher: Dixie Fried.* New York: Vertigo – DC Comics, 1998.
———. *Preacher: War in the Sun.* New York: Vertigo – DC Comics, 1999.
———. "New York's Finest." *Preacher* #6 (September 1995). New York: Vertigo – DC Comics.
———. "To the Streets of Manhattan I Wandered Away." *Preacher* #26 (June 1997). New York: Vertigo – DC Comics.
Garcia, Robert. "The Animated Adventures: Batman." *Cinefantastique* (February 1994): 68.
Gelder, Ken (ed.). *The Horror Reader.* London: Routledge, 2000.
Haynes, Roslyn D. *From Faust to Strangelove: Representations of the Scientist in Western Literature.* Baltimore, MD: Johns Hopkins University Press, 1994.
Kitson, Niall. "Rebel Yells: Genre Hybridity and Irishness in Garth Ennis & Steve Dillon's *Preacher.*" *The Irish Journal of Gothic and Horror Studies* 2 (March 2007). http://irishgothichorrorjournal.homestead.com/PreacherEnnisDillon.html (18 September 2007).
Leerssen, Joseph Th. "'The Cracked Lookingglass of a Servant': Cultural Decolonization and National Consciousness in Ireland and Africa." *Europa und das Nationale Selbstverständnis: Imagologische Probleme in Literatur, Kunst, und Kultur des 19. und 20. Jahrhunderts*, edited by Hugo Dyserinck and Karl Ulrich Syndram. Bonn: Bouvier, 1988, 103–18.
Mac an Ghaill, Máirtín. "The Irish in Britain: The Invisibility of Ethnicity and Anti-Irish Racism." *Journal of Ethnic and Migration Studies* 26.1 (2000): 137–147.
Mahoney, Dennis F. "From Caligari to Strangelove: The German as (Mad) Scientist in Film and Literature." *Analogon Rationis. Festschrift für Gerwin Marahrens zum 65. Geburtstag*, edited by Marianne Henn and Christoph Lorey. Edmonton: University of Alberta Press, 1994, 419–32.
Moench, Doug (w), Don Newton (p), Alfredo Alcala (i). "Bedtime Stories." *Batman* #379 (January 1985). New York: DC Comics.

_____. "One Hat Madder." *Batman* #378 (December 1984). New York: DC Comics.
Morrison, Grant (w), Dave McKean (a). *Arkham Asylum: A Serious House on Serious Earth.* New York: DC Comics, 1989.
Reichstein, Andreas. "Batman — An American Mr. Hyde?" *Amerikastudien/American Studies* 43.2 (1998): 329–50.
Ross, Andrew. "Ballots, Bullets, or Batmen: Can Cultural Studies Do the Right Thing?" *Screen* 31.1 (Spring 1990): 26–44.
Rucka, Greg (w), Shawn Martinbrough (p), Steve Mitchell (i). "Unknowing Part One." *Detective Comics* #758 (July 2001). New York: DC Comics.
_____. "Unknowing Part Two." *Detective Comics* #759 (August 2001). New York: DC Comics.
_____. "Unknowing Part Three." *Detective Comics* #760 (September 2001). New York: DC Comics.
Schultz, Nancy L. "Introduction." *Veil of Fear: Nineteenth-Century Convent Tales*, by Rebecca Reed and Maria Monk. West Lafayette: Indiana University Press, 1999.
Uricchio, William, and Roberta E. Pearson. "I'm Not Fooled by that Cheap Disguise." *The Many Lives of the Batman: Critical Approaches to a Superhero and his Media*, edited by Roberta E. Pearson and William Uricchio. New York: Routledge, 1991, 182–213.
Vonnegut, Kurt. *Cat's Cradle*. New York: Delta, 1963.
Zacharasiewicz, Waldemar. *Das Deutschlandbild in der amerikanischen Literatur*. Darmstadt: Wissenschaftliche Buchgesellschaft, 1998.

# 12

## *2000AD*: Understanding the "British Invasion" of American Comics

*Ben Little*

The mid–1980s marked a watershed for American comics. Alternately dubbed "an unprecedented renaissance," "the third movement," or the start of "the revisionary superhero," there is little doubt that something changed in the mindset of the comics industry that suggested that the old rules of what was allowed and disallowed, the boundaries of creativity and content, changed (McCue and Bloom 3; Klock 2f). One indication of the shift was the increasing willingness of big publishers to release titles without prior submission to the comics code, which had been the main shackle to conformity, severely constraining creators. Other factors for change were the increasing experimentation with different styles or the acknowledgement of the market for older readers who remained invested in their favorite characters and their comics collections well into their 20s and 30s.

The comics that came out of this period drew on a wide range of influences both inside and outside of mainstream American comic books. The underground comics of the 1960s and 1970s and their descendants in the independent comics of the 1980s are one source of inspiration, as are the design sensibilities of Japanese manga (notable in Frank Miller's work). French science fiction, particularly in the repackaged form of *Heavy Metal* magazine, offered a different range of ideas and styles. Yet the most significant influence on American comics were the large number of creators that left the UK to work on many of the titles that have come to be considered the defining works of the period. In some respects the 1980s saw not simply a progression to a new stage in the history of American comics, but a merger of two national traditions.

The emergence of the field of Anglo-American comics is what will be explained and contextualized here through a look at *2000AD*, the weekly UK magazine that launched the careers of many of the creators in question. This will then be brought into focus through a close look at the trope of poverty in Alan Moore and Ian Gibson's *The Ballad of Halo Jones*.

The influx of British talent to U.S. comics publishers paved the way for a fertile exchange of ideas, techniques and approaches that went beyond a simple notion of national influences. Moreover many of these creators continue to work for U.S. publishers to this day and have been followed by a second generation of British talent. Richard Pells states that the process of cultural intermingling between Europe and America is intricate:

> Americans are as affected by European products and fashions as Europeans are influenced by American technology and mass entertainment. The result is a complex interaction between different and increasingly heterogeneous cultures and societies [Pells xv].

The British-American relationship, however, is closer and more nuanced than that between the U.S. and the rest of Europe. While this can initially be attributed to a shared language and colonial history, it grew even closer with the political convergence that occurred during the 1980s under the stewardships of Margaret Thatcher and Ronald Reagan. Richard Dumbrell argues that the personal and political closeness between the two "was intense, and unprecedented in recent history" (89). He goes on to argue that, by the time Alan Moore was writing comics for U.S. publishers, "by some measures the US and Britain [...] seem[ed] to constitute a distinct 'culture area'" (32).

The "discovery" of British comics creators in the United States represents a similar phenomenon to the impact that British artists had on American pop music in the 1960s, following the success of the Beatles, both in terms of their popular appeal and their comparative radicalism:

> The Beatles managed to be avant-garde and commercial at the same time. After their spectacular tour of the United States in 1964, the directors of America's record companies realized that Britain was a hotbed of musical innovation. Producers signed any British group they could find to a recording contract. American radio programs featured the latest British music. American singer-composers like Simon and Garfunkel tried to emulate the artistry of the Beatles. Soon, American and British groups sounded indistinguishable. By the 1970s, a transatlantic style had emerged, combining elements of British and American popular music [Pells 319].

To demonstrate the strength of this parallel we can make a short list of some of the British talent who had or were continuing to work with American publishers by 1995: John Wagner, Alan Moore, Dave Gibbons, Alan Grant, Eddie

Campbell, Grant Morrison, Warren Ellis, Garth Ennis, Steve Dillon, Neil Gaiman, Dave McKean, Kevin O'Neill, Bryan Talbot, Ian Gibson, Brian Bolland and many more. In the same way as the British music scene of the 1960s developed out of exposure to, and reinterpretation of, American popular music, so the changes that occurred in comics in the 1980s cannot be seen as a simple case of one group of creators influencing another. British comics had changed in the late 1940s and early 1950s, inspired by an influx of American publications imported for GIs stationed in the UK.* Moreover, the British creators involved in *2000AD* had been immediately influenced by both the American mainstream and underground U.S. artists such as Robert Crumb, Jaxon, Gilbert Shelton et al. In fact, many of the *2000AD* writers and artists had been involved in the British underground comics scene largely inspired by its American counterpart (cf. Sabin 55). Thus, over time, the process has been one of reciprocal influence and innovation, so that by the mid–1980s we can talk of the emergence of a transatlantic Anglophone comics culture. One way this convergence has been described is as the "darkening" of the comics industry, as the tone of many comics became more cynical, and favorite characters more sinister. What will be suggested here is that far from being a purely stylistic shift, creators were taking their medium more seriously and were, with due concern, responding to the significant political and social changes occurring on both sides of the ocean in their work.

Until the mid–1980s, American comics were imported to Britain or reprinted in special British editions (for instance, under the auspices of Marvel UK—which also produced original material) without a corresponding export of UK comics back to the United States. In this way, the importance of the work done in the UK prior to the emergence of this joint culture has largely been ignored, marketed under the auspices of a "genius" creator such as Alan Moore, or considered irrelevant in commentaries of the period.† Consider how Alan Moore's starting work on *Swamp Thing* is described in the corresponding Wikipedia article: "Moore, then relatively unknown, had at that time *only* written several stories for *2000AD*, *Warrior* and *Marvel UK*" (my emphasis). Moore's *Swamp Thing* is significant because it represents the

---

*Cf. Pumphrey 12, 13. Since 1950 the old-established comics have been joined by many new ones. Undoubtedly the most interesting newcomers are those produced by Hulton Press—Eagle, Girl, Robin and Swift. These comics were planned by Marcus Morris, a clergyman, who, although new to the business, induced the Hulton Press (also new to comics publishing) to produce Eagle. These new comics have been enormously successful. They are interesting because they use a technique new to British comics. It is the technique of the American comic, which makes the picture tell the story. Captions are reduced to a minimum and are placed in balloons that emerge from the characters' mouths. The traditional British comic has captions under the pictures and some balloons. The new technique integrates the pictures, making the story develop from frame to frame.*

†*The exception here is Roger Sabin's excellent* Adult Comics: An Introduction, *which demonstrates the historical importance of* 2000AD *and the "Britpack."*

first mainstream comic for decades to consistently not be submitted for approval to the industry regulator: the Comics Code. To suggest that this rejection of the censors in American publishing would come from an unknown, untested and relatively inexperienced comics creator understates the professionalism and market awareness of the editors at DC Comics. It was because of the quality and sophistication of Moore's early work that DC were prepared to take such a step.

In fact industry insiders acknowledge that comics such as *2000AD* in the UK were radically ahead of the United States at the time, yet fail to understand the landscape from which they emerged. Tom DeFalco, editor-in-chief of Marvel Comics from 1987 to 1994, suggests that the maturity of European comics was precisely due to their lack of a comics code:

> In Europe, they never had the McCarthy era that we had. They never had that 1950s era. Consequently, their publications never twisted toward just the children's medium. Consequently they have a whole adult comic-book industry over there and there are regular monthly and weekly comic books, for adults [McCue and Bloom 94].

DeFalco clearly is misinformed. Comics on both sides of the Atlantic have experienced censorship in the post-war years and onward. John A. Lent indicates that censorship in the 1950s was a very international affair with at least 20 countries engaging in their own version of the campaign against American horror comics (9). In Britain and France the censorship of the 1950s manifested itself at a governmental level, rather than through industry self-regulation, with laws passed in both countries specifically limiting the content of children's comic books. British censors were at least as severe, if not more so, than their American equivalents, especially seeing as Britain lacks constitutional first amendment guarantees. Censorship in Britain continued into the late 1990s, one example being the consistent attacks under obscenity charges suffered by Manchester publishing house Savoy for their *Lord Haw Haw* and *Meng and Ecker* comics (cf. Mitchell).

However, British creators' response to limitation of the content of their work was distinct enough to those in the United States to bring about the changes that led DeFalco to call comics such as *2000AD* "adult material." Led by Pat Mills and John Wagner, British comics excelled at finding ways to bring out serious issues under a guise seemingly flippant enough to slip past the conservative guardians of public taste. The learning experience of the boys weekly *Action,* which collapsed under pressure from censors in 1976, had been a catalyst for the less directly controversial approach of *2000AD* (Barker 1989, 3). The significant difference was the insistence of *2000AD* editors and writers, Mills and Wagner, to produce material that was political, instead of simply more "realistic," and their vehicle was children's comics even if their audience ended up being much older.

To understand *2000AD*, however, we must first understand how its predecessor *Action* failed. Martin Barker states that "[*Action*] stood at the edge of a very radical politics — and that couldn't be allowed" (Barker 1990, 49). It ruffled the feathers of a status quo that was quick to challenge dissidence wherever possible (the non-art status of comics making them an easy target). *Action* showed contemporary youth getting into scrapes with malevolent authority figures and coming out on top. It put what would now be seen as antisocial behavior into the context of the protagonists' lives. Barker states that

> [*Action* ran afoul of] the renewal in the 1970s of the activities of moral pressure groups such as Mary Whitehouse's National Viewers' and Listeners' Association, and the Responsible Society[...]. These two groups were the most vociferous, representing the kind of new moralism associated by many with the rise to power of Margaret Thatcher [1990, 7].

*Action* was violent, subversive and, more importantly (according to Steve MacManus, editor of *2000AD* in the 1980s), "the first working class comic" (Barker 1990, 6). The moral pressure groups backed up by the right-wing press didn't know what to make of it, and the calls for censorship were initially matched by a grudging respect for *Action*'s commercial success.

This respect, however, evaporated in what Barker identifies as the key moment in the campaign against the comic. In the story "Look out for Lefty," the footballer protagonist's punk girlfriend Angie just happened to throw a coke bottle from the terraces at another player at a particularly inopportune moment:

> This all happened at a time when football violence was once again hitting the news headlines, culminating in a riot at a "friendly" between Aston Villa and Glasgow Rangers. Seizing the opportunity, the critics went for the throat. The football league and leading officials were primed to complain: "World Cup referee Jack Taylor denounces comic!" [Barker 1990, 7].

Yet it was not that the comic simply showed football violence; it was a girl's involvement that caused the real controversy. Thatcherite social rhetoric and the rise of the moral pressure groups were about preserving the traditional role of the family in a changing society. Stuart Hall and Martin Jacques state that this included the "centrality of women's domestic role" (Hall and Jacques 14). Angie challenged not only this idea of the domestic role of women, but also the basic concepts of femininity that such an idea is founded on. Angie was as tough, as foul-mouthed and aggressive as any of the men in the strip and had a relationship with the protagonist, Lefty, that worked on an equal basis. If any one character was the step too far for *Action*, it was Angie, and it would not be until Evey in Moore and Lloyd's *V for Vendetta* and Moore and Gibson's *Halo Jones* that a female character with such vim would feature in the pages of British comics.

Angie is a profoundly political character and marks the shift in political terrain that was going on throughout the 1970s and 1980s. The historical framing of politics around questions of class, which was so central to *Action*, was subtly changing to a new radicalism that embraced at its heart questions of gender, race and anti-authoritarianism. These tropes, which would become established political touchstones in *2000AD* and filter into American comics, are one of the significant changes in comics of the 1980s. Yet in mid–1970s Britain, Angie was too much, too soon for an establishment that still saw boys comics in the mode of the 1950s comic *Eagle*, which emphasized traditional Christian values and militaristic virtues.*

Nevertheless, *Action* paved the way for its influential successor. *2000AD* exceeded the political vigor of its precursor without attracting the same kind of criticism.† When something is censored, it is brought materially into the political sphere, but it must then change its approach. As Gershon Legman describes the process,

> The censor's unequivocal "You must not!" is seldom answered with an uncompromising "I will!" Ashamed to oppose the censor's morality, and afraid to contravene his authority, the writer's first reaction is to evade the censorship, to see what can be sneaked through, what can be gotten away with, what can be disguised just enough to pass the censor but not so much as to escape the audience[...]. [But] having buffooned to the end of the censorship tether — and it is short — the only recourse for both artist and audience is transvaluation, displacement, the siphoning off of the suppressible urge for expression elsewhere [Barker 1984, 75].

*2000AD* was the response of British creators to the politicization of their medium. Its success rests upon its ability to manage issues of censorship, bring in an older readership and consistently question the authoritarianism and values of the new status quo, particularly as it moved into the 1980s. This was achieved through three main changes from *Action*.

Firstly, as a commercial response to its growing popularity in film, *2000AD* tapped into a long tradition of political science fiction. This is Leg-

---

*Interestingly, Dan Dare, the main character in *Eagle*, featured in *2000AD*, yet was too conservative for the tone of the magazine and was eventually dropped.

†This is not to say *2000AD* did not attract any censorship or media criticism. The *Guardian* newspaper was initially particularly harsh in its criticism. Moreover, having learned lessons on *Action*, the senior management were far more cautious about strips that could attract controversy. A famous example is a strip featuring a war between McDonald's and Burger King that was dropped due to fears of a lawsuit.

man's "transvaluation" and "displacement": the movement of content into the fantastic in order to deprive the censors of a direct line of attack. Within 20th-century literature we can identify a clear chain of such literary practice that leads from Yevgeny Zamyatin's *We* through George Orwell, Aldous Huxley, Philip K. Dick, Ursula LeGuin and through the 1980s up to the present with writers like William Gibson and Neal Stephenson. In *2000AD* that merger of politics and science fiction made its way into the comics medium. The magazine's writers and artists used the paradigm of the future to play out current concerns and possible teleologies of contemporary social practices. As Adam Roberts puts it: "SF does not project us into the future: it relates to us stories about our present" (Roberts 35).

*2000AD*'s politics was always at the forefront of the writers' and artists' minds. In a recent interview for the BBC online magazine, writer Alan Grant makes this explicit:

> Many of the stories we wrote were taken from the headlines of the newspapers. We just put a futuristic spin on them. There were genuine social problems, particularly from the Thatcher days. It was obvious to us that Britain and the whole world was turning into a right-wing society [qtd. after Roher].

Science fiction stories were less offensive to the critics on the right who could not see just how political they were. They failed to credit comics with enough sophistication to see that the fantastical environments were allegories for the changing society of the 1980s.* Pat Mills explains this:

> On one level *2000AD* was almost a retreat, because I'd been so badly mauled on *Action*, it was like, ok, let's go into science fiction. We can say they're all robots, mutants and it's all in the future, so it doesn't actually matter and that's what we did [Resonance FM].

Thus science fiction in *2000AD* can be seen as secondary to the political content: it was a vehicle to avoid censorship as much as an end in itself.

The second key difference between *Action* and *2000AD* was the latter magazine's mode of address. Barbara Wall's distinctions between single address (targeted specifically at an audience of either children or adults), double address (at children or adults at different times throughout the text) and dual address (at children and adults at the same time) are very useful to help make sense of this here (cf. Wall). One of the key changes in *2000AD* was its increasing adoption of the dual address mode. Unlike *Action*, which despite its political awareness was very much focused on its target demographic, *2000AD* started to engage in narratives that, while internally logical to any ten-year-old reader, would be peppered with references that make sense only to a far

---

*\*Ironically it then attracted criticism from the left, most notably from the* Guardian *newspaper, who expressed outrage at its simplistic "bad guys" portrayal of the Soviet Union.*

more adult audience. Dual address became the primary mode of the comic and gave the writers and artists a framework to explore increasingly complex issues in a style that did not alienate its younger readers.

This complexity was necessary to come to terms with the third factor in *2000AD*'s success: its ability to adapt to the changing political milieu of the late 1970s and 1980s. Stuart Hall describes this change as the disintegration of the left in the fallout of Thatcher's phenomenal and unlikely success. Instead of a unified class-based politics with its teleologies in socialism, the rise of the new right forced the left to instead consider "questions about moral conduct, about gender and sexuality, about race and ethnicity, about ecological and environmental issues, about cultural and national identity" (Hall 8).

This sociopolitical shift can be seen in the movement from *Action* to *2000AD* and beyond into the comics that British creators would go on to publish in the United States. As we have seen, *Action* was firmly positioned by its writers and artists as a working-class comic. This is a direct reflection of the politics of its conceptual founder, Pat Mills. His work for *Battle* (a weekly war comic) and in some cases for *2000AD* relies explicitly on representing the tensions between the classes. Mills' serial *Charley's War* for *Battle* magazine reframed World War One as a conflict about middle-class officers sending working-class foot soldiers over the top to their death: a conflict he portrays as far more acute than the one between Britain and Germany. Likewise, in his first *ABC Warriors* stories in *2000AD*, we see exactly the same scenario — except that the foot soldiers are now robots and the officers fight through battlefield simulations rather than from a bunker out of range of the artillery.

Yet Mills also helped start the new style of politics found in *2000AD*. *Nemesis the Warlock* was his take on race, religion and cultural imperialism; and *Slaine* tapped into the growing popularity of the New Age movement with its interest in Neo-Paganism and the ancient myths, religions and folklore of the British Isles, just as it was coming into direct conflict with Thatcher's government. Nevertheless, Mill's work rarely captured the fragmentation of traditional political positions. His stories usually had an internal consistency that made for a good narrative, but presented a Manichean "good guys/bad guys" politics that failed to represent either the coalition nature of the Thatcherite project or the collapse of the traditional categories on the left.

One story that managed to truly engage with the spirit of the times, and did so exceptionally well, was Alan Moore and Ian Gibson's *The Ballad of Halo Jones*. This comic clearly demonstrates the three primary reasons for *2000AD*'s success. It is a sophisticated text published in three separate storylines or books between the years 1984 and 1986. The comic charts the adventures of an 18-year-old girl (Halo Jones) from the Hoop, a "poverty reduction" district of New York — a giant ghetto moored off Manhattan in the Atlantic

Ocean. The three books narrate distinct periods of her life: the first focusing on life in the Hoop, the second depicting Halo's first year as a waitress aboard a luxury space cruise ship, and the third showing her as an infantrywoman in a brutal imperialist conflict. The science fiction setting functions effectively as a stand-alone universe with various details adding to the effect. From the political struggle between dolphins and humans, to the concept that this 50th-century setting is a turbulent time in history being studied from the even more distant future, to the strength of Gibson's visualizations of a crumbling society that despite its technology is collapsing in upon itself, all help to create a credible universe for Halo to explore.

This consistency enables Moore's writing to engage in a steady stream of commentary upon the politics of the 1980s. Not all of this is directly analogous with the changes in Britain and the United States during the rise of the new right. Instead, Moore uses historical criticism to contextualize contemporary concerns. Said criticism is also key to the dual address mode that is prevalent throughout the comic. While the narrative would make sense to a younger reader through its internal consistency, the extra-textual references are directly aimed at an older readership. The conflict in the Tarantula Nebula, for instance, is clearly an interpretation of the Vietnam War.

There is a second kind of dual address at work here, too. Jones has alternately been described as "possibly the first feminist hero in comics" and as an "everywoman," both of which fail to accurately capture what Jones meant for a comic like *2000AD* (Wikipedia "Halo Jones"). The 1980s audience of *2000AD* was still predominantly male, and while Jones is a believable female character, to position her as a feminist or a neutral cypher for women in general is not really the point. She sits on a line between being an attractive, although not overly sexual, female action heroine, designed to appeal to men, and yet has complex and believable relationships with the women around her that owe much to the girls comics of the time. In this way she functions to create a second level of dual address, that between men and women. This may seem like a fairly simplistic argument about gender, but it is a function of the marketing expectations of the editors. The comic is carefully balanced in its gendered address, so much so and so well achieved that these commercial considerations may not be immediately obvious to a readership meeting it for the first time in a collected edition. Halo was *2000AD*'s first female protagonist and as such was carefully managed as a project to engage more women with the comic, but without alienating its male core market.* The question

---

*In an interview Ian Gibson suggests that the editors were concerned that the lack of violence in the second book on the cruise ship would put off 15-year-old boys, and thus more action was injected in the form of an attempted hijacking (see Twomey).*

of gender is central to the third way in which *The Ballad of Halo Jones* exemplifies the success of the *2000AD* formula. This is the fragmentary approach to politics, specifically the alignment between different contemporary issues without recourse to a unified ideology. It can be seen in the way the comic addresses the question of poverty as a direct response to the politics of the era, entwined in its portrayal of women.

Poverty is one of the main focuses of the first book and returns as a key theme in the third. In the second, it is conspicuous through its absence, as Halo lives among the mega-rich. The first book, based entirely in the Hoop, depicts a ghettoized society made up predominantly of women and minorities: riots are an everyday occurrence. If the riot forecast says "fine," then "dress for Armageddon," as Rodice, Halo's best friend, says to her on a routine yet perilous shopping expedition (Moore and Gibson 24). In uniting the unemployed, women and ethnic minorities, Moore and Gibson were identifying the main groups that were hardest hit by Thatcher's rise to power. The government's shift from the social democratic consensus of state ownership of major industries to free markets and monetarism meant that the economic emphasis had moved from full employment to low inflation. One effect of this was the highest level of unemployment since the great depression. Moreover, the impact was spread unevenly throughout society, as with the new right's emphasis on domesticity and its narrow definitions of British culture, single women and minorities (as well as skilled laborers in manufacturing areas) soon found themselves at risk of becoming part of a permanent underclass. When race riots exploded across the UK in the early 1980s, Thatcher declared that the "problem had nothing to do with either race or unemployment, but was a problem of public order" (Gamble 117). Moreover, the demonization of single mothers in the later years of Thatcher's government is foreshadowed here.

Halo's environment reflects the teleology of this situation, encapsulating how, rather than dealing with the problem, the Conservative government chose to suppress it, changing the role of the police from crime detection and prevention to an institution meant to preserve social order. The Hoop is a physical form of social control, and the shopping trip that dominates book one demonstrates just how effective it is. Yet while the comic is clearly attacking the potential outcome of such a system, it is ambivalent about the way to deal with it. Jones escapes from the Hoop, but only through the internal logic of a Thatcherite morality. Braving wealthy vigilante groups who kill the rights-less "hoopsiders" for sport, she leaves her confines legitimately and goes begging for work. That she then finds traditional "women's work" as a waitress and escapes without aid from the state makes the message extremely difficult to see as a form of political resistance.

There is a resignation to the injustices of society in the comic despite a consciousness of its failings. Jones is not a revolutionary; she is an ordinary woman making the most of a bad situation, playing by the rules and refusing to be a victim. This is why we can question the description of her as a feminist: she operates entirely within the bounds of a repressive social milieu, making no attempt to change the political parameters that constrain her life. Her escape from the Hoop becomes a success story of the system, not a radical step against it. She does not challenge the options available to her as a woman, but accepts and operates within the range of choices she is given.

The Hoop becomes a science fiction parody of Thatcherism's nightmare scenario: a vision of how a society could cope with the creation of a massive group of the permanently poor. The extreme measures Halo must go to in escaping the ghetto and the excesses of the world of the rich she joins aboard the Clara Pandy bring into focus the basic injustice of such a system. In this way, this vision of the future becomes a lens used to exaggerate an issue in order to render it into conceptual caricature. To suggest a way to break that system, to change it, would undo the portrait of this society. It would make its injustices trivial if they were easily resolved. Instead, the world of Halo Jones stands complete and open for a reader to interpret, understand and reconnect to the 1980s Britain to which it refers.

This is part of a wider trend in British popular culture in the 1980s, where parody and pastiche became central ways of raising public awareness of political issues. Dick Hebdige suggests this was an enabling technique that gave politics back to the consumers of popular culture:

> Pastiche and collage can be valorised as forms which enable consumers to become actual or potential producers, processors and subjects of meaning rather than the passive bearers of pregiven "messages" [211].

In the aftermath of the failure of the radical counterculture projects of the 1960s and 1970s and the triumph of Thatcher-Reaganism, comic books became a site where readers could re-engage with texts that appealed directly to their experience of the political in everyday life.

Although the three ways *2000AD* developed this kind of political discourse from its predecessor, *Action*, are significant within comics, it should also be mentioned that the changes outside of comics helped to a large extent as well. As *markets* and *choice* became the key words in economic life, censorship and government intervention in a commercial activity such as publishing were increasingly frowned upon. This was perhaps one of the areas that exposed the paradoxes that sat at the very heart of Thatcher's alliance between economic liberals and social conservatives. If *2000AD*'s creators got smarter and sharper in the wake of censorship, so their censors found that their calls for "tasteful" media were often at odds with public demands.

Nevertheless, the sorts of methods and techniques identified here became common in Anglo-American comics. The types of narrative pioneered in *2000AD* are not the sole influence on the changes in comics of the 1980s, but the magazine's resonance can be felt in such a variety of celebrated works ranging from Frank Miller's *Batman: The Dark Knight Returns* or Moore and Gibbons' *Watchmen* in the 1980s right up to contemporary comics like Mark Millar and Bryan Hitch's *The Ultimates,* Bill Willingham and Mark Buckingham's *Fables* or Warren Ellis and Ben Templesmith's *Fell.* This is without mentioning the vast array of titles now written or drawn by British creators for whom *2000AD* remains the key starting point in their career as comics professionals.

BIBLIOGRAPHY

"The Ballad of Halo Jones." *Wikipedia.* http://en.wikipedia.org/w/index.php?title=The_Ballad_of_Halo_Jones&oldid=194038938 (14 September 2007).
Barker, Martin. *A Haunt of Fears: The Strange History of the British Horror Comics Campaign.* London: Pluto, 1984.
_____. *Action: The Story of a Violent Comic.* London: Titan, 1990.
_____. *Comics: Ideology, Power and the Critics.* Manchester and New York: Manchester University Press, 1989.
Dumbrell, John. *A Special Relationship: Anglo-American Relations in the Cold War and After.* London and New York: Macmillan, 2001.
Gamble, Andrew. *The Free Economy and the Strong State.* 2nd edition. London: Macmillan, 1994.
Hall, Stuart. *The Hard Road to Renewal: Thatcherism and the Crisis of the Left.* London and New York: Verso, 1988.
Hall, Stuart, and Martin Jacques. "Introduction." *The Politics of Thatcherism,* edited by Stuart Hall and Martin Jacques. London: Lawrence and Wishart/Marxism Today, 1983.
Hebdige, Dick. *Hiding in the Light: On Images and Things.* London and New York: Routledge, 1998.
McCue, Greg, and Clive Bloom. *Dark Knights: The New Comics in Context.* London: Pluto, 1993.
Mills, Pat. "I'm Ready for My Close-Up: 2000AD — Then...." http://podcasts.resonancefm.com/archives/620 (22 September 2007).
Mitchell, David. "The Horror of It All. An Introduction to Savoy Comics." *Savoy Publishing Online.* http://www.savoy.abel.co.uk/ (14 May 2007).
Moore, Alan, and Ian Gibson. *The Ballad of Halo Jones.* Oxford: Rebellion, 2005.
Pells, Richard. *Not Like Us: How Europeans Have Loved, Hated, and Transformed American Culture Since World War II.* New York: Basic Books, 1997.
Pumphrey, George H. *Children's Comics: A Guide for Parents and Teachers.* London: The Epworth Press, 1955.
Roberts, Adam. *Science Fiction.* London and New York: Routledge, 2000.
Roher, Finlo. "30 Years of the Future." *BBC News Online.* http://news.bbc.co.uk/1/hi/magazine/6390731.stm (14 May 2007).
Sabin, Roger. *Adult Comics: An Introduction.* London and New York: Routledge, 1993.
"Swamp Thing." *Wikipedia.* http://en.wikipedia.org/w/index.php?title=Swamp_Thing&oldid=200063647 (14 September 2007).

Twomey, Seán. "The Ballad of Halo Jones — The Creation of an All-Time Classic." http://homepage.eircom.net/~twoms/halo1.htm (24 May 2007).

Wall, Barbara. *The Narrator's Voice: The Dilemma of Children's Fiction*. London: Macmillan, 1991.

# 13

## Whatever Happened to All the Heroes? British Perspectives on Superheroes

*Karin Kukkonen and Anja Müller-Wood*

In the late 1980s the superhero comic was past its Golden and its Silver Age. "Truth, justice and the American way," the catchphrase of Superman, had lost its credibility, and Spider-Man's mantra "with great power comes great responsibility" had become a triviality. Things had changed. Scholars proclaimed a new age of superhero comics, which still lacks a common name in comics studies. It is an age of disillusionment, an age of irony, an age of question marks.

Two works are generally held to mark the beginning of this new age: Frank Miller's *The Dark Knight Returns* and Alan Moore's *Watchmen*, both published in 1986. One is written by an American, the other by an Englishman. While the social and political situation in the United States after Vietnam and Watergate and the country's position as one of the antagonists of the Cold War certainly are an important factor in the development of superhero comics, it should not be overlooked that many of the seminal works in superhero comics at that time were not written by U.S. authors.

The "Second British Invasion"* of U.S. popular culture took place on the field of superhero comics in the late 1980s when Britons like Alan Moore and Neil Gaiman wrote ground-breaking works like *Watchmen* or *The Sandman*. Some time later, Warren Ellis, Grant Morrison and others followed to complete the invasion party. These British authors turned out to be a lot less reverent toward U.S. superheroes than their U.S. counterparts. For example, in Warren Ellis' *Planetary 2*, "To Be in England, in the Summertime," we have

---

*See Berry for the term "Second British Invasion."

a decrepit superhero who looks like a rabid Superman crying: "I didn't want to find out that instead of getting my powers from a transcendent scientist-mentor, I was grown from the DNA of Aryan super-athletes and Hitler's personal sex midgets!" Neil Gaiman's *The Sandman* features a superhero whose only powers are delusions of grandeur (see *The Doll's House*). These British authors meet the U.S. superheroes with little respect. They see them from an outside perspective. Even though the United States and Britain share a common language, the cultures of the two countries are vastly different. When it comes to superhero comics, British readers and authors may have read just as many comics as their U.S. counterparts, but the heroes are not theirs: Captain America, Superman or Wonder Woman would never be mistaken for subjects of Queen Elizabeth, just as much as James Bond is no CIA agent.

Due to these cultural differences, British authors have a more distanced perspective on superheroes than their U.S. counterparts. We believe that this different perspective and its inclusion into the superhero discourse through the influential works of British authors is a decisive factor in the development of this new age of superheroes. In this essay we will trace different strategies by which British authors bring their own distant perspective into the discourse on superheroes and, thus, foster an atmosphere of disillusionment, irony and question marks.

## ALAN MOORE'S *WATCHMEN*

*The tombs of the past have been dismantled....*
—Alan Moore, "Planetary Consciousness"

Despite its restrained aesthetics of nine panels a page and its scheme of primary colors, both of which are strongly reminiscent of the classical superhero comics, *Watchmen* marks a clear and thorough break with the traditional image of the superhero. *Watchmen* not only shows its heroes with all their private troubles and neuroses, which is nothing special since the Silver Age and its denizens Spider-Man, Hulk or The Thing; the comic moreover questions the justification of superheroes to take the destiny of society into their own hands. "Who Watches the Watchmen?" is one of the central questions of the comic. What are the checks and balances for superheroes? And what happens when society rejects its champions? *Watchmen* answers: Then superheroes have to accept that they do not act on behalf of others but rather to live out their own fantasies and neuroses and to please their own vanities.

*Watchmen*, and this is the main point here, questions the mythological status of superheroes. Roland Barthes introduced the notion of the contemporary myth as a "système semiologique sécondaire" (687), a secondary semiotic system that seems consistent in itself and that renders cultural constructions natural. The myth of the superhero as the defender of society is not questioned: Superheroes are good folk. They defend the weak and wretched against evil machinations and doomsday devices. To apply a term the Russian cultural and literary theorist Mikhail Bakhtin developed in *Problems of Dostoevsky's Poetics*, the superhero myth is monologic. There is only one perspective to the superhero and that is all. Alan Moore now manages to break this myth by giving us different perspectives in *Watchmen*. Moore employs narrative strategies that provide the reader with different perspectives at the same time. This strategy, which Bakhtin calls polyphonic, is the opposite of the monologic storytelling of classical superhero narratives, and Moore shrewdly employs the special capabilities of the medium for this task: The different modes of perception that comics address through image and text allow the medium to present different, even conflicting, information at the same time and, thus, provide its readers with different perspectives. Time and again, Moore juxtaposes the dialogue of one storyline with the imagery from another in the same panel: the newsvendor's rants on the state of the world interlace with the action of the comic his customer reads. Similarly the retelling of a joke in the snippets of Rorschach's diary serves as a commentary on images from the life of The Comedian (II, 26f.). We have a TV show where the physical prowess of public superhero Adrian Veidt is celebrated and the everyday superheroes Dan and Laurie become intimate in their living room (VII, 13ff.). The discourses of physical achievement and love-making, of public display and the most private of experiences, are juxtaposed and start commenting on each other both on the level of image and written text. Different angles put each other into perspective.

    A second characteristic of Moore's polyphony in *Watchmen* is that he does not take a stance as an author. Moore likes to stress in interviews how averse he is to "baby-bird moralising," to feed his audience with his opinions (see Eno and Csawza). He does not favor one particular perspective, which monologic storytelling would do, but stands back and, for example, lets his characters discuss whether Veidt's killing of 5 million people to bring about world peace was justified (XII, 9ff.).

    Moore's third strategy to break the mythic coherence of the superhero is pointing out the different hero discourses that interact in his superheroes' identity. The character of Adrian Veidt is a good case in point: Veidt is also known as Ozymandias, the Greek name of Rameses II. This points to the discourse of ancient god kings on which Veidt's role model Alexander the Great fashioned himself. In the context of English literature, Ozymandias refers to a sonnet of the same name by Percy Bysshe Shelley, which uses the fragmented remains of a gigantic statue of the pharaoh to reflect on overreaching on a grand scale. Veidt also strikes us with his Nietzschean belief in the power of will, the Riefenstahl aesthetics of his TV performance and the gigantic interior of his offices. Associative images of an Aryan Übermensch are thus evoked. The English translation of Übermensch, Superman, and the discourse connected to this particular superhero comes into play when we learn that Veidt likes to retreat to his own Castle of Solitude in the Arctic wastes, just like Shuster and Siegel's comic book hero.

Alan Moore thus breaks the myth of the superheroes by providing his readers with different perspectives, not imposing his authorial stance on their opinion and pointing out the historicity of the superhero discourse.

## Warren Ellis' *Planetary* and *NextWave*

> *stones taken to pave a way into whatever awaits in the comic field's future.*
> — Alan Moore, "Planetary Consciousness"

Alan Moore's countryman Warren Ellis continues, it seems, with *Planetary* where *Watchmen* left off and goes well beyond it. Ellis keeps the distinction of discourses and a plurality of perspectives in *Planetary*. Still, he strives to reintegrate the centrifugal elements Moore identifies, the stones of the dismantled tombs of the past, into a new coherent structure, a (possible) path into the comic field's future. In *Planetary*, Ellis develops the structure of "The Snowflake," a myriad of different worlds of popular culture that are all individual and all have their own perspective but still are connected in this overarching structure.

The stories of *Planetary* lead readers into the different realms of popular culture. Every issue has a special theme, be it Japanese monsters (*Planetary 1*: "Island"), Hong Kong films of the heroic bloodshed genre (*Planetary 1*: "Dead Gunfighters") or James Bond espionage glamour (*Planetary 2*: "Cold World"). As the Planetary team moves through these different worlds, Ellis can put them into perspective. James Bond stories are one way to contextualize the world, superhero comics another (*Planetary 2*: "Magic and Loss"). While Moore juxtaposes the perspectives of individual characters, Ellis contrasts different contexts of popular culture.

In the story "Night on Earth" (*Planetary: Crossing Worlds*), Ellis brings the historicity of the superhero, already implicit in Moore's *Watchmen*, to the point: We follow the adventures of Elijah Snow, Jakita Wagner and The Drummer through different levels of reality, where they meet the different incarnations of Batman through the decades. After an encounter with the camp Batman we know from the 1960s TV series (identifiable both through imagery and manner of speech), they run, among other versions, into the Batman from *Dark Knight Returns* and the upstanding 1970s Batman until they can contain the madman John Black, who has caused what Ellis calls a "partial universe collapse." Ellis' storytelling is deconstructive; it destroys the mythic naturalness of Batman being one identifiable character. On the other hand, Ellis' multiverse structure links these different layers and gives us a coherent background.

Where Moore's *Watchmen* dismantles the "tombs of the past," Ellis tries to pave a way into the comic field's future through reassembling the individual stones he finds in the plentiful quarry of popular culture. Both authors, however, bring a foreign perspective to what is possibly the most American of all comics genres and, thus, deal severe blows to the naïve naturalness of the U.S. superhero.

Ellis has recently continued his deconstruction of the superhero genre in the 12-issue *Nextwave* series published by Marvel—an explosion of violence and color peppered with Pythonesque absurdities from which even the last trace of cool still discernible in *Planetary* has been culled. In Ellis' own words, *Nextwave* is "an absolute distillation of the superhero genre. No plot lines, characters, emotions, nothing whatsoever. It's people posing in the street for no good reason. It is people getting kicked, and then exploding. It is a *pure* comic book, and I will fight anyone who says otherwise. And afterwards, they will explode" (Weisbrod). This is also the gist of the comic's morality-disavowing motto, "healing America by beating people up," and a line in the series' own theme song (which can be downloaded from the internet): "it's like Shakespeare but with lots more punching."*

The *Nextwave* squad consists of a cast of superheroes pilfered from the Marvel universe: Monica Rambeau, a female Captain Marvel (and a black one to boot); Aaron Stack, a spoof of Machine Man; Elsa Bloodstone, the daughter of Hyborian monster hunter Ulysses Bloodstone; The Captain, who recalls any previous superhero named Captain; and Tabitha Smith, who is modeled on Boom Boom from *New Mutants* and Meltdown in *X-Force*.† Realizing that their new client—a shady multinational called The Beyond Corporation—is a cover of S.I.L.E.N.T., a terrorist cell that Nextwave used to fight, the agents quit their employer H.A.T.E., not without having first stolen a trusty Shockwave Rider for their missions. Apart from clashing with Fin Fang Foom (a Marvel lindworm in purple underpants filled with no genitals), a corrupt-police-officer-turned-car-devouring Goliath and the Broccoli Men, Beyond's eerie plant-androids, the squad is also busy fighting their for-

---

*http://www.marvel.com/publishing/stories/nextwave/NextWaveFinal.mp3
†As explained by Ellis himself in an "afterword" in the book edition of the series.

mer boss, Dirk Anger. This character who is, of course, modeled on Nick Fury is an erratic psychopath whose arsenal contains deadly Koala bears and homicide crabs — weapons too ridiculous to pose a serious threat to Ellis' disrespectful protagonists. At the end of issue six, we see him, à la Norman Bates, a whimpering wreck with a penchant for his mother's clothes.

If Ellis takes his superheroes down a peg or two by reducing their *enemies* to absurdity, he is also busy undermining the Nextwave squad's own superhero credentials (without, however, diminishing their astounding powers and hence attractiveness for a comic artist). He does so mainly by extending the historical perspective already introduced in *Planetary* by turning the series' overarching archaeological conceit against the *Nextwave* protagonists. This happens for instance through soap opera–style flashbacks to scenes from the characters' past, which shatter the homogeneous identities they like to project. Monica Rambeau's repeated smug comments on the absurdity of the agents' tasks and their use of violence ("when I ran the Avengers we didn't kill people" [19]) are challenged when she is shown as a child, incinerating a stray dog by giving it a brief gamma laser glance. "Monica Rambeau, leader of the Nextwave Squad," we are told elsewhere, "lies all the time" (108). The Captain, we learn from a similar flashback, received his superpowers from aliens who had discovered him in a state of absolute inebriation in a dark alleyway. To return the favor, he immediately tries his new powers on them — and then is sick all over the altruistic aliens as he bends down over their prostrate bodies to search for their credit cards. Aaron Stack, finally, is one of a discontinued series of robots, some of which were deployed, though rather unsuccessfully, as priests visiting the elderly. Despite this fact Stack's hubris ("I'm a unique robot intellect," he protests in one panel [101]) makes him the perfect butt of his team's practical jokes (if not plain brutality) — whom he insists on addressing (as he thinks, dismissively) as "fleshy ones."

In contrast to counterfactual postmodernism, which celebrates such acts of revisionism as a political strategy (see especially Hutcheon 62–92), Ellis uses these flashbacks to highlight the absurdity of the characters' claims. Their supernatural powers are offset by their grotesque personalities, which are shaped by baser instincts and desires rather than absolute virtue. But it is not only Ellis' agents that are grotesque, but also the world in which they live and work is Rabelaisian,* fusing the hypermodern with the visceral, the techno-

---

*The comic here recalls the material bodily principle as described by Mikhail Bakhtin in Rabelais and His World: "In grotesque realism [...] the bodily element is deeply positive. It is presented not in a private, egoistic form, severed from other spheres of life, but as something universal, representing all the people. As such it is opposed to severance from the material and bodily roots of the world; it makes no pretense to renunciation of the earthy, or independence of the earth and the body. We repeat: the body and bodily life have here a cosmic and at the same time an all-people's character; this is not the body and its physiology in the modern sense of these words, because it is not individualized. The material

logical and the disgusting. Here, towns bedecked with towering skyscrapers have names like Abcess, North Dakota and Sink City, Illinois. Of course, these names insinuate the even more abyssal underworld the superheroes have to fight — Fin Fang Foom, for instance, whose gastric tract becomes the site of Aaron Stack's mission against the monster when it is sweeping the city of Abcess. Although this miasmic milieu seems to provide a contrastive backdrop against which Stack's transhuman abilities emerge with particular clarity, these abilities are turned against themselves, as Stack transmogrifies into something akin to a Swiss army knife in order to whip up the contents of Fin Fang Foom's stomach.

Despite their triumphs, the agents remain shallow and superficial. The elegiac style of recent American superhero comics with their messianic messages and weighty dialogue (consider for instance Mark Waid's *Kingdom Come* [1996], which eerily anticipated some of the visual heroism that accompanied the events of 11 September 2001) is here replaced by flat and stylized characters whose juvenile jargon and imbecilic chatter is meant to annoy. Always on her mobile phone gossiping about doubtful personalities like "Jessica" (Simpson) and "Paris" (Hilton), Tabitha Smith sounds like a contemporary American teenager.

These reductions also allow Ellis to cash in on cultural stereotypes pervasive in both UK and U.S. culture. A running joke is Tabitha's ongoing squabble with the stalwart British character Elsa Bloodstone, even at the most inappropriate moments — for instance, as the two are fighting Anger's deadly Samurai androids. Upon Elsa's matter-of-fact count: "I make it six [Samurais] each," Tabitha retorts: "Don't you try and impress me with your English counting. You know I growed up [sic] in a trailer park" (117). This clash of old and new world may be read as a tongue-in-cheek hint at the "Second British Invasion" of the American comic scene, in progress since the 1980s. The remarks are aimed at taking some of the sting out of this popular culture conflict, but Ellis here also suggests that self-deprecating humor might be the only way of rejuvenating American comic art. For that to happen, however, superheroes must come down to earth, as it were.

In chapters five and six of the first volume, Ellis takes this idea quite literally. Out on yet another mission, the Nextwave squad lands on the Beyond Corporation's "war garden"— the outdoor plant where the corporation grows their vegetable androids, the Broccoli Men. As the agents are busy destroy-

*bodily principle is contained not in the biological individual, not in the bourgeois ego, but in the people, a people who are continually growing and renewed [...]. This exaggeration has a positive, assertive character. The leading themes of these images of bodily life are fertility, growth, and a brimming-over abundance. Manifestations of this life refer not to the isolated biological individual, not to the private, egotistic 'economic man,' but to the collective ancestral body of all the people" (19).*

ing the reeking creatures — "digging for victory," as Elsa puts it with a gesture of jingoistic Britishness (a deeply British in-joke that might go unnoticed by some readers)[5] — they are attacked from the sky with Dirk Anger's spectacular weaponry. They manage the situation with the aid of their superpowers and a bunch of shovels. The sudden intrusion of real life — in the form of gardening equipment — into the plot is both absurd and disillusioning. Whereas laser rays and other gimmicks usually serve to divert attention from the actual violence superheroes commit, these shovels emphasize the material humanness of Ellis' protagonists. Violence is one of the unfailing features of this comic. The penultimate panel of the first volume depicts Stack being given a good thrashing by the other members of the team with their shovels. Silhouetted against the light of the setting sun, the scene of in-group violence turns into grotesque kitsch. This is also emphasized by the tag superimposed over the panel: "nextwave is love" (137). Ellis' self-ironic stab at the harmonizing function of traditional superheroes acts as a reminder of the actual brutality underpinning their actions — and those of all superheroes, however righteous their aims.

## GRANT MORRISON'S *VIMANARAMA*

> *The more things change, the more they stay the same.*
> —Vimanarama 3, 45

In Ellis' colorfully vibrant world of political incorrectness, there is little space for hope and heroic grandeur — sentiments which Grant Morrison's *Vimanarama*, our final example, still exploits. A three-issue series published by Vertigo in 2005, *Vimanarama* tells the story of Ali, a young Muslim living in Bradford in Northeast England, whose life is beset with numerous problems, one of them being an impending arranged marriage. But worse is still to come, as Ali, in the attempt to rescue his baby nephew from a gaping hole that has mysteriously opened up underneath his father's corner shop, unleashes the forces of darkness, led by the terrible Ul-Shattan — who promptly sets out to destroy the human world. To the rescue comes Ben Rama, semidivine leader of the Ultra-Hadeen, ancient superheroes engaged in a fierce struggle with the forces of darkness, but matters are complicated when Rama falls in love with Sofia, Ali's future wife. Her rejection of his offer to join him in the supernatural world — as well as, implicitly, her rejection of

---

*The "Dig for Victory" campaign was started immediately at the beginning of World War II to increase the production of agricultural goods by motivating owners of private gardens to turn them into allotments. See for instance http://www.bbc.co.uk/dna/h2g2/A2263529.

immortal superhero status — almost leads Rama to perish with love sickness and abandon his task of rescuing the planet. In the end he pulls himself together just in time to vanquish the forces of evil.

No less colorful and stylish than Ellis' *Nextwave*, Morrison's comic is brimful with multicultural allusions. The title refers to the "Vimana," a mythical flying machine described in the ancient literature of India (and literally meaning "aircraft" in Hindi), said to have existed in the Rama empire thousands of years ago. The figure of Ben Rama is taken from the Hindu epic Ramayana (c. 11 AD), where he is a popular prince considered an incarnation of Vishnu. Other, more popular (and vague) references — to Bollywood aesthetics and life in the North of England (where it always rains) — abound. And while Ali is a teenage–Everyman complete with zip-up jersey, designer stubble and an undefined sense of ennui, his father is the kind of graying patriarch stereotypically associated with Asian family structures. In a trope typical for the superhero genre, Morrison stages a brief but baroque encounter between the everyday world and the supernatural.

Essentially a "post–9/11 comic" in inspiration,* Morrison's absurd romance revisits the metahuman conflicts depicted in, again, a comic like *Kingdom Come*. Although he ultimately privileges the ordinariness to which life returns after the apocalyptic clash of the superpowers, the benevolent powers of Ben Rama nevertheless lead to an improvement of normal life — admittedly in a somewhat absurd way, as what he leaves the Bradford mortals are "fridges that run on prayer, telepathic telephones, and the sky filled with vitamins" (3, 45). Superhero magic is here reduced to the splendid icing on the cake of normalcy. The final panel of the third issue also reveals who will benefit most from this magic. It shows Ali in defiant easy rider pose on a space glider on the way to the moon (into which a group of teenagers had crashed a "two-man Bright Vimana"). He is wearing Rama's somewhat too bulky space uniform and imitates his laughter in an archetypal gesture of stubborn defiance in the absence of physical power. Of course, if a real space glider is not available, a good comic book may do. Hence *Vimanarama* might be read on a metalevel as a self-referential celebration of the enduring escapist power of the comic medium, which provides alternative worlds to sweeten life in the here and now.

Morrison's compromising take on superheroes is echoed by his equally compromising view of multicultural Britain, where radically different lifestyles coexist — the suicidal Ali and his devout brother, Omar, the sexy Sofia in hip–

---

*See Brady. Morrison points out in this interview that the "the seed [for this comic] was planted after 9/11 when I started reading up on Muslim culture in an effort to comprehend the world's political and religious situation a little more clearly."

ster pants and women wearing the hijab. "There are devout Muslims in the book and there are couldn't-care-less Muslims so everyone gets a shout" (Brady). Yet despite his own affirmation of the universality of the plot,* and the media's rather positive review of the comic,† historical events give the exclusively Pakistani context in which the comic is set a somewhat more disturbing tinge.

The fact that the city of Bradford, where the comic is set, was the site of some of the most harrowing race riots in 2001, foregrounds how idealizing Morrison's perspective is. In view of the terrorist attacks in July 2005 in the UK, taking place only one month after the publication of the final issue of his comic and carried out by young men who uncannily resembled Morrison's Ali, the naïveté underpinning this ideal becomes glaring. This association also puts in perspective his avowed aim of "taking all the pomp and high holiness of one of the world's greatest religions [...] and turning it into a Jack Kirby comic" (Brady). One is left to wonder whether Muslim fundamentalists would want to share the joke.

The absolutism of the clashing supernatural worlds portrayed in Morrison's comic is echoed in a disturbing way by radical contrasts in the here and now. If Ul-Shattan's invectives against humanity (which he likens to maggots) uncannily resemble the diatribes that we know only too well from the messages of Islamic fundamentalists, then the vague multiculturalism of contemporary Bradford is no less disconcerting, as it, too, sparks radical positions. While Morrison attempts to defuse any form of nascent fundamentalism with a hefty dose of humor, real life might be less compromising. Hence Ali's devout and diligent brother, Omar, squarely admits that he does not get Ali's jokes: "I have no sense of humor, Ali. You know that" (1, 6). Yet it is not only this dire literalism that is worrying but also Ali's latent extremism, which is illustrated by his pledge that he will commit suicide should the wife his parents have chosen for him turn out to be ugly. This suggests that he, too, might be harboring a suppressed potential for violence (even though he is less willing to turn this against others). Only the fact of mortality ultimately puts a stop to these extremes and unites Ali, Omar and their father in Nirvana — from which they all return, better, more contented and happier people (and without becoming martyrs to their personal causes).

---

*"I think the story is human enough at its core to mean something to anyone who's ever been a teenager in the grip of immense and ridiculous forces beyond one's control or understanding" (Brady).

†See, for example, Martin Wainwright, "New Take on Life in Bradford," The Guardian (11 February 2005) (http://arts.guardian.co.uk/print/0,,5124626-110427,00.html), or Tina Sharma, "Vimanarama: British Pakistani Saves the World in New Comic!" Asians in Media (20 February 2005) (http://www.asiansinmedia.org/news/printable.php?article=824).

## Conclusion

Since the 1980s, British comic artists have successfully deconstructed the superhero myth as propagated by the American comic industry. This deconstruction included the American attempts to review the superhero genre, be it by depicting their protagonists' inner turmoil and neuroses (*Dark Knight Returns*) or by enhancing their mythical potential (*Kingdom Come*). Whether the British artists have used an elaborate polyphony that demythologizes the superhero myth by placing it at the center of a web of conflicting perspectives, that uncovers its historicity or portrays superheroes with a sense of humor for which the epithet "British" is the only appropriate one, these comics put a question mark to the old certainties of the genre like "truth, justice and the American way" or "with great power comes great responsibility." Yet they also prove that superheroes are alive and kicking — even after Captain America's sad and sudden demise.

## Bibliography

Bakhtin, Mikhail M. *Problems of Dostoevsky's Poetics*. Minneapolis: University of Minnesota Press, 1984.
\_\_\_\_\_. *Rabelais and his World*. Bloomington: Indiana University Press, 1984.
Barthes, Roland. "'Mythologies,' suivi de 'Le Mythe, aujourd'hui.'" *Roland Barthes. Œuvres completes*. I. Paris: Éditions du Seuil, 1993, 561–724.
Berry, Michael." The Second British Invasion." http://www.sff.net/people/mberry/gaiman.htm. (4 September 2007).
Brady, Matt. "Inside Morrison's Head: Leaving Marvel, *Vimanarama* and More." *Newsarama*, 11 August 2003. http://forum.newsarama.com/archive/index.php/t-5087.html (4 September 2007).
Ellis, Warren et al. *Nextwave: Agents of H.A.T.E. Vol. 1: This is What They Want*. New York: Marvel, 2006.
\_\_\_\_\_. *Planetary: Crossing Worlds*. La Jolla, CA: Wildstorm, 2004.
\_\_\_\_\_. *Planetary 1: All Over The World and Other Stories*. La Jolla, CA: Wildstorm, 2000.
\_\_\_\_\_. *Planetary 2: The Fourth Man*. La Jolla, CA: Wildstorm, 2001.
\_\_\_\_\_. *Planetary 3: Leaving the 20th Century*. La Jolla, CA: Wildstorm, 2004.
Eno, Vincent, and El Csawza. "Alan Moore Interview." 1988. *Feuilleton*. http://www.johncoulthart.com/feuilleton/?p=53 (4 September 2007).
Gaiman, Neil, et al. *The Sandman 2: The Doll's House*. New York: Vertigo, 1995.
Hutcheon, Linda. *The Politics of Postmodernism*. London and New York: Routledge, 1993.
Kukkonen, Karin. *Neue Perspektiven auf die Superhelden: Polyphonie in Alan Moores Watchmen*. Marburg: Tectum, 2008.
Miller, Frank, et al. *Batman: The Dark Knight Returns*. New York: DC Comics, 2002 (1986).
Moore, Alan. "Planetary Consciousness." In Warren Ellis et al., *Planetary 1: All Over The World and Other Stories*. La Jolla, CA: Wildstorm, 2000.
Moore, Alan, et al. *Watchmen*. New York: DC Comics, 1987.
Morrison, Grant et al. *Vimanarama* 1–3. New York: Vertigo, 2005.
Waid, Mark. *Kingdom Come*. New York: DC Comics, 1996.
Weisbrod, Aaron. "Recapping an Evening with Warren Ellis @ heroes con 06." *Newsarama* 7 June 2006. http://forum.newsarama.com/showthread.php?t=76010 (4 September 2007).

# 14

# A Cornerstone of Turkish Fantastic Films: From *Flash Gordon* to *Baytekin*

*Meral Özçınar*

The history of the comics medium in Turkey is a long and troubled one. Despite the fact that parents in Turkey do usually not approve of them, comics are highly popular with children and have a considerable standing in the media landscape. Both thematically and formally, Turkish comics have been greatly influenced by a number of Italian and American serials that were imported in the past. But these works were not absorbed without important changes made to the foreign concepts. The Turkish political system, which regarded anything coming from abroad as a threat to the national identity, tried to "localize" comic books as quickly as possible, that is, to adapt and rewrite them to suit a Turkish background. The influence of nationalist ideology thus made itself clearly felt both formally and content-wise. Originally blond heroes were given dark hair and the names of characters and places were changed into more familiar, Turkish terms. A typical example is the transformation of the character Flash Gordon into the Turkish hero Baytekin. *Flash Gordon* was welcomed with great enthusiasm by Turkish audiences, but only after the series' original concept had been "domesticated," that is, changed to suit ideological aims. The popularity of comics reached a new height when a wave of adaptations of foreign films hit Turkish cinema screens in the 1960s and 1970s, and a new genre in Turkish cinema was thus created. The marriage of the sometimes endearing technical and formal insufficiencies of the Turkish film industry with the rich imagination of comics brought forth what could be called the "Turkish fantastic movie" or, to use the term commonly used in Turkey, the "costume adventure movie."

Comics have played an important role in the cultural socialization of children in Turkey for several decades now. A common Turkish saying, which might sound familiar to comic fans everywhere, states that "the only books which are read without knowing how to read are comics." Typically, Turkish readers can be divided into two categories, those whose reading started with an ubiquitous children's book called *Pollyanna* and those who learned their letters with the help of comics. Among these two options, the latter is certainly remembered with greater fondness. It can also be assumed that almost everybody in Turkey goes through a comics reading phase at least once in their lives. Yet, comics are at the same time patronizingly frowned upon and seen as inevitable an element in the process of growing up as football. In other words, everybody reads comics at some point in his or her life but later the grown-up readers do not want them to be read by youngsters. While this paradoxical attitude toward comics with its ensuing "clash of generations" still occasionally surfaces in the West, it is much the general opinion in Turkey. As Turkish school children do not heed the elders' admonitions more than Western teenagers, comics are still hidden in many school textbooks so students can peruse them clandestinely during class.

The first comics published in Turkey were called "novels" or "movie novels." The aim behind this curious choice of terminology was to make this slightly dubious form of literature respectable by associating it with established media and genres. In a similar fashion, the term "paper cinema" was later coined because comics are printed on paper and, at least from a rather superficial point of view, appear to take their narrative conventions and formal means from cinema. Once again, the effort to make use of the popularity of the cinema is rather transparent. It is also of importance in this respect that popular Turkish comics serials such as *Baytekin*, *Bayçetin* and *Tarkan* were all made into serials for the cinema, with a total of 32 episodes altogether. My aim in putting such emphasis on the names given to comics when they first arrived in Turkey is to demonstrate that they met with opposing reactions. From this point of view, the terminological confusion also seems to provide a key to the mentality that informed the ideological counterreactions against the new medium. Comics first published in newspapers in America achieved popularity in Turkey when they were reprinted in magazine form in the 1930s. At the same time, as they became popular in the kids' magazines, comics came to have a bad reputation among parents who were keen on providing their children with a good education. Their quasi-instinctive opposition marked the starting point of an aggressive public campaign against comics and their partial banning. The slogan of this particular movement for censorship said, "Taking good care of children is not an economical matter, but a moral one." Public reactions to comic books were so volatile because many people believed that the magazines printing them only adhered to capitalist principles in their crafting of the stories. It was also a widespread belief that the books did not teach the moral principles of the regime in power, or were even opposed to them. Indeed, the fact that comics' origins lay abroad impinged greatly on the regime's doctrine of cultural nationalism. In other words, to the adherents of the anticomics movement, the growing popularity of comics was just another symptom of the spread of Americanism. Consequently, various kinds of opposition emerged. The different authoritarian regimes of the 1930s intervened to domesticate American comics. In Turkey, the localization of the stories even went so far as to making the blond characters dark-haired: Flash Gordon thus became Baytekin.

In Turkey, *Flash Gordon* was first published in 1935 in a magazine called *Çocuk sesi*, and the title of the comic would later be changed to *Baytekin*. The title character's name was not the only one to be tinkered with. The original American character going by the name of Dane Arden was changed into Yıldız, and Zarkov became Çetinel. *Baytekin* affected the youth of that period profoundly, both in comic book and movie form. The series was first published under the name of *Super Gordon* in 1971. Its main character was presented as "the pilot of the future." At the bottom of the comics pages, propaganda slogans could be found, such as: "Our future is in the sky," "Help strengthen the Turkish Air Forces," or "Let's strengthen our Air Forces." Sadi Konuralp comments:

> *Flash Gordon* was brand new for the comics reader because of the quality of the drawings and the good use it made of its science fiction scenario. Consequently, it had a remarkably big audience in Turkey. This great reader interest lead other publishing houses to develop fake *Flash Gordon* serials. A publication called *Uzay* produced an adventure serial called *Angry Tessie*. Its first installment was first published in issue 28, dating from August 30, 1971. Both in drawing and in content, it was an obvious appropriation of the *Baytekin* concept. Some panels of this comic, printed without any authorial signature underneath, are clear swipes of drawings in the *Baytekin* story "Lieutenant Volkan." Another fake *Super Gordon* adventure was published under the name of "455 Escaping," starting from issue 31 on September 20, 1971. Here, figures from a comic probably made in Great Britain were modified. [Flash] Gordon's and Draver's faces replaced the heads of the characters of the original story. The ratio between the head and the body has not been well calculated, with amusing anatomical results [356, my translation].

These interventions reflect the political and social atmosphere of the period. Political worries, the manipulation of society by way of political speeches, and psychological warfare caused widespread pessimism and further encouraged the regime in its authoritarian mentality. The economical recession all over the world and a certain lack of confidence in the Turkish people were considered as evidence of the imminent danger the regime found itself in.

The new regime that would come into place was to reject its political inheritance and renew almost every part of society, but it was not in power yet. Instead, in an attempt to ensure the continuity of the system, the governing powers once again came to rely on their customary defensive reflexes. For that reason, comics coming to Turkey were filled with nationalist figures, so much so, in fact, that they faced the danger of entirely losing their original identity. Ideologically, this process of nationalist censorship was justified in the following way:

> In order to mobilize the nation [...] the child should be educated as a prospective adult who is supposed to contribute to the [national] effort. This education should enable the child to take part in the collective conscience and to consider itself part of a national community which depends on cultural and emotional cooperation [Cantek 28, my translation].

These comics, which were much informed by the general atmosphere of the country at the time, told moral stories. When the 1940s with the battles of World War II arrived, the country (which was not prepared for the war) was forced to cut down on almost everything. Restrictions on the use of paper prevented newspapers from being published, and comics were equally affected. Consequently, the Turkish comics boom slowed down. But this would not prove the only stumbling block in the development of the medium in Turkey. As a result of Atatürk's death in 1938, fears that the now-inefficient political regime might collapse increased, and the public measures taken against comics in the West, especially in America, found their counterparts in Turkey as well. One of the most important reasons for these reactions were the nationalist fears generated by the fact that American culture was adopted by the Turkish people with great ease and speed. Consequently, Vedat Nedim Tör, Turkey's Frederic Wertham, started a crusade against comics. His campaign resulted in the shutdown of the comics magazines. Most of the artists became unemployed.

It would take until the 1950s for comics in Turkey to enjoy their very own golden age. Newspaper circulation increased with the help of the popular comics that were printed on their pages. Of course, nationalist factors also played a great role in this increase. As a matter of fact, these years were the period when home-grown heroes gradually took center stage. In the 1950s, a Turkish comics hero called *Pekos Bill* enjoyed high circulation numbers. But coinciding with the publication of the series' 70th issue, it was banned. Its supposedly harmful psychological effects on children were cited as the reason for the censorship. Comics' opponents were once again gaining in power. In fact, it was not just comics that were opposed, but all of the newly emerging entertainment culture. Comics, which occupied a remarkable place in popular culture and provided well-deserved doses of escapism for their audience, were rejected by certain factions of society just like any other cultural influence from abroad. The conflicting groups that were to dominate public discourse about comics for the following years emerged during this decade, but the ascent of popular culture could not be stopped, despite the great number of opponents.

After *Pekos Bill*, another comic book that enjoyed great success was a Western serial called *Tommiks Texas*. It quickly rose to great fame. In fact, the series was so successful that its title was adopted as a general term for comics. With the further contribution of American movies, cowboy stories became remarkably popular. Turkish movies started to emulate this quintessentially American genre faithfully. The unfavorable attitude toward American culture displayed in the 1930s was replaced by admiration for American movies. The trend toward Turkish-made Westerns started in 1967. It would last for seven years, and about 50 films of this sort would be shot. These films, most of which were cheaply produced, nevertheless proved highly successful. Giovanni Scognomillo remarks on the subject:

> This sort of costume film, which was made with complete disregard for historical accuracy, is similar to the so-called "Byzantine Westerns," especially in how much these films are informed by clichés of the old west. Supposedly, only the decorations and the costumes are changed in our country. As in the American Westerns, where the villains are the "Redskins" who scalp their enemies' heads, the Byzantines are defined as sinful infidels and the villains in this type of historical adventure [qtd. after Agah Özgüç 196, my translation].

This period also was the time when comics were first made into films. *The Red Mask* and *Kinova* are the most well-known examples.

The 1960s were the decade during which Turkish national identity was questioned. A Turkish comic book called *Karaoğlan* became famous. It served as a model for other comic book creators and thus gave birth to a number of new serials called *Tarkan*, *Kara Murat* and *Malkoçoğlu*. At the same time, comics were once again attacked as an ideological means of American imperialism. American cultural influence also made itself felt in other areas such as music and cinema. Commonly, the opponents of American culture would raise the same arguments against it over and over again, criticizing its escapist aims, its insistence on material values and its supposedly hypocritical optimism. As a reaction against the rise of more liberal, leftist views, which were symbolized by comics hero *Karaoğlan*, new types of strips were produced that were intended to spread conservative and nationalist ideas.

These new nationalist comics took their basic formal and narrative cues from serials made in the West, but added new local content both in regard to the art styles employed and to the stories they told. Their creators made abundant use of Turkish history, changing historical facts to suit their ideological aims and to flatter their audience's ego. The historical heroes were portrayed as unbeatable, and seemingly, that was just what the public wanted. The hero protagonist had all qualities to perfection. At the same time, the villain was absolutely certain to lose in the end. The protagonists would fight magnificently and prove excellent lovers. It comes as no surprise that beautiful young ladies would inevitably fall in love with them. As a matter of fact, the most significant common ground of all these nationalist heroes probably was their relationship with women. All of them would have a love affair during each and every one of their adventures. Most times, a princess or a queen ruling a foreign country would fall in love with the protagonist. Also, while the main character was shown to be perfect, the supporting characters tended to represent human weaknesses.

One of the quintessentially "Turkish" heroes was *Kara Murat*, a dark-haired, strong man with a moustache. His adventures were drawn by Abdullah Turan and written by Rahmi Turan. In the eyes of the middle class, he was the most powerful hero, a reputation built especially on his later screen incarnation by actor Cüneyt Arkın in a series of films. The supporting characters of both the films and the comic books were generally weak. The main character was young, aged about 20. He was tall and lean. Supporting characters, on the contrary, were bald, fat or ugly. The main characters would go out with beautiful women, whereas the bit players would only be left with the ugly ones. In these comics, which flirted with nationalist sentiment, certain racist tendencies can also be detected, which were meant to bait readers: commonly, all characters who did not belong to the Turkish nation were portrayed as being cruel or merciless.

By and by, the operation of localization that had been so crucial in the preceding years proved insufficient because the problem lay not only with foreign heroes or so-called cultural imperialism. In almost every branch of the Turkish art world, western views had never truly been adopted. Consequently, even though Turkish comics imitated a specific form from abroad, a suitable indigenous use of the medium had not been found. The result was that Turkish comics could never go beyond being mere copies of the Italian or American originals. Turkish comics never proved truly creative in and of themselves, and they never exerted the same cultural influence their foreign role models did. Their creators also failed to develop sophisticated visual narration. This may again be traced back to the fact that the visual arts had never fully developed in Turkey. Instead, oral culture continued in its dominance. In comics, however, the reader wants to follow both the visual and the verbal narration but Turkish comics severely neglected visual narration and foregrounded verbal narration instead. Much that should have been narrated visually was thus left to the reader's imagination. As in many Turkish films, verbal narration was preferred to visual narration in comics.

History-based films generally reflect the political climate of the period they were made in, apart from telling stories about the events, occurrences and people of the past. Historical stories, at times, are used as an arena for the battles between different ideological approaches. That is why, when examining these comic-based Turkish films, it becomes apparent that their historical plots are used to transport the various political and social currents of the period the films were released in. These heroes and their adventures also point toward diverse cinematic ways of looking at history. It can be said that the cinema knows three different approaches toward historical subjects. There are films that represent history in a fantastical manner, as well as films that attempt to accurately reflect historical truth, and finally, there are films that approach history from an ideological point of view. Fantastic films rarely treat any specific historical moment, place and person. At best, they are based on a vague historical backdrop or on legend. Although the story of a historical figure is told, the filmmakers will manipulate the historical facts of his or her adventures at will. The themes of these films are usually love, adventure and valorous deeds. The films in the second category admit to a considerably greater responsibility toward history. Their approach is mainly different from that of the purely fantastic films in that their setting is firmly based on historical facts. In the third category of films treating historical subjects, the creators' main aim is to approach an actual historical event from an ideological point of view. Here, for instance, heroism is defined according to the respective ideology's political anxieties. The Turkish films adapted from comics serials and shot during these years — for example, *Karaoğlan*, *Tarkan*, *Malkoçoğlu* and *Kara Murat*— are all based on historical events and figures. These films, which offer a mixture of heroism, action, adventure and sex, exhibit features of both the fantastic and the ideological type of historical filmmaking.

The exaggerated heroes and stories of Turkish comics provided the raw materials for a wave of new fantastic films in Turkey. These movies also took up comics' sometimes questionable approach toward history. From the late 1960s, Turkish comics were adapted for the cinema as serials (32 films were made altogether). From the marriage of the endless possibilities of the fantastic cinema and the world of comics a new genre emerged, the so-called "costume adventure film." These films, like Hollywood's so-called "B" movies, or cheaply made genre fare from Italy, India, or Hong Kong, were produced in a cost-effective factory system. The films would be made in very little time and with a very limited budget. The same historical sets, camera angles, narrative techniques and music would be used and recycled in a whole number of films. Sometimes, shots would be pilfered from foreign films and inserted into Turkish productions, as in the case of *Dünyayı Kurtaran Adam* ("The Man Who Saves the World"), which tells the story of an alien invasion. In this film, which has become a cult picture, shots from the original *Star Wars* were inserted into the Turkish material starring Cuneyt Arkın. In this manner, a science fiction setting could be established at next to no cost.

In 1966, the first installment of a film serial called *Malkoçoğlu* was released and became highly popular almost instantly. Following in its footsteps was the serial *Kara Murat*, its first installment released in 1970. It was based on a concept rather similar to *Malkoçoğlu*'s. Unsurprisingly, Cuneyt Arkın was cast the title character in both series. Arkın's athleticism dictates the tone of both films, and their success in turn made Arkın an indispensable mainstay of costume adventure films of this kind. No real awareness of history is displayed in the filmmakers' choice of stories and characters. History serves only as decoration or picturesque background. Instead, these films put their emphasis on narrative momentum, the story's fantastical atmosphere and their primitive ideological point of view. To give a few examples: Malkoçoğlu meets Kazıklı Voyvoda, fights against the crusaders, and woos the daughter of the Hungarian King. Kara Murat, another heroic character portrayed by actor Fatih Sultan Mehmet, hunts his enemies mercilessly, but he is also proficient as a lover. According to this particular character, "love is the greatest favor God has granted us!" In one of the films, he dances to Johann Strauss' "The Blue Danube" waltz, which was composed approximately 400 years after the historical events represented in the film.

*Karaoğlan*, on the other hand, occupies a special place among the films of its genre. Apart from being based on heroic stories, these films also tell the story of a young man from Middle Asia. This Turkish youngster is so naïve as to make him an instant figure of identification for any audience. Surprisingly, though, he is rather witty in comparison with other adventure heroes like Tarkan. During a fight, he tells his opponent: "You seem to like music, because you hold your sword like a clarinet!"

The more traditional *Tarkan* comics, created by Sezgin Burak, were adapted for the screen by director Mehmet Aslan. In these films, Tarkan generally and somewhat monotonously fights for a treasured artifact, for example, a golden sword or a beautiful woman. Alongside his companion dog, he experiences endless adventures and emerges victorious from almost all of them. The comics version shows a rich imagination at work, but technical insufficiencies caused significant trouble in the screen adaptation, which resulted in many unintentionally humorous scenes.

In fact, most of the costume adventure films were just as ridiculous as the *Tarkan* series. Their heroes were brave and strong, so strong, in fact, that they could beat a whole army on their own, scale high castle walls in one leap, kill a handful of men with one strike of the sword and finally make all the beautiful women fall in love with them. These heroes were inspired by historical novels or publications that, in turn, took their material from the legends and events of the past. Dialogue in these films was often inadvertently comic, so much so that everybody in Turkey knows at least a few particularly funny lines by heart. Goofs and clearly visible mistakes, inevitable in films made in such a short time and with a limited amount of money, thus came to characterize the costume adventure film. But despite these obvious shortcomings, these films' political subtext demands to be taken seriously.

> Like the historical comics, the costume adventure films depended on a nationalist message and made-up history. The pseudo-historical premise of these films gave the filmmakers both the opportunity to create a fantastic setting for the hero's adventures and the possibility to expound crude sentiments of Turkish nationalism which originated from a propaganda version of history or were supported by the mangled version of history created by the film itself [Cantek 20, my translation].

The heroes of these films, like their comic book counterparts, symbolized superiority and invincibility. They were constantly engaged in battle. The general structure of the films' plots can be divided into three segments, that is, the hero's departure, his heroic actions and his triumphant return. Themes are repeated again and again. As Umberto Eco puts it: "The main characteristic of popular stories like comics is the renovation of a series of events according to a kind of scheme arranged beforehand. This scheme which repeats itself endlessly is based on an unnecessity" (21). Eco is writing about American and Italian serials here. Turkish comics and adventure films differ somewhat from those in the common aim behind this eternal repetition of heroic deeds, which was to form a perspective for national identity. The costume adventure films that transported certain concepts of Turkish national identity for a mass audience made use of the medium as a means to provide people with psychological support. In other words, adventure films were used to soften the impact of a traumatic political history. Most of the iconography of these costume adventure films was taken directly from comic books. The settings used in the films (dungeons, inns, palace gardens, etc.) and the accessories (swords, knives, flags, etc.) were identical with the comics props. Suat Yalaz, a former comics artist who made films in those years, employed the same themes in his films that had previously informed his comics. His *Karaoğlan* series is a good example. Here, Yalaz invented most of the characteristics that would later be used as clichés in other costume adventure films.

Errors and ridiculously exaggerated fantasy worlds are the main features of the costume adventure films. It is impossible to think of them without these shortcomings. The re-appearance of dead characters on the screen, the stilted dialogue and action scenes taken from other films are some of the features the costume adventure films would never relinquish. The primitive nature of the films is also reflected in the narrative perspective of the films (and comics). "I" (as in the Turkish protagonist) and "the other" (as in the foreign villain) are presented as essentially unchangeable. The hero is shown to be proud, honorable and unbeatable, whereas the foreign characters are physically and emotionally weak. Similarly, the frequently encountered figure of "the other hero," whom the protagonist meets somewhere on his way, is usually introduced as a character with feminine tendencies. This kind of essentialism arises from fears of losing values in the process of Westernization. In Turkey, not only those representing Western values but also women were "the other" in those days. The "other" had to exhibit specifically bad qualities so that the group that perceived itself as "essentially Turkish" could develop its mechanisms of defense.

These nationalist themes of costume adventure films and comics serials were mixed with other themes such as freedom, independence and male solidarity. This is the essential paradox at the core of these artifacts of Turkish popular culture: the costume adventure films and the comic books they were based on were, on the one hand, really contributing to the idea of liberty and individual freedom. They suggested that everyone might be able to depart on adventures of their own. But on the other hand, these films and comic books also fetishized male dominance and solidarity. Their male heroes, while hurrying from one adventure to the next, taught patriarchal and nationalist lessons. The legacy of these films dating from the 1960s and 1970s is clearly visible today: they were the inspiration for modern Turkish fantastic films produced with the help of 3D animation and much more sophisticated technology today. As can be seen by the example of this more sophisticated renaissance, the old serials seem to have retained their ambivalent power. Whether comics are savagely criticized or exalted enthusiastically, they have always provided us with a refuge where we could meet fantastically incorrect, hilariously omnipotent and stylistically imperfect heroes.

BIBLIOGRAPHY

Brockmeier, Jens, and Donal Carbaugh. *Narrative and Identity Studies in Autobiography, Self and Culture.* Amherst: University of Toronto Press & Freie Universität Berlin / University of Massachusetts Press, 2001.

Cantek, Levent (ed.). *Çizgili Hayat Kılavuzu* [Guide of Stripped Life]. Istanbul: İletişim Yay, 2002.

Coté, J. E., and C. G. Levine. *Identity Formation, Agency, and Culture — A Social Psychological Synthesis.* Mahwah, NJ: Lawrence Erlbaum Associates, 2002.

Daniels, Les. *DC Comics: Sixty Years of the World's Favorite Comic Book Heroes.* Boston: Bulfinch, 1995.

Eco, Umberto. *Anlatı Ormanlarında Gezinti.* Istanbul: Can Yay, 1995.

Freeman, Mark. "Why Narrative? Hermeneutics, Historical Understanding, and the Significance of Stories." *Journal of Narrative and Life History* 7 (1997): 169–76.
Harvey, Robert C. *The Art of The Comic Book: An Aesthetic History*. Jackson: Mississippi University Press, 1996.
Keller-Cohen, Deborah, and Judy Dyer. "Intertexuality and the Narrative of Personal Experience." *Journal of Narrative and Life History* 7 (1997): 147–53.
Konuralp, Sadi. "Flash Gordon." http:// www.seruven.org (10 April 2007).
Ozguç, Agah. *Türlerle Türk Sineması* [Turkish Cinema with Styles]. Istanbul: Dünya Yay, 2005.
Sabin, Roger. *Adult Comics: An Introduction*. London: Routledge, 1993.

# 15

# From Capes to Snakes: The Indianization of the American Superhero[1]

## Suchitra Mathur

If one was to believe the international media buzz, the Indian superhero is a brand-new twenty-first-century product. Of course, there is some debate here about who exactly *is* the first Indian superhero. While the producers of the film *Krrish* (2006) would like us to believe it is their eponymous masked hero, others point to Gotham Entertainments' *Spider-Man: India* (launched in 2004). And then there's Virgin Comics, a partnership between Richard Branson's Virgin group and India's Gotham Comics, which has a stable full of superheroes — from Devi to Sadhu. However, as the Indian media, especially the informal sector of Indian bloggers, have been at pains to remind us, the Indian superhero has been around for much longer. Exactly how much longer is once again a matter of debate. There are some who would like to push this date of origin back into pre-history, pointing to mythical characters such as Hanuman (the monkey-god) as the original Indian superheroes (cf. Haldipur). Others, more rooted in comic book culture, point to various characters launched by Indian comic book publishers in the late 1970s and 1980s. Of these, Nagraj, the 1986 Raj Comics creation, appears to best fit the established conventions of the superhero genre as defined by the tradition of the American superhero. But, as Lang and Trimble remind us, "it is logical to assume the American monomythic hero is different from the heroes of other cultures" (158). How and when, then, was the Indian hero transformed into the Amer-

---

*I would like to thank my undergraduate students at IIT Kanpur, especially Vinod Khare, for introducing me to Nagraj comics and providing invaluable insights (as ardent fans and followers) into the world of Raj Comics' superheroes.

ican superhero? And is this transformation a sign of the infamous McDonaldization of the world, or does it point toward a more positive form of cultural globalization where the global is linked to the local in a relationship of mutual exchange and empowerment? I will here attempt to answer these questions by situating Nagraj within Indian sociocultural history in general, and comic book history in particular.

The Indian comic book tradition is relatively young. Apart from the appearance of a few characters appearing in single-frame cartoons in the early part of the 20th century, Indian comics did not really establish themselves as a distinct genre until the 1960s when Anant Pai began the Amar Chitra Katha (henceforth ACK) series. A distinctly nationalist enterprise, the ACKs are a retelling of Indian myths, legends and history in the form of graphic narratives that create a visually coherent "Indian" cultural tradition. In terms of both style and content, these comics self-consciously set themselves apart from the Anglo-American comic tradition. And an important aspect of this distinctiveness is the definition of heroism in the ACKs, which studiously stays away from the anonymous masked crusader figure of the American superhero. Instead, these Indian comics depict their larger-than-life heroes as easily recognizable representative figures rooted in a specific sociocultural context. However, the superhero figure was not entirely absent from the Indian comic scene during this first phase of the Indian comic tradition. Along with ACK, the 1960s also saw the establishment of two comic book publishers in India — Diamond Comics (1960) and Indrajal Comics (1964), both of which primarily published American superhero comics such as *Superman*, *Spider-Man*, *Phantom* and *Mandrake*, often in Hindi translation. What was conspicuous by its absence during this period was the creation of any specifically Indian superhero. Diamond Comics' Chacha Choudhry, with a "faster-than-computer mind," was a successful problem solver, but his super-intelligence is combined with the disarmingly human physique of an elderly gentleman, which is far from the muscle-rippling form of the conventional superhero. And Sabu, another character in the same series, though endowed with the requisite strength as well as "super" origins (he is from Jupiter), is merely a side-kick who never emerges from the shadow of Chacha Choudhry to act as an independent superhero.

It is not until the late 1970s, 1978 to be precise, that both Diamond and Indrajal comics came out with identifiably Indian superheroes — characters that have a "selfless prosocial mission, who possess superpowers, advanced technology, mystical abilities, or highly developed physical and/or mental skills" (Coogan, qtd. in Emmons). While Indrajal created Bahadur, a reformed dacoit who has vowed to fight against all kinds of criminal elements in society, Diamond brought out Fauladi Singh, a humanoid robot engaged primarily in fighting aliens attacking earth. Interestingly, neither of these characters corresponds faithfully to the conventions of the American comic superhero genre. Coogan's definition, for example, continues beyond the "prosocial mission" and "superpowers" to define the superhero as one "who has a superidentity and iconic costume [...] and can be distinguished from characters of related genres (fantasy, science fiction, detective, etc.) by a preponderance of generic conventions." The 1970s Indian comic superheroes violate many of these conventions. While Bahadur has neither an iconic costume nor a secret identity, Fauladi Singh is primarily a science fiction figure engaged in fighting futuristic alien invasions rather than dealing with crimes afflicting the contemporary world. These first Indian superheroes, therefore, appear to point toward the development of a distinctly indigenous superhero tradition that shares with the ACKs a self-conscious distancing from the Anglo-American comic tradition. Instead, this figure of the Indian superhero appears to draw more obviously upon another indigenous popular culture tradition, namely, Hindi cinema. The 1970s was the decade that saw the emergence of Amitabh Bachchan as *the* Indian superstar, the unbeatable action hero whose portrayal of the "angry young man" single-handedly fighting against every kind of social evil effectively redefined the idea of heroism within Indian popular culture. Though endowed with no identifiably superhuman powers, this action hero is nonetheless "super" in his victory against extraordinary odds, in the way he stands head and shoulders above all his contemporaries, in his unswerving integrity, which wins him the support of the entire community, though no one is able to provide much practical aid in his crime-fighting activities. It is no wonder, then, that in the 1980s Indrajal comics cashed in on this phenomenon by creating Supremo, a comic superhero version of Amitabh Bachchan.

Interestingly, however, the portrayal of Supremo draws upon several features of the American superhero that had been conspicuously absent in earlier Indian comic book superheroes. While drawing upon Amitabh Bachchan's hit action films for characters and even plot lines, *Supremo* transforms the recognizable young hero from the neighborhood into a masked crusader, complete with costume and secret identity, who emerges as a crime-fighting superhero only at night while remaining incognito during the day. This transformation may be seen as symptomatic of a cultural shift in the Indian superhero tradition in the latter half of the 1980s. In 1987, for example, Shekhar Kapur released *Mr. India*, often touted as India's first SF film, but more remarkable for its redefinition of the Indian superhero as an "average Indian" who has special powers bestowed on him by science, in this case the ability to become invisible. This "Mr. India" is not only very much the extraordinary lone crusader with a secret identity á la American superhero, but is also played by an actor, Anil Kapoor, who has a very different screen image than Amitabh Bachchan. In contrast to Bachchan's towering 6'3" height and deep baritone voice that consolidated his "angry young man" image, Anil Kapoor is an average 5'11" with the kind of looks that early in his career pegged him as a romantic hero. Kapur's choice of Anil Kapoor as the protagonist of his superhero film clearly signals a cultural shift in the Indian monomyth of the action hero. Interestingly, the year after the release of *Mr. India*, Amitabh Bachchan himself appeared in a film, *Shahenshah* (1988), which is also premised upon the idea of an ordinary man with a costumed secret identity as a superhero. This telling departure from the then-existing Bachchan tradition, following so closely in the footsteps of *Mr. India*, does indicate an Americanization of the Indian superhero concept in the very medium — that is, film — where it was first consolidated in the popular imagination. And this cultural shift was clearly not restricted to the world of Hindi cinema. It is in 1986 that we have the establishment of Raj Comics, a special subsidiary of an existing publishing firm, which launched itself under the banner of being "the home of Indian action superhero comics" with Nagraj as their vanguard inaugural superhero figure.

According to Sanjay Gupta, one of the concept creators of Nagraj, the main inspiration behind the creation of this superhero was Spider-Man. It was in the early 1980s that Spider-Man first appeared on Indian television as a cartoon serial that immediately gained tremendous popularity. Sanjay Gupta fondly recalls Sunday mornings spent watching this show and how this slowly led to the desire to create an Indian counterpart to this superhero. The influence of Spider-Man on Nagraj is obvious — starting with the animal motif that is most clearly visualized in the costume and background story that traces the origins of both superheroes to science labs, to technical details like snakes shooting out of Nagraj's wrists in imitation of Spider-Man's web-shooting wrists. As with Spider-Man's webs, these snakes become the chief source of Nagraj's powers, including the all-important ability to "fly" by swinging on snake ropes. Even the ethical framework of the story of origin, which governs the superhero's role and purpose in society, is similar. Spider-Man's transformatory experience of Uncle Ben's murder (which makes the latter's statement "with great power comes great responsibility" his guiding principle) is echoed in Nagraj's encounter with Baba Gorakhnath, a "guru"-figure who guides Nagraj toward using his powers for the good of society. All these details that build up Nagraj's profile as a superhero are clearly distinct from the earlier tradition of Indian superheroism as embodied in Amitabh Bachchan films as well as comics such as *Bahadur*. Although some aspects of Nagraj do not appear to be derived directly from Spider-Man, these variations often can be traced back to other American superheroes rather than any specifically

Indian superhero tradition. Nagraj's snakey look, for example, is not achieved by a costume; it is his "skin," which has developed snake-like qualities as a result of ingesting the ashes of a powerful shape-shifting snake. As a result, Nagraj, unlike Spider-Man, cannot shed his "costume" to look like an ordinary citizen. Instead, he has to put on "normal" clothes, especially a long overcoat, when he goes out into society and needs to disguise his exceptionality. Visually, this strategy is reminiscent of Phantom, whose costume, though not a biological part of his body, is almost never taken off, and who dons a disguising overcoat whenever he needs to leave his jungle home to enter "civilization." Similarly, later in the *Nagraj* series, Nagraj adopts a secret identity as Raj, an ordinary bespectacled man, deadly scared of snakes, who works for a large media company—an obvious echo of Superman's alter ego, Clark Kent, in both looks and profession. *Nagraj* thus clearly signals the Americanization of the Indian superhero, a telling example of the cultural dynamics of neocolonial globalization. Though the latter is often associated with the specific policies of economic "liberalization" promulgated in 1991, these economic policies are themselves rooted in the import liberalization "reforms" of the 1980s (Kurien 95). In the cultural sphere, this 1980s orientation toward foreign imports in the field of production is evident in Indian television, which, while remaining exclusively under government control, opened its doors to foreign programming by telecasting serials like *Spider-Man* and *Star Trek*. This shift from education to entertainment as the official purpose of television may be seen as indicative of a modernization that then became the catchword of the Rajiv Gandhi administration, which took over the reins of the country in 1984. The flagship of this modernization was the telecom sector and expertise for this transformation came from the United States. While collaboration with the United States was not in itself a new thing, the amount of publicity given to it and the valorization of the United States as a desirable model for imitation did result in a noticeable shift within the popular cultural discourse. It is this shift that I see exemplified in *Nagraj* and the emergence of the Americanized Indian superhero.

This shift, however, should not be taken as an indication of the successful establishment of a neo-imperial American cultural hegemony. Popular culture, as Stuart Hall reminds us, "is neither, in a pure sense, the popular traditions of resistance to these processes [of domination and reform]; nor is it the forms which are superimposed on and over them. It is the ground on which the transformations are worked" ("Notes on Deconstructing 'the Popular'" 456). The *Nagraj* comics embody such a negotiation between containment and resistance in an India where growing U.S. influence through a "liberalized" consumerist economy coexists with a resurgent militant nationalism allied to Hindu fundamentalism. This discourse of cultural nationalism, officially named "Hindutva," has invented an Indian tradition that is a curious amalgamation of Hindu scriptures and mythologies along with popular legends that are given a specifically Hindu spin. It is this last set that is particularly relevant to *Nagraj*, which draws upon the folklore of *ichchadhari nagas*— shape-shifting snakes — and combines it with the Naga cult of Hinduism. In Hindu mythology, snakes, especially the nag (cobra), are revered as protectors and worshipped as symbols of prosperity and fertility. The festival of Naag-Panchmi, for instance, is dedicated to the snake goddess and is celebrated across India by feeding snakes on the fifth day of the month of Shravan. But in addition to this specifically Hindu mythology regarding snakes, there also exist legends about *ichchadhari nagas* that have no direct relationship with the idea of the naga as a divinity. These legends tell the tale of a breed of snakes that over millennia have developed the power of shape-shifting and can thus exist in the form of both humans and snakes. Romantic stories about the mutual loyalty of *ichchadhari naga* couples (who always avenge the unlawful death of their partners) and the precious magical "*mani*" (jewel) set in the hood of the male nagraj (king cobra) permeate the popular imagination and have found frequent expression in the world of Hindi cinema. Significantly, in all such myths and legends, snakes are viewed positively, which completely inverts the Western Judeo-Christian association of snakes with evil, an association that is qualitatively different from the mundane negative feelings (found as much in India as in the West) aroused by a potentially life-threatening creature. Interestingly, a certain kind of malicious duplicity *is* associated with snakes in certain parts of India; in Hindi, for instance, the idiom "aasteen ka saanp" refers to the traitor within the family. But this association, as well as the more general mortal fear of snakes, is usually limited to the most colloquial Hindi word for snakes, namely, "saanp." The more sanskritized "sarp" as well as the specific term "naag" are largely free from such negative associations. This linguistic divide is clearly evident in the *Nagraj* comics where the narratorial voice uses the word "nag" to preface everything related to the superhero, while referring to his snake-powers as "sarp shakti"; it is only the villainous characters who cry out "saanp" in horror when they are attacked by Nagraj's snake army, thus confirming their adversarial position within the cultural/moral framework of the comic world.

According to Sanjay Gupta, the main reason he and his brothers chose snakes as the totem figure for their first superhero was to counteract the very natural fear of snakes that is deeply rooted in people. Nagraj's use of snakes not only as instruments of justice but also as considerate agents in helping innocent people out of their difficulties was intended to develop a healthy friendly attitude toward snakes in the readers. This claim, supported to a large extent by the copious use of live snakes as do-gooders in every *Nagraj* comic, signals a significant departure from the American superhero tradition where animal totems, when evoked (as with Spider-Man and Batman), are restricted almost completely to a symbolic function that draws upon their stereotypically known characteristics without invoking their physical presence within the comic world. Nagraj, on the other hand, in addition to having snake powers (real and mythical) such as poisonous breath and the ability to hypnotize others through the power of his gaze, also has close association with multiple live snakes who actually reside in miniature form within his body and are largely responsible for his invincibility. Such a symbiotic relationship between the animal and the human, which practically blurs the boundary between the two, is often associated with "primitive" cultures, more specifically with the East in general, and with India in particular. By making this snake-man association the foundational feature of their first superhero, the creators of Nagraj obviously Indianized the American superhero. Nagraj thus becomes not a slavish copy of the American original, but a "mimic" superhero who is, in Homi Bhabha's terms, "almost the same but not quite" (86). And this "not quite" variation is a result, not of faulty imitation, but of the deliberate invocation of an Indian cultural framework, of an indigenous knowledge system that transforms the contours of a Western cultural icon.

But can this transformation really be regarded as part of the discourse of cultural nationalism? Or is it only window-dressing — an exotic orientalism that ostentatiously dresses up the superhero in recognizably Indian garb while its conceptual core remains American (cf. Rohit Gupta)? While the folklore of *ichchadhari nagas* is largely restricted to indigenous popular culture, the association of India with snakes, especially cobras, is one of the most recognizable stereotypes within orientalist discourse. The very first *Nagraj* comic, in fact, abounds in the invocation of such orientalist stereotypes, ranging from the gold idol of a goddess that is mysteriously protected by ferocious snakes, the miraculous transformation of an ordinary-looking child into a snake-man when he is fed the ashes of an *ichchadhari naga*, to the all-powerful *sadhu* (sage), whose untold mental powers far exceed any known physical powers as embodied in Nagraj. Such specific plot devices, but more importantly, the overarching mythical worldview that they represent, are very much part of a well-established orientalism that clearly demarcates the rational/scientific/modern West from the nonrational/mythical/traditional East. From this perspective, *Nagraj* appears to be no different than *Bombaby*, an American comic that also draws upon orientalist stereotypes regarding Indian mythology and culture (cf. Basu). There is, however, a crucial difference between the two — the difference in intended audience, and consequently, the impact of such so-called orientalist material. While *Bombaby* is clearly meant for a Western, specifically, American, audience (as is evident by its place of publication and distribution), *Nagraj* is very much confined not just to an Indian readership, but more specifically to a vernacular readership, since very few Nagraj comics have been translated into English. And this regional specificity means that while for the majority of the audience of *Bombaby*, the "Indian" elements would have the flavor of alien exotica, for the readers of Nagraj, the entire worldview, from *ichchadhari nagas* to powerful *sadhus*, would hold the appeal of familiarity, of a cultural affinity based on easy recognition rather than estrangement. The self/other dichotomy that underpins the reception of an "Indian" comic character in the United States is completely missing in the Indian reception of *Nagraj* which, for its intended reader, is very much part of "self" identity. In fact, *Nagraj* comics can be seen to function as a way of consolidating this "self" through the codification of a specific "Indian" cultural identity. It is this codification that makes *Nagraj* part of the discourse of cultural nationalism that gained currency during the 1980s.

This cultural codification is governed by an ideology of nativism whose invention of "India" is closely related to the orientalist construction of India. Largely ignoring the complex multicultural history of the subcontinent and its sociopolitical dynamism, this definition of "Indian" culture traces its origins to a mythical pre-history and gives it an explicitly, and exclusively, Hindu gloss. Both these elements are evident in the portrayal of Nagraj. Not only does this superhero have close connections with the mythical species of *ichchadhari nagas*, but also his individual origins are in themselves ambiguous, shrouded in mystery and becoming progressively more mystical. The first comic in the series, which is simply entitled "Nagraj," merely makes the hero the abandoned illegitimate child of a rape victim who has subsequently been looked after by a temple priest (who happens to be an *ichchadhari naga*) until the evil Professor Nagmani finds and adopts him for his own purposes. But even this shallow grounding in social realities — the passing reference to rape and the priest's desire to nurture Nagraj into an avenger of his mother — is soon undermined in subsequent comics where Nagraj is associated with Nagdweep, the home of *ichchadhari nagas*, and is crowned their king. This mythical dimension of Nagraj's adult life is then, by the mid–1990s, extended to his origins when, in the volume "Khajana," Nagraj is revealed to be the boon-child of royal parents who was miraculously saved by the snake-god Kaljayi, the family deity, from certain death, and then mysteriously hidden for over 40 years before being found by Professor Nagmani in an abandoned temple. Interestingly, the verbal narrative of this origin story does locate these events within a temporal framework, tracing Nagraj's birth to the early part of the 20th century. But the visuals accompanying this narrative depict Nagraj's birthplace and parents in terms that, by the conventions of comic art established by the *Amar Chitra Kathas*, place them within the realm of ancient mythical India. Mystical royal origins combined with a mythical iconography, thus, clearly place Nagraj outside history. At the same time, the abundance of temples, Devis (goddesses), and Sadhus of different hues in the life-history of Nagraj, as well as more generally, in the plot lines of the comics, roots the entire series in an explicitly Hindu ambience. Even the moral framework governing Nagraj's crime-fighting activities is given a specific Hindu definition when, in the second comic of the series, Nagraj declares himself to be playing the role of "Rama" in destroying the evil Lanka-like network of terrorists who are the contemporary "Ravana." This invocation of Rama most clearly connects *Nagraj* to the discourse of cultural nationalism that began in the 1980s, whose central icon is Rama, its agenda, the re-establishment of Ram Rajya in India, and its symbolic fight, the reclaiming of Ramjanmabhoomi (the birthplace of Rama).

This valorization of a mythical Hindu past does not, however, make this discourse backward looking. Far from indulging in any sentimental nostalgia, this brand of cultural nationalism has a militant focus on the present, on a time when various forces, both internal and external, are alleged to pose a threat to this Hindu identity. The rarefied mythical past is invoked only as a source of strength, as the basis for an identity that enables action in the here and now. Nagraj, the superhero, lives very much in the present; he lives in Mahanagar, a modern Indian city, and fights international terrorism, a very modern form of "evil." Nagdweep, the home of *ichchadhari nagas*, of which Nagraj is the elected King, and Takshaknagar, the birth-city of Nagraj, whose treasure he receives as its rightful heir, are both far removed from this modern India — the first in space, the second in time. His knowledge of these two places, and his association with those belonging to them, are the source of his powers, but these are used to fight evil in the modern world. And this evil, as mentioned earlier, is primarily claimed to be "terrorism," a term and a phenomenon that came to the forefront of Indian popular consciousness in the 1980s with the Khalistan movement that resulted in the assassination of Prime Minister Indira Gandhi by her own bodyguards and the bombing of Kanishka that killed all 329 people on-board an Air India flight from Canada. The global links of terrorist networks, which became obvious during investigations into the airline bombing, and the apparent inability of established security forces to contain this threat to "national integrity," clearly overdetermine the emergence in India, at this particular historical juncture, of a superhero like Nagraj. An extraordinary "man" whose powers derive from a mythical Hindu past but who is launched into the world through a terrorist network, Nagraj embodies the intertwining of the past and the present within this discourse of cultural nationalism. Even at the visual level — in the physical portrayal of Nagraj — we can see the intermingling of tradition and modernity.

While his snake-skin and flashing gold earrings establish his links with ancient mythical traditions, his suit and shades as Raj, the public relations officer at Bharati Communications, place him firmly within the modern global corporate world. Interestingly, it is Nagraj's ancient treasure that makes it possible for him to launch Bharati Communications, an enterprise whose purpose is twofold — to act as a sound economic investment that will allow the treasure to grow, and to provide "good" programming (read "Indian" rather than "Western") to Indian television viewers. The modern spirit of entrepreneurship as well as the power of the visual media are both openly embraced by this discourse of cultural nationalism, signaling its comfortable coexistence with a First World–dominated capitalist globalization and its accompanying consumerism.

Nagraj, thus, is very much an "Indian" creation, a topical 1980s cultural product, that can be read neither as a simple slavish imitation of Spider-Man, nor as a self-conscious postcolonial subversive mimicry of the American superhero tradition. Instead, it may be seen as a occupying a third category — a native "adaptation" — that is neither an attempt to catch up with nor a form of talking back to the metropolitan "original." Instead, it is an Indian version of a commercially successful American cultural product, which, nevertheless, stands independently; reading (and enjoying) Nagraj comics does not require any familiarity with Spiderman or any other American superhero. In this respect, Nagraj is significantly different from the "foreign collaboration" superhero creations that have appeared more recently on the Indian comic scene; whether it is the film *Krrish*, Gotham Comics' *Spider-Man: India*, or the various production of Virgin Comics, all of which are firmly rooted in a global economy at every level, from production to consumption. *Nagraj*, on the other hand, remains local, published from a basement facility located in the semi-urban outskirts of Delhi, retailed through railway bookstalls and fast-disappearing corner stores, and read by a vernacular population that remains on the periphery of the urban-cosmopolitan, upwardly mobile Indian "middle class."

How these comics are actually read by this audience — whether Nagraj is "decoded" from a "dominant-hegemonic position," through a "negotiated version" or in terms of an "oppositional code" (Hall, "Encoding, Decoding" 101–03) — is the subject of another study. But I would like to end with a quick look at one example of how the "encoding" of the Nagraj series in terms of its content adopts a strategy of negotiation rather than either total acceptance or radical rejection with respect to the two dominant cultural discourses — the American superhero tradition and Hindu cultural nationalism — that inform its comic universe. The issue under consideration relates to the "national" identity of Nagraj. In the over 120 Nagraj comics published so far, there is no reference to Nagraj as a specifically "Indian" superhero, as a defender of either "India" or of the "Indian way of life." Nagraj's constituency at all times is referred to more generally as "samaj" (society), and though midway through the series Nagraj does settle down in Mahanagar (a fictional Indian city), his sphere of activities continues to be global. And this lack of explicit national affiliation extends to the comic's visual representations. Apart from a two-part series that focuses on the Taj Mahal, there is no iconographic invocation of India in the comics, either in terms of the artwork or the inking; neither national symbols nor the tricolor scheme of the Indian flag makes any noticeable appearance in individual story frames or the cover pages of *Nagraj* comics. This absence is a significant point of difference from the American superhero tradition, where red, white and blue as well as the "American way" permeate the comic universe of characters such as Superman and Spider-Man (see Jewett and Lawrence 313, Scott 330). At the same time, this absence also silences an important element in the discourse of cultural nationalism whose visual media articulation is awash with waving tricolors and references to "Indian culture," "Hindutva" and the like. One way of understanding this lacuna in the Nagraj comics is in terms of its aforementioned rootedness in the local rather than the global or even the national. The Nagraj universe is regionally familiar within its circulation range, but such regional identity does not require an explicit national affiliation. And this local identification, as mentioned earlier, is very much in terms of a Hindu worldview, so the absence of any explicit invocation of the nation does not actively undermine the discourse of cultural nationalism. However, the affiliation of Nagraj within the comic world with either the local (Mahanagar, or the residents of Nagdweep) or the global (from Africa to America, with help from people of various nationalities), while conspicuously skipping over the national, may also be seen to make Nagraj an embodiment of the "glocal"— a third space that is relatively autonomous with respect to the hegemony of both corporate globalization and militant nationalism. It is this possibility, enabled by the implicit dialogism of the Nagraj comics, that makes Nagraj much more than just an Indianized American superhero; it makes Nagraj symptomatic of vernacular popular culture as a precariously poised space for the articulation of alternate identities and discourses of empowerment.

BIBLIOGRAPHY

Basu, Samit. "The Indian Superhero." Posted 3 July 2006. http://samitbasu.blogspot.com/2006/07/indian-superhero.html (3 August 2007).
Bhabha, Homi. "Of Mimicry and Man: The Ambivalence of Colonial Discourse." *The Location of Culture*. New York: Routledge, 1994, 85–92.
Emmons, Robert A., Jr. "Modernism and the Birth of the American Superhero." Last Updated 19 October 2005. http://www.sequart.com/articles/?article=704 (3 August 2007).

Haldipur, Vrushali. "Indian Superheroes? That's a Myth!" *The Times of India*, 21 July 2004. Available at http://timesofindia.indiatimes.com/articleshow/785204.cms (3 August 2007).
Hall, Stuart. "Encoding, Decoding." *The Cultural Studies Reader*, edited by Simon During. New York: Routledge, 1993, 90–103.
_____. "Notes on Deconstructing the Popular." *Cultural Theory and Popular Culture: A Reader*, edited by John Storey. New York: Harvester, 1994, 455–66.
Jewett, Robert, and John Shelton Lawrence. "The Problem of Mythic Imperialism." *The Journal of American Culture* 2.2 (Summer 1979): 309–20.
"Khajana." *Nagraj* series. Written by Anupam Sinha and Hanif Azhar. Artwork by Anupam Sinha and Vitthal Kamble. Edited by Manish Gupta. Raj Comics No. 60 (n.d.).
Kurien, C. T. *Global Capitalism and the Indian Economy*. New Delhi: Orient Longman, 1994.
Lang, Jeffrey S., and Patrick Trimble. "Whatever Happened to the Man of Tomorrow?: An Examination of the American Monomyth and the Comic Book Superhero." *The Journal of Popular Culture* 22.3 (Winter 1988): 157–73.
Mathur, Suchitra. "Personal Interview with Sanjay Gupta, Founder of Raj Comics." 8 March 2007.
"Nagraj." *Nagraj* series. Written by Parshuram Sharma. Artwork by Pratap Mulik. Edited by Manish Chandra Gupta. Raj Comics No. 14 (n.d.).
Scott, Cord. "Written in Red, White, and Blue: A Comparison of Comic Book Propaganda from World War II and September 11." *The Journal of Popular Culture* 40.2 (April 2007): 325–43.

FILMOGRAPHY

*Mr. India*. Dir. Shekhar Kapur. Starring Anil Kapoor, Sridevi. Producer Boney Kapoor. 1987.
*Shahenshah*. Dir. Tinnu Anand. Starring Amitabh Bachchan, Meenakshi Sheshadri, Pran. Producers Bitu Anand, Tinnu Anand, Naresh Malhotra. 1988.

# 16

# The Roving Eye Meets Traveling Pictures: The Field of Vision and the Global Rise of Adult Manga

*Holger Briel*

In the West (and I use this word in the broadest possible sense), readers of comics have been on the move. In recent times, it seems many of them have traveled from Donald Duck's Duckburg, Calisota, to Tokyo, Japan. By now manga (Japanese comics) are dominating global comic consumption. The West continues to be awed by the size and complexity of the Japanese manga market. In Japan, many manga books appear weekly, bi-weekly or at least monthly, with print runs of up to 6 million each. Since 1995, when the circulation figure for all manga in Japan was a staggering 1.59 billion, the Japanese market has remained relatively stable, dipping slightly only recently. The annual Japanese manga market is estimated at around $5 billion (cf. Watts). Unlike in the West, almost half of all manga are destined for the adult market (cf. Schodt 83). Top manga artists can easily draw seven-figure annual salaries, and publishers make vast amounts of money in the process. In comparison, according to Thomas Dartige, *Bandes Dessinées* manager for the French book, video and audio seller FNAC, the best-selling French comic book of all time was *Le Galère d'Obélix* with 2,950,000 copies sold (cf. *Fous de BD*). However, this figure has to be seen in the context of the trans-age phenomenon of *Asterix* itself. Other comics in France simply cannot match such huge sales figures. The second-highest-selling comic only achieved 670,000 copies (*Fous de BD*). For adult comics, the figures are even lower. In the United States, adult comics engender print runs between 15,000 and 30,000 copies only (cf. Gehr).

Something else the West has not been able to emulate is the versatility of the Japanese comics market. Magazines about gay love produced exclusively for young women (*June*, circulation 100,000), magazines for very young boys (*Coro Coro*, circulation 800,000), magazines for adolescent boys (*Weekly Boys Jump*, circulation 6,000,000), women's erotic manga (*Fixx* and *Comic Amour*, the latter's circulation being 430,000), manga for young mothers (*Yan Mama Comic*, monthly circulation 130,000) and even manga from the AUM sect are available. The most successful serialized stories then appear as complete story books of their own, bringing in additional revenue. Furthermore, fan involvement is also much higher than in the West. While there are fan conventions, the involvement of Japanese fans goes much further; their conventions are huge events with hundreds of thousands of participants. But fan involvement does not stop there. A phenomenon which has only recently appeared in the West is devotee art (*dojinshi*), in which enthusiasts write and paint their own stories based on characters of a certain cult series, or continue a series after its demise. These fan manga themselves sometimes become hugely popular, either in printed form and or on the Internet.

While the rest of the world is no match for such dedication, it is catching up fast. In 2005, manga were a $180 million market in the United States; in Germany, every month 50 new manga appear and thereby capture about 50 percent of the German comics market, a figure holding true for most of Europe. The 2004 sales figures for France, one of the mainstays of European comics production, show that manga had captured more than 20 percent of the market and accounted for almost $50 million in revenue.* Even more recently, in January 2007, manga for the first time completely dominated the comics sales charts in France.

Despite their popularity, problems with the reception of manga abound. Here are only three examples: Until very recently, manga were received in the West as a distinct and exotic "other" when compared to Western comics such as those from the Franco-Belgian school or the American one. The case is, of course, not that simple. One could argue that Japanese comics took this very detour via Duckburg as well. An example: 150 years ago, big eyes were not usually considered to be a sign of beauty in Japan. They are, at least partly, a foreign element in Japanese aesthetics, having been introduced after the opening of Japan to the West in the second half of the 19th century and with further Americanization starting in the 1950s. In effect, then, one of the few defining features of manga that Westerners agree on, the large eyes of manga protagonists, are "fake foreigners" (cf. Donald Richie, passim), as they come out of the Western tradition. This should right away lay to rest any argument along the lines of an essentialist orientalism. It is therefore not a sim-

*http://www.lovemanga.co.uk/date/2005/10/26/). See also Masters.

ple comparison of "them vs. us," but the inquiry has to go much further than that.*

Secondly, one of the doyens of comics research in Germany, Bernd Dolle-Weinkauf, in his 2006 essay on the globalization of comics points out the cultural intertextuality of manga, correctly calling them a "mix" of styles (n.p.). This is certainly true; however, this statement can also only be a beginning. It does not absolve one from finding out what the exact historical and social situation for the mixing of these ingredients was and still is. What is not addressed by Dolle-Weinkauf is that any particular mix is also the local at any given time, with very finicky parameters. The roots of manga by far transcend any cultural mix imported into Japan. They can be traced back to the *Animal Scroll* of the 12th century, a popular satire on the clergy and Japanese society.† Perhaps the most famous forerunners of today's manga artists was the painter Hokusai (1760–1849), whose woodcuts of the 19th century, among them the *36 Views of Mount Fuji* and *The Great Wave at Kangawa*, proved to be a vast visual treasure trove for manga. But the real manga explosion did not happen until the 1950s, and admittedly, foreign sources played a major part in this development. Japan had taken on board the serialization of comic strips from American sources and tweaked this medium to its own needs. And lastly, such a view contributes little to the explanation of why this particular local mix is so successful today all over the world.

A third example: In his 1999 *Système de la Bande Dessinée* (hereafter BD), Thierry Groensteen, otherwise one of the best structuralist analysts of comics, is equally challenged to add manga to his *carrées sémiotiques*. He rightly states that BD are not an object, but a "champ," a field (BD 21), thereby opening up the discussion of different styles and philosophies. For him the BD image is always "un art de fragment et un art de enchaînement" (BD 26).‡ But then he also speaks of the "solidarité conique" of the solidarity of the text and image within a frame, its self-identity in the frame and its reliance on the "bande horizontale" the horizontal order of appearance, as a primary order. While Western comics are also, more and more, breaking out of these molds, I would very strongly claim that neither conic solidarity nor a horizontal reading are as definitive for manga as they are in the Western comic tradition.

---

*In this context, it is worth remembering that the first modern manga is generally considered to be Osamu Tezuka's 1947* New Treasure Island, *taking the Westerner Robert Louis Stevenson's* Treasure Island *as a model. Tezuka is considered to be the father of modern-day manga and became famous with the long-running* Astro Boy *series.*

†*Many parts of the animal scroll, such as the Choju Giga, the Scroll of the Frolicking Animals, are attributed to Kakuyu (also know by his honorary title, Toba Sojo), 1053–1140 (cf. Priest 1953, passim).*

‡*This* enchaînement *that Groensteen claims for comics is also true when looking at the larger picture. In effect, the history of pictorial art can be read as a global comic strip, with picture following upon picture.*

When receiving non–Western comics, that solidarity is shattered. Western sequencing, both visual and narrative, is at least questioned, if not obliterated, by manga.

The question to be answered then is, why this recent Japanese domination of otherwise rather diverse comic cultures? Is it simply the "otherness," and particularly the violence and sexual depictions that attract Western readers, as is often suggested? Is it the cuteness of the characters? Is it the narrative technique? The answer is an elusive one, consisting of various cultural, artistic, religious and economic facets. Within the remit of this contribution I will attempt to sketch some of these facets, but a definitive answer will have to await further study. As such, my remarks can best be prolegomena to a deeper study of the subject. To further focus this text, I have chosen to leave aside the large offering of manga for children and adolescents and concentrate on adult manga instead. Of course, as is the case in Japan as well, the transition from adolescent to adult wares is fluid.

## Viewpoints

Among other factors, manga's arrival was eased by a change in Western readership. While children's comics had gone mainstream in the 1970s, a new comic genre began to appear in the 1960s, at first in the United States, as a reaction to the stringent U.S. comics code introduced in the early 1950s. Those were underground comics, with decidedly adult themes. Robert Crumb, Gilbert Shelton, Larry Welz and others led the way, publishing in small, subversive, bad-quality and small-print-run magazines. Starting from these small circles, a whole alternative network began to appear whose software included music, films and comics, fittingly often sold in head shops. Roger Sabin says of the comics culture of this era:

> The underground is best understood as a product of the profound social changes that racked the West in the 1960s and 1970s[...]. At the centre of these developments was a generation that viewed society as essentially reactionary and bellicose, and which instead interested itself in pacifism, sexual freedom, minority rights and perhaps, most notoriously, the benefits (spiritual or otherwise) of drugs[...]. In America, the first undergrounds can be traced to the mid 1960s — self-published, small-scale affairs, which were often not intended for wider distribution[...]. At the same time, individual "alternative" strips found a home in the American counter-culture newspapers [Sabin 36–37].*

---

*The fact that it was mainly underground publishing had to do with the early 1950s war against comics, culminating in the censorship of almost all violent and sexual content. For an impression of the severity with which this war was fought, cf. the 1948 "Code for the Comics" from Time magazine.

In Germany, it was mostly the magazine *U-Comics* that followed this American example, published by *Volksverlag*, a publishing house associated with the "drop-out" movement (cf. Dolle-Weinkauf 286). In France it was *Fluide Glacial*, founded by Marcel Gotlib in 1975. Teenagers and young adults, having grown out of their childhood comics and weaned on underground texts, were then ready for further adventures in adult comics. As an example, in the 1970s in Switzerland the comics magazine *PIP International*, with its mostly sexual topics, already moved into the direction *Penthouse* comics would go in the 1980s.* In the 1980s, on the back of such successful Japanese children's cartoons as *Astro Boy* or *Speed Racer*, manga and anime arrived first in the United States and then in Europe. In this respect, an interesting research area yet to be explored would be the influence of American underground comics on manga themselves.†

But exactly who were/are manga's audience in the West? It seems very clear that one of the main draws of Japanese comics was their perceived exoticness, and with it, the promise of a new (comic) culture. Making these manga available in Europe and the United States was not all that easy. In his topical essay, *Translating Comics*, Rota mentions a few problems in comic translation from the Japanese:

> As in Japan nearly all comics are in black and white, publishers colored them for the North-American market, which, in contrast, publishes almost everything in full color. However, Japanese comic authors usually employ cross-hatchings and chiaroscuros in a massive way, in order to compensate the absence of color; the mingling of these graphic techniques with colors created a disagreeable outcome, and the effect of both colors and cross-hatchings was spoiled. Soon publishers (and readers, of course) realized this inconvenience, and nowadays no Japanese comic is published in the United States in color. Nevertheless, there are some cases in which the coloring of a black-and-white comic can produce good results, or even improve the original work: Katsuhiro Otomo's *Akira*, for instance, is much appreciated in the edition colored by Steve Oliff for Marvel Comics (thanks to the graphic style of the author, less rich in cross-hatchings), and this version is well known in Western countries today. The peculiar charac-

---

*Cf. http://www.comicguide.de/pics1/large/38757.jpg. Of course, this diversification of the comics market would not only drift off into sleazier areas. Another offshoot, into a very different direction, was the rise of feminist comics. The anthology* Twisted Sister, *based on a comic created by Diane Noomin and Aline Kominsky in 1976, might serve as an example. Furthermore,* Wimmen's Commix *(1972ff) would pick up on 1970s feminist trends and continue to propose feminist issues. With regard to Japanese women and sexually explicit manga, see Shamoon, who gives a compelling interpretation of why explicit eroticism for women in Japan might be more acceptable than for women in the United States. For an interpretation of gender relations in manga, see Izawa. A look into female super heroines in U.S. comics is taken by Klähr and enlarged upon by Merino.*

†*Speed Racer was the series with which in the 1970s Japanese anime came to Germany. However, it was broadcast only for a few weeks, and then very quickly pulled as it supposedly carried "excessive violence."*

ter of the North-American market, which is dominated by super-hero comics, constitutes another cultural barrier. Curiously enough, what in other countries are considered mainstream subjects (familiar settings and comedy, for instance), are here considered minor genres, and are usually published in black and white by small houses. However, super-hero stories, which constitute the bulk of the production of comics in the United States, include many sub-genres, ranging from adventure to horror and from science fiction to magic [Rota 2004, 451–52].

It became clear from the onset that with the introduction of Japanese manga not only did they have to be altered (e.g., the famous *flipping* and *flopping*, of changing the Japanese writing and style to the Western left-to-right format), but their Western markets would also insist on receiving them in different ways and forms. It is worth remembering that comics formats in the West generally differ and range from French deluxe albums and Italy's b/w comics, to a mix of forms, books and magazines in Germany. One example of such a transcultural shift is the German edition of Walt Disney's stories of Donald and Mickey, Walt Disney's *Lustige Taschenbücher*, which started in 1967 and is still running today. While the content is of U.S. origin, the format itself was taken over from the Italian edition and only then proved to be popular.

No matter how tricky these more practical aspects of manga reception were, other, more basic questions in their regard would require answers. The main question is this: How well does such an assembly of text and image translate from one culture to another? What kinds of processes play a role here? While we readily accept that most words need translation in order for them to be understood in another language, is this also the case with images? Are they in need of translation as well?

In his challenging and comprehensive text, *Das echte Bild*, the art historian Hans Belting readily concedes that signs/words are in need of a certain (linguistic) convention in order to be understood. However, images exert more power on their own account (Belting, *Das echte Bild* 8). The commonplace phrase "A picture is worth a thousand words" might be cited to further underline this fact. And indeed, many a philosopher has agreed with this statement. One of the most profound theories of perception came form Maurice Merleau-Ponty. In one of his famous phrases, he rejects the Cartesian model of (self-)understanding and states: "It is not enough to think to see" (Merleau-Ponty, *Phenomenology of Perception* 270). For him, to truly see goes beyond cognition and triggers responses inaccessible via enlightenment philosophy. He declares the primacy of perception over cognition, thereby strengthening the significances of objects vs. the thinking subject. In this respect, the eye is very different from the ear, which is a passive instrument, whereas the eye actively seeks out and excludes/includes materials in its view, thereby pretending to be dealing with objective phenomena.* In this way, the innocent "to see" always already is "to theorize what one sees."

This is of course not to say that we do not interpret what we see. Humans tend to do this continually in a subconscious way, but according to Merleau-Ponty, there are at least two different modes of perception: Perception is effected either through *associative* or through *focused* attention. Focused attention happens when there is a strong directive bond between our mind and the items viewed, for example, when attempting to find our way on the road. Our vision will search out items that experience has taught us will help us in our quest to find the way — road signs, topographical particularities, etc. Associative perception, on the other hand, would celebrate the being lost on the road, as it is only then that we will truly be open to the images presenting themselves to us. Merleau-Ponty readily admits that the first kind of perception is necessary, but that the second has been overlooked for too long. I would claim the second one as particularly fruitful when perceiving the culturally "other" image.† It is the open road of these phenomena that intrigues us, questioning our pedestrian understanding of things. Furthermore, with his insistence on the relationship between the sensor and the sensed, Merleau-Ponty is able to do justice to both: the sensor in her/his individuality and the sensed as an object, but an object of a very special kind:

> Our experience of perception comes from our being present] at the moment when things, truths, and values are constituted for us; that perception is a nascent Logos; that it teaches us, outside of all dogmatism, the true conditions of objectivity itself; that it summons us to the tasks of knowledge and action. It is not a question of reducing human knowledge to sensation, but of assisting at the birth of this knowledge, to make it as sensible as the sensible, to recover the consciousness of rationality. This experience of rationality is lost when we take it for granted as self-evident, but is, on the contrary, rediscovered when it is made to appear against the background of non-human nature ["Primacy of Perception" n.p.].

---

*Cf. Wohlfahrt 1994. In a similar vein, Lacan had claimed as early as 1964 that the view point (point de regard) is not to be found in geometral space and always already inheres the ambiguity of a jewel (Lacan 65–66). Before Lacan, Wittgenstein had argued for different ways of seeing, privileging the "Sehen-als," an aspectual mode of seeing in need of linguistic interpretation, to be closely linked with a critique of a particular way of seeing an object and also of the object itself (cf. Sample 216f).

†Others have also taken these ideas onboard, for example, Chris Jenks when he differentiates between seeing and observing. For him, much of our modern preoccupation with over-scientification and reification of human concerns stems from the confusion of those two ways of seeing. And in an application to cinema, Laura Marks wants to reclaim visual apperception from an objectifying view by coining the phrase "haptic visuality." Waldenfels, building on Max Imdahl's theories (233–35) differentiates between "sehendes Sehen" and "wiedererkennenndes Sehen" (innovative seeing vs. mere recognizing seeing).

In perceiving, rather than in just observing, we put significance back into the perceived object, thereby doing it much more justice than by mere deduction. Sensation is here understood as *co-existence* between object and subject. Merleau-Ponty even speaks of this act of perception as "voyance," a perceptive act defying rationality. He also uses the concept of the *pli*, the fold, as a metaphor to describe this relationship of seeing and the seen further, whereby the unseen achieves founding status over the seen (Merleau-Ponty, "Eye and Mind" 262). Within the field of perception, these folds allow us to make discoveries and draw conclusions that would otherwise not be possible. They are only possible because the visible is dependent on its opposite, the invisible. Without the latter, the former could not exist. In this vein, the description of the non–Western reception of manga might be described as the reading of a *palimpsest*, as a document written over many times. The original writing (and many of its cultural subplots) has been erased and overwritten. Much of it has become invisible or at least indecipherable. And yet, the power of the image continues to live on despite, or perhaps because of, much of its previous sense being invisible.

To take this further, in a text from 1998, *Der Ort der Bilder*, the art historian Hans Belting uses the concept of palimpsest to describe how the individual becomes the sole reserve of vanishing pictures in a medial society: "Wir reisen unaufhaltsam im anonymen Verkehrssystem der Räume und kommunizieren im weltweiten System der Netze. In dieser neuen Welt verschwinden Orte aber nicht spurenlos, sondern bilden ein mehrschichtiges 'Palimpsest'" (38).

Manga traveling from Japan are precisely such "already scraped" and overwritten texts by people, epochs, fads and interacting cultures. When they arrive in the West, they receive yet another layer of reception by specific subjects in a specific historic situation. Of course, in the traveling process, much of the cultural referents are lost or at least altered. But this is a general occurrence that happens in any translation. However, there are ways of softening this loss, as much is gained in the transference as well. Rather than decrying the loss of cultural referents, for Belting, these traveling pictures are one of the last resorts in which fading local cultures might survive:

> Im Global Village stoßen wir auf einen Bewohner, der immer auch Einzelgänger, Reisender und auf seinen Reisen Partisan ehemaliger lokaler Kulturen ist. Er bleibt der Ort der Bilder, die ohne ihn im Leeren zirkulieren würden[...]. Der nomadische Weltbürger, der an keinem geographischen Ort mehr zuhause ist, trägt Bilder in sich, denen er noch einmal einen Ort mit vergänglichem Leben, mit seinem eigenen gibt ["Der Ort der Bilder" 39, 41].

In a telling passage, Belting uses the image of a Malaysian rice field as an example and contends that as *aesthetic product* it nowadays almost only exists away from Malaysia ("Der Ort der Bilder" 45–46). Might I be so bold as to suggest that Japanese (visual) culture as an *aesthetic product* also survives if not best, at least very well, in the pages of manga?

One last concept might also prove helpful here. It is the one proposed by the art theoretician Erwin Panofsky. In *Studies in Iconology,* he differentiates between pre-iconographic, iconographic and iconological interpretations (15–32). Pre-iconographic interpretation would simply look at the composition of an image in terms of color, lines, shapes and similar imagistic vocabulary. An iconographic interpretation would require the knowledge of "sujet," historic period and perhaps also artist. Lastly, the iconological interpretation would then build on the previous two and open up new ways of seeing an image. It seems that the first two steps might very well be possible when viewing a document from another culture. The third step, the iconological interpretation, might differ considerably when comparing receptions from within a culture as when receiving it as a culturally other. However, if one has taken the second step, the third kind of interpretation, even if differing considerably from a more "native" one, cannot be considered wrong. Indeed, as Belting suggested in the passage quoted above, the non-native interpretation might reveal things a native one cannot.

While nobody would doubt the global power of images, there are nevertheless important provisos to be made. Depending on where one is situated in this world, the associations evoked by an image might be very different. To take the globally "most valuable brand" as an example: the poster of a Coca Cola bottle will evoke different reactions from viewers in the United States than from those in Iran. And while this has to do with more recent histories, it clarifies the point I am trying to make: pictures are perceived in a very particular and culturally dependent way.*

## Stories of Seeing — The West

In Western history, images have been dealt with in very specific ways. Their receptions are connected to the history of linguistic signs. In many ways, the history of images moves between pure idolatry and abject rejection. In his aforementioned texts, Belting argues that the adoration of images came to a halt for the first time with the reception of the Ten Commandments by Moses, a text supposedly manufactured by the only true god and replacing

---

*Arthur Danto is one of the philosophers who insist that there exists a global picture language (Danto 2004, 144). I would agree with him, but only up to a certain point. As the above-cited example illustrates, even the same image can evoke rapidly different reactions. And yet, this universality still exists, albeit in a more limited form. One might think about the iconicity applied by a company such as the furniture shop Ikea. Their wordless manuals are designed to work anywhere, with people expected to be able to follow iconic instructions only. However, this works only once they've been introduced to Ikea's "language," which admittedly is a very basic one, but one that needs to be learned nevertheless.*

the worship of images. Words superseded images. This would remain the case until Jesus was born. Within the Christian cosmology, with his birth, word had become flesh. But while this should have put to rest the argument once and for all, this was hardly the end of the story. A battle would commence which is still continuing today, with the dominance of media by the word or the image at stake. For the first 300 to 500 years after Jesus' birth, words clearly had the upper hand.* It would take until A.D. 500 to find paintings of Jesus, and even until the Renaissance to find nonreligious paintings in the West. And while there existed several iconoclastic movements, the image always returned triumphant.† In this regard it is worth remembering that the visual adoration of Christ was not a new artistic moment but had had secular predecessors in the painting and sculpting of emperors and nobles.

With a deeper feeling of iconicity relegated to the Eastern Church as early as the late first millennium, the onset of the Renaissance changed the situation even further. With the arrival of the Gutenberg era in particular, images lost their remaining truth claim to, by now omnipresent, writing. Belting describes the resulting situation for paintings as "enlightened iconoclasm," with paintings having lost their remaining claim to any supernatural religious status.‡ Their supernaturality and truth claim would however not be lost, but would return in the guise of the aesthetic of the sublime. In the Renaissance and Reformation, dealing with religious images would get even more complicated. As the word had become the new fetish, paintings were also asked to take sides. Painters had to decide whether they wanted to paint in a Catholic or in a Protestant way, in each case following certain stringent conventions. And the winning ways of the book would permeate paintings even further. Paintings started to become formatted like books, with the triptych on the alter changing into a diptych reminiscent of an opened book, as was the case with many of Cranach's paintings. Already here we can see that the reception of paintings differed in major philosophical aspects from user group to user group and depended on which kind of iconographic background one hailed from. Still, one has to keep in mind that all these different approaches originated from the same cultural realm.

Another development that would take place during the Renaissance and undermine any seeming truth content of paintings was the introduction of perspectivism in Italy by Leon Battista Alberti (1404–1472), the painting

---

*Cf. Bauch, who he traces the reduction of the image (Jesus on the cross) to a sign (the cross) in the name of Christianity.

†The issue mostly revolved around the divine nature of Christ and how this could be banned onto a canvas. As in Islam, many influential church fathers believed it to be sacrilegious to paint a god.

‡This claim to divine intervention still existed in the Byzantine Orthodox Church, for instance with the acclaimed Acheiropoietos (an icon reputedly not made by human hands).

technique in which closer objects would be painted in larger forms than objects further away in order to give a painting depth.* From now on, painters could claim to be nearing representational truth only if they "lied" in the process of painting the picture.† Equally important, there existed another moment in paintings that undermined any "truth-claim": letters as signifiers of either an accepted source, such as the initials of the evangelists, the INRI itself, or, and this brings us to the modern age, the initials or the name of the painter.

More so than ever before, paintings became artifacts positioned between the ambiguity of life and mediality. And this mediality would increase further as the auratization of the initials of religious figures gave way to the auratization and market capitalization of painters' initials on their paintings. Any signature would take away from the illusion of the painting, becoming a fetishizing manner of assigning value to a painting. In Japanese and Chinese traditional painting the illusion of truth had never existed in such a form. Perhaps sensitized to the issue by the fact that ideogrammata bear a much closer resemblance to paintings than the Latin script, traditional Chinese and Japanese paintings always prominently incorporated letters and comments within their frames. In this way, what was deemed an illusion in the West, that is, the painting as true image or representation of a certain reality, had never really existed as such in the East. Hence, it was much easier for the Eastern visual tradition to accept the *Picture/Image* of comics than it was for the West, where an iconoclastic distrust of the image lingers on even today.‡

## STORIES OF SEEING—JAPAN

The history of seeing was encoded in Japan quite differently.§ And while many similarities exist between the Western and the Eastern ways of viewing

---

*While Alberti is usually credited with having "invented" the theory of perspectivism, its practice can already been observed in Giotto's frescoes around 100 years prior to Alberti, and even in frescoes stemming from Pompeij.

†Incidentally, this "lying" of the painting would put it into close proximity to the then emerging narrative form of the novel, which ever since its invention by Cervantes was also charged with "lying" about reality. It seems that these kinds of "lies" are dangerous to any powers that be as they are questioning traditional patterns of interpretation. In a more general stance, and in Lacan's wake, Bernhard Lypp has pointed out that a mirror always offers us the alternative that: 1) whatever we see in a mirror is true representation or 2) whatever we see in a mirror is a lie, because we cannot be in two places at the same time (cf. 436–39).

‡Proof of this is the still-continuing fight of conservative newspapers such as Le Figaro, The Times or the Frankfurter Allgemeine Zeitung *against pictures, and colored ones at that, on their front pages, an area traditionally reserved for sense created by linguistic symbols alone.*

§*The following can of course only be a brief and unjust rendition of the vast topic of Japanese art. For a more extensive treatment of this topic, I would direct readers to the texts by Mason, Sadao, Ohashi, Lambourne and Yamamoto listed in the bibliography.*

images, one has to be aware of major differences as well. Early Japanese art depicted Buddhist religious imagery, which had been introduced to Japan by A.D. 552 at the latest. Pictures were even used in death rites, with the belief being that if a dead person held a picture of Buddha in his/her hands, a direct entry into Buddhist paradise would be assured. In a further step, and similar to the West where imperial adulatory paintings were taken as a model for Christian iconography to follow, Japanese painting began to combine Shinto and Buddhist elements in portraiture. While it had been considered "unrighteous" to portrait a person's face during the Heian Period (A.D. 794 to 1185), from the 14th century A.D. onward portraits of priests abounded. But similar to secular movements in Europe, paintings of landscapes (in Japan inspired by Zen Buddhism) became abundant during the 15th and 16th century, replete with a move toward perspectivism as exemplified by Josetu's painting "Catching a catfish with a gourd" from the early 15th century. Furthermore, portraits of courtiers (*Onna-e*) and of battles (*Otoko-e*) broadened popular "sujets."

But the tastes of the wider public also began to be taken more seriously. *Fuzokuga* paintings, depicting scenes from common life, began to appear. Within this field there was also created the mass market wood print, *Ukiyo-e* ("pictures of the floating world"), which would prove to be vastly popular during the Edo period (1603 to 1868) and become a forerunner of manga. *Ukiyo-e* is a wordplay on the homophone term "Sorrowful World," the world of death and rebirth Buddhists sought to escape and left behind by life affirming artistic manifestations. Its topics were thoroughly urban, oftentimes erotic in nature (*shunga*), harkening back to Chinese models, with pictures about kabuki theatre, brothels and courtesans as staple fare. These were popular with commoners and liberally enjoyed by men and women alike. The shogunate did not take kindly to such depictions however, and in the 17th and 18th centuries attempts at censorship were made (1661 and 1772). But only later, in the 19th century, would such topics be toned down in favor of floral elements and landscapes, helped once again by the censorship act of 1842. However, through the introduction of photography this particular depiction of sexuality had started to lose its edge anyway, and would have to wait until the 20th century to be revived through adult *jū hachi kin* ("18-restricted") manga and anime.

As a general point, one can underline the fact that, based on Chinese models, sexuality as depicted in paintings was very common in Japan and was much more widely accepted than was the case in Western art. Thus, while many historic art movements were similar to those in the West, particularities such as a different attitude toward the depiction of nudity within Japanese visual history need to be given due credit.

## Technology

Now that we have looked at the distinctly different histories of seeing in the cultures of the West and Japan (and to a lesser degree, of China and Korea), it is time to turn to the specific conditions under which postmodern receptions of culturally others take place. By the 1980s, Japan had begun to economically dominate the West. Japan was on the rise, was selling cars and electronics as never before, for a while even threatening American economic hegemony. In turn, it also came to be seen as a fascinating cultural other. One outcome was the thematic reliance on broadly Japanese subjects that often manifested a strong reliance on mytho-technological themes, leading to new genres such as cyberpunk. Manga is a prime example of this new influx of the Japanese imaginary. In addition to this the Internet began to appear in the early 1990s, making the distribution of images a matter of seconds. It might be argued that the influx of Japanese manga would have never been as strong, or at least would have taken much longer, if this means of distribution had not existed. Much of manga and anime are now consumed via the internet, rapidly changing the preferred mode of access.

But this was just the setting. It has already been hinted at that technology plays an important part in the reception of images. In the history of visuality one would have to name the inventions leading up to and comprising photography and moving images. Much of what has been labeled the "iconic turn" can indeed best be attributed to technological advances that would in turn lead to new ways of seeing. Increasing visual stimulation is a hallmark of postmodernism, signs usurping the place of pure letters, emoticons speaking of our techno-emotional status quo, Ikea symbols ruling our global private, furnished lives. Conversely, Dadaism and Surrealism had flagged up the infiltration of pictures by words. Hybridizations followed text into image, image into text, to varying, ever-changing degrees. Yet these hybrid pictures are not the same as yesterday's. As a result of technology, human vision is continuing to undergo substantive changes. These changes in vision have their roots in the beginning of the 19th century. Jonathan Crary argues convincingly in *Techniques of the Observer* that alterations in Western vision were preceded by the unbundling of the senses at the end of the 18th century and then furthered by technological inventions of the 19th century. Continuing the paradigm shift that Giotto and Alberti had initiated for art and subjective seeing, the stereoscope, in a much more scientific way, would make people realize that what is seen is not "out there" in reality, but is rather synthesized in their mind. Humans have been trained to "see" by their new visual aids ever since.

The philosopher Vilém Flusser coined the phrase "Techno-Bilder," techno-pictures, for this new cultural material, of which photographs are the earliest examples. Describing a pansocial phenomenon (but he could as well be describing manga), he speaks of the decline of linear codes and the rise of new kinds of visual codes:

> Die Behauptung, dass das Alphabet und ähnliche Codes gegenwärtig eine viel kleinere Rolle beim Programmieren der Menschheit spielen als früher, während die Bedeutung technisch erzeugter Bilder ständig wächst, scheint auf den ersten Blick weit weniger beunruhigend zu sein als die Behauptung, die Menschen könnten immer weniger dialogisieren und seien zunehmend von Massenmedien programmiert. Betrachtet man jedoch die Sachlage näher, so stellt sich heraus, dass es sich beim Umbruch der Codes um eine Umwälzung des Daseins handelt, die so radikal ist, dass sie nur mit jener verglichen werden kann, welche zum geschichtlichen Dasein führte. Nur ist eben unsere Lage so beschaffen, dass die Radikalität der Revolution, an welcher wir teilhaben, von den Kommunikationsstrukturen verdeckt wird [Flusser 224].

The sheer mass of pictures necessitates a rethinking of the relationship pictures — text. For Flusser, this new situation calls for "techno-imagination," for the ability to view these constellations discerningly. This new technological seeing has far-reaching consequences, encompassing reinterpretations of time, space and epistemologies. And, one might add, this new visuality also has a strong Japanese touch. Nicholas Mirzoeff observes:

> A younger generation takes the digital gaze for granted. On the Cartoon Channel, the hugely popular digitally animated figures of the Power Puff Girls deal up the punishment of the bad guys once reserved for male superheroes alone. The Power Puff Girls lack the ripped muscles of earlier Avengers but are drawn in the style of Japanese anime with vast eyes perched on insignificant. These digital eyes emit blasts of unspecified energy at their enemies, much like the mutant Cyclops and Storm in the 2000 hit film *The X-Men*, based on a long-standing Marvel Comics series. The Power Puff Girls are pixilated panopticism, in which the body is a vehicle for visual surveillance unhindered by a self or an identity [11].

Mirzoeff aptly describes the dangers of relying excessively on the visual as the only interpretation of the world. It is the belief in the infallibility of the gaze that needs correction. Viewing the other might help. In this respect, comics, and then especially those that originate from the "Other," are a case in point.\*

Not only do they force their audience to confront new "Vor-Stellungen," but to renegotiate one's own visual decoding mechanisms. At their best, they question one's own vision, one's culture, one's perceptions and notions of the

---

\**After all, Roland Barthes in his* L'Obvie et l'obtus *already describes BD as "mettent en scène un nouveau signifiant" (56). While he had mostly the Franco-Belgian comics of his time in mind, his phrase fits even better when applying it to manga.*

appropriateness of interpretations. Manga lend themselves especially well to this new visuality, as they favor the move away from the narrative, lexical code. In the West, ideogrammata were received as pictorial and not as lexical elements of the panels. At least for non–Japanese speakers, their abundance functions as a surplus visual code, at once heightening the need for visual decoding and subtracting from the narrative one. This is the case not only as a result of their formatting, but also because of their contents.

## VIOLENCE

As already mentioned in regard to the anime series *Speed Racer*, the Japanese depiction of violence has been problematic in the West, perhaps in Europe more so than in the United States. But important points must be raised here. First of all, violence in a Japanese context invariably is of the localized, fantastical kind. Frederic Schodt, along with Scott McCloud — perhaps the most respected manga scholar in the West — underlines this thesis by stating:

> To a high school student in Japan, the notion of getting hold of a AK-47 and mowing down the teachers in his school is clearly absurd, a fantasy. But to a high school student in Los Angeles it is a distinct possibility[...]. The point here is that the inherent stability of modern Japanese society — in particular the stability of family life — may give people more leeway in their fantasy life. And a vivid fantasy life may act to defuse some of the more primal impulses that occasionally come over all of us [51].

This also happens to be the official position of the Japanese government, although censorship continues to be an issue.

Similarly, one could argue that manga are also an escape mechanism from the highly hierarchical, ritualistic and connotative Japanese society. The further away from reality, the better. However, Schodt's belief in the stability of Japanese society seems a bit optimistic. It is true, crime rates are very low when compared to those in the West, but negative attitudes, such as misogyny, do not figure in the official statistics. At the same time the loosening of traditional ways of life, oftentimes initiated by young women having been educated in the West and refusing to go back to these ways upon their return to Japan, alone does not make for a "stable" society. Having said that, Schodt's example is nevertheless not without merit. The argument here is that the fantasy is too removed from life to allow for imitation. A similar and, I believe, successful argument was made with regard to the depiction of violence in the Quentin Tarantino film *Pulp Fiction* (1994). By now, the Tarantino style has become accepted as a fantastic genre sui generis in the West.

There were no more such discussions for his *Kill Bill 1 and 2* (2003–2004) films and his double feature, *Grindhouse* and *Death Proof* (2007), which by far surpassed his earlier film in terms of gallons of blood spilt. But while violence was an issue, sexual depictions received much more attention.

## SEX

Arguably, it was two feature films that raised Western consciousness to Japanese-style animation. The first one was Katsuhiro Ôtomo's *Akira* (1988) and the groundbreaking anime saga *Urotsukidoji — Legend of the Overfiend* (1987–1989) by Toshio Maeda. The latter in particular introduced a new genre of adult anime to the West: tentacle sex. It arguably became the most infamous adult Japanese anime of all time. Why did it enjoy such a success? It could not have been the plot:

> Demons, known as the Machi, have begun appearing in Japan as well as Man-Beasts, known as the Jujinchi. Two siblings of the Jujinchi, Amano and Megumi Jyuko, have come in search of The Overfiend within a young student named Tatsuo Nagumo, a shy lech, who they believe may bring the Jujinchi, the Machi and human race into a promised eternal kingdom based on an old Jujinchi prophecy. Nagumo has begun a relationship with a young cheerleader by the name of Akemi Ito after she is raped by a demon. She begins to understand the circumstances behind Nagumo's destiny. But opponents have begun to conspire against Nagumo, Akemi, and the Jyukos. Could The Machi, Jujinchi, and human race, see the beginning of a New World, or witness The End of The World as we know it?*

Regarding its inception, it is worthwhile referring back to Dolle-Weinkauf and his "intercultural mix." In a recent interview, Toshio Maeda explained that the film had been made before the 1993 easing of sexual censorship laws prohibiting the depiction of the male sex organ. So he had been looking for something legal to take the penis' place:

> At that time [pre–*Urotsuki Doji*], it was illegal to create a sensual scene in bed. I thought I should do something to avoid drawing such a normal sensual scene. So I just created a creature. [His tentacle] is not a [penis] as a pretext. I could say, as an excuse, this is not a [penis], this is just a part of the creature. You know, the creatures, they don't have a gender. A creature is a creature. So it is not obscene — not illegal.
>
> Drawing intercourse was, and is, illegal in Japan. That is our big headache: to create such a sensual scene. We are always using any type of trick.†

---

*http://imdb.com/title/tt0108461/plotsummary (15 October 2007).
†http://www.bigempire.com/sake/manga1.html (15 October 2007).

I don't think this is enough of an explanation though. I would contend that only in a society that already has a predilection for monsters and is used to interacting with octopods such images might arise. And indeed, Japan was such a society. There was nothing arbitrary about this topic showing up in Japanese society. For the Japanese, such depiction would not be a new phenomenon. The depiction of intercourse between a woman and octapodia has a long tradition, going back to Hokusai and his "Dream of the Fisherman's wife."*

Of interest here is the fact that the enjoyment seems mutual and not forced as it mostly is in modern-day depictions of the same *ur-myth*. And it is embedded in the story of an abalone diver named Tamatori, who steals a jewel from the sea king and is then pursued by his minions. The sexual scenes in this story are described as mutually satisfying and Edo-period audiences would have understood them as such. Here, a religious element also plays a role. During the Edo period, Shinto religion replete with animism was resurfacing in Japan, thereby legitimizing such images even further. In terms of anime and manga, other examples of tentacle and/or appendage sex include *La Blue Girl*, *Injukyoshi* ("Obscene Beast Teacher"), *Alien from the Darkness* and *Advancer Tina*.†

I have already hinted at intra–Japanese attempts to enforce censorship of sexually charged images. And indeed, the perceived "weirdness" and "dirtiness" of Japanese adult manga has always drawn the most criticism and interest in the tabloids of the West. Sex piques the interest and sells; this was the case for photography, film, and also the Internet. This is not to say that Japan has a general laissez-faire attitude toward sexual depictions. It is to say, however, that certain manifestations of sexual depiction are historically and culturally more sanctioned than perhaps somewhere else. Japan has always had strong censorship. It was only as recently as 1946 that freedom of the press was legally guaranteed, but for Japanese manga censorship had been intact until the late 1980s:

> Manga had until then observed the explicit prohibitions against overt depictions of sexual intercourse and adult genitalia (derived from an interpretation of Article 175 of Japan's very vaguely worded obscenity laws) as well as a general, more implicit social consensus about what was proper and what was not [Schodt 53].

This led to a surge in sexually explicit material. In 1993 the last censorship law fell, and depictions of pubic hair and sexual organs were legalized, the

---

*http://upload.wikimedia.org/wikipedia/commons/4/44/Dream_of_the_fishermans_wife_hokusai.jpg (15 October 2007)

†For a further treatment of the entwinement of sex and aesthetics, see Yamamoto's explanation of the Japanese term iki (n.p). For more sensationalist accounts, see Gehr and Watts.

former itself an example of a strange prohibition from a Western point of view. This particular prohibition had already led to an extraordinary phenomenon, where Japanese manga were sent abroad to be de-barred (the affected areas in the panels had always been censored with a black bar), and then sent back to be consumed, a re-retranslation with culturally vertiginous effects. Oftentimes, censorship is still hinted at, but rather ironically. Another concession to the Western, especially U.S. market, is the following notice added to manga sold outside of Japan: "All characters [...] are aged 18 years of age or older. No actual or identifiable minor was used in the creation of any character depicted herein" (qtd. Garrett 144). I leave it to the reader to decide how much sense this one makes. The fight over censorship, however, is still continuing in today's Japan in the guise of the harmful books act.*

When it comes to sex, it is worth remembering that just as with visuality, there is no universal sexuality. Western sexuality, as well as other localized sexualities, are themselves always historical constructs.† In her book *Der Wille zur Lust*, Svenja Flasspöhler reminds us how the Western subject of sexuality was created through very specific historic situations: The French Revolution, the perceived death of God and the rise of the subject gave rise to a new, de Sadean writing component. The philosopher Michel Foucault had of course already elaborated on how the modern subject had arisen. Flasspöhler extrapolates from his theories of power and perversion, but underlines the difference between the will to lust and the will to knowledge, which she rates higher. However, she also has to concede that more recently the difference between sexual and aesthetic stimulation has been eroded (cf. Flasspöhler 10). One could also remark that the difference between simulation and stimulation exists in a single "t." Suffice it to say that since and through de Sade, Western art has added the outright pornographic to its repertoire of tropes as a central mechanism for a new, nonmetaphysical subject. In her criticism of the fake reality of pornography, Flasspöhler is unable to differentiate further between various strands of such mediated products. Pornography itself is not a monolithic and culture-independent unit, but rather culture dependant. The reality of adult manga and their erotic imagery outside Japan can therefore also only be fractured, estranged. And since most adult manga are consumed via the Internet, one might even speak of an estrangement of the technological kind.

Lastly, the differentiation between pornography and erotic art has always been a difficult one, if not fatally flawed from the start. Yet, one can certainly make certain observations regarding the appearance of such material. Since 1993, "Adults-Only" labels had to be put on the covers of adult-themed manga

---

*Cf. "A History of Shojo, Loli, and Harmful Books."
†Cf. the texts by Lucie-Smith and O'Toole.

in Japan. When searching for manga on the Internet, one is invariably pointed toward commercial providers dealing in all kinds of categorized pornography. It is fair to say that most commercially viable sex sites have some kind of manga available, neatly partitioned into several segments — tentacles, monsters, gay sex, domination, submission and even straight sex. When looking at single-frame *hentai*, these pictures do not attempt, and herein lies the crux of the story, to give sexual depictions any narrative, let alone sociocultural grounding. Oftentimes, the story the panels tell is destroyed, engorging one of its subtexts into its only raison d'être. Other *hentai*, as comic stories, are not solely concerned with sexual aspects and keep panels intact and/or provide co(n)-texts, thereby, I would argue, at least making an attempt to giving a more rounded picture.

## Ways Forward

Over the last 25 years or so, comics have also been following this iconic turn and have generally emphasized visuality over text. Groensteen rightly asserts that: "[l]'évolution esthétique de bande dessinée depuis un quart de siècle a été dans le sens d'une libération de l'image" (BD 192). Artists such as Moebius, Enki Bilal, Alan Moore, Milo Manara and others might serve as examples.* This movement toward visual predominance had played manga's way, as it is assumed that a picture book with many frames without text is more easily accessible than a conventional Western comic with a stronger textual base. That this assumption is fallacious has, I think, by now been demonstrated. Their visual surplus, particularly the visual usage of the ideogrammata and other Japanese lexical indices, could be read by non–Japanese as *pictorial* rather than as *textual* markers and serve as further proof of the increasing power of the image. Thereby, what Groensteen asserts for all comics is especially true for manga: "Montrer et raconter sont, pour le dessin narrative, une seule et même chose" (BD 192).

One might also state that the West is haunted by the abstraction of the letters of the alphabet because writing has forgotten its visual beginnings and has been suppressing images (and thereby its own history) ever since. In Japan, this relation is rather more conciliatory and one might constitute a tacit agreement between picture and ideogram. However, even this agreement is not final. A case in point is the tradition of those Haiku that are hung on trees so that nature could modify the writing. And Belting ("Der Ort der Bilder"

---

*Incidentally, these are also the only well-known Western comic names in Japan. Yet, their sales figures demonstrate how low their market performance is. In his* Nouvelle Manga Manifesto *Boilet relates the sales figure of only 6,000 copies for one of Bilal's comic books in Japan (Boilet 2001).*

49) tells us of Chinese cliff writing, a way to combine lexis and nature, whereby any writing on nature would invariably be changed by nature itself.

It was again Frederic Schodt who attempted to define the basic difference between Western and Japanese comics when he wrote: "Until recently, many mainstream American comics still resembled illustrated narratives, whereas Japanese manga were a visualised narrative with a few words tossed in for effect" (26). Schodt argues convincingly why manga are such an elaborate cultural system in Japan:

> [In Japan] a 320-page manga-magazine is often read in twenty minutes, at a speed of 3.75 seconds per page. In this context, manga are merely another "language," and the panels and pages are but another type of "words" adhering to a unique grammar. Japanese say that reading manga is almost like reading Japanese itself. This makes sense, for manga pictures are not entirely unlike Japanese ideograms, which are themselves sometimes a "cartoon," or a streamlined visual representation of reality (Schodt 26).

Leaving aside the problematic notion of language being a "representation" of reality, it is nevertheless worthwhile keeping in mind that it is through the emulation of the ideogrammatic roots of the Japanese language that manga has become a mainstay of Japanese culture. And this is also a pivotal point when it comes to their reception in the West: these linguistic roots are not present and hence challenge one's vision, when a translation of reading processes becomes necessary, a remembering of the differences in cultural material available and its processing in the two cultures in question.

One possible reaction of Western artists to the dominance of manga is to incorporate manga styles in their own work, a development that is increasing in Europe and the United States. Another reaction is for the artist to move to Japan. A case in point is the Frenchman Frederic Boilet, who in 2000 issued a *New Manga Manifesto*. He concedes the draw of manga, argues for the Western adaptation of more self-drawn, fan art and then proposes a new gendering of manga, turning "le manga" into "la manga." From a French viewpoint, he reasons:

> Having only been used in the French media for a few years, "le manga" is unfortunately already perceived in a very stereotypical way by both the public and the media. Manga in its masculine form is shorthand for a cheap Japanese comic book for children and teenagers, that is simultaneously violent and pornographic: the Japanese equivalent of the sleazy imported Italian comic books of the past....
>
> We're well placed with our own "BDs" and "comics" to know that stereotypes die hard once they've become associated with a word [n.p.].*

---

*Here, Boilet is certainly pointing out important intercultural facts. Unfortunately, he falls into a stereotypical trap himself in that he "others" sleaze by assigning it an Italian background when it comes

Beyond "le" manga, essentially Japanese comics for a public mostly composed of teenagers, there is "la" manga, referring to Japanese comics d'auteur that are adult and universal, that speak of men and women and their daily life: a manga closer, for example, to the films of Yasujirô Ozu and Jacques Doillon or to the novels of Yasushi Inoue than to *Sailor Moon* or Luc Besson.

Boilet refuses to pit the two styles against each other and searches for common ground:

> When one looks at "la" manga and BD d'auteur, that is to say more adult manga and BDs, the differences almost completely disappear. While many series targeted at specific audiences can only attract their respective fans (either of BD or manga), who are already familiar with, or nostalgic for, the codes and mannerisms of the genre, smooth and innovative albums by Fabrice Neaud or Kiriko Nananan seem to me perfect for readers of BD and manga, specialists and neophytes, French and Japanese people alike [Boilet n.p.].

Boilet argues for a depiction of "the universal realm of daily life." And indeed, so-called slice-of-life manga have become much more popular in recent times, and while incorporating violent and sexual elements, go beyond any such narrow topic. Boilet's own work is also not shy when it comes to sexual situations. Granted, the sexual and violent is inherent in the inception of any technology and perhaps culture, and anime and manga series such as *Death Note* and *Battle Royale*, to name only two very successful recent manga and anime of the more violent kind, will remain popular. But then there exist series such as *Genshiken* (2002–2006), which actually make fun of the other genres and are able to successfully hold their own in the Japanese and, increasingly, the Western markets as well.

The non–Japanese reception of manga is a forceful example of what has been called *cosmopolitanism* (cf. Tomlinson, passim), this globalization arrived at through the global reception and variable local reinterpretation of certain cultural artifacts.* In order to make this phenomenon an enriching experience, learning to go beyond its granted entertainment value is imperative, that is, the refiguring of cosmopolitanism as a *critical* practice. Cultural differences continue to exist despite globalization, and counterfertilizations are quickly becoming the norm. The framework of the analyses of power structures within these "trance-ferences" is helpful in revealing the mercantile interests inherent in mass media production and distribution, no matter where on earth; another panel of this story portrays and betrays its audience, insisting on having changed their vision, immaterially and materially.

---

*to comics. This is despite the fact that other countries, including France, have always had their own share of "sleazy" comics.*

*\*See also the excellent remarks by Featherstone et al. on the globalization of culture (passim).*

In order to understand the rise of manga in the West, one has to look at the conditions prevalent in the Western comic markets at the time. Reasons for their rise were the powerful, seminal texts, an audience ready for new reading/viewing adventures, the technological status quo of society, globalization and the general and still increasing rise of the global visual. Through the use of new visual techniques, human vision might perhaps return to a more primordial sharing of visionary perception, something philosophers such as Merleau-Ponty had always argued was the case already, but which had been decidedly obscured and even altered through the rise of different cultures, or *Ways of Seeing*, as John Berger had titled his influential text. A fear such as Heidegger's, that the world as image, as depiction, would arrest the dynamics of being, are perhaps overly vigilant. Images themselves are highly complex objects that carry within themselves a history and a dynamic of their own. Manga can play an important role in exemplifying this moment. They are no pure pictures. They themselves have undergone multicultural changes during their own genesis, and they also require of their non–Japanese readership a questioning of their own modalities of perception, and this not only in viewing an (exotic) image, but even more so in decoding them. The postmodern visionary is on its way to becoming global not because everybody is seeing the same pictures, but because the *means* of diffusion are becoming omnipresent and synchronous. On the back of this global distribution process, the local returns, adapts and changes content, as the cases of Boilet and his "la manga" and other non–Japanese mangaka aptly demonstrate. Lacan's "appetite of the eye" will and should not be arrested, but it can be trained to include some healthy consumption habits. Manga will certainly have their share in this endeavor. In any case, they rightly lay to rest the West's illusion of being the only global culture.

BIBLIOGRAPHY

"A History of Shojo, Loli, and Harmful Books." http://comipress.com/article/2007/07/17/2307 (15 October 2007).
Barthes, Roland. *L'Obvie et l'obtus*. Paris: Seuil, 1982.
Bauch, Kurt. "Imago." *Was ist ein Bild?* edited by Gottfried Boehm. Munich: Fink, 1994, 275–99.
Belting, Hans. *Das echte Bild. Bildfragen als Glaubensfragen*. Munich: Beck, 2005.
\_\_\_\_\_. "Der Ort der Bilder." *Das Erbe der Bilder*, edited by Hans Belting and Lydia Haustein. Munich: Beck, 1998.
Berger, John. *Sehen*. Reinbek: rororo, 1974 (German translation of *Ways of Seeing* [1972]).
Boehm, Gottfried (ed.). *Was ist ein Bild?* Munich: Fink, 1994.
Boilet, Frédéric. "Nouvelle Manga Manifesto." http://www.boilet.net/am/nouvellemanga_manifeste_1.html (15 October 2007).
"Code for the Comics." *Time*, 12 July 1948.
Crary, Jonathan. *Techniques of the Observer*. Cambridge MA: MIT Press, 1990.
Danto, Arthur. "Abbild und Beschreibung." *Was ist ein Bild?* edited by Gottfried Boehm Munich: Fink, 1994. 125–47.

Dartige, Thomas. "Fous de BD, ces Français—An Interview with Thomas Dartige." *The Guardian*, 28 October 1997.
Denzin, Norman K. *Images of Postmodern Society*. London: Sage, 1991.
Dolle-Weinkauf, Bernd. *Comics*. Basle: Beltz, 1990.
_____. "Comics und kulturelle Globalisierung. Historische und aktuelle Tendenzen." http://www.comicforschung.de/tagungen/06nov/06nov_dolle.html (15 October 2007).
Featherstone, Mike (ed.). *Global Culture*. London: Sage, 1990.
Flasspöhler, Svenja. *Der Wille zur Lust. Pornographie und das moderne Subjekt*. Frankfurt: Campus, 2007.
Flusser, Vilem. *Kommunikologie*. Frankfurt: Fischer, 1998.
Gravett, Paul. *Manga. Sixty Years of Japanese Comics*. New York: HarperCollins, 2004.
Gehr, Richard. "Caught Looking. Sex Comics Come Again." *Village Voice Literary Supplement*, December 1992.
Groensteen, Thierry. *L'Univers de Manga*. Paris: Casterman, 1996.
_____. *Système de la bande dessinée*. Paris: PUF, 1999.
Holmberg, Carl B. *Sexualities and Popular Culture*. London: Sage, 1998.
Izawa, Eri. "Gender and Gender Relations in Manga and Anime." http://www.Mit.edu:8001/afs/athena.mit.edu/user/r/e/rei/WWW/ (15 October 2007).
_____. "The Romantic, Passionate Japanese in Anime: A Look at the Hidden Japanese Soul." http://www.Mit.edu:8001/afs/athena.mit.edu/user/r/e/rei/WWW/manga-romanitcism.html (15 October 2007).
Jenks, Chris. "The Centrality of the Eye in Western Culture: An Introduction." Chris Jenks (ed.). *Visual Culture*. London: Routledge, 1995.
Klähr, Alexander. "Frauenbilder in der grapischen Literatur. Vorüberlegungen am Beispiel amerikanischer Superheldencomics." http://www.comicforschung.de/tagungen/06nov/06nov_klaehr.pdf (15 October 2007).
Knigge, Andreas C. *Comics. Vom Massenblatt ins multimediale Abenteuer*. Reinbek: Rowohlt, 1996.
Lambourne, Lionel. *Japonisme: Cultural Crossings Between Japan and the West*. London and New York: Phaidon, 2005.
Lucie-Smith, Edward. *Sexuality in Western Art*. London: Thames and Hudson, 1991.
Lypp, Bernhard. "Spiegel-Bilder." *Was ist ein Bild?* edited by Gottfried Boehm. Munich: Fink, 1994, 411–42.
Maeda, Toshio. "Interview." http://www.bigempire.com/sake/manga1.html (15 October 2007).
Marks, Laura. *Touch: Sensory Theory and Multisensory Media*. Minneapolis: University of Minnesota Press, 2002.
Mason, Penelope. *History of Japanese Art*. New York: Prentice Hall, 2005.
Masters, Coco. "America is Drawn to Manga." *Time*, 10 August 2006.
Merino, Ana. "Women in Comics: A Space for Recognizing Other Voices." *Comics Journal* 237 (2001). http://www.tcj.com/237/e_merino.html (15 October 2007).
Merleau-Ponty, Maurice. "Eye and Mind." *Merleau-Ponty: Basic Writings*, edited by Thomas Baldwin. London: Routledge, 2004, 290–324 [French original 1961].
_____. *Phenomenology of Perception*. London: Routledge, 2004 [French original 1945].
_____. "The Primacy of Perception." http://www.tameri.com/csw/exist/merleau.shtml (15 October 2007) [originally published 1945].
_____. *The Visible and the Invisible*. Translated by Alphonso Lingis. Chicago: Northwestern University Press, 1969.
Mirzoeff, Nicholas. "The Subject of Visual Culture." *The Visual Culture Reader*, edited by Nicholas Mirzoeff. London: Routledge, 2002.
Mitchell, William J. Thomas. *Iconology. Image, Text, Ideology*. Chicago: University of Chicago Press, 1986.
Moliterni, Claude, and Philippe Melot. *Chronologie de la Bande Dessinée*. Paris: Flammarion, 1996.

Ohashi, Ryosuke. "Zum japanischen Kunstweg — Die ästhetische Auffassung der Welt." *Das Erbe der Bilder*, edited by Hans Belting and Lydia Haustein. Munich: Beck, 1998, 149–62.
O'Toole, Laurence. *Pornocopia: Porn, Sex, Technology and Desire*. London: Serpent's Tail, 1998.
Panofsky, Erwin. *Studies in Iconology: Humanistic Themes in the Art of the Renaissance*. New York: Harper & Row, 1962.
Priest, Alan: "A Note on Japanese Painting." *The Metropolitan Museum of Art Bulletin* (New Series) 11.8 (April 1953): 201–240.
Richie, Donald. *The Image Factory: Fads and Fashions in Japan*. London: Reaktion Books, 2003.
Robins, Kevin. *Into the Image*. London: Routledge, 1996.
Rota, Valerio. "Translating Comics, Translating Cultural Differences." *Translating in the 21st Century: Trends and Prospects*, George Androulakis. Thessaloniki: University Studio Press, 2004, 449–55.
Sabin, Roger. *Adult Comics*. London: Routledge, 1993.
Sadao, Tsuneko. *Discovering the Arts of Japan: A Historical Overview*. Tokyo: Kodansha International, 2003.
Sample, Colin. "Sprachliche Interpretation und projektive Wahrnehmung." *Auge und Affekt. Wahrnehmung und Interaktion*, edited by Gertrud Koch. Frankfurt: Fischer, 1995, 202–29.
Schieb, Jörg, and Uwe Kauss. *Sex in den Computernetzen*. Frankfurt: Ullstein, 1996.
Schodt, Frederik. *Dreamland Japan. Writings on Modern Manga*. Berkeley: Stone Bridge Press, 1996.
Seldes, Gilbert. *The Seven Lively Arts*. New York: Sagamore Press, 1927.
Springer, Claudia. *Electronic Eros*. Austin: University of Texas Press, 1996.
Tomlinson, John. *Globalisation and Culture*. Cambridge: Polity, 1999.
Waldenfels, Bernhard. "Ordnung des Sichtbaren." *Was ist ein Bild?* edited by Gottfried Boehm. München: Fink, 1994, 233–52.
Watts, Jonathan. "Japan in Grip of Blood-soaked Cartoon Film." *The Guardian*, 5 November 1997.
Wohlfahrt, Günter. "Das Schweigen des Bildes." *Was ist ein Bild?* edited by Gottfried Boehm. München: Fink, 1994, 163–84.
Yamamoto, Yuji. "An Aesthetics of Everyday Life — Modernism and a Japanese Popular Aesthetic Ideal, *Iki*." http://purl.org/yuji/papers/papers-e.htm (15 October 2007).

# 17

## *Kawaii* vs. *Rorikon*: The Reinvention of the Term *Lolita* in Modern Japanese Manga

### Dinah Zank

Originally made famous as the name of a literary character, *Lolita* has today developed into a multifaceted term. Psychology, literature, comics or youth subculture — all these fields advance their own definitions of *Lolita*. This is especially true in the case of Japan, where affection for adolescent girls, as well as the development of a protected and idealized image of adolescent girlhood (*shôjo bunka*), has a tradition that can be traced back at least to the early Edo period (1600–1868), if not further. From this source has sprung a decidedly distinctive girls culture, which is nowadays characterized by a highly stylized, cute and childlike appearance and behavior (*kawaii*). *Kawaii* has spread not only through a variety of Japanese subcultures but is now also visible in mass media, especially in manga — a medium that has a decisive impact on the aesthetic perception of most Japanese from their early childhood.

With the recent global success of Japanese comics, the graphic and cultural vocabulary of manga has become common coinage around world, but to gauge the actual dimension of the connected phenomena one still has to turn to Japan. On the streets of Tokyo or any other Japanese city one can spot many adult women wearing pink "Hello Kitty" accessories or come across frilly-dressed girls who proudly call themselves *Lolitas*.

It is interesting to note that the word *kawaii* cannot only be translated as something (innocently) "cute" but also as (decisively not so innocently) "sexy." It does not, therefore, surprise that *kawaii* is also omnipresent in the Japanese erotic industry. In erotic manga, a genre called *rorikon* (an abbreviation of "Lolita complex" in Japanese pronunciation) focuses on the clearly sexual depiction of adolescent-looking girls in *kawaii* style. Despite the often-cited Japanese licentiousness in cultural matters, *rorikon* has ignited fierce discussion among Japanese critics for more than three decades now.

The new wave of manga that has been sweeping across Europe and America since the middle of the 1990s has brought both Japanese connotations of the term *Lolita* (the "cute" and the "sexy") to the West. Where it had been almost impossible to imagine a (female) youth subculture based on embracing the concept of *Lolita* in the Western understanding of the term, the modeling influence of Japanese manga has led to a shift in perception among European youths and has sparked off the development of a *Lolita* girls subculture. However, this new subculture is often wrongly associated by outsiders with the original Western concept of *Lolita*. It is thus important to first trace the significant differences in the development of the term in the West and Japan when discussing *Lolita* in the context of Japanese comic culture.

In Europe, the concept of *Lolita* first appeared in 1916 in the eponymous German short story by Heinz von Lichberg as the pet name for the main character, Dolores. This story provided the model for Vladimir Nabokov's novel *Lolita* (1955), which immediately became one of the most famous and controversial works of modern literature. The plot of this novel is as famous as it is simple: Humbert, a middle-aged man, is hiding in the 1940s in America from the Nazi regime and moves into the house of the single-parent Charlotte and her 12-year-old daughter, Dolores, whom he calls Lolita. The girl reminds him of his long-gone first love, Annabel Leigh, and he decides to marry the mother to be able to stay with her daughter without arousing suspicion or producing complications. When Charlotte suddenly dies in an accident, he is afraid to lose his stepdaughter and takes Dolores with him on an aimless trip from motel to motel. Humbert and the girl become lovers, but Humbert is still trying to exert some kind of fatherly authority, which leads to their relationship becoming increasingly violent. Dolores starts to take money from Humbert for sexual favors and later on elopes with Quint, another man several years older than she is. When Humbert discovers that Quint is abusing Dolores for the filming of pornographic material, he decides that he has to kill him.

Nabokov's successful novel — but also the earlier version by von Lichberg, which differs in many important details from the later adaptation by Nabokov (in von Lichberg's story, for example, Lolita is not a real girl but an ethereal adolescent goddess in an oil painting) — provided for a lot of controversial discussion among psychoanalysts. As part of Siegmund Freud's and C.G. Jung's remapping of the human psyche, the term *Lolita complex* was introduced in the early 1920s into the European discourse on sexual taboos and resulting neuroses. Jung described the *Lolita complex* as a sexual fixation of an adult man on an adolescent girl which is neither still child nor yet woman. In theory, the *Lolita complex* is caused by the trauma of a man losing his first love during his own adolescence, or it results from an excessively strong (and sexual) relationship of a man with his daughter. From the perspective of the girl, her affection for the older man grows out of an equally strong relationship to her father (the so-called *Elektra complex*). Freud, on the other hand, viewed the *Lolita complex* as a kind of sexual perversion that is caused by male fear of a self-confident adult woman or *femme fatale*, which leads to the male need to dominate a weak young woman. The mixture of sexual fascination and disgust, of lust and neurosis described by Freud and Jung has consequently shaped the Western perception of the term *Lolita*, especially since the topic was readily picked up and exploited by the entertainment and erotic industry. As a consequence, the term *Lolita* gained a mainly negative meaning, variously connected with pedophilia or mature women acting innocent and vulnerable to seduce men.

In Japan, by contrast, the development of the term took a slightly but significantly different route. The first Japanese version of Nabokov's *Lolita* was published as early as 1956, but there are no signs that a problem-dominated discourse like the one in the West was ever sparked off by the book. One reason for this may have been that Japan had by then already developed its own, positively connoted kind of idealized girls culture (*shôjo bunka*) in the Meiji-period (1868–1912) and the first half of the 20th century.* Neither child nor married wife, the adolescent girl, for a preciously short period of time, stood outside the rigid Japanese social structure, thus gaining an exceptional position of freedom away from the daily duties and usual expectations of society. The idealization of this status in *shôjo bunka* was influenced by the glitteringly romantic Takarazuka theater, which, to the present day, is performed only by female actors. Another influence were early women's and girls' magazines, which infused female Japanese culture with the Western poetry and art of Romanticism, of the Pre-Raphaelites, and of Symbolism.† This led to the world of adolescent girls being romanticized and mystified not only in fiction and art but, in turn, also in daily life.

Early examples of *shôjo bunka*'s essentially peaceful dream world of adolescent girls are the magazines *Jôgaku zasshi* (established in 1885 as a proto-feminist support for the education of girls by Iwamoto Yoshiharu),‡ and *Shôjo kurabu* (established in 1923 by Takabatake Kashô as a female follow-up to

---

*For an overview over the development of shôjo bunka from 1868 to 1920, compare Gomarasca 33–35.

†Similar processes of adaptation of European art into Japanese manga are still going on today, as can be seen in Yamato Waki's illustration of the death of Yugao in the series "Asakiyumemishi" (1980–1993), which recalls J.E. Millais's painting "Ophelia" (1852). For Waki's drawing, see http://digilander.libero.it/smosites/asaki/AG_08.jpg.

‡For further information on Iwamoto and the Jogaku zasshi, see Brownstein.

the boys' magazine *Shônen kurabu* from 1909). The graphic vocabulary of, for example, Dante Gabriel Rossetti (1828–1882) or John Everett Millais (1829–1896) was thus imported to Japan and blended with traditional Japanese visual narratives. After World War II, influences of American Pop Art underwent a similar process of assimilation into Japanese comics, and the influence of Western art is still very visible in contemporary manga aimed at young girls and women (*shôjo manga*).

Compared to the early 20th century, the situation of girls regarding their education has, of course, dramatically changed and with it also the daily life of the adolescent Japanese girl. In reality, the transitory period between childhood and adulthood is not any longer only the dreamy "eye of the storm" and "just care about your first love" phase idealized in *shôjo bunka*. In modern Japan, teenage girls find themselves living through the often-criticized "exam hell" of middle school, where emancipated young women struggle as hard as their male counterparts for a place at a top-ranking high school, which is a prerequisite for professional success later in life.

But even though times have changed, the mystified image of the adolescent girl's world still looms large in the Japanese mind, and this might explain why Nabokov's novel with Humbert's urgent wish to reconnect to the sensation of his first love and the combination of this with his affection for the adolescent Dolores did not cause much of a stir in Japan. It simply fitted too well into the narrative structures of *shôjo bunka* and consequently has not come to be viewed from the angle of a perverted pedophilia but as an emotionally understandable story of a man wishing to reclaim part of his youth lost during the war by living through his first love again. In Japanese eyes, Humbert's journey thus appears not so much as a guilty flight from persecuting authorities but as a search for a place where to live his dreams, a place he finds by entering the peaceful world of the young girl.

Naturally, the concept of the *Lolita complex* as developed by Freud and Jung is also well known in Japan. But instead of connecting *Lolita* automatically with the *Lolita complex*, both terms remained separated from each other. While *Lolita complex* (*roricon*) came to signify the sexual attraction of a young woman (no matter whether the man is older or of the same age), *Lolita* developed into an essentially positive synonym for the adolescent girl herself. In the Japanese sense of the word, a *Lolita* is sweet and adorable, a young woman idealized to the point of perceiving her as living on a different, unearthly plane. A *Lolita* has to be cared for, and she has to be protected from the ugly sides of daily live. This idealization of the *Lolita* as an innocent and ethereal creature, who deserves adoration from others while staying entirely passive and never drawing attention to herself intentionally, is the main difference in the understanding of the term *Lolita* in the West and in Japan.

This also explains why we find two different interpretations of *Lolita* in the world of Japanese comics. The two views are represented in two distinct manga genres, which are, although very similar in their graphic vocabulary, completely different in context and content. *Kawaii-kei* (i.e., "cute style" or "systematically cute") is a subgenre of *shôjo manga* and directed at a female audience, aged between 14 and 25 years, while *rorikon* is a subgenre of pornographic adult manga, directed at a mature male audience.

During the great manga boom of the early 1980s in Japan, amateur manga (*dôjinshi*) appeared on the comic market and earned their place alongside the professionally published manga. This also became visible in the presence of *dôjinshi* at comic conventions and on the shelves of comic stores. In contrast to the work printed by professional publishers, these manga did not have to care about most of the censorship laws. Accordingly, erotic manga production directed at the male audience of the emerging and quickly spreading *otaku* culture* flourished. *Rorikon* started as a small insider market at Tokyo's comic convention, *Komiketto*, but it is today one of the most successful genres of erotic manga in Japan and maybe in the world.

According to a survey of *The Japan Times* from December 2005, many *otaku* prefer a virtual girl to a real one because virtual girlfriends do not cause trouble, have no expectations and — on top of that — have a nearly perfect appearance (see Kaoru). The childlike appearance of female *rorikon* characters is rooted in the glorification of girls culture in Japan and therefore shares the graphic vocabulary of *shôjo manga*, which create a pastel, harmonic and secure refugium for the reader. The development of the *rorikon* style is also indebted to a specifically Japanese censorship law prohibiting the depiction of pubic hair but not the depiction of genitals in photography and drawings. *Rorikon* is consequently firmly linked with the attraction of a girl looking — but not necessarily being — adolescent.

On the other hand, a female counterpart to the *rorikon* genre developed in the context of girls manga along with the rise in popularity of *kawaii* consumer goods and the hype of girls culture in the mass media. In what was originally meant as a statement against the debasing of female characters in adult manga, a group of young female coplayers embodied *rorikon* characters at the *Komiketto* convention in Tokyo in 1983 and thus unintentionally started a fashion trend that has grown over the years into the *Lolita* subculture of contemporary Japanese metropolises. The new trend was soon adopted for the mass media by pop idols like Matsuda Seiko and other artists (see Gomarasca 40f). The participants in this now fashionable, slightly feminis-

---

*Otaku *literally means "house" or "safe retreat" and describes extreme hardcore fans who retreat from normal social life to life entirely inside the virtual spaces of manga, anime, and video games.*

tic subculture initially called themselves *burikko* (i.e., "fake child," an originally derogatory term describing a woman who dresses as a girl to get the attention of men), but are nowadays much more positively referred to as *rori*. Today, this subculture has also completed the transformation from a mere fashion trend to a complete counterculture of Japanese youths, who rebel against the conformity of the mainstream and still find one of their main platforms in *shôjo manga*.

Typically, teenagers and young adults create a childlike dream world for themselves that is reminiscent of illustrations from children's book classics like Lewis Carroll's *Alice in Wonderland*, fairy tales of the brothers Grimm, or classical Japanese romances like, for example, *Tales of Genji*, a book that dates from the Heian period (794–1185). With what is a new version of the "no future" attitude, the *rori* refuse to grow up and fulfill the expectations of Japanese society (see Kinsella 96). At the same time the exceptional position of adolescent girls in Japan has enabled the *rori* to adopt a post-feminist philosophy of not fighting for equality of the sexes but looking at girls or young women as naturally superior beings. Aspects traditionally viewed as feminine, like grace, beauty, light-heartedness, and cuteness, are embraced as the essence of the new movement. The *Lolita* subculture, which now also increasingly includes boys, thus makes use of a tradition that dates back to the aesthetics of 11th-century court culture in Japan and mixes this tradition with European aesthetics, for example, of the French court in the 17th century or the Victorian age.

A weekly manga series created by Mitsukazu Mihahara in 2002 for *KERA* magazine shows that this ancient tradition is very much present in the mind of the youths. The series was designed like a Tarot game, and two accompanying texts were written by the bestselling author and professing male *rori* Takemoto Novala.* Freely translated, the first text reads:

> This chamber is my kingdom.
> It shelters many different subjects.
> I'm not only a princess.
> I'm the ruler of this chamber's kingdom
> for eternity [10].[†]

The second text deals with the merits of being born as a girl and the flaw of being born as a boy. It thus becomes the confident manifesto of a female *rori*.

> Because I'm a girl I won't carry any heavy things. Because I'm a girl, I merely like to eat sweets. Because I'm a girl, I won't pay any attention to things I don't

---

*For the original Japanese text and images see Mihara/Takemoto 152–53.
[†]First published in Mihara, Chokoleeto 10–11. The original Japanese text is: "Kono heiya wa watashi no kuni. Kerai datte takusan iru no yo. O-hime sama nanka janai wa. Watashi wa konokuni no eien no shihaisha na no."

like. Because I'm a girl, I'll take more than two hours to choose my clothes and hairstyle, put on my shoes, piercings, rings and make-up.

[...] I'm glad not to have been born as a boy. In the old days, boys were viewed as special because they can do a lot of hard work. But today, they only read and watch porn and toy with themselves. One does expect that they will someday work as employees of large firms and will be called idiots if they aren't able to contribute to their country's economic growth. One also does expect that they will be able to protect their wife and children.

[...] I, on the contrary, will never ever change, no matter whether I'll stay single, get married, or will have children. I'm glad not to have been born as a boy, for I'm a princess. I'm an empress. God save the Queen! [Mihara/Takemoto 152, my translation].

Even if this text ironically plays with the clichés common in the glossy weekly girls magazine it was published in, it still gives an impression of the self-concept of the *Lolita* subculture. It expresses the views of the *rori* on job perspectives and the restrictions of adult life in Japan. Against the expectations of Japanese society they hold their determination to remain forever in the dream world of *shôjo bunka* instead of fitting into a society that seems to offer nothing but duties and restrictions. This escapist attitude, which is combined with a proud display of "girl power" and individualism, is the main feature of the modern Japanese *rori*.

Despite its relative popularity, the *Lolita* subculture has retained the character of a counterculture and is still usually seen as a fringe phenomenon even in Japan. Its unruly character is also evident in the fact that the movement is still marginalized by the authorities and often thought to be connected with juvenile delinquency. The undisputed center of the Japanese *Lolita* culture is the Harajuku district in Tokyo, which has often inspired art movements, music and lifestyle trends over the last decades — in Japan and beyond. The personal, handwritten notes of the manga artists, which appear in almost every comic, show that most of the usually female manga artists of the *kawaii-kei* are actively involved in Tokyo's *Lolita* subculture. The comic fans read in these notes, for example, about the artist's recent visit to a rock concert or her favorite design label, about her preferred manga series and her recently bought accessories.* In addition to this, the closeness to the *Lolita* subculture also shows in the plots of the comics, in the chosen aesthetics of the whole manga and especially in the design of the characters. The style of drawing usually employed has been described with the terms *kawaii-kei* or *ultra-*

---

*\*Tomoko Hayakawa, author of the series* Perfect Girl — Yamato Nadeshiko Shichi Henge, *for example, proclaims herself a fan of the Japanese rock bands Sads and Baroque in each volume of her series. She also dresses her characters in the fancy stage outfits of her favorite musicians and the clothes of hip designer labels who follow the* Lolita *trend. Hayakawa is by no means exceptional in this excessive fan behavior but rather acts along the lines of what is common practice among* shôjo manga *artists.*

*kawaii*, which means, as already mentioned above, "systematically cute" or "cute concept" and has shaped an entire subgenre of Japanese *shôjo manga*. Aesthetics and classical design characteristics of *shôjo manga* like overlarge, sparkling eyes, overlapping and floating panels, or symbolic decorative elements are adopted in *kawaii-kei* and then supplemented with cute accessories borrowed from child culture like strawberries, cherries, little flowers, bunnies, or cuddly toys. The fashion worn by *kawaii-kei* characters is especially striking. It is often reminiscent of elaborate court dress of the Rococo or Victorian era. It is the same frilly, fluffy fashion that the real *Lolita* girls wear on the streets of Tokyo, a style that gives both the manga and the *Lolitas* a nostalgic, fairytale look. This nostalgia for childhood aesthetics in *kawaii-kei* is enhanced by the almost exclusive use of pastel colors or, in the case of black-and-white illustrations, by the avoiding of sharp contrasts through the use of an extra-large spectrum of grayscales. The character design of— even by manga standards — extremely oversized eyes, a very small mouth and an almost completely round face is combined with the doll-like, frilly clothing and thus often gives the impression that the characters are little children, even if they are — as indicated by the storyline and by the usual marginal notes — at least 13 or 14 years old.

A comparison between *kawaii-kei* and the erotic *rorikon* genre quickly shows that both genres use the same kind of aesthetics and employ similar sign stimuli. But where in *rorikon* manga the private parts of the characters are usually clearly visible, this is never the case in *kawaii-kei*. Explicit sexual interaction that goes further than a shy "first kiss" is the exception in *kawaii-kei*. In addition to the special graphic make-up, the guiding principle in this genre is the impression of *moe*, a specifically Japanese aesthetic concept that can be translated as "blossoming" and entails a sensual but mainly spiritual perspective that focuses on the moment when a girl first recognizes her womanhood. The concept of *moe* is part of the Japanese tradition of the idealization of adolescent girls, and a famous modern example is Sakura's innocent but longing adoration for her elder brothers' friend Yuki in CLAMP's *Card Captor Sakura* (1995). Sakura's admiration for Yuki is quite different from the loving attention with which she looks after her brother, but her relationship with Yuki is not explicitly sexual either. Her love for him is depicted as pure and — this is typical of *moe*— as much more spiritual than physical. With this aspect of *moe* in mind, one can hardly be surprised to find this kind of "blossoming love" transgressing the usual borderlines of heterosexual love. This can be seen, for example, in Shaoran, Sakura's (male) classmate, who is also in love with Yuki and therefore continually quarreling with Sakura. At the same time, Sakura's (female) classmate, Tomoyo, admires her the same way as Sakura admires Yuki. Her obsession with her best friend goes so far that she idolizes her like a pop star and constantly records her actions on video. The concept of *moe* is thus translated in *kawaii-kei* manga into a concept of devoted love for one's best friend or an idol (this could be a movie star but just as well an elder schoolmate). According to the tradition of *moe* this devotion is depicted as more intense and on a higher, more spiritual level than the feeling for a sexual partner.

A more controversial and sexual take on *kawaii-kei* and *moe* is presented in CLAMP's *Chobits* (2000). This manga was first published in a men's weekly called *Young Magazine* but then published as *tankôbon*, that is, in book format, by Tokyopop, who cater for both male and female readers. CLAMP had previously been known for their splendid *shôjo* style illustrations and opulent, romantic fantasy stories. As could thus be expected from CLAMP, *Chobits* includes most of the common elements of *shôjo manga* and *kawaii-kei* in its arrangement, character design, and story line. A closer look reveals, however, that CLAMP here consciously explore the grey zone between *kawaii-kei* and *rorikon*.

In the manga, a *ronin\** named Hideki finds a computer in the shape of a beautiful adolescent girl and takes her home with him. He is somewhat embarrassed to find that her power switch is situated right between her legs. The moment he switches the android on, she instantly regards Hideki with unblemished adoration. The only word she seems capable of saying is "chi" and thus Hideki names her Chi. Although Chi does not appear to have any programs installed in her, she seems to be able to learn from experience. After a while, Chi begins to develop feelings for Hideki that "persocons" (person-computers) are not supposed to possess. As Hideki also starts to feel something for her, the series then mainly explores the nature of "persocons," human interaction with them, and the nature of love in general. When Chi discovers a couple of romantic picture books of mysterious origin, they seem to awaken something deep inside her. The books inspire her to find the "person just for me," a euphemism used in the series to refer to "one's true love." In the whole series, Chi is presented as very special and, according to the genre conventions, she can thus be expected to find her true love in the course of the series and with that also her own identity.

The pin-up-like poses of Chi, who is mostly clad in frilly mini-skirts, in combination with her childlike, innocent and vulnerable appearance make her a model *Lolita*. As a newly booted persocon she is completely unconscious of her effect on men and is thus unintentionally involved in a lot of sexually

---

\**In Japan, the term* ronin, *which originally referred to a masterless Samurai, is nowadays used for a student who has just graduated from college but has not been able to get into university yet, due to failed entrance exams. These youngsters have to kill time for another year, working in part-time jobs and preparing for the next round of entrance exams.*

charged situations that ironically imitate typical *rorikon* scenarios. This includes unthinkingly changing her clothes in front of a public audience or trying to make her "owner," Hideki, happy by posing like the *rorikon* girls from his porn magazines.

The fifth volume of the Tokyopop series deals primarily with Chi's special semi-consciousness and contains some very interesting scenes, which shall be analyzed in the following. Chi is kidnapped in this volume by a computer freak who wants to find out how she works because she is in fact the only persocon who is able to feel and learn from experience instead of being programmed or relying on a preinstalled operating system. In the ensuing action, which again imitates *rorikon* scenarios, some scenes occur that are very typical for *shôjo manga* and thus identify the comic as not only directed at a male audience but geared in equal measure — if not even more so — to the tastes of a young female readership.

When her abductor searches for her control mechanism, Chi states that only the "one person for her" (this is of course her "first and true love," Hideki) is allowed to touch her there. When Hideki later appears on the scene, Chi guides Hideki's hand between her legs and repeats this statement. If this picture was seen isolated from the rest of the story, one could easily assume that this is the opening of an erotic scene from a *rorikon* manga. Yet Chi is in fact getting Hideki into a severe moral conflict entirely untypical of *rorikon* manga. He and the readers know all too well that it is Chi's power switch that lies between her legs, and so Hideki has to decide if he wants to retain her love or to have sex with her. The latter would erase her memory and consequently her feelings for him due to a loss of power. Following the genre conventions of *shôjo manga*, Hideki chooses "love" and so *moe* — the passionate longing that stops short of the sexual touch — suddenly dominates the previously *rorikon*-like scene. *Moe* here even takes a more complex and intense form than, for example, the rather conventional character constellations of *Card Captor Sakura*.

A second indicative scene occurs in the same volume when Chi's kidnapper considers using her as a sex doll and tries to grab her between the legs. Instead of reacting with submissive passivity like a typical pliant *rorikon* character, Chi defends herself by capturing him with electric wires, a scene that makes for an excellent, gender-inverted parody of the tentacle sex scenes of Japanese porn manga.*

Such parodic moments are no rare cases in *kawaii-kei* manga. For example, the cover of the first volume of Utatane Hiroyuki's erotic manga "*Cool*

---

*\*See* Chobits, *Vol. 5, pp. 68–71, 84–85 and 88. For a discussion of the tradition of tentacle sex scenes in Japanese manga, see also Holger Briel's chapter in this volume.*

*Devices*," which shows two girls in a cat and bunny outfit stroking each other in a sensual way, has a parodic copy in an art book by the girls manga artist Koge Donbo. To understand the symbolism of the images, one has to know that the animal outfits relate to traditional Japanese iconography. Bunny and cat go together as antagonists, a contrast in which the bunny is viewed as truly naïve and cuddly while the cat is a symbol of sensuality hidden behind a mask of innocence. So it is not surprising that a Japanese slang term for having sex is "nyan-nyan suru," which means "to mew." Donbo uses the sexual context of these two iconic animals by placing them next to the superstylized child bodies of the main characters of her own manga *Pita Ten*. In a parodic move Donbo casts the animals in the conventional role of "little angel and little demon on the shoulder," a device that is often used to represent moral conflicts in manga. With this she also indicates that the characters in her comic might look like innocent children but are not necessarily sexually naïve anymore.

It transpires from all this that the difference between *kawaii-kei* and *rorikon* does not only lie in the presence or absence of erotic elements but rather in the way in which they are used. The genre distinction depends much on whether sex is viewed from a male or female perspective. This gendered perspective, which is visible for example in the choice of "camera angle" in the panels or by the plot structure, depends not only on the creators of the manga but also very significantly on the intended readership. The term *Lolita*, which is applied to both *kawaii-kei* and *rorikon* manga, accordingly has come to describe two connected but significantly different concepts. As has been shown above, the Japanese have adopted the term *Lolita* over the decades to their indigenous tradition. *Rorikon* employs the *Lolita* image much along the lines of its original, male-dominated meaning (as defined by Nabokov's novel and psychoanalytic discourse). Yet the term has also been fused with *moe*, a concept of aesthetic sensibility that has long been part of the Japanese cultural tradition. This has allowed for a positive female perspective on the *Lolita* image and has sparked off a new genre of girls manga and a whole subculture.

As manga are now translated and published all over the world, this reinvented female reading of the term *Lolita* is also spreading worldwide. The situation in Germany can be taken as an example. Over the last five years the number of young girls publicly calling themselves *Lolitas* and dressing like their Japanese pop music and manga idols has risen from zero to an estimated 15,000.* Against a background of economic difficulty and social tension at the beginning of the 21st century, Germany has seen a massive rise in the phe-

---

*This steep rise is evident from a recent count on* Animexx e.V., *Germany's biggest internet forum for manga fans.*

nomenon, which has been described in Japan as *otaku* culture. Along with this escapist movement, the connected interest in the Japanese *Lolita* subculture and *kawaii-kei* manga has become an important feature of German youth culture and continues to grow. *Kawaii-kei* and the self-confident *Lolita* subculture seem to hold an irresistible charm especially for female teenagers, a charm of bright and colorful childhood nostalgia and timeless security that is used as a defense against the vague imagination of bleak prospects, which has always haunted teenagers. It remains to be seen whether this new, redefined *Lolita* movement will continue to grow more and more popular over the next decade or whether it will turn out to be a short-lived fashion. Much depends probably on the self-perception of young women. It is safe, however, to say that it is at the moment a colorful, subversive and exciting cultural phenomenon that is no longer restricted to fringe circles in Japan but spreading all over the world.

BIBLIOGRAPHY

Brownstein, Michael C. "*Jogaku Zasshi* and the Founding of *Bungakukai*." *Monumenta Nipponica* 35:3 (Autumn 1980): 319–36.
CLAMP. *Chobits*, Vol. 5. Cologne: Egmont Manga & Anime, 2006.
Gomarasca, Alessandro. "Sous le Signe du Kawaii." *Poupées, Robots — La Culture Pop Japonais*. Paris: Éditions Autrement, 2002.
Hayakawa, Tomoko. *Perfect Girl — Yamato Nadeshiko Shichi Henge*. Ongoing series, 16 volumes published so far. Hamburg: Tokyopop, since 2004.
Kaoru, Shoji. "Sweetness Counts for Women in Search of Geeks." *The Japan Times* 13 December 2005. http://search.japantimes.co.jp/member/member.html?ek20051213ks.htm (1 October 2007).
Kinsella, Sharon. "Dessins à risques: Les *otaku* et le manga amateur." *Poupées, Robots — La Culture Pop Japonais*, edited by Alessandro Gomarasca. Paris: Éditions Autrement, 2002.
Mihara, Mitsukazu. *Chokoleeto*. Tokyo: Index Communications, 2005.
Mihara, Mitsukazu, and Novala Takemoto. "Tarot: The Lolita Pass or Pass for Lolita — Grand Glass." *KERA* 41 (February 2002). Tokyo: Nouvelle Goo, 2002.
Nabokov, Vladimir. *Lolita*. Paris: Olympia, 1955.
von Lichberg, Heinz. "Lolita." *Die Verfluchte Gioconda. Grotesken*. Darmstadt: Falken, 1916.

# 18

## Mangascape Germany: Comics as Intercultural Neutral Ground

*Paul M. Malone*

Japanese comics, or *manga*, have become as hugely popular in Germany over the last decade as they have elsewhere in the world. The context of this popularity, however, and the manner in which it is being commercially exploited, are markedly different in Germany from the circumstances in North America or much of Western Europe, and not merely because the *manga* boom occurred in Germany somewhat later than in the other western nations.

The German comics scene has historically been relatively small. Tim Pilcher and Brad Brooks' *Essential Guide to World Comics*, for example, devotes entire chapters, each over 30 pages, to the comics production of the United States, Great Britain, Japan and France respectively; while Germany, in a chapter entitled "Continental Comics," occupies a mere two pages (three, including German-speaking Switzerland; 189–91). This accurately reflects Germany's status as a net importer of comics culture, to the extent that as of 2006, in Bernd Dolle-Weinkauff's reckoning, "less than 10% of the contemporary comic production [in Germany] is of German origin" ("Attractions" 1). Despite pioneering work in the German territories in the 1800s, such as Wilhelm Busch's famous *Max and Moritz* (1865), "the crucial events that marked the comic in its development [in other countries]—the adventure comic, the comic book, etc., occurred precisely during [the years of Nazi rule under Hitler]," and graphic storytelling in Germany therefore remained "stuck in the nineteenth century" (Gasser 24).* Curiously, while the Nazis exploited almost every mass medium available for propaganda purposes, particularly in

---

*\*All translations from the German are my own; Japanese names are given in Western fashion, with the family name last.*

order to indoctrinate Germany's youth, they showed no interest in producing or disseminating anything like comic books (Fix 165).

These widespread cultural prejudices had little to do with National Socialist ideology. Even after the Second World War, the influx of American superhero and crime comics in the hands of occupying soldiers only hardened the conviction of many German parents and authorities that the victors possessed a far more impoverished and decadent culture than the vanquished (Springman 414): comics were not only resented as a cultural imposition, but also reviled as *Schmutz und Schund* ("smut and trash") that would reduce children to violent, pathological illiterates. As West Germany became more autonomous politically, these criticisms, leveled not just against comics but oftentimes against popular culture in general, ultimately led to a law against "disseminating publications that endanger youth" (*Gesetz über die Verbreitung jugendgefährdender Schriften*) in 1953 (Gasser 25). Even more draconian laws were passed in East Germany soon afterward (Knigge, *Comics* 222).

During the 1950s in the west, essentially conservative artists such as the popular adventure artist Hansrudi Wäscher, with his blond, lantern-jawed hero, *Sigurd*, and the Disney-inspired entrepreneur Rolf Kauka, with his funny animal comic *Fix und Foxi*, managed largely to escape censure and censorship (Dolle-Weinkauff, *Comics* 117–25; 154–57). Other cartoonists, such as Roland Kohlsaat and Manfred Schmidt, published their work in glossy magazines such as *Stern* (Kohlsaat's *Jimmy das Gummipferd*, or *Jimmy the Rubber Horse*, appeared in *Sternchen*, the children's supplement, from 1953 to 1977) and *Quick* (where Schmidt's Sherlock Holmes satire, *Nick Knatterton*, reigned from 1950 to 1961) rather than in separate comics, thus evading the youth endangerment law (Knigge, *Comics* 219–20). These varied and fragmented success stories ultimately failed to contribute to a united and viable West German comics culture.

In the 1960s, however, the rise of a youth-oriented popular counterculture in reaction to the conservatism of the previous decade gradually raised the profile of comics among an audience not primarily of children, but rather of young male adults with rebellious tastes. The publishers catering to this interest were largely originally foreign firms, directed from abroad, selling imported wares: Egmont Ehapa Verlag (founded in Denmark in 1878; established in West Germany in 1951) had long been a licensee of the Walt Disney characters, and in 1968 it acquired Goscinny and Uderzo's *Astérix*, which became hugely popular in German translation (Dolle-Weinkauff, *Comics* 220–21); while Carlsen Verlag (also founded as a Danish firm, in 1899) set up a West German branch in 1953 and moved from children's books into comics in 1967, when it licensed Hergé's *Tintin* (in German, *Tim und Struppi*, which also became a long-term success; Knigge, *Alles* 53). *Donald Duck* and

*Astérix* in particular became popular reading for members of the counterculture, along with the underground "comix" of Robert Crumb and his compatriots (Fix 168, 183; Dolle-Weinkauff, *Comics* 286; Gasser 24, 27).

By the early 1980s, these movements had finally created a comics consumer culture strong enough that indigenous comics artists began to make names for themselves; arguably the most successful, in commercial terms, were humorous artists such as Brösel (the *nom de plume* of one Rötger Feldmann), with his beer-swilling slacker character, *Werner* (1981); Ralf König, whose provocative queer themes found a surprisingly large audience in works like *Schwulcomix 3* (*Gay Comix 3*; 1985); and Walter Moers, who veered from charming comics for children to edgier fare such as *Das kleine Arschloch* (*The Little Asshole*; 1990). In contrast to these artists' popularity, there was a relative dearth of serious adventure or action comics from German artists (Knigge, *Comics* 309–10).

By coincidence, the early 1980s also saw the first appearance of Japanese-style *manga* comics in Germany, when Keiji Nakazawa's autobiographical *Hadashi no Gen* (*Barefoot Gen*) was published as an anti-war treatise by Rowohlt Verlag in 1982 under the title *Barfuß durch Hiroshima*. However, its publication by a firm not generally associated with comics, and under an imprint (*rororo aktuell*) reserved for political texts by such authors as Che Guevara, Bertrand Russell and Mao Zedong (Dolle-Weinkauff, "Attractions" 1), meant that Nakazawa's work went unnoticed by comics readers, while regular *rororo* readers were likely to be put off by "the combination of cute pictures and a truly frightening but moving story" (Jüngst, "Japanese Comics" 87). At the end of the decade, Shōtarō Ishinomori's economic treatise in *manga* form, *Nihon Keizai Nyūmon*, translated into English as *Japan, Inc.*, appeared in German translation as *Japan GmbH* in 1989, published by the business-oriented Rentrop Verlag and, therefore, also overlooked by the comics market (87). Like almost all early Western translations of *manga*, both *Barfuß durch Hiroshima* and *Japan GmbH* were "flipped": the pages, and hence the pictures, were reversed in printing to accommodate reading from left to right in Western fashion, rather than right to left as is normal in most Japanese books, including *manga*.

The first German comics publisher to try its hand at *manga* was Carlsen, who began publishing Katsuhiro Ōtomo's science-fiction epic *Akira* in 1991 in an edition that was not only flipped, but colorized to conform to Western comics practice. In fact, the pictures were taken from the United States translation published by Marvel Comics, though the text was translated directly from the Japanese. *Akira* remained a small but steady seller for a decade, but without reaching an audience outside the established comics community (89).

After several more such false starts, the real German *manga* wave finally began in 1997–1998, thanks to two series: the boys' action comedy (or *shōnen manga*) *Dragon Ball*, by Akira Toriyama, and Naoko Takeuchi's girls' romance fantasy (or *shōjo manga*), *Sailor Moon*. Both *manga* were tied to *anime* TV series and collateral merchandising in a manner that broadened their appeal, and both were printed in black and white, like the Japanese originals. But while *Sailor Moon* (published by Feest Verlag, later absorbed by Ehapa) was flipped and translated from previously published English or French editions, Carlsen's edition of *Dragon Ball* was not only translated directly from the Japanese, but also printed unflipped, so that the reader had to get used to reading right-to-left. As in other countries, this quickly established itself as the gold standard for "authentic" translations of Japanese *manga*, and flipping became an unacceptable and counterproductive practice (91). Ironically, *Dragon Ball* had first been offered to Ehapa, but its reluctance to produce an unflipped edition had offended the Japanese rights holder, Shueisha—who took their property to Carlsen instead and refused to do business with Ehapa for another six years (Rosenbach 78).

The success of these two *manga* started a boom in interest, which quickly threw into starker relief the troubles that were now plaguing the comics industry in the newly reunified Germany. After a strong start and rising cultural acceptance of comics at the beginning of the 1990s, the major publishers had expanded too quickly and saturated the market (Gasser 28; Knigge, *Alles* 69–70). By 2001, as the news magazine *Der Spiegel* reported, poor sales had forced the cancellation of both *Superman* and *Fix und Foxi* by their German publishers, while *Mickey Mouse* and *Asterix* were similarly failing to meet sales expectations. Already in 2000, however, sales of *manga* had surpassed those of western comics, in what Joachim Kaps, at the time Carlsen's editor in chief, described as "a dramatic upheaval" (*ein dramatischer Umbruch*; Rosenbach 78).

With the handwriting on the wall, the established comics publishers began aggressively cornering the *manga* market, entering into partnerships with Japanese publishers and acquiring well-known titles with great speed. Carlsen snapped up such series as *Astro Boy, Battle Angel Alita, Dr. Slump, Dragon Ball, Fruits Basket, Gravitation, Naruto, Neon Genesis Evangelion, One Piece, Tenchi Muyo* and *Yu-Gi-Oh!* Ehapa, under its new imprint, Egmont Manga & Anime (or EMA), licensed *Card Captor Sakura, Cowboy Bebop, Fushigi Yugi, Ghost in the Shell, Great Teacher Onizuka, Gundam, Inu Yasha, Love Hina, Maison Ikkoku, Oh! My Goddess, Pokémon* and *Ranma ½*, among others. A relative newcomer also joined the fray: Panini Verlag (an Italian company founded in 1954) had put down roots in Germany only in 1974; it was mainly known as a publisher of sports stickers until the mid–1990s, when it was briefly owned by the American Marvel Comics and became their European licensee. Now Italian-owned again, Panini publishes both Marvel and DC Comics in Germany, as well as *The Simpsons*; its Planet Manga division hurried to acquire titles like *Berserk, Beyblade, Burst Angel, Fist of the North Star, Full Metal Panic, Hellsing, King of Bandit Jing, Lone Wolf & Cub, Nadesico, Paradise Kiss, Real Bout Highschool, Silent Möbius* and *Tenjo Tenge*. All three firms also publish Korean *manhwa*, which share a similar aesthetic but are printed and read left-to-right, like western comics.

The manner in which the major German comics publishers have colonized the *manga* market is in marked contrast to the North American example, where smaller niche publishers such as Viz Communications were founded to serve the growing *manga* readership (Vollbrecht 458), generally catching the mainstream comics publishers napping and leaving them to play catch-up with mixed success.

To further build their readership, both Carlsen and Egmont (though not Panini) publish monthly magazines with serialized *manga* chapters to introduce new series and artists to readers, similar to the practice of Japanese publishers (Jüngst, "Japanese Comics" 99). These chapters, if they prove popular, are then usually collected into later paperback publications. Carlsen founded the *shōnen* magazine *Banzai!* in 2001; Ehapa retaliated with its own *Manga Power* the following year. A *shōjo* counterpart to *Banzai!*, Carlsen's *Daisuki* began appearing in 2003, the same year that Ehapa brought out *Manga Twister*, which eventually displaced its stablemate, *Manga Power*. By 2005, a licensing disagreement with Shueisha forced Carlsen to cease publication of *Banzai!*, but *Daisuki* survives to the present.

The landscape was shaken up somewhat in 2004 with the arrival of Tokyopop Deutschland. With experience and an almost exclusive focus on *manga* inherited from its American parent (founded in 1999), and under the leadership of former Carlsen head Joachim Kaps, the German Tokyopop quickly overtook the relatively passive Panini to compete directly with Carlsen and EMA for market share. Though many of the properties published in America by Tokyopop U.S. were already in other hands in Germany, the German branch lost no time in bringing out popular series such as *Beck, Bleach, Comic Party, Cromartie High School, DearS, Death Note, Ichigo 100%, Peace Maker Kurogane, School Rumble* and *Sgt. Frog*. However, Tokyopop was also prepared to compete with Carlsen and EMA on another front.

For the importation of *manga* as a subculture also entailed the importation of a strongly do-it-yourself-oriented sense of fandom, in which every consumer of *manga* is potentially also a producer. Brian Ruh has examined the importance of "fan-to-fan pedagogy" in the maintenance of cultural competence among *manga* fans in America, whose "identification with characters in Japanese comics or animation ... prompts them to want to create their own stories using similar methods" (Ruh 378). In Japan, this desire is the basis of the huge *dōjinshi* or amateur comic/fanzine scene, a major focus of fan activity and a potential springboard for amateur *manga* artists into the professional publishing world (380–82). A large number of how-to books aimed at this audience of aspiring artists have been published in Japan, and both translations of these manuals and American knock-off versions have become popular in the English-speaking world (383–86). Most of these instructional books, regardless of their origin, have also been translated and published for markets in Europe, including Germany, where a 2003 survey carried out by the fan magazine *MangasZene* found that two-thirds of *manga* fans also drew their own comics (Holzer et al. 6).

In keeping with this mentality, Carlsen, Ehapa and Tokyopop have not only licensed real Asian *manga* and *manhwa*, but have also cultivated home-grown artists via competitions that can lead to publication in anthologies, magazines, or in paperback form. As a result, in Heike Jüngst's words: "Becoming a *mangaka*, a *manga* artist, has become a job today's German children dream of" ("Japanese Comics" 99). Carlsen, for example, publishes a yearly anthology entitled *Manga-Talente* (*Manga Talents*) since 2002; EMA, in conjunction with Germany's largest annual anime and manga convention, Connichi, has been producing the anthology *Shinkan Special* every year since 2003; and Tokyopop's *Manga Fieber* (*Manga Fever*) is now in its third volume since 2005. These contests are similar to the activities of U.S. publishers (note in particular Tokyopop U.S., with its contest-based anthology, *Rising Stars of Manga*, described in Ruh 387–89), but a distinct contrast to Germany's neighbor France, for example, where the *manga* boom is just as much in evidence, there are probably more *manga* publishers — mainstream and niche combined — and the same instructional manuals are available; yet there has been little or no attempt to promote French beginners as prospective *mangaka*.

There were precedents for young Germans hoping to break into *manga* publishing. In 2001, a Hamburg-born Japanologist had published a two-volume *manga*, *Bloody Circus*, with Carlsen. Jürgen Seebeck (born 1961) had been working as a translator with his wife, Junko Iwamoto-Seebeck, on Carlsen's editions of *Akira* and *Dragon Ball*, and had taken up drawing himself, publishing in several magazines until 1997, when he began the series of short stories that became *Bloody Circus*. Before their print publication, Seebeck's vignettes had actually appeared in Japan as "*E-manga*" thanks to the Japanese publisher Kodansha (Holzer et al. 7); despite this pedigree and a good deal of Japanese visual content, however, *Bloody Circus*' full-color artwork and generally "European" artistic style were not entirely accepted as "authentic" by German *manga* fans (Jüngst, "Manga" 251–52).

Carlsen had better luck, at least at first, with Robert Labs (born 1982), a talented young artist who had won a competition for comics based on the *Tomb Raider* video games, published short *dōjinshi*, and completed an apprenticeship at rival Ehapa. Labs' proposal to Carlsen for his own *manga*, *Dragic Master* (the first word combines "dragon" and "magic," with a soft "g"), was accepted, and the first volume appeared in 2001 (Holzer et al. 7). Far closer to the typical *shōnen* fantasy action style in both plot and appearance than Seebeck's work, *Dragic Master* showcased both Labs' strengths and weaknesses. He is capable of producing panels and even whole pages of great beauty and skillful composition; given the short production schedule, however, such work often alternates with rushed and sloppy sections, particularly toward the end of the book (Jordan and Thau). Before a second volume of *Dragic Master* could be published, Labs began another series, the more science-fiction-oriented *Crewman 3*, in installments in *Banzai! Crewman 3* showed the same weaknesses as its precursor, though its visual style at its best was reminiscent of Labs' influences, Akira Toriyama and Eiichiro Oda (creator of *One Piece*). *Crewman 3* was collected in two paperback volumes (2003 and 2004), but its hurried conclusion bespoke premature cancellation; only afterward was Labs able to produce a second volume of *Dragic Master* (2005), which likewise wrapped up its storyline far too abruptly. Despite these disappointments, Labs had become a minor celebrity as a "star" of the German *manga* scene (Holzer et al. 7). Nonetheless, he had also found the *manga* style too restrictive and the readership too hostile to any deviation from expectations (Kögel); he gave up his Japanese influences, and completed his next work for Carlsen, *The Black Beach: Ein Surfermärchen* (*A Surfer's Fairy Tale*; 2005) in a visual style more reminiscent of American cartoons.

EMA's first attempt to publish a German *manga* failed even more signally: *Naglayas Herz* (*Naglaya's Heart*; 2002) was written by Stefan Voss and drawn by Sascha Nils Marx (born 1965), who was already working as a professional advertising illustrator (Holzer et al. 8). Voss' script is a genial and often witty pastiche of *shōnen*-style fantasy quest adventures, with a close resemblance to Rumiko Takahashi's *Inu Yasha*. Marx's clumsy artwork, however, defeats the script at every turn, puncturing sight gags and reducing most of the action scenes to incoherence. Despite a cliff-hanger ending, there was no continuation — possibly due to Marx's trouble meeting deadlines — until 2005, when a second volume appeared from the much smaller Christian Solar Verlag (Jüngst, "Manga" 259). In the case of both Labs and Marx, the overwhelming workload of producing many pages of artwork on a short schedule, and without the uncredited assistants who aid professional *mangaka* in Japan (Ruh 384), was clearly an important factor in the ultimate failure of their projects.

As Heike Jüngst has pointed out, most of the German *mangaka* who followed in the footsteps of Labs and Marx have been young women ("Manga" 251), either near the end of their high school studies or at the beginning of their postsecondary education; moreover, almost all of the artists in this group have won the chance to be published in the various publisher-sponsored competitions. The preponderance of female artists is itself a sign of the most notable change wrought by the arrival of *manga* in the comics market in most western countries: finally, after decades of comics produced primarily for a male audience, *manga* included a range of themes and genres that appealed to girls and young women as well, thus virtually doubling potential readership (Dolle-Weinkauff, "Attractions" 4–5; Jüngst, "Manga" 258; Hickley), but also requiring female artists as role models, thus justifying the publishers' training them — which is in fact far more expensive than licensing genuine *manga* (Böckem 11).

Carlsen, for instance, discovered Judith Park (born 1984), publishing her tale of near-incest, premature death and cloning, *Dystopia: Love at Last Sight* (2004), and *Y Square* (2005), a comic tale about a student who has no luck with women, and the gay admirer who helps him land a dream girl; Nina Werner (born 1986), author of *Jibun-Jishin* (a tale of adolescent guilt and cross-dressing whose title might be rendered as *I Myself*; 2006); and Christina Plaka (born 1983), creator of the story of a struggling Japanese grunge band named *Prussian Blue* (2004).

EMA published *Orcus Star* (2005), a gender-bending variation on the Orpheus myth by Gina Wetzel (born 1985); *Catwalk* (2006), the story of an albino fashion model, by Alexandra Völker (born 1986); the supernatural comedy *Freaky Angel* (2006), by Lenka Buschová (born 1987); and *Mon-Star Attack* (2006), an absurd alien invasion parody by DuO (joint pseudonym for a pair of young women who call themselves Asu and Reami, born in 1985 and 1986).

When Joachim Kaps left Carlsen for Tokyopop, Christina Plaka followed him, taking *Prussian Blue* with her under the new title *Yonen Buzz* (2005); shortly afterward, the existence of a Neo-Nazi musical group in the United States named Prussian Blue also impelled Plaka to change her band's name to the less euphonious Plastic Chew (Jüngst, "Manga" 257). Plaka was joined by newcomers Detta Zimmermann (born 1987), creator of the magical fantasy *Iscel* (2006), and Anike Hage (born 1987), whose *Gothic Sports* (2006) tells the story of a young outsider's attempt to form an unauthorized high-school soccer team. The list of German *mangaka* and their publications continues to grow at all three publishers (as well as at several smaller presses), though women continue to far outnumber men (Dolle-Weinkauff, "Attractions" 5; Jüngst, "Manga" 257).

The contest-bred *mangaka* of this group, however, like Labs, Marx and Seebeck before them, continue to be beholden to a thoroughly institutionalized but deeply problematic ideal of "authenticity." The very term *mangaka*, which is so frequently used to refer to these German artists by their publishers, the wider press and scholars alike, is a token of this ideal: as Brian Ruh says of the American scene, "the use of the Japanese language is intentional — it distinguishes manga creation as separate from the other types of comic art and serves as a marker of authenticity" (383).

German *manga* are in fact permeated with such "markers of authenticity"; all of these artists' works conform to at least some of the visual and generic tropes of established *manga* styles, particularly those of *shōjo manga*. For example, much use is made of visual elements such as a single giant sweatdrop on characters' heads, signaling anxiety; the X-shaped throbbing forehead vein, representing anger; or simplification and distortion of facial features (sometimes of the entire body) to show extreme emotion of various kinds (see Jüngst, "Manga" 257). Likewise, stories tend to be set in Japan, or in a non-specific locale that could be Japan, though exceptions include Park's *Y Square*, which takes place in Korea; Zimmermann's *Iscel*, set in a kind of alternate medieval Europe; and Hage's *Gothic Sports*, with an unspecified but contemporary European setting. Even when the location is unclear, there is a tendency for characters to be given Japanese (or pseudo-Japanese) names, as is the case in Wetzel's *Orcus Star* and Buschová's *Freaky Angel*, whose protagonists are named Maiko and Hikari, respectively; again, there are exceptions, including again Zimmermann and Hage's works, but also Völker's *Catwalk*, where either Western or completely invented names are the rule.

One element most typical of *shōjo manga* that also characterizes most of these German *manga* is the direct address from author to reader in sidebars within the story, where the artists give background information about the creation of the book, about particular scenes or characters, or about themselves. As Jüngst points out,

> They also use these boxes for the typical humble excuse that is so popular with Japanese female mangaka: They tell the readers how horrifyingly bad the manga is and how grateful they are that the readers have nevertheless chosen to buy and read it. Virtually all female German mangaka do this ["Manga" 253].

Here, however, Jüngst overstates her case; Zimmermann and Hage, for example, do not include such asides, while Robert Labs regularly does.

Of course, the most obvious sign of this false authenticity remains the reversed reading direction, which is now so enshrined that even Judith Park, who is of South Korean background, draws flipped Japanese-style *manga*, rather than in the left-to-right *manhwa* style (Jüngst, "Manga" 253). This reversal is forcibly drawn to the attention of anyone who foolishly opens a *manga* like a western book; all three major publishers provide reminders like the following in both translated and original German *manga*:

> TOKYOPOP: Stop! This is the end of the book! ... To be able to follow the story in a manner that's undistorted and true to the original [*sic*], you'll have to do like the Japanese do and read from right to left....
>
> CARLSEN: Halt! This isn't the first page! This is a comic in Japanese style, and since in Japan they read from back to front and from right to left, you'll have to open this book from the other side....

EMA's warning actually reminds you in both Japanese and German:

> Sutoppu! Koko wa kono manga no owari dayo. Hantaigawa kara yomihajimete ne! Dewa omatase shimashita! "Catwalk" no hajimari hajimari!
> Manga Chiimu
> Stop! This is the end of the *manga*. Please begin at the other end! And that's enough introduction, now it's time to start "Catwalk"!
> Your *Manga* Team

As Jüngst has pointed out, this last strategy is doubly inauthentic: if you can read Japanese, Romanized or not, you likely do not need to be told where to open your *manga* ("Japanese Comics" 92). However, this also underscores the manner in which German-language *manga* imitate not original Japanese models, but rather those models as already translated; thus becoming what Jüngst elsewhere calls "simulacra" or "pseudo-translations" ("Manga" 258).

The idea of producing an original work that must pretend to be a translation encapsulates the tension between conforming to a supposedly exotic aesthetic and simultaneously being promoted as "local talent" for a relatively small market. The negotiation between these opposing poles poses challenges for some artists — as it certainly did for Robert Labs, for example.

And yet this ideal of "authenticity" also creates a kind of virtual community that we might call, with apologies to Arjun Appadurai, the "mangascape," a space where "cultural material may be seen to be moving across national boundaries" (Appadurai 33; see also Wong 26; Ruh 377). In the case of the German mangascape, the priority given to a superficial authenticity in the *manga* form de-emphasizes the actual ethnicity of the *mangaka*, and thus creates an exotic but neutral meeting place for artists of differing backgrounds to contribute to a field that has become "multicultural" beyond the simple opposition of Germany and Japan.

For the German publishers' promotion of home-grown artists, expensive as it is, is easily explained as a vital element in their struggle for economic survival, by reaching and maintaining a previously practically untapped female audience. The residual effect, however, which has gone almost unnoticed, has been the creation of a multiethnic and multicultural in-group that no longer functions merely as an audience, but that feels it has a participatory stake in an aspect of German culture, however marginal and "exotic." Even a cursory glance at the names of entrants who have achieved publication in the various contest anthologies provides a fascinating cross-section of the modern German population: names such as Simone Xie (Basel), Nhung Vu (Munich), Tian Yang (Braunschweig), Nam Nguyen (Pforzheim), Ying Zhou Cheng (Bad Neuheim), Luisa Velontrova (Luckenwalde), Reyhan Yildirim (Brühl) and Eri Maruyama (Erkrath), to list only a few. Such non–German names may not belong to a majority of the contestants, but they are heavily represented among the winners and honorable mentions; whether they are citizens or only residents of Germany, in this context, is irrelevant. Judith Park herself, arguably one of the most successful of these artists, has been described as "a South Korean, but born in Duisburg and living in Düsseldorf" (Holzer et al. 11) — an apparently absurd statement to anyone unaware of Germany's pre–2000 nationality laws, under which nationality was based on descent and not birthplace.

Allegiance to the conventions of an already imported, migrant medium thus unites these disparate artists and allows them equal and active participation in German-language culture without regard to their ethnicity, in a manner very different from the *manga* scenes in either the Anglophone countries or in France. One observer has proclaimed *manga* in Germany "the chance for a healthy comics scene where there is finally something on offer for younger people" ("Riesenaugen"); but it appears that there may well be far more on offer, and to more people, than has previously been acknowledged.

BIBLIOGRAPHY

Appadurai, Arjun. *Modernity at Large: Cultural Dimensions of Globalization.* Minneapolis: University of Minnesota Press, 1996.
Böckem, Jörg. "Sind die süüüß!" *KulturSpiegel* 9 (2006): 8–11.
Dolle-Weinkauff, Bernd. *Comics: Geschichte einer populären Literaturform in Deutschland seit 1945.* Weinheim/Basel: Beltz, 1990.
\_\_\_\_\_. "The Attractions of Intercultural Exchange: Manga Market and Manga Reception in Germany." *Mobile and Popular Culture in Asia.* Asia Culture Forum 2006. http://www.cct.go.kr/data/acf2006/mobile/mobile_0402_Bernd%20Dolle-Weinkauff.pdf (5 September 2007).
DuO. *Mon-Star Attack.* 2 vols. Cologne: Egmont Manga & Anime, 2004–2005.
Fix, Marianne. "Politik und Zeitgeschichte im Comic." *Bibliothek* 20.2 (1996): 161–90.
Gasser, Christian, ed. *Mutanten: Die deutschsprachige Comic-Avantgarde der 90er Jahre.* Ostfildern-Ruit: Hatje Cantz, 1999.
Hage, Anike. *Gothic Sports.* Hamburg: Tokyopop, 2006.
Hickley, Catherine. "Asterix Retaliates as Asian Comics Invade the European Market." *Bloomberg.com.* 26 October 2005. www.bloomberg.com/apps/news?pid=71000001&refer=europe&sid=a6BN0d.7Ttr0 (14 March 2006).

Holzer, Steffi, Martin Jurgeit and Sascha Krämer. "Es muss nicht immer Japan sein: Mangas aus deutschen Landen." *Comixene* 78 (2004): 6–14.
Jordan, Martin, and Sascha Thau. "Comicgate-Interview: Robert Labs — Der Dragic Master im Gespräch." *Comicgate*. Undated. http://www.comicgate.de/robertlabs.htm (9 May 2006).
Jüngst, Heike. "Japanese Comics in Germany." *Perspectives: Studies in Translatology* 12.2 (2004): 83–105.
_____. "Manga in Germany — From Translation to Simulacrum." *Perspectives: Studies in Translatology* 14.4 (2006): 248–59.
Knigge, Andreas C. *Alles über Comics: Eine Entdeckungsreise von den Höhlenbildern bis zum Manga*. Hamburg: Europa Verlag, 2004.
_____. *Comics: Vom Massenblatt ins multimediale Abenteuer*. Reinbek bei Hamburg: Rowohlt, 1996.
Kögel, Thomas. "Interview mit Robert Labs." *Comicgate*. 16 December 2005. http://www.comicgate.de/content/view/224/76/ (9 May 2006).
Labs, Robert. *Crewman 3*. 2 vols. Hamburg: Carlsen, 2003–2004.
_____. *Dragic Master*. 2 vols. Hamburg: Carlsen, 2001–2005.
Marx, Sascha Nils, and Stefan Voss. *Naglayas Herz*. Berlin: Egmont Manga & Anime, 2002.
Park, Judith. *Dystopia: Love at Last Sight*. Hamburg: Carlsen, 2003.
_____. *Y Square*. Hamburg: Carlsen, 2004.
Pilcher, Tim, and Brad Brooks. *The Essential Guide to World Comics*. London: Collins & Brown, 2005.
Plaka, Christina. *Prussian Blue*. Hamburg: Carlsen, 2002.
_____. *Yonen Buzz*. 3 vols. to date. Hamburg: Tokyopop, 2005.
"Riesenaugen sorgen für Comic-Boom." *Stern.de*. 26 August 2003. http://www.stern.de/unterhaltung/comic/337086.html?eid=501566&nv=cb (9 March 2006).
Rosenbach, Marcel. "Frische Ware aus Fernost." *Der Spiegel*, 5 March 2001: 77–78.
Ruh, Brian. "Creating 'Amateur' Manga in the US: Pedagogy, Professionalism, and Authenticity." *International Journal of Comic Art* 7.2 (2005): 375–94.
Seebeck, Jürgen. *Bloody Circus*. 2 vols. Hamburg: Carlsen, 2000–2001.
Springman, Luke. "Poisoned Hearts, Diseased Minds, and American Pimps: The Language of Censorship in the Schund und Schmutz Debates." *The German Quarterly*. 68.4 (1995): 408–29.
Vollbrecht, Ralf. "Manga & Anime." *Jahrbuch Medienpädagogik 1*, edited by Stefan Aufenanger, Renate Schulz-Zander and Dieter Spanhel. Opladen: Leske & Budrich, 2001, 441–63.
Werner, Nina. *Jibun-Jishin*. Hamburg: Carlsen, 2006.
Wong, Wendy Siuyi. "Globalizing Manga: From Japan to Hong Kong and Beyond." *Mechademia 1: Emerging Worlds of Anime and Manga*, edited by Frenchy Lunning. Minneapolis: University of Minnesota Press, 2006, 23–45.

# Interdisciplinary

The following chapters have their origins in a set of interconnected workshops held at the "Comics as Nexus of Cultures" conference, which took place in Lambrecht, Germany, in May 2007. The workshops tied in with the overall topic of the conference by negotiating the special role of comics as being situated and thus mediating between different age groups, between different media cultures, between high art and entertainment, between different regions of the world, and between different academic disciplines. In contrast to the mostly analytical papers held at the conference, the workshops took a more practical approach directed at concrete planning. We felt that the presence of many comics experts, of academics from various fields, and of educators of different professions presented a great opportunity to grapple with some urgent topics surrounding the field of "comics studies."

Four separate but interconnected workshops were held. The participants of the first workshop engaged in a discussion on the possibility, and maybe necessity, of developing a refined "toolbox" of methods and approaches for the analysis of comics, a toolbox that could be equipped with instruments from various academic disciplines (see Haberkorn and Kukkonen's report). While this workshop thus developed something like a methodological outline for a course in "comics studies," a second group concentrated on how comics can be used as teaching tools (in schools and universities) and how comics literacy could be taught both in schools and in already existing academic programs. Two separate groups then took this as a basis to develop units on comics for the widely taught introductory courses in Literary Studies and Film Studies (see the reports by Berninger and Rauscher). In this context, we were especially grateful to also have a linguist among us who could speak at greater length of her experiences in using comics and cartoons in an introductory course on English linguistics. We think that Christina Sanchez's practically oriented paper on this topic effectively complements the session plans that were the result of the workshops.

Naturally, the organizers of the conference and the authors of the reports are highly indebted to all the participants of the workshops for their lively, creative, and also critical input. Special thanks go to Ulrike Behlau for her invaluable note-taking during the proceedings.

# 19

# Workshop I: Toward a Toolbox of Comics Studies

## Karin Kukkonen and Gideon Haberkorn

This is an attempt to capture what was a very lively and insightful workshop on the possibilities and pitfalls of establishing a theoretical framework for comics studies. The participants were Jochen Ecke, Mario Gomes, Dan Hassler-Forest, Josh Lambert, Ben Little, Paul M. Malone, Suchitra Mathur, Anja Müller-Wood, Jan Peuckert, Mareike Späth, Dirk Vanderbeke and Dinah Zank. We thank them for their contributions to the workshop, and thus, to this essay. Special thanks to Jochen Ecke, Mario Gomes and Mareike Späth.

### 1. Problems

#### 1.1 The Paradigm of the Hammer

> *If the only tool you have is a hammer, every problem will begin to look like a nail.*
> Abraham Maslow

Maslow's insight into human psychology neatly sums up the dilemma of developing a theoretical approach to comics. As scholars from many different academic fields turn to comics, they bring the tools of their trade with them. As every set of tools brings an inbuilt bias with it and scholars from different fields view comics with their own specific set of preconceptions, the interdisciplinary appeal of comics can become a double-edged sword.

If art historians look only at the images, film scholars consider only the sequences and literary critics talk about nothing but words, each group looses two-thirds of the comic's meaning potential. This leads to the common misunderstanding that comics are nothing but a bastard art form: "[A]n easy-going intermixture of drawing and text forms the staple of young readers today, the comic book, where one art continually feeds on the other, so that the deficiencies in each art by itself are less noticeable," as Northrop Frye puts it (186). Frye, like many others, approaches comics with the separation of images and words firmly in mind. Lessing's *Laokoon* (1766) laid the groundwork for this understanding. According to Lessing, pictorial art works with space, and literature is the art of time. However, modern media like film or comics work both with images and words, challenging this overly classicist separation of the arts, and calling for a more collaborative theoretical project.

The hammer of simplification is not only wielded by those who concentrate on one formal element of the comic, but also by those who reduce the rich variety in the contents of comics to one aspect. If the only characteristic of comics you analyze is their "exalted code" (cf. Weidenmann), you will ultimately start reading realistic, even sober comics from this perspective. Early comics like *Ally Sloper* (1884) or *The Yellow Kid* (1894) show of course that they have developed from caricatures, yet in the century that has passed since their publication, comics have come a long way from these roots. You can approach comics like *Tintin* or *Astérix* in terms of caricature, but talking about Moebius' work from this perspective would be inappropriate. You can analyze comics as diverse as *Kingdom Come*, *Hellblazer* or *Tarzan* in terms of religion, myth and savior figures (cf. Savramis for *Tarzan*), but using this approach on *Fables* or *Strangers in Paradise* would be wrong.

All of these approaches are valuable tools of analysis, yet, as soon as they become hammers driving in screws, they are worthless. Comics are too varied a field to allow for one thematic approach only, and they are too complex as a medium to be grasped through one classical field of media studies either.

### 1.2 The Catch-All System

While following too narrow an approach is problematic, trying to construct a catch-all system for comics analysis comes with its own difficulties. The most common generalizing approach to comics is semiotics, which allows us to perceive the individual elements of the comic as signs creating meaning through different channels like image, word and sequence. It also allows us to connect the comics text to its cultural context, since the meaning of signs is usually culturally determined.

If used with discretion, as demonstrated in the works of Groensteen or Eco ("Steve Canyon"), semiotics are a very valuable approach to comics. However, as soon as we try to establish a general system of comics semiotics, the trouble begins: Can we analyze both images and words with a theory based on linguistics? Which is the smallest meaning-carrying unit in the images of a comic? The line or the pixel? Which are the units we can determine in any comic? In treating these problems, many comics scholars turn their systems into a mousetrap or a maze. They either reduce their system to a limited number of basic types, which do not cover a good part of the comics production and thus defy the idea of a catch-all system, or — as it is the case a lot more often — they create a catalogue of categories so extensive that the system's practical use becomes questionable (cf. Krafft or Köhn). The complexity of the interaction between individual elements, be they image, word or sequence, is the basis of the system that is comics (Groensteen 28). To truly acknowledge this fact might make the construction of a catch-all theory for comics seem a daunting, if not impossible, task, inviting criticism from all sides. However, it may not even be necessary to create such a Swiss army knife of comic theory.

## 2. THE TOOL BOX APPROACH

Comics studies travel between the Scylla of reduction and the Charybdis of overcomplexity when it comes to theory. Assembling a collection of critical tools, a "toolbox of comics studies," would be an appropriate solution to this dilemma. Such a toolbox could hold the wealth of thematic and disciplinary approaches that scholars from different academic fields choose to bring to comics. More general theoretical structures like semiotics, narratology or rhetorics also have a place in the box. If these approaches and structures are used as tools in order to solve a specific problem, they yield valuable results. By holding a variety of approaches, the toolbox emphasizes the necessity of carefully choosing an appropriate tool for a certain task, rather than always using the same one.

In the course of the workshop, the toolbox was stocked with a wide and varied array of problem-oriented tools. These tools do not form a universal key, but rather a ready set of means to solve specific problems. The discussion we started during this workshop is by no means over: The toolbox is always open for new tools, or for new uses the traditional ones could be put to.

### 2.1 Production and Reception

Comics are cultural artifacts and physical entities — they are created, produced, manufactured, and consumed. The theoretical analysis of both the production and the reception of comics is an important part of comics studies.

Comics can be mass produced by large media companies, as are the classical superheroes, or they can be independent productions issued through small presses or self-publishing (cf. Jeff Smith's *Bone* or Dave Sim's *Cerebus the Aardvark*). They can be produced by a lone artist, or by a large team. Thus the artistic process of creating a comic can be much more complex than that which leads to the average novel. Since many individuals like writers, pencillers, inkers, letterers, colorists, but also editors are involved, determining "the author" of a comic is more difficult, and of questionable merit.

When it comes to the reception of comics, one of the central issues is how comics *can be read*, what specific challenges they pose and what specific opportunities. As this belongs to realm of poetics, we will put it aside for the moment and come back to it under that heading later.

Another question entirely is how comics *are actually read*. Here, empirical research might supplement classical reader response criticism, hermeneutics or more idiosyncratic approaches like psychosemiotics (cf. Packard). Results of qualitative field work could shed light on the sociological dimension of comics: Who buys which kind of comics? What kinds of communities of "fanboys and true believers" does their reception foster (cf. Pustz)? How readily available is a specific comic? How are comics circulated? What is their reputation in society?

Cultural differences also play an important role when it comes to the reception of comics, be it on the level of reading conventions — both Japanese manga and Arabian comics (cf. Douglas and Malti-Douglas) are read from right to left — be it concerning the necessary cultural background knowledge for decoding the comic's imagery. Different cultural communities develop different cultures of comics, different forms and different styles. Social Anthropology, Cultural Studies as well as Art History can provide useful tools for tackling these problems.

Both the production and the reception of comics are important fields in which much original research is possible. The toolbox therefore contains methods for investigating how the artists involved create a comic, how the publishers produce and distribute it, how customers acquire it, and how they then consume or read it.

## 2.2 Form and Content

The divide between form and content has been a virulent problem in criticism of all forms of art for a very long time. Can form be separated from content? Does a certain subject matter require a specific form in which to unfold, or could the content of an epic poem be told just as well in the form of the Sunday newspaper strip?

Some comics, like *Kabuki* or *Promethea* foreground their formal aspects and, thus, achieve what Shklovsky, called the *defamiliarisation effect*. They stress their quality as a work of art over their narrative. There are authors like Alan Moore or Frank Miller with a very distinct *écriture*, who have developed a distinctive personal style even though they work in the streamlining environment of U.S. superhero comics. Other comics, however, try to render their style as inconspicuous as possible. They apply a highly conventionalized form in order to appear transparent as a medium — the "natural" way of telling a story.

Form can be analyzed through poetics and rhetoric but also with the help of the linguistic distinction between the paradigmatic and the syntagmatic (see Benveniste for an elaboration of the terms' background in linguistics). The syntagmatic axis presents the connection of individual elements in sequence, while the paradigmatic axis presents the range of possible elements from which the author has to choose when designing the comic. Talking about reading practices, we could say that the syntagmatic axis represents the linear sequence of panels and the paradigmatic axis the nonlinear composition of the entire page. In both cases, the syntagmatic axis stresses the linear, the conventional, the naturalized; the paradigmatic axis stresses the nonlinear, the eye-catching, the artistic.

There are comics that are mainly a formalist extravaganza, just as there are those that "only" want to tell a story. In the end, form and content are always interconnected aspects, and their separation is a critical fiction. Often, it is a necessary critical fiction because it allows to isolate various aspects of a work. In reality, however — in comics maybe to a greater extent than in any other medium — style *is* content.

### 2.3 Poetics and Rhetoric

The classical fields in the study of literature in which form is analyzed and catalogued are poetics and rhetoric. Both have established a catalogue of devices used, in literature and oratory respectively, to achieve certain effects and to express certain contents. A similar catalogue of devices exists, implicitly, for comics. The spatial arrangement of elements on a page is significant, as is the flow between panels, inside panels, from speech balloon to speech balloon. The structure and shape of the speech balloons hold meaning. Gutters can vary in width, which can in turn be the same all over the page or vary between different panels. Text is usually presented in all caps, using font size, exclamation marks and bold types to indicate loudness, and typeface to indicate tone of voice and even accent. Panels can be detailed or sparse, small or large. Placement, size, and richness in detail of panels can influence the speed with which pages are read. Thus, large, detailed pictures can effectively achieve slow motion, while small and sparsely illustrated pictures can convey fast-paced action. The consistent use of these devices forms conventions that seem natural and thus create a "suspension of disbelief" for the duration of the reading process.

It is here that poetics and rhetoric intersect with the study of reception and culture. No comic exists, as it were, on an otherwise blank canvas. Rather, it is embedded in a cultural background, and read in the context of the reader's mental landscape. A comic, like any other work of art, is a collection of gestures, in the sense that a gesture exists where "a speck of behavior" collides with "a fleck of culture" (Geertz 6). If the comic gestures toward a (fictional) world (cf. Culler 157), comics studies must not only look at that world, but also examine the gestures. The analysis of comics always has to consider both the *what* and the *how*, and structuralist narratology provides a useful terminology for the latter project.

Narratology distinguishes between *discourse* and *story, expression* and *content* (cf. Chatman), thereby identifying elements of structure and elements of manifestation (verbal, cinematic, pictorial, etc.) in a narrative. The structural elements allow us to classify and categorize the story being told. The elements pertaining to manifestation can be used to describe the comic-specific formal elements we can compile under heading of a poetics or rhetoric of comics, a body of "knowledge of the general laws that preside over the birth of each work" (Todorov 6). If Eco's description of the novel as "a machine for generating interpretations" (*Postscript* 2) can reasonably be extended to all works of art, then a toolbox of comics studies needs to contain tools for taking the machine apart, examining the bits and pieces, and finding out how they help the machine do what it does.

## 3. Pandora's Boxes

Comics make for a wide and varied field, and in studying it, we are likely to encounter more questions than answers, and some questions are less likely to lead to more questions rather than answers, and many answers are likely to be unsatisfactory. In the case of some questions, no tool seems to fit — every hammer is too clumsy and every screwdriver is too delicate. These are the Pandora's Boxes of comics studies, tempting us with the promise of heated and productive discussion, yet threatening with the inconclusiveness and the quicksand of neverending debate. Three of these Pandora's Boxes were brought on the table during the discussion in the workshop.

*Can there be a definition for comics, one that is meaningful and useful?* Is such a definition really necessary? Would it be enough to move toward a definition? What would count as progress? Right now, what we have is a number of debates rather than satisfactory answers. It is easy as well as pointless to get bogged down in such debates, and they should not dominate comics studies. Perhaps a thorough description of what comics *do* instead of the inevitably essentialist debate of what they *are* can suffice.

*Does a pen have to be involved in the creation of a comic?* Can it use photographs, without becoming a photo-novel instead of a graphic novel? What about comics that take photos and play with them, digitalize them, rework them? At what point do photos become pictures?

*Is the comic a medium, or a discourse?* Is it a multimedia event, combining pictures and text? What is a medium? The usual answer to this question is: a means for communication. But is a medium defined by the channels of perception it uses, or rather by the materials and processes involved? Do we mean cognitive or sensual perception? If a medium is defined by the mental means of perception, there is a clear difference between the standard novel and the standard comic, because one uses text, the other pictures and text — which are decoded by different parts of the brain. Yet both are perceived via our visual senses, so in the context of sensual perception, novel and comic are one and the same medium. If the medium is fundamentally a technology, or a product of technology, then again, novel and comic are incarnations of one and the same medium: They could be described as different discourses in the medium of print. The medium mediates; it stands in the middle between a sender and a receiver. The discourse is a mental framework, an arena of expression, the context in which meaning is produced. Film is a medium, and radio, and television, and print. If you film words without movement or animation, the product will still be a film. If you print a book of pictures instead of words, it is no longer a novel. And what about the much-touted "digital convergence"? As soon as all media are the product of the same computer, are they then all the same medium?

## 4. Conclusion

Rather than offering a catch-all system for comics studies, a universal key for reading comics, we have argued for a ready set of means to solve specific problems, a collection of critical tools, a toolbox of comics studies. By holding a variety of approaches, the toolbox emphasizes the necessity of carefully choosing a tool appropriate to the task, rather than always using the same one. While this may not avoid the problem that every tool carries an inbuilt bias, it draws attention to that fact, which we hold to be a step forward in the right direction.

The areas for which the toolbox will need to provide effective tools are wide and varied. Comics are cultural artifacts and physical entities — they are created, produced, manufactured, and consumed. Comics, like all works of art, are the intersection of form and content. Like all cultural products, they exist within the web of their culture, incomprehensible if isolated from that context. They are collections of gestures, complicated assemblages of bits and pieces which can be disassembled, labeled, and examined carefully. They can be the source of productive discussions as well as fruitless arguments. Much of the way toward a satisfactory toolbox still lies largely ahead, and parts of it are sure to be messy. But who said it should not be so? The snares are not obstacles on the path; they are the path. They might seem to hold us back, but they actually provide the means for development.

BIBLIOGRAPHY

Benveniste, Émile. *Problèmes de la linguistique générale*. Paris: Gallimard, 1966.
Chatman, Seymour. *Story and Discourse: Narrative Structure in Fiction and Film*. Ithaca: Cornell University Press, 1978.
Culler, Jonathan. *Structuralist Poetics: Structuralism, Linguistics and the Study of Literature*. New York: Routledge, 2002 [1975].
Douglas, Allen, and Fedwa Malti-Douglas. *Arab Comics Strips. Politics of an Emerging Mass Culture*. Bloomington and Indianapolis: Indiana University Press, 1994.
Eco, Umberto. "Lektüre von 'Steve Canyon'" *Apokalyptiker und Integrierte: Zur kritischen Kritik der Massenkultur*. Frankfurt a. M.: Fischer, 1984, 117–59.
———. Postscript to *The Name of the Rose*. Orlando: Harcourt Brace, 1984.
Foucault, Michel. *The Archaeology of Knowledge*. London: Routledge, 2002 [1969].
Frye, Northrop. "Literature and the Visual Arts." *Myth and Metaphor: Selected Essays 1974–1988*. Charlottesville and London: University Press of Virginia, 1991, 183–95.
Geertz, Clifford. "Thick Description: Toward an Interpretive Theory of Culture." *The Interpretation of Cultures*. 1973. London: Fontana, 1993, 3–30.
Groensteen, Thierry. *Système de la bande dessinée*. Paris: Presses Univ. de France, 1999.
Köhn, Stephan. *Traditionen visuellen Erzählens in Japan. Eine paradigmatische Untersuchung der Entwicklungslinien vom Faltschirmbild zum narrativen Manga*. Köln: Harraossowitz, 2005.
Krafft, Ulrich. *Comics lesen: Untersuchungen zur Textualität von Comics*. Stuttgart: Klett-Cotta, 1978.
Lessing, Gotthold Ephraim. *Laokoon oder Über die Grenzen der Malerei und Poesie*. Stuttgart: Reclam, 2003 [1766].
McLuhan, Marshall. *Understanding Media: The Extension of Man*. Massachusetts: MIT Press, 2002 [1964].
Packard, Stephan. *Anatomie des Comics: Psychosemiotische Medienanalyse*. Göttingen: Wallstein, 2006.
Puszt, Matthew. *Comic Book Culture: Fanboys and True Believers*. Jackson: University Press of Mississippi, 1999.
Savramis, Demosthenes. "Der moderne Mensch zwischen Tarzan und Superman." *Comics und Religion: Eine interdisziplinäre Diskussion*, edited by Jutta Wermke. München: Fink, 1976, 110–20.
Shklovsky, Viktor. "Kunst als Verfahren" *Russischer Formalismus. Texte zur allgemeinen Literaturtheorie und zur Theorie der Prosa*, edited by Jurij Striedter. München, 1971 [1932].
Todorov, Tzvetan. *Introduction to Poetics*. Minneapolis: University of Minnesota Press, 1981 [1968].
Weidenmann, Bernd. "Der exaltierte Code der Comics." *Comics zwischen Lese- und Bildkultur*, edited by Bodo Franzmann. München: Profil, 1991, 60–65.

# 20

# Workshop II: Comics in School
## *Mark Berninger*

The role of comics in education is already considerable, but it is largely unacknowledged. The potential of comics as an educational medium is vast but still only partially realized. It is still a rare exception that comics are specifically dealt with in school or academia and are thus addressed on the same level as literature, theater, art, or film.* This leaves room for an analysis of the reasons for this situation but it also creates the wish to acknowledge the existing role of comics in education, to stress the possibilities inherent in the use of comics in school teaching and academic courses, and to promote comics as a topic of analysis, again both in schools and academia. The following essay attempts to tackle all these objectives as they all formed part of the workshop from which it originates. It must necessarily remain a sketch or rather a first attempt at covering so extensive a field. We hope that the discussions in the workshop as filtered through this essay might spark off further discussions elsewhere that will result in new and refined descriptions, concepts, and practical planning.

### THE ROLE OF COMICS IN EDUCATION

The reasons for the role comics play in education shall be outlined here with a few brief strokes. Teachers tend to look at comics with a suspicion that is still rooted in debates waged in the middle of the 20th century when comics, especially in America, were considered to be potentially dangerous for young

*In recent years the number of academic courses including work on comics has risen and a number of art colleges in America and Japan now offer courses in comics design (see the NACAE homepage for details). However, comics studies and comics art classes remain a severely neglected field in the academic world, which so amply caters for those interested in literature, drama, film, etc.*

people in several ways.* They were accused of both reducing literacy by replacing "proper reading," and of morally endangering children and teenagers through the themes of violence, sex, and crime, which they address. The specific pictorial and narrative style that comics use was also considered offensive as it was seen as aggressive, reductive, and ultimately deficient in artistic quality. Finally, the argument that comics encourage escapism was, and still often is, brought forward.

This negative reaction cannot surprise as it resembles the attacks all newly emerging media, genres, or artistic styles have to face. It is, however, astonishing how long-lived prejudices against comics have proved to be. This can partly be explained with the fact that, unlike other new media, comics have remained primarily a youth (sub)culture. While, for more than 100 years now, almost every child and teenager has read comics, people have tended to "grow out of comics" and look at them with disdain (or sometimes with a certain nostalgia) later in life.†

On the other hand, this rootedness in children's and youth culture also makes comics especially attractive for teachers. Comics simply form an excellent tool to reach and interest children and teenagers. This has led to a fairly extensive use of pictorial narratives in school. Comics are usually employed not for their own sake, though, but simply as stepping stones toward different goals, for example, when a story told in pictures is used to entice pupils to write a "proper story" (in words), an exercise that probably everyone has experienced in school. Like films, comics combine the visual with the narrative and have thus been employed in school in a way that makes use of their visual appeal to introduce narrative and welcomes them as an attractive vehicle to transport content.‡ While this positively stresses the mediating quali-

---

*The notorious paragon of the 1950s anticomics movement was of course Fredric Wertham, whose 1954 book, The Seduction of the Innocent, *virtually silenced all the positive approaches toward comics in the classroom, which had been slowly spreading in the 1940s. See Yang for details.*

†*Individual exceptions naturally prove the rule. General exceptions can be found in comics cultures that cater explicitly for an audience beyond children and teenagers. Japanese mangas for adults are a case in point, of course, as are the artistically elaborated albums of the bande dessinée for grown-ups in France and Belgium. In America, the 1992 Pulitzer Prize for Art Spiegelman's Maus has somewhat turned the tide and showed that "comics have grown up" (Yang). The ensuing terminological debate about "comics" (for children) and "graphic novels" (for adults) indicates, however, how heavily comics still have to battle against prejudice.*

‡*Some illuminating examples can be cited from the academic world: James Kakalios, professor of physics at the University of Minnesota, started to spice up his lectures with examples of comics in 2001. The resounding success in motivating students that way made him develop a full-blown course and finally a bestselling book on* The Physics of Superheroes *(2005). A similar project is "The Periodic Table of Comic Books," which is hosted at the Department of Chemistry at the University of Kentucky and supervised by John P. Seleque and F. James Holler. The German professor Felix Herzog has recently begun to use the same method in a similarly dry field: law. His textbook on criminal law works with a series of 30 cases depicted in comics.*

ties of comics, it has also proved a limiting force. Comics have thus again come to be seen in a reductive way, this time as the proverbial lump of (motivating) sugar that makes the medicine of (serious) content go down.

Finally, new developments in the theory of education have lead to a reevaluation of comics in the classroom. Research on different types of learners has stressed the necessity to reach learners through their specific channels and to develop their special learning strategies. Where visual learning had previously been sidelined as only an initial step toward "higher" forms of acquiring knowledge, it is now stressed as one of the central elements of all learning processes. Similarly, learning through narrative and creative work is no longer seen just as an adornment of abstract cognitive strategies but as an integral part of successful teaching. Professional educators have also formulated the necessity to adapt teaching to the media reality of the 21st century, which does not just comprise books and newspapers. One of the central skills pupils should develop according to most new school curricula is "media literacy."

For the role of comics in the classroom, these developments again have proven to be a double-edged sword. While comics are ideal tools to engage visual learners, to reach pupils through narrative, and to involve them in creative work, they have also often been identified as "old-fashioned" when compared with the "new media" (esp. film) that have come to be so vigorously promoted in teaching. This sadly overlooks the mediating qualities of comics, which could well help to bridge the gap between traditional literacy and new media literacy.

## Pros and Cons

The short survey above has already highlighted some of the specific strengths of comics in teaching, but it has also shown the difficulties comics face in the classroom. A table of arguments in favor of and against an increased use of comics in education might be helpful to give the debate a systematic frame.

| + | − |
|---|---|
| An awareness of the existence of different media and their specific conditions is the basis on which media education rests. Comics are a widespread medium and should therefore be considered. Comics are also a prime example of multimedia. | Among the varied and growing field of media, comics tend to be overlooked. They lack the traditional backing of literature or drama in school and they appear less "trendy" than new electronic media. |

| + | − |
|---|---|
| Comics promote visual learning. They engage visual learners and provide a counterpart to auditory learning and traditional reading. | If they are used simply as illustrations, comics are superfluous as a single photograph or image is sufficient. |
| In contrast to films or theater, comics are permanent and not performance-bound. This makes them effective teaching tools as they can be read at different speeds by pupils and can be discussed while they are still visible. | The performative aspect of films or theater is lost. The physical circumstances of reading comics are similar to reading literature (seated, individual, silent, etc.). The auditory channel is not used in comics. |
| Printed comics are not dependent on electronic equipment, which makes their handling in class easy and allows for easy re-reading at home. | The availability of comics is still somewhat of a problem. High-quality comics can be expensive and are not always easily available. Parents are also often reluctant to spend money on comics. Budget (school) editions of comics classics are still a desideratum, though they begin to appear. |
| Comics are a hybrid medium consisting of visual and narrative aspects. They can function as a mediator between literature and visual art. | Comics could be seen as blurring the boundaries between different media. They are often considered "neither fish nor flesh," not real literature, not real film, and no "real" art. |
| Comics are not restricted to the printed page; indeed, they translate much better into electronic media than literature. They also share many aspects of film. Comics thus form an excellent bridge between traditional media and new media. | Comics are usually not perceived as part of the electronic media. Many teachers might solely depend on their own comics socialization, which relied on print. The similarity of comics and film storyboards might be overlooked. |
| The reading of comics is very intuitive and informs other media literacy. In contrast to reading literature, most pupils can be expected to be readers of comics, and teaching can build on their experience. | The specific comics literacy has to be refined through training like all other literacy to gain a full understanding of texts. Pupils may not find this very engaging, and teachers might not possess refined comics literacy themselves. |
| Comics can mediate between "highbrow" and "lowbrow" culture. | The image of comics as "lowbrow," as a medium for people who cannot read properly, still persists. |

| + | − |
|---|---|
| Comics are great motivators in teaching, especially for pupils who are not very interested in traditional texts and teaching methods. Part of this motivation springs from the use of specifically "youth culture" texts. his acknowledges the pupils' being different (not adult) and their role as participants in their own cultural scene. | If comics are regularly used as textbooks, they might lose their specific appeal as the joke of using them is spoiled and the idea of bringing something different and special into class might get lost. On the other hand, comics might simply be used a motivating gags. |
| Comics are ideal for interdisciplinary education at schools, for example, in projects that involve art, language arts, computing skills, background research, etc. | There is a danger that, due to traditional training, no teacher and no specific subject feels particularly responsible for comics. Teachers of literature might see them as "deficient literature," art teachers as "deficient art" etc. |
| The drawing and writing of comics is a great creative project, especially as it can be done in groups, which brings out the different individual strengths of the pupils. | As with all creative group work, it is difficult to clearly assess the knowledge gained or to give grades. Many teachers, due to lack of training, might also be unable to assess the qualities of the pupils' work. Art teachers might relish the artwork but have difficulties with marking narrative qualities, etc. |
| Comics are ideal for presentations to parents and peers. They are accessible, easy to insert in a presentation, and motivate the audience. | As comics still suffer from being regarded as infantile, they might be regarded as unacademic in presentations. |
| Comics are especially effective in language learning. They are ideal tools for exercises in language production if the speech bubbles are removed. | Comics are usually relegated to the initial steps of language learning. The complexity of comics is thus glossed over. |
| Comics are also very helpful in foreign language training as words and images support each other and help to bridge language deficits. This provides an easy access to foreign language texts. | The assistance of the images could be seen as "watering down" the difficulty of the language exercise. Comics might also promote a "half-reading" of the text, since it is often fairly easy to get the general drift of the story, but much more difficult to understand the comic in its entirety. |

| + | − |
|---|---|
| Foreign comics (even in translation) are also an ideal medium for the introduction to foreign cultures. They combine specific cultural traditions with the depiction of everyday life in other countries. | Comics are often seen as contributing to the "mishmash" of cultures, for example, to the Americanization of European culture. As their specific value is still often overlooked, the ubiquitous mangas are often not seen in the West as a chance to access Japanese culture, but as a new wave of globalized kitsch. |
| Comics are intricately linked with youth culture. This gives them their vitality and subversive potential. | Comics are intricately linked to youth culture. This limits their scope and often makes them part of commercialized media campaigns. |
| As comics grow out of youth culture, they often address topics characteristic for the problems and experiences of teenagers. | Comics are still largely associated with the superhero genre, which has created the idea that they formulate mostly male adolescent fantasies of unlimited power. The tradition of Western comics is very much male-dominated and offers little of interest for girls. |
| Like most media, comics can be applied to all possible subjects. Comics contain the entire spectrum of human experience. | Complex comics might be perceived by pupils as "heavy reading" where they expected straight entertainment. There are few comics that deal in an academic way with abstract, scientific material. |
| A substantial and growing body of theoretical material on comics exists. Scott McCloud's *Understanding Comics: The Invisible Art* is an ideal introductory textbook. | Access to secondary sources on comics is still problematic. Many libraries lack even the most basic works (of both primary and secondary literature). Systematic academic research on comics is still rare. |

## Conclusions

What follows from this? The first aspect that becomes evident here is that many of the strengths and weaknesses of comics in education either depend on the hybridity of comics as a medium that combines aspects of the visual and the literary or are linked to comics' intimate connection with youth culture. The task at hand is to build on the strengths of comics and promote them as effective classroom tools. At the same time, educators also have to be aware of the weaknesses of comics. These weaknesses should be counterbalanced, especially where prejudice is involved, but not negated. Comics are not a "remedy for all diseases" and are not suited for all purposes. In many cases, they should be used in conjunction with other media to be most effective. This, in turn, stresses one of the greatest potentials of comics: to mediate between different discourses and to facilitate access to other fields.

However, comics in the classroom should not be reduced to this role. It should be the objective of all comics experts to stress the artistic quality of comics, which still often goes unnoticed. The development and refinement of a canon of comics is the essential next step. If this happened excessively at the expense of comics' rootedness in youth culture, for example, by strictly separating high art "graphic novels" from low quality "comics," much of the teaching potential of this medium would be lost.

It is therefore another task at hand for comics experts and teachers to embrace comics' proximity to popular culture and to be open to new developments. The advance of mangas in the Western world offers, for example, the almost unprecedented chance to interest children in Japanese or Korean culture. In the wake of the manga boom many Western teenagers have even begun to learn Japanese of their own accord. On the other hand, mangas also allow for the previously difficult inclusion of girls in classwork with comics. Teachers might be surprised to find their female pupils very much versed in shôjo mangas, where themes of interest for girls are widely covered.*

The current development toward a greater inclusion of popular culture and new media in classroom work offers a great chance to promote comics as an educational tool, also because they might help to bridge the unnecessary and unproductive confrontation between "traditional literacy" and "new media literacy." The same goes for the opposition of canonical texts and popular culture. To achieve this, teacher training in the field of comics has to be improved. Special attention should be drawn to the diversity of comics, and teachers should be made aware of the often-overlooked qualities of popular comics. They should also be made familiar with the immense artistic value of less well-known comics. Ultimately it is therefore necessary to further develop comics studies in academia. Examples for this will be outlined in the following chapters.

*Indeed, it seems as if the manga boom in the West comes to be mainly female dominated. The fact that, for example, in Germany the shônen (boy) manga magazine Banzai *has ceased publication while its shôjo (girl) opposite,* Daisuki, *is thriving is an indicator for this. Another case in point is the coplayer movement, which is much dominated by female teenagers. See also the essay by Zank on* Lolitas *in this volume.*

BIBLIOGRAPHY

Herzog, Felix. *Strafrecht Illustrated: 30 Fälle aus dem Strafrecht in Wort und Bild.* Hamburg: Merus, 2007.
Kakalios, James. *The Physics of Superheroes.* New York: Gotham, 2005.
McCloud, Scott. *Understanding Comics: The Invisible Art.* New York: Harper Collins, 1994.
NACAE [National Association of Comic Art Educators] homepage. http://www.teachingcomics.org/ (24 May 2007).
Seleque, John P., and F. James Holler. "The Periodic Table of Comic Books." 1996–2005. http://www.uky.edu/Projects/Chemcomics (24 May 2007).
Yang, Gene. "Comics in Education." 2003. http://www.geneyang.com/comicsedu/ (24 May 2007).

# 21

# Workshop III: Teaching Comics and Literary Studies — Neil Gaiman and Charles Vess' "A Midsummer Night's Dream"

*Mark Berninger*

It has been outlined above that comics are an excellent tool to facilitate and diversify access to other media. In the following session outline, the "A Midsummer Night's Dream" episode from Neil Gaiman's *The Sandman: Dream Country* (1991, artwork by Charles Vess) will be used as an example how a session on comics can be integrated in an introductory course in Literary Studies at university undergraduate level. The episode by Gaiman/Vess has been chosen because it is easily accessible, relatively short (only 22 pages\*) and self-contained. The high artistic quality of the comic and its connection with Shakespeare were of course other decisive points why this particular text has been selected.

### Course Context

The course plan of most "Introduction to Literary Studies" classes contains a unit on Elizabethan drama due to Shakespeare's unrivaled position as the world's most important dramatist. This is where the specific session on "A Midsummer Night's Dream" by Gaiman/Vess could most easily be inserted. Ideally, the Shakespearean *Midsummer Night's Dream* has already been read

---

\**This counts just the "narrative" pages, which are numbered from 3 to 24 by Vess. Reference in the following will be to these page numbers. In the collected edition of The Sandman, these are the pages 65–86 of volume 3* [Dream Country].

in class and central features of Elizabethan drama have been introduced. The session on the comics version by Gaiman/Vess then serves as a revision and expansion of the material already covered. We assume this as the general frame for the session plan but, as will be indicated below, the proposed session can easily be adapted to different circumstances and course formats.

Instead of revision, the session can also serve as an introduction to Elizabethan drama and Shakespeare in general or specifically to *A Midsummer Night's Dream*. A pre-reading activity could in this case consist of collecting bits of the widespread general knowledge on Shakespeare and his plays in class. The following discussion of the Gaiman/Vess comic could then build on the context thus established. A probably more interesting alternative is not to introduce the text at all and leave it to the students to discover and explore the Shakespearean connection. After all, the name Shakespeare does not appear until page 9 of the episode, and part of the fun in reading the Gaiman/Vess comic lies in the gradual uncovering of the parallels to the Shakespeare text.

## Teaching Aims

A main aim of the session is to generate or deepen interest for the class topic (Elizabethan drama, Shakespeare, *A Midsummer Night's Dream*) by approaching it from an unusual angle. The comics version can provide a variant to and supplement the close reading and cultural context routines that usually dominate Literary Studies classes. It thus facilitates or broadens access to Elizabethan drama. The session also increases the specific understanding of *A Midsummer Night's Dream* as key scenes of the play are highlighted in the comic and supplemented with additional visual and narrative information. This leads to an improved recollection of the play and a deepened discussion of its central themes. The introduction of the biographical context of Shakespeare's life allows for an exploration of this topic with all the historical research, guess-work, myth-making and fictionalization that surrounds it.

The introduction of a Shakespeare adaptation in class also serves to focus on the process of adaptation in general and to create an awareness for the problems connected with concepts like authorship, intertextuality, originality, or fidelity to the original. This could also prove a starting point for an exploration of central elements of postmodernism.

The discussion of a comics text necessitates the introduction of comic-specific terminology, which in turn allows for a contrasting analysis of narrative means and structures by comparing the comics text with a novel, drama, or film. An improved understanding of narratology is thus another aim of the session, as is an increased ability to describe texts objectively and to form a critical opinion. The intermedial aspect of an adaptation from drama to comics also highlights the specific character of different media and thus helps to broaden and combine traditional literacy and new media literacy.

In the context of a Literary Studies class, the session also introduces a key phase of English literature and contributes to its understanding. If the session is used with non-native speakers of English, it also supports language training and facilitates the approach to Shakespearean English.

PRE-READING ACTIVITIES

Before the episode by Gaiman/Vess is introduced in class, the Shakespearean play should have been read and the following aspects should already have been discussed in some depth:

- the function of Puck and his ambiguous character (with a special focus on his interaction with Oberon and on Puck's epilogue)
- the contrast and interaction of fairy world and human world (e.g., by taking the relationship of Titania and Bottom in the scenes II.1.122ff and IV.1.1ff as an example)
- the symbol of the dream (e.g., by a close reading of Theseus' and Hippolyta's reflection on dreams in V.1.1ff)
- the play-within-the-play and its functions

Ideally, the conflict between Titania and Oberon has been especially highlighted and the significance of the "Indian Boy" pointed out in a close reading of II.1.60–145. It is also helpful if an introduction to Elizabethan drama has already taken place and the following aspects have been covered (in descending order of significance):

- boy actors playing female roles
- commercial aspects of Elizabethan theater
- London-based companies and touring the provinces
- material aspects of the Renaissance stage (costumes, stage setup, backstage action as reflected in metadrama, etc.)
- the tradition of clown actors in Elizabethan theater

The comic is understood more easily if the biography of Shakespeare, especially the significance of his son, Hamnet, has already been introduced. However, all these layers of background information could also form part of a gradual further exploration of the topic after the session has been taught (see below).

The following session plan consists of two parts, which take 45–60 minutes each (depending on how much time is given to the students for developing their own ideas or how heavily the teacher dominates and leads the session). The two parts can be taught together in a (fairly packed) 90-minute session or as two separate sessions. In the later case, which is preferable, the whole comic should be read between the two parts. An in-class reading of the entire comic is also possible at the beginning of part two, but it takes about 25 minutes and consequently eats brutally into the class discussion scheduled for the second part. If both parts of the session are taught en suite, then the complete comic should have been read as homework before the session starts.

## Session Part One: How to Read a Comic

Depending on the set-up of the group and the point in the course plan at which the session is taught, it might be necessary to start with an "icebreaker" question. The teacher could bring a number of comics to class, show them and ask: "Is this literature? Why? Why not?" Usually there will be some students in class who defend comics as literature while a majority will argue against an incorporation of comics in the literary canon. The teacher should, however, be ready to support both sides with good arguments (playing "advocatus diaboli" if necessary) when the discussion becomes lopsided in either direction. If the chosen comics range, for example, from mangas, *Mickey Mouse*, and *Superman* to Belgo-French albums (e.g., by Moebius or Enki Bilal) and graphic novels (e.g., *Maus* or *Blankets*), the ensuing discussion might be directed into developing and questioning the distinction between "high" vs. "low" or "popular" vs. "artistic" comics. This could, in turn, inform a general discussion on the definition of literature and the establishment of a canon, which has probably already been part of the course anyway. If desired, this could easily be expanded into a full session of its own (e.g., with group work on the differences between the various comics or the restaging of the 1950s debate about the dangers and chances of comic reading as a role-play). In the framework of the given session, however, the discussion should stick to a spot-light character and not last for too long.

As an alternative to the "Is this literature?" opening, the teacher could show one of the famous Roy Lichtenstein paintings based on a comics image and ask "Why is this art?" This approach has the advantage that it probably takes the students by surprise and steers them away from the topic of literature for a while, which might start an entirely fresh discussion. If the teacher wants to take a more personal and less provocative approach, the session could also start with asking for the specific comics experiences of the students (Do you read comics? Have you read comics? Did you enjoy them? Why have you stopped reading them? etc.). This opening naturally proves most effective in small to medium-sized groups where students are less afraid of relating and discussing personal experiences.

The opening discussion should then be channeled by the teacher into the development of a rough mind map on comics that covers the constituent parts of comics as a medium (panel, lettering, gutter, page setup, line, coloring, etc.). If the teacher wishes to expand this, different schools and authors, connections to related genres (literature, art, film), genre subdivisions within the field of comics and other information could be added. The mind map should then be developed into a description of comics, which could follow Scott McCloud's definition of comics as "sequential art" (the relevant passages from *Understanding Comics* could be provided as supplementary reading at home or used directly in class).

This should be followed by a short lecture from the teacher that introduces the terminology relevant for the description of comics so far as this has not been done already in connection with the mind map.* The teacher should then outline some possibilities of what could be looked for especially in the interpretation of comics in contrast to other media, for example, the use of the gutter, the arrangement on the page, the page break, the use of color, static image vs. dynamic action, the use of speech bubbles, etc. This should be underlined with examples drawn from a variety of comics, or — to simplify the preparations for this session — again with the help of McCloud's *Understanding Comics*.

The next step is to distribute sample pages of comics for analysis in groups of three to four students. The aim of this group work is to apply the terminology which has just been introduced and thus secure knowledge gained through practical work. If the Gaiman/Vess comic has been read before the session, then the sample pages could come from the episode.† Pages 3 through

---

*Terminology can be selected from the "list of terms" supplied by Andrei Molotiu in his "History of Comic Book Art" course description (see bibliography). Illustrative material can be taken from McCloud. Naturally the selection of terms depends on the outline of the whole course. In a Film Studies class, terms like "framing," "medium shot," "canted framing," "shot/reverse shot sequence," etc. can be taken for granted, while narratological terms like "diegesis" and poetic devices like "metonymy" or "synecdoche" have probably already been introduced in a Literary Studies course. Depending on the focus and intensity the teacher chooses here, this part of the session can thus either serve as revision under different colors or as a means to expand on analytic terminology.

†Good sample pages are 3, 4, 5, 6, 11, 15, 22, and 23. As an alternative, each group could pick the page from the comic that they find most interesting.

6, as they form the opening of "A Midsummer Night's Dream," could be included in the material distributed for analysis even if the comic is not yet known to the students. Other sample pages should then be selected from different sources.* The phase of group work should close with a short presentation of the results to the whole class by each group. If this takes too long, the findings could also be turned into very short essays (ca. 100 words) as homework, which could be collected (and marked) or distributed among the students for discussion.

## Session Part Two: Gaiman/Vess and Shakespeare

If the session is split up into two separate sittings, then this second part begins with a short recapitulation of the territory already gained, for example, by discussion of one or two of the mini essays or by a joint analysis of a new sample page, for example, the opening of "A Midsummer Night's Dream," if this has not been done so already by a group. As the comic by Gaiman/Vess has now been read in its entirety by the students, the session can then proceed with a direct comparison with Shakespeare's *A Midsummer Night's Dream*. This could be done again as group or partner work, or as a plenary discussion. Leading questions could be:

- Which scenes from the play are highlighted in the comic?
- Which central themes of Shakespeare's play receive special attention in the comic?
- Where does Gaiman/Vess's version differ from the usual perception of the play?
- Which aspects have been added to Shakespeare's text by Gaiman and Vess?
- How does Peaseblossom in Gaiman/Vess differ from Peaseblossom in Shakespeare?
- What is the role of the frame narrative in the comic and how is it connected with Shakespeare's play?
- What is the role of the character Dream (who is also called "Lord Shaper" by the fairies)?

---

*Paul Gravett's* Graphic Novels — Everything You Need to Know *offers a host of sample pages that could easily be copied and distributed. Good examples to contrast with Gaiman/Vess's work would be Ware's* Jimmy Corrigan *(Gravett 24f), David B.'s* Epileptic *(Gravett 28f, see also the chapter by Engelmann in this volume), Sacco's* Palestine *(Gravett 68f, see also the chapter by Vanderbeke in this volume), Moebius'* The Airtight Garage *(Gravett 90f), and Woodring's* The Frank Book *(Gravett 136f). If the teacher wants to put special emphasis on the specific style of Neil Gaiman and wishes to introduce Dream as a character, then the sample pages from* Sandman *that are reproduced in Gravett (98f) could be used.*

- Which comic-specific means do Gaiman and Vess employ to underline all this?

The following aspects should emerge from the discussion of these questions: Gaiman weaves his tale around Shakespeare's play. He creates a frame narrative that explains the special character of *A Midsummer Night's Dream* (and by implication also of *The Tempest*) as inspired by the Lord of Dreams. This accounts, among other things, for the fact that *A Midsummer Night's Dream* "is one of the small group of plays in which Shakespeare appears not to have depended upon already existing narrative material. [...] [W]e know of nothing that would have provided the main story of *A Midsummer Night's Dream*" (Wells 14). The frame narrative also hints at a number of historical details connected with Shakespeare's life: the plague in London, the death of Christopher Marlowe, the members of Shakespeare's troupe of actors (e.g., William Kemp and Henry Condell), and finally the death of Shakespeare's son, Hamnet.

Thematically the frame narrative is connected to Shakespeare's play in numerous ways that mirror, invert, and vary elements of the play. Where, for example, the mechanicals in Shakespeare rehearse their play in the woods and perform at the Athenian court, the actors in Gaiman/Vess have rehearsed in London and now perform in the wilderness for the court of the fairies. The identities of the actors and their roles become blurred, most obviously so in the case of Hamnet/The Indian Boy. In a metadramatical turn that mirrors Shakespeare's play-within-the-play, the audience of the performance in Gaiman/Vess is identical with the characters embodied on stage (Auberon, Titania, Puck, Peaseblossom, etc.). This also introduces an element of reinterpretation of Shakespeare's play, as some of the fairies in the audience do not appear as they are usually represented in productions of the Shakespeare play. Instead of the beautiful little girl with wings into which Victorian interpretations of the fairy world has turned her, Peaseblossom is a rather ghastly and nightmarish figure more reminiscent of a tree than a human being.

The fairies in the audience also take over the structural function that the mechanicals have in Shakespeare's play, that is to provide an additional level of comedy through travesty. This is highlighted on page 18 of Gaiman/Vess, when Peaseblossom proclaims that the performance he witnesses "[i]ssa wossname, travelogue? Nah. Travesty. That's it."

The fact that Shakespeare's comedy is dangerously close to tragedy due to the mischief Puck is playing on the humans is underlined by another narrative turn that Gaiman/Vess introduce. After he has put the actor incorporating him to sleep, the Puck of the fairy audience takes over his own role in the performance of Shakespeare's troupe. The epilogue of the play, which in

Shakespeare is a classical example of *captatio benevolentiae*, thus turns Gaiman/ Vess into a sinister and foreboding scene, which underlines the malicious character of Puck and points toward later appearances of this character in *The Sandman* (see also the remark "Robin Goodfellow's present whereabouts are unknown," which closes the episode). The significance of this is underlined by the use of color in the comic, which moves from a bright opening to darker and darker tones to end with an entirely dark panel on page 23.

The contrast between dream (fairy) world and reality, which is so essential to Shakespeare's play, is highlighted in Gaiman/Vess by the stark color contrast of page 23 and 24, where the darkness spread by Puck with the turning of the page (Gaiman and Vess here use the physical outline of the comic to great effect) changes into a sunny and green morning. The events of the night then seem only a bad dream but, as in Shakespeare's play, their influence is still felt. Although the colors in the final panels are similar to the opening panels of the comic, which gives the comic a circular character, the shadow of the dreams looms on in the form of the impending tragedy surrounding Hamnet. Interestingly it is Shakespeare in the Gaiman/Vess comic who utters the words "Foolish fancies, boy" (24) when Hamnet alludes to the strange experience he has had. This echoes the discussion between Theseus and Hippolyta about the significance of dreams and their connection to poets and madness in V.1.1ff, a passage from the play that Gaiman was naturally keen to include, highlight, and vary in the comic. It is therefore singled out here for close reading.

Pages 19–21 show how Gaiman and Vess integrate the discourse on dreams in the comic. The monologue of Bottom after he awakes at the end of act IV, scene 1, in Shakespeare ("I have had a most rare vision") forms the frame of page 19 in Gaiman/Vess. It is slightly abbreviated and split into two page-wide panels at the top and bottom of the page. Inserted between and overlapping these two panels is a tight dialogue of four square panels between Dream and Titania, which is thus indicated as going on parallel to the stage action. The topic of this dialogue are the doubts that notoriously haunt Dream in *The Sandman*. He mentions "the price" Shakespeare will have to pay for "getting what he wants" and thus foreshadows the ending of the comic. The dark mood of Dream's musings is underlined by the black speech bubbles with wavy edges, which always characterize him in *The Sandman* but here form an especially strong contrast to the other characters. Page 19 is also the point from where the increasing darkness sets in, which leads to an almost complete loss of color on page 23.

Page 20 starts with the opening of act V of Shakespeare's play and juxtaposes the brightly lit action on stage (panel 1) with the reverse shot of a dark and gloomy audience. This undermines the famous "fine frenzy" monologue of Theseus (played by Shakespeare in Gaiman/Vess) which — at a surface level — dismisses the significance of dreams. In Gaiman/Vess the dark figures of the fairies with their glowing red eyes make clear that dreams are much more than an "airy nothing" (V.1.16). The dream topic is developed further on page 21 in a dialogue between Dream and the king and queen of the fairies. Auberon, who now resembles Theseus in his line of argument, says, "We thank you Shaper. But this diversion, although pleasant, is not *true*. Things never happened thus." To this Dream replies with a curtsy to Titania: "Oh, but it IS true. Things need not have happened to be true. Tales and dreams are the shadow-truths that will endure when mere facts are dust and ashes and forgot." From this dialogue, which has again been inserted as parallel to the stage action, the comic returns at the bottom of the page to the performance of *A Midsummer Night's Dream*, ironically with Hippolyta's metadramatical remark, "This is the silliest stuff that I ever heard" (V.1.207). This is countered by Theseus' enigmatic "The best in this kind are but shadows; and the worst are no worse, if imagination amend them" (V.1.208-9).

The fact that this commentary within the play mirrors the preceding dialogue between Dream and the fairy rulers is underlined by the juxtaposition of Dream and the fairies facing right and toward the reader and the actors facing left and away from the reader. The contrast between the sphere of the fairies and the human (theatrical) world is stressed through a difference in size (Dream and the fairies are shown in the medium shots and close-ups that are typical for dialogue passages, whereas the actors are depicted in a long shot) and by the use of the panel borders and background. While Dream and the fairy rulers are enclosed in panels with clear black frames and a tense dark background of foliage, the actors hover in an unbordered white field.

On the following page the stage action and the audience (fairy) action cease to run parallel to each other and begin to merge. This is indicated by the blending of the previously brightly colored stage action into the bluish and dark tones of the fairy action. The Auberon in the audience now assumes the function of Oberon in *A Midsummer Night's Dream* in calling the fairies (especially Puck) to leave. But instead of the nuptial blessing of Shakespeare's play (V.1.381ff), the mischievous Puck rebels and decides to stay as "the last hobgoblin in a dreary world" (22). This is the turning point of the story, which is captured in panel 4 on page 22, where Puck discharges the mask of the theatrical character Puck, which he has taken on earlier. As the goblin thus becomes himself again, the theatrical order is lost. A disoriented Shakespeare in the role of Theseus asks "What's happening?" and the page ends in a dramatic panel showing a blinding blast of light that spreads underneath the preceding panels. What follows are the two epilogues already described above, the epilogue of Puck from Shakespeare's play, which is turned into a dark omen, and the return to the frame narrative of the comic.

## Points for Further Exploration and Adaptation to Different Course Formats

When the session on the Gaiman/Vess episode has ended with a close reading of the comic, there are a still a number of points left that could be used for a further development of themes. Most of the following suggestions, however, presuppose a course format different from the normal "Introduction to Literary Studies" class, which usually does not allow for lengthy (multisession) explorations of individual topics.

The most logical direction into which teaching could be developed after the session would be an exploration of *The Sandman* as a whole or maybe specifically of the volume *Fables and Reflections*. As *Fables and Reflections* consists of a collection of self-contained but interconnected stories, it provides additional material that can easily be tailored to any time slot available. The reading questions by Rocco Versaci on *Fables and Reflections* provided on the NACAE (National Association of Comic Art Educators) homepage indicate directions into which the discussion of the other stories might go. Bender's *The Sandman Companion* offers a wealth of additional material on the whole comic series.

As has been indicated above, the session on "A Midsummer Night's Dream" by Gaiman and Vess could also be used as a starting point to discuss the specifics of Elizabethan theater, the historical background of the late 16th century, or Shakespeare's biography if this has not already been done before the session. This could be connected with another, thematically more specific point raised by the comic, namely the fictionalization of "the Bard." The comic's treatment of Shakespeare's biography offers the possibility to discuss the contrast of historical reality and fictionalized past. An interesting companion text to explore the development of "Bardology" further is Peter Barnes' play *Jubilee* (2001), which deals with the introduction of the Shakespeare festival at Stratford-upon-Avon by David Garrick in 1769. On a more general level, this could lead to an analysis of Shakespeare's history plays, to Walter Scott's concept of the historical novel, and to contemporary historical metafiction (see Hutcheon and Engler/Müller) in a course focusing on representations of history in literature.

If the teacher wants to expand on the Shakespearean references in Gaiman's comics, but *A Midsummer Night's Dream* for some reason proves impracticable as a point of reference in a specific course, then the "Tempest" episode from *The Sandman: The Wake* (1996) might serve as an alternative. If the two "dream play" episodes, which were designed by Gaiman as direct counterpieces, are taken together, the session outlined above can be expanded into a unit of two (long) sessions.

Naturally, the session as it has been outlined above could also form part of a course entirely devoted to Shakespeare. Beyond the obvious possibilities for integrating the comic in such a class, another interesting point for further discussion could spring from the passage on the significance of dreams, which has been analyzed above. Dream's remarks on page 21 in Gaiman/Vess could form the basis of a discussion of the "immortality through poetry" theme, which is one of the main topics of Shakespeare's sonnets, for example, in the famous sonnet no. 18 ("Shall I compare thee to a summer's day") or in the only slightly less well-known sonnet no. 55 ("Not marble, nor the gilded monuments").

The session on Gaiman's comic, either in a longer or short format, can also be embedded in various more specific literature classes at undergraduate or graduate level, for example, in a course on postmodernism or, more specifically, on contemporary Shakespeare adaptations, for example, in combination with Tom Stoppard's *Rosencrantz and Guildenstern Are Dead* (1996), Terry Pratchett's *Wyrd Sisters* (1988) and *Lords and Ladies* (1992), or Jasper Fforde's *Something Rotten* (2004).

If the session plan is changed slightly, the Gaiman/Vess comics can also be used in an introductory course in Theatre Studies or a Film Studies class which deals, for example, with Shakespeare adaptations. Connections to film versions of *A Midsummer Night's Dream* can easily be drawn, for example, to the 1999 adaptation starring Kevin Kline and Michelle Pfeiffer (dir. Michael Hoffman) or freer adaptations like *Sommarnattens Leende* (1955, dir. Ingmar Bergman) and *A Midsummer Night's Sex Comedy* (1982, dir. Woody Allen). Equally, similarities to the use of the Shakespearean play as an intertextual reference in films like *Dead Poets Society* (1989, dir. Peter Weir) could be highlighted.

This could also be integrated in a course that deals with adaptation in film and highlights the interaction of film and comics. The following session plan, which was also developed in the Lambrecht workshops and has been spelled out by Andreas Rauscher, deals specifically with this topic.

BIBLIOGRAPHY

Barnes, Peter. *Jubilee*. London: Methuen, 2001.
Bender, Hy. *The Sandman Companion*. London: Titan, 2000.
Engler, Bernd, and Kurt Müller. *Historiographic Metafiction in Modern American and Canadian Literature*. Paderborn: Schoeningh, 1994.
Gaiman, Neil. *The Sandman: Fables and Reflections*. New York: Vertigo, 1993.
Gaiman, Neil, and Charles Vess. "A Midsummer Night's Dream." *Sandman* #19. *The Sandman: Dream Country*. New York: Vertigo, 1991.
\_\_\_\_\_. "The Tempest." *Sandman* #75. *The Sandman: The Wake*. New York: Vertigo, 1999.
Gravett, Paul. *Graphic Novels. Everything You Need to Know*. New York: Collins Design, 2005.

Hutcheon, Linda. *Narcissistic Narrative: The Metafictional Paradox*. New York: Methuen, 1984.
McCloud, Scott. *Understanding Comics: The Invisible Art*. New York: HarperCollins, 1994.
Molotiu, Andrei. "History of Comic Book Art — Course Schedule." http://www.teachingcomics.org/syllabi/19.pdf (24 May 2007).
NACAE homepage. http://www.teachingcomics.org/ (24 May 2007).
Versaci, Rocco. "Reading Questions: Neil Gaiman's *Sandman: Fables and Reflections*." http://www.teachingcomics.org/studyguide/studyguide4.php (24 May 2007).
Wells, Stanley. "Introduction." *A Midsummer Night's Dream*, by William Shakespeare. Edited by Stanley Wells. London: Penguin, 1995, 7–37.

# 22

# Workshop IV: Teaching Comics and Film Studies — Ang Lee's *The Hulk* (USA 2003)

*Andreas Rauscher*

In the late 1990s and early 2000s a significant change in the popularity and the aesthetics of comic book adaptations has been noticed and not only by aficionados of the art form. Recent developments in CGI (computer-generated images) have resulted in a vast variety of new approaches towards the adaptation of comic books. Films like *Sin City* (USA 2005) by Robert Rodriguez and Frank Miller were shot entirely in front of a green screen, which was later replaced with computer graphics recreating the moody, noir-inspired set pieces from the graphic novel of the same title. The superhero genre reached new heights by offering different takes on well-known series, from a darker and more realistic version of Batman (*Batman Begins*, dir. Christopher Nolan, USA 2005/2008) and the psychologically motivated everyday troubles of *Spider-Man* (dir. Sam Raimi, USA 2002/2004/2007) to fun movies featuring *The Fantastic Four* (dir. Tim Story, USA 2005/2007).

Nevertheless ambitious directors did not only employ the new technological possibilities to achieve more impressive visual effects as one would expect from a state-of-the-art blockbuster movie but at the same time they used them in order to create innovative synergetic effects combining the spatial perception of the printed image with the mobile frame of the moving image. The resulting cross-over between cinematic codes and well-known comic book stylistics provides an accessible and promising starting point for a discussion on the similarities and differences between both media that can be used in different academic courses on the subject of comics and film.

The following chapter outlines a few suggestions in what way this subject could be included in an introductory class on film studies as well as in a course on the aesthetics of comic books. The sample analysis discussed on the following pages focuses on the stylistic approach of Ang Lee's *The Hulk*, released by Universal Pictures in 2003. This film takes a rather unconventional approach toward a mainstream comic book adaptation by self-consciously breaking with established directing styles in order to give the film a distinctive look based on traditional comic books. After a short introduction featuring some ideas on how to prepare the session, the essay will take a closer look on a sequence from the film and its defining stylistic devices. The last paragraph offers several points for further discussion in class.

## INTRODUCTION AND PREPARATION

Before the session, the complete film *The Hulk* by Ang Lee, available on DVD from Universal Home Entertainment, should be screened for the class. Additionally, the students should read the first ten pages of Scott McCloud's *Understanding Comics*, including his definition of comics as "sequential art," as well as the discussion of cinematic framing methods featured in *Film Art— An Introduction* by David Bordwell and Kristin Thompson for homework (the relevant pages are pp. 182–207).

An effective way to get the students involved at the beginning of the lesson is to discuss if they are familiar with the character of Bruce Banner/the Hulk, what makes him different from other (traditional) comic book heroes and if they know predecessors from literature or film to which the Hulk could be related to. In this context, Frankenstein's creature, reflected in the hostility the Hulk experiences from government officials, civil mobs and military forces, and the split personality of Dr. Jekyll and Mr. Hyde, echoed in the Hulk's civil identity of scientist Bruce Banner, should be mentioned in particular. The focus on misunderstood heroes has become a trademark of Marvel comics from the early 1960s on and should be summarized in a short survey as well. If the topic is divided into several sessions, the differences between the Golden and the Silver Age, exemplified by comparing, for example, a *Superman* comic strip from the 1930s to an issue of *The Amazing Spider-Man* from the 1960s or 1970s, would be well-suited for an additional oral presentation prepared by a group of students.

A second step in the introduction of the topic would be to discuss what films based upon comic books the students are familiar with. If only current productions are known by the class, it would be helpful to mention predigital efforts like the *Superman* series (USA 1978/1980/1984/1987) by Richard Donner and Richard Lester, the two *Batman* films (USA 1989/1992) by Tim

Burton or *Dick Tracy* (USA 1990) by Warren Beatty, all of which had to rely on architecture, make-up, costume and set design in order to create the artificial look associated with traditional comic books. In order to provide an appropriate impression of this aesthetic style screenshots from the films and excerpts from comic books can be presented to the class. The differences between analogue and digital comic book adaptations should be discussed before approaching the analysis of *The Hulk*. Topics of relevance include the use of digital backgrounds like the recreation of Times Square in the first *Spider-Man* film or the unusual perspectives created by the combination of CGI shots and real footage. If several sessions are available it would be helpful to show select scenes like the fight between Spider-Man and the Green Goblin from Sam Raimi's *Spider-Man* (USA 2002) to the class.

The discussion should not focus on technical details but consider significant differences between analogue and digital filmmaking on a more general level. An interesting topic would be, for example, if the use of digital effects contributes to a more complex illusion of reality or if the employment of techniques more characteristic of animation than of feature films creates a rather artificial atmosphere. The pros and cons of this debate can be used as groundwork with regard to the sample sequence from *The Hulk* and to the question of which stylistic elements of Ang Lee's visual composition remind the class of comic book aesthetics.

For the session, a handout featuring some important key terms for the analysis of a film has to be prepared. This should include the basic definitions of shots (long, medium, close-up), of framing, of sequence, and of split-screen. These can be taken from the glossary included in Bordwell's and Thompson's *Film Art*:

*Framing*: The use of the edges of the film frame to select and to compose what will be visible onscreen.
*Sequence*: Term commonly used for a moderately large segment of film, involving one complete stretch of action. In a narrative film, often equivalent to a scene.
*Shot*: In the finished film, one uninterrupted image, whether or not there is mobile framing.
*Split-screen*: Stylistic device often employed in films from the 1970s to show two simultaneous events within the same frame [190–194].

In addition to introducing those key terms, the principles of continuity editing should be explained. Helpful examples can be found in Classical Hollywood productions, for example in many films by director Alfred Hitchcock such as the opening sequence of *The Birds* (USA 1963). The film opens with a scene shot on location in San Francisco and then switches to footage recorded on a sound stage at the Universal studios. The change between the two sets occurs during a shot in which actress Tippi Heddren passes a commercial ad filling out the whole frame for a short moment. In this way the audience does not necessarily notice that two separately recorded scenes were used to build the whole sequence. In film history, continuity editing has been regarded as one of the trademarks of the Classical Hollywood style. As explained by Bordwell and Thompson, continuity editing tries to keep up the illusion of spatial and dramatic unity:

> The basic purpose of the continuity system is to allow space, time, and action to continue in a smooth flow over a series of shots[...]. First, graphic qualities are usually kept roughly continuous from shot to shot. The figures are balanced and symmetrically deployed in the frame; the overall lighting tonality remains constant; the action occupies the central zone of the screen [231].

On a visual level there are many similarities between films and comic books, especially since graphic novels like *Watchmen* by Alan Moore and Dave Gibbons or *The Dark Knight Returns* by Frank Miller began to emulate cinematic trademarks like camera movements and editing patterns in the mid-1980s.

In comic books, references to film syntax can imitate the smooth flow that, according to Bordwell and Thompson, continuity editing had on traditional film audiences. But nevertheless the fragmentation of the visual narrative by the panel structure remains, even if graphic novels become similar to the story-board for a film. This basic difference between both media can be introduced in a comprehensible way by discussing the key terms for film analysis summarized on the handout. While the framing of an image is important for films and comic books as well, it is quite difficult to find an equivalent for the uninterrupted image of a cinematic shot in a comic book.

## Discussing the Sequence

It is characteristic of the films of director Ang Lee (*The Ice Storm, Crouching Tiger Hidden Dragon, Brokeback Mountain*) that he brings a keen sense of stylistic devices to his new perspectives on traditional genre topics. In *The Hulk* he combines the psychological update of traditional horror motives taken from the source material with a reflection on the formal differences between films and comic books. Not only focusing on the superhuman skills of the Hulk, which are characteristic of heroic fantasy, Lee's film offers several innovative compositions that provide an interesting sample of the complex relationship between visuals on page and on screen.

The sequence discussed here occurs mid-way through the film and indicates a significant turning point in the story.* Having being imprisoned by military forces under the command of General Ross (Sam Elliott), the prejudiced father of his love interest Betty (Jennifer Connelly), scientist Bruce Banner (Eric Bana) turns into the Hulk. During an action scene, the misunderstood monster escapes from the secret research lab into the desert. In comparison to huge set pieces in conventional blockbuster productions, Lee, who at first tried to put the sequence in chronological order, decided to give the action an almost abstract quality by way of unconventional editing. On the audio commentary of the DVD, the director explains that he was aiming for a "larger-than-life cutting style."

One of the most striking devices Ang Lee uses throughout the film, and which features prominently in the selected sequence, is the split-screen effect. He uses this rather old-fashioned device in order to emulate the panel structure of a traditional comic book on screen. In one shot of the sequence, he even divides the image into many multiframes of equal size that resemble the structure of a printed page from a comic book. David Bordwell explains the traditional function of the split-screen effect as follows: "In this process, two or more images, each with its own frame dimensions and shape, appear within the larger frame. From the early cinema onward, this device has been used to present scenes of telephone conversations[...]. Multiple-frame imagery is also useful for building suspense[...]. We gain a godlike omniscience as we watch two or more actions at exactly the same moment" (Bordwell and Thompson 187). In some sequences Ang Lee follows the traditional use of split-screen mentioned by Bordwell by showing two characters like Bruce Banner and his estranged father, played by Nick Nolte, during a phone conversation or by presenting a relationship of cause and effect by connecting two events taking place in different places within the same frame. Although in those scenes the film provides the audience with knowledge about events taking place in separate locations, the use of split-screen also transcends the effect of an implied omniscient narrator. It raises the awareness of comic book syntax, for example when a smaller frame is moved within a larger shot as if the camera were imitating a reader's gaze looking at a series of panels.

Several scenes present the same person from different angles, for example, three shots of Sam Elliott as General Ross combined within one frame. The viewer does not gain any further knowledge from this composition. Rather, the redundancy of the visual content is meant to be reminiscent of the way in which panels are arranged in comic books. On the printed page the repetition of the same visual content within several panels can create the impression of passing time. According to the syntax of comic books, this

---

*The relevant time code for the sequence is 01:28–01:33 (DVD version of the film).

device can be considered as the equivalent of a slow-motion effect. Since the temporal structure of a comic can only be hinted at in an abstract way by the repetition of similar images, it must be constructed in the mind of the reader. In a film, a similar use of images within a split-screen composition disrupts the continuous temporal flow of 24 frames per second. Retransferred to the cinema screen, the visual composition of several frames showing similar phases of the same action does not fulfill the function of illustrating the passage of time like in a comic book any more. It rather illustrates the differences between both media.

Scott McCloud explains in his definition of comics as sequential art: "Each successive frame of a movie is projected on exactly the same space — the screen — while each frame of comics must occupy a different space. Space does for comics what time does for film" (7). Ang Lee's editing of *The Hulk* illustrates this definition in an innovative and sophisticated way. Instead of using it as a tongue-in-cheek reference to stylistic devices popular in thrillers from the 1960s, the director tries to find new ways to raise the consciousness for the configuration of time and space in films and comic books.*

Apart from the use of split-screen compositions, Ang Lee also resorts to a whole variety of other stylistic devices to create what he calls a "combination of comic book translation and horror film."† After watching the sample sequence and discussing its characteristic use of split-screen effects, other visual elements reminiscent of comic book aesthetics should be named by the students. For example, the inclusion of bright, almost neon colors, which is not very typical for a hidden military base, and the very stylized sound effects support the overall impression of the "larger-than-life" style of superhero comics.

One of the most obvious approaches toward the look of comic books is the use of freeze-frame when Banner's evil adversary, Talbot (Josh Lucas), is hit by the Hulk and suddenly stops in mid-air in a panel-like frame (at time code 1:33). In comparison to those eye-catching visuals, there are, in addition, rather more hidden devices meant to recall the aesthetics of a comic book: the occasional rapid change of distance between the camera and the portrayed action from one shot to the next is, like the split-screen effect, reminiscent of the images presented in panels. Another technique, employed by Sam Raimi in his *Spider-Man* films as well as by Ang Lee in *The Hulk*, is the jerky pan-

---

*If the sequence is discussed in an introductory course to film studies this might offer a good opportunity to discuss the split-screen effect in regard to film historical developments, for example, from its characteristic use in a classical action drama like John Frankenheimer's* Grand Prix *(USA 1966) to its nostalgic use in Quentin Tarantino's tribute to Blaxploitation cinema,* Jackie Brown *(USA 1997) and its representation of a disturbed state of mind in Bruce MacDonald's experimental teenager drama* The Tracey Fragments *(Canada 2006).*

†*Cf. the audio commentary on the DVD version of* The Hulk *(Universal Home Entertainment, 2003).*

ning of the camera in several scenes (for example during the sample sequence at time code 1:32). Since it is difficult to notice the digitally created distortion in movement, occurring when Talbot enters the hallway in which the Hulk has been trapped on a first viewing, the scene should be shown several times. Similar to the effect created by jump-cuts, made famous by Jean-Luc Godard in *À bout de souffle/Breathless* (France 1960), which interrupt the flow of a film by consciously leaving out parts of a character's or an object's natural movement, jerky panning disturbs the viewer's perception of the action. Just like the split-screen effects refer to the panel structure in comics, the use of jerky panning is reminiscent of the representation of movement in a comic book, which can only be depicted in a fragmented way either by using so-called speed lines within a panel or by adding the second phase of a movement within the next panel. On a more general level the camera position and angles used throughout *The Hulk* imitate the framing of comic panels as well. Instead of using highly dynamic hand-held cameras or the so-called steadycam system, stylistic choices that have become regular elements of many recent action films like *Mission Impossible 3* (USA 2006) and the *Bourne* series (USA 2002/2004/2007), Lee favors long and medium shots to present the action. The mobility of the camera within the frame seems to be rather limited. Instead of relying on mise-en-scène, which focuses on the staging of the events for the camera (including set design, lighting, and the choreography of the actors) and uninterrupted movements, in *The Hulk*, Lee is more concerned with the principles of montage, which echo the function of the "gutter," the elliptical space between two panels, in comics. If the analysis of the film is part of a film studies introduction, this discovery could also provide an interesting starting point for a discussion on why editing and reduced camera movements are maybe closer to the syntax of comic books than an elaborate mise-en-scène (which is nevertheless crucial in making the fictional world believable).

## Further Topics for Discussion

The discussion of the sample sequence can be extended to other questions for further sessions. Here are a few examples that can be varied according to the field of studies the course is part of:

- *The Hulk* turned out to be not as successful as Marvel and Universal Pictures had expected. What could be the reason for the film not having enough crossover appeal to mainstream as well as art house audiences? Do the rather abstract formal elements like the use of split-screen and

freeze-frame affect the audience's empathy with the main character negatively?
- Does Ang Lee offer a personal view on the material? Are there motifs, for example the focus on family structures, that connect to other films by the same director?
- Can Lee's directing style be compared to the individual approach taken by well-known comics artists and writers like Alan Moore or Frank Miller when they take on a popular superhero character like Batman for a stand-alone graphic novel?
- Ang Lee employs digital effects to break with the tradition of continuity editing and focuses on the cinematic recreation of traditional comic book aesthetics instead. In what other ways can technological developments be used to create a new synergy between film and comics? How does Sam Raimi use digital effects in his *Spider-Man* films? What sequences could be compared to the self-conscious approach taken by Lee, and are there also other situations that use digital effects in the tradition of classical continuity editing?
- Comic artists and writers like Frank Miller (*Sin City*), Dave McKean (*Mirror Mask*) and Enki Bilal (*Immortal*) became directors of their own material. Does this personal involvement influence the visual style of the finished film, and in what ways can digital technology help to make the transition from comics writer and/or artist to director succeed?

These are only a few examples to discuss the growing connections between film and comic books. Whether the boom of comic adaptations during the early-to-mid-2000s will continue or not, the synergetic effects achieved during those years indicate that the topic does not belong exclusively to film or literary studies but should be considered within the larger frame of ongoing interdisciplinary research projects.

FILMOGRAPHY

*Batman*. Dir. Tim Burton. Starring Michael Keaton, Jack Nicholson. Warner Bros. Pictures, 1989.

*Batman Begins*. Dir. Christopher Nolan. Starring Christian Bale, Michael Caine, Liam Neeson. Warner Bros. Pictures, 2005.

*The Birds*. Dir. Alfred Hitchcock. Starring Rod Taylor, Tippi Heddren. Universal Pictures, 1963.

*The Bourne Identity*. Dir. Doug Liman. Starring Matt Damon, Franka Potente. Universal, 2002.

*The Bourne Supremacy*. Dir. Paul Greengrass. Starring Matt Damon, Franka Potente, Julia Stiles. Universal, 2004.

*The Bourne Ultimatum*. Dir. Paul Greengrass. Starring Matt Damon, Julia Stiles, David Strathairn. Universal, 2007.

*Breathless [À bout de souffle]*. Dir. Jean-Luc Godard. Starring Jean-Paul Belmondo, Jean Seberg. 1960.

*Dick Tracy.* Dir. Warren Beatty. Starring Warren Beatty, Charlie Corsmo. Touchstone Pictures, 1990.
*The Fantastic Four 1–2.* Dir. Tim Story. Starring Chris Evans, Jessica Alba. 20th Century–Fox, 2005/2007.
*Grand Prix.* Dir. John Frankenheimer. Starring James Garner, Eva Marie Saint, Yves Montand. MGM, 1966.
*The Hulk.* Dir. Ang Lee. Starring Eric Bana, Nick Nolte, Jennifer Connelly. Universal Pictures, 2002.
*Immortal.* Dir. Enki Bilal. Starring Linda Hardy, Thomas Kretschmann, Charlotte Rampling. TF1 Films, 2004.
*Jackie Brown.* Dir. Quentin Tarantino. Starring Robert De Niro, Samuel Jackson, Pam Grier. Miramax, 1997.
*Mirror Mask.* Dir. Dave McKean. Starring Stephanie Leonidas, Jason Barry. Jim Henson Productions, 2005.
*Sin City.* Dir. Robert Rodriguez and Frank Miller. Starring Mickey Rourke, Elijah Wood, Clive Owen. Dimension, 2005.
*Spider-Man 1–3.* Dir. Sam Raimi. Starring Tobey Maguire, Kirsten Dunst. Columbia: 2002/2004/2007.
*Superman.* Dir. Richard Donner. Starring Christopher Reeve, Margot Kidder. Warner Bros. Pictures, 1978.
*The Tracey Fragments.* Dir. Bruce Macdonald. Starring Ellen Page, Libby Adams. Shadow Shows, 2007.

BIBLIOGRAPHY

Bordwell, David, and Kristin Thompson. *Film Art. An Introduction.* 7th edition. Boston: McGraw-Hill, 2004.
McCloud, Scott. *Understanding Comics.* New York: Harper Perennial, 1993.
Miller, Frank: *The Dark Knight Returns.* New York: DC Publishing, 1986.
Moore, Alan, and Dave Gibbons: *Watchmen.* New York: Titan Books, 1987.

# 23

# Comic Linguistics: Comics and Cartoons in Academic Teaching*

## Christina Sanchez

I am a linguist, and I am a comic lover. As I am trained academically to compare and contrast entities with regard to their similarities, differences and potential combinability, it follows almost inevitably that I should try to reconcile those two interests. In my own teaching, the central aims are the transmission of knowledge about linguistic phenomena and linguistic training in general. In this chapter, I wish to demonstrate that comics and cartoons[†] can be used in various ways to support those aims. As these art forms represent a combination of both text and image, with the image as the perceptively more salient part, they can be used in many contexts where images are traditionally employed. Seeing that language is its central preoccupation and research interest, linguistics is predominantly language- and text-based. In contrast to many other academic disciplines, such as art history, archaeology or geology, it cannot draw on many inherent visual or even haptic stimuli — for example, paintings, pot shards or pieces of rock. Therefore, comics and cartoons constitute perfect teaching material for linguists by permitting an increased involvement of the visual channel in addition to the printed or aural texts that are traditionally dealt with. After discussing some general advantages of comics and cartoons as teaching material, I will suggest how these art forms can be drawn on in linguistics courses.

---

*I am grateful to my former English teacher, Wolfgang Preuß, for swamping me and my fellow pupils with funny cartoons during my school days, thus showing me that they can be successfully employed in a teaching context. Another thank you goes to Mike Marks for permission to include his cartoon in this volume.

†Following Eisner (1985), the term comic is used here to refer to the sequential arrangement of more than one frame containing images and words, while the term cartoon refers to a single-frame entity. An intermediate category is formed by comic strips, which are arranged sequentially like comics, but which consist of a fairly small number of frames.

## WHY COMICS AND CARTOONS ARE IDEALLY SUITED AS TEACHING MATERIAL

The most important reason why comics and cartoons are ideally suited as teaching material is that they are intrinsically motivating.* In contrast to textbooks, which only a few students will consider spending their spare time with, comics are frequently read as a leisure-time activity (cf. *Medienpädagogischer Forschungsverbund Südwest* 5, 6). Thus, their introduction in the academic context may remind the students of positive private experiences. This claim may be further supported by the strong link that comics still bear to children as a target audience. For instance, the *Longman Dictionary of Contemporary English*, which is aimed at an English-learning audience, defines a "comic" or "comic book" as "a magazine for children that tells a story using comic strips" (LDOCE s.v. *comic*). Even though this statement may be criticized for its generality, the definition, which is simplified to meet its audience's needs, underlines stereotypical ideas about comics, namely that they are mainly read by children. While this may indeed be true of some comics, such as the *Bussi Bär* type, others, such as *Pin Up*, have a purely adult — or at least teenage — target audience. Many sequential works of art, though, have a fairly mixed readership. This is particularly true of humorous comics, such as *Asterix* or the *Calvin and Hobbes* strips. As a fair share of those comics and cartoons that are suitable as teaching material for linguistic purposes is read by children and adults alike, the students presented with comic/cartoon material may associate them with pleasant childhood experiences.

Comics and cartoons are now firmly situated on a level between high and low culture — but this was not always the case, as sequential art had a really bad reputation only a few decades ago. For instance, the formerly common opinion that reading comics makes people stupid is reported in Welke (8, 9), and Fröhlich Kämpf and Ramseier print the letter of a teacher who considers comics rubbish (6). In the meantime, comics have gained a high degree of acceptance as an art form. This is evidenced by the fact that there are now several festivals celebrating the so-called ninth art, such as the *Festival International de la Bande Dessinée d'Angoulême* and the biannual *Comic Salon* in Erlangen, Germany. Moreover, the awarding of the *Max und Moritz Prize*, Germany's most important comics award, is widely reported in the national press. However, this newly gained public esteem seems to apply more to adult than to children's comics, and less so to cartoons. For these reasons, one may claim that on a global level, comics and cartoons are still associated

---

*See Müller (2007, 33) for a discussion of the advantages of intrinsic motivation, such as remembering the learned items longer.

with subversion, at least to a certain degree — which makes them appear like a kind of break from academic content, something less serious than the usual teaching material, something that students can simply enjoy. In short, by being mediators between young people and adults, between high and popular culture, comics and cartoons are ideally suited as an intrinsically motivating teaching material that can draw students' attention to demanding linguistic phenomena in a playful way.

## Functions of Comics and Cartoons as Teaching Material

Apart from serving as intrinsically motivating items, comics and cartoons can fulfill several other didactic functions, some of which they share with images. Among the various didactic functions of visual items reported by Hawelka and Wendorff (138), the raising of attention is the first one mentioned. Not surprisingly, cartoons are often used as the starting point for lessons in the school context. On the academic level, Alberternst recommends using cartoons as a stylistic device in the introduction of academic lectures or courses to raise attention and to make a transition to the main part of the course session (87). The importance of attention-raising becomes clear when one considers that information that is to be stored in long-term memory must enter short-term memory first and be processed there — the requirement for this being that attention is focused on it (cf. Mietzel 245).

Another function of comics and cartoons that is often chronologically close to that of attention-seeking is their function of encouraging speech production (cf. Reinfried 418). In other words, the situation depicted in the comic/cartoon serves as a stimulus to verbal reaction by the students. This function is of particular interest where students are inhibited by the presence of a very large audience, so that a visual stimulus may serve as an encouragement by offering a structure or a shared basis to build their own statements on.

Other functions of comics and cartoons rely on their combination of images and language. Thus, they situate utterances, that is, what particular speakers say, in a context. This multimedial quality of comics and cartoons is particularly useful in the teaching of pragmatics, the branch of linguistics dealing with the meaning and effect of utterances and their conditions of use in particular communicative situations (Herbst, Stoll and Westermayr 168). Sequential art can be used to draw students' attention to such aspects as necessary extralinguistic world knowledge or situational constraints (cf. Bublitz 135).

Another very important argument in favor of the use of comics and cartoons in an academic context lies in the fact that the combination of images and language results in improved memorization (cf. Hawelka and Wendorff 140). This effect is reinforced by laughing: as new information is remembered better when it is connected to emotions, preferably positive ones,* funny comics and cartoons may contribute to the students' learning process. However, comics and cartoons should not be made use of simply for their own sake, but always with a particular didactic aim (cf. Hawelka and Wendorff 141). Furthermore, they should not be overused in teaching. They can only conserve their intrinsically motivating force if they are used sparsely. Otherwise, they will come to be viewed as standard teaching material, with all the ensuing associations.†

## COMICS AND CARTOONS IN LINGUISTIC TEACHING

Comic strips and cartoons being very short, they are usually better suited for use in class than the typically book-length comics — but of course, there are exceptions. For instance, McCloud's metacomic *Understanding Comics* (1993) was among the texts on the reading list for a semiotics course I once taught. In his second chapter, "The Vocabulary of Comics," McCloud discusses different types of signs. Even though he uses the terms *symbol* and *icon* in this context, his definitions do not coincide with the more common ones by Peirce (1955), which had been previously treated.‡ In this context, a comic fulfilled the function of a course text whose content was discussed in class.

More commonly, though, I use cartoons or comic strips as illustrative examples by showing a transparency or a PowerPoint slide that everyone in the audience can look at simultaneously. As I have a preference for funny cartoons or comic strips, the students typically react with amusement or even laughter, so that I can ask what they find amusing. Their description of the funny aspect in the particular cartoon or comic strip then serves as a transition into a particular topic. I shall restrict myself to a single example here, but it seems that there are comics and cartoons to illustrate all kinds of lin-

---

*Cf. http://arbeitsblaetter.stangl-taller.at/EMOTION/EmotionEntwicklung.shtml (13 August 2007).

†*This can be compared to the analysis of poems, where the wrong kind of teaching and forced interpretation may eventually result in the pupils'/students' aversion to this art form (cf. Rojahn and Schneider 29,30).*

‡*Thus, while Peirce defines* iconicity *as a sign's representation of its object mainly by its similarity (Peirce 105), McCloud uses the word* icon *"to mean any image used to represent a person, place, thing or idea" (McCloud 27).*

278  COMICS AS A NEXUS OF CULTURES—INTERDISCIPLINARY

An illustration of phonemic difference in German ("Camouflage, Miller! Not warning clothes!") (Mike Marks, "Untitled Cartoon." *www.querbilder.de/comix/197/197.html* (13 August 2007). ©2007, Mike Marks).

guistic phenomena.* One very common concept in phonetics and phonology, which deal with speech sounds, is the *phoneme*. It is defined as the basic unit of language that brings about a change in meaning and can be determined by a so-called minimal pair test: if two chains of sounds differ by a single sound in the same position, and if these two chains of sounds correspond to the form side of two words with different meanings, each of the two distinctive sounds is a phoneme (cf. Gimson 44, 45).

A German cartoon by Mike Marks illustrates this phenomenon nicely. The cartoon depicts a higher-ranking member of the army yelling "Tarnkleidung, Müller! Nicht Warnkleidung!"—that is, "Camouflage, Miller! Not warning clothes!"—at a naked subordinate, dressed only with a triangular traffic sign announcing danger, white-and-orange tape around the neck and a white-and-orange traffic cone as a hat. This combination of text and image shows very clearly that the word-initial sounds /t/ in the German word "tarnen" and /v/ in the German word "warnen" make all the difference between the verb "to camouflage" and the verb "to warn."

Cartoons need not necessarily serve merely to introduce a new topic. In the lesson following the introduction of particular linguistic phenomena, comic strips can also be used as stimuli for revision by asking which of the concepts treated during the previous meeting can be applied to the scene

---

*Teaching English linguistics to German-speaking students, I mainly use English comics and cartoons, but if a particularly good specimen is in German, I employ it nonetheless.

depicted in the cartoon. For example, Grice suggests that a cooperative principle rules conversation between speakers (45, 46). He proposes several maxims that are typically followed in conversations, such as being relevant, making one's contribution as informative as required and making it one that is true. When these maxims are violated, the hearer can make different inferences. There is a *Calvin and Hobbes* strip in which Calvin is sitting at the dinner table, looking suspiciously at his food, and he asks, "What's this?" His father's reply, "Taste it. You'll love it," leaves him unsatisfied, and he pushes away his plate, thinking, "You *know* you'll hate something when they won't tell you what it is" (Watterson 7). In this particular cartoon, Calvin's father is violating the maxim of quantity because he is not making his contribution as informative as required: he does not reveal what the food is, thereby attracting his son's suspicion. Calvin's experience tells him that in some cases, a speaker who quietly and unostentatiously violates a maxim will be liable to mislead (cf. Grice 49). The cartoon can thus be used to practice applying linguistic theory and terminology to an everyday language statement about communication.

Another way of integrating comics and cartoons into teaching is by using them as the basis for exercises. In linguistics courses on translation, practical exercises make a welcome change and allow for a more profound understanding of the problems that can arise during translation. Compared with the translation of texts, the translation of comic strips and cartoons involves the additional challenge that the target language text needs to suit the pictures. This can represent a real problem when the original text involves plays on words. Gary Larson cartoons are particularly well-suited for this task. For instance, the English word "bad" can mean "evil" as well as "decayed," among other things. In one of Larson's cartoons, both meanings are combined: we can see an open fridge in which a bowl of potato salad is holding up a gun and aiming at a bottle and a jug standing with their hands raised into the air. The cartoon's caption says: "When potato salad goes bad" (Larson 262). My students' first attempt at translation was the German word "böse," but this is not entirely satisfactory, as it only renders the "evil" aspect. They quickly noticed that the different facets of meaning of a word and its possible translation equivalents need to be checked against the extralinguistic pictorial context. After realizing this, the students arrived at the ideal translation equivalent "schlecht," which can be used both in a moral sense and in the sense of "decayed." The notion of polysemy* and context-sensitivity of translation equivalents can thus be illustrated very clearly with the help of comic art.

Another way in which comic strips and cartoons can be used is as dec-

---

*Polysemous words have more than one meaning (cf. Palmer 100).

orative elements.* Placed on handouts, they support the memorization of a particular worksheet by providing a mnemonic anchor. Thus more visually oriented students may remember years later that a particular exercise was on a handout with a cartoon about oranges in the bottom right corner. This mnemonic aid effect can be expected to be even stronger if the cartoons are related to the topic of the worksheet, for example, when a text about global English is decorated with a cartoon about the attitude of the English toward their language, and when this phenomenon is addressed in class. Decorative cartoons on examination papers may provide a moment of comic relief and ease the examinees' initial tension, and beyond the classroom, hung on the notice-board outside a university teacher's office with a few brief instructive notes, they may make waiting time pass more quickly and efficiently for students attending office hours.

Last but not least, comics and cartoons can be used in the way pictures have been traditionally used in primary schooling, namely as a reward. Some comics and cartoons can even supply a link between a particular season or holiday and linguistic content. Shortly before Christmas, the linguistics teacher can show the students comics, comic strips or cartoons that are related to linguistics — as a kind of immaterial Christmas "present," but also with the function of revision. Thus, a cartoon in which a character complains to his note-taking secretary, "If I say *Merry Christmas, Happy Holidays*, or *Season's Greetings*, I'm going to offend someone. Just say, *Bah Humbug*!" (Randy Glasbergen, www.glasbergen.com/images/cmas2.gif) can round off the discussion of political correctness in a sociolinguistics course right before the holidays.

## Summary and Conclusion

Comics and cartoons are intrinsically motivating. Students enjoy their usage in class. In addition, they are useful as exemplifications and can serve as mnemonic aids. I have suggested a variety of ways in which comic art can be integrated in the academic teaching of linguistics and can encourage all linguists whose style is compatible with comics and cartoons to use them in their academic teaching every once in a while.

### Bibliography

Alberternst, Christiane. "Rhetorik für die Hochschullehre." *Förderung von Kompetenzen in der Hochschullehre. Theoretische Konzepte und ihre Implementation in der Praxis*, edited by Birgit Hawelka, Marianne Hammerl and Hans Gruber. Kröning: Asanger, 2007, 85–106.
Bublitz, Wolfram. *Englische Pragmatik. Eine Einführung*. Berlin: Erich Schmidt, 2001.

*Comics do not lend themselves to this usage because of their length.

Chandler, Daniel. *Semiotics: The Basics.* London: Routledge, 2002.
Eisner, Will. *Comics and Sequential Art.* Tamarac, FL: Poorhouse, 1985.
Fröhlich, Arnold, Rolf Kämpf and Ernst Ramseier. *Handbuch zur Medienerziehung. Comics.* Vol. 2. Zurich: Sabe, 1983.
Gimson, A.C. *An Introduction to the Pronunciation of English.* London: Arnold, 1962.
Glasbergen, Randy. "Untitled Cartoon." www.glasbergen.com/images/cmas2.gif (17 August 2008).
Grice, H.P. "Logic and Conversation." *Syntax and Semantics* 3. *Speech Acts*, edited by P. Coole and J.L. Morgan. New York: Academic Press, 1975, 41–58.
Hawelka, Birgit, and Jörg A. Wendorff. "Medien in der Hochschullehre." *Förderung von Kompetenzen in der Hochschullehre. Theoretische Konzepte und ihre Implementation in der Praxis*, edited by Birgit Hawelka, Marianne Hammerl and Hans Gruber. Kröning: Asanger, 2007, 137–50.
Herbst, Thomas, Rita Stoll and Rudolf Westermayr. *Terminologie der Sprachbeschreibung. Ein Lernwörterbuch für das Anglistikstudium.* Ismaning: Hueber, 1991.
Larson, Gary. *The PreHistory of The Far Side. A 10th Anniversary Exhibit.* London: Warner, 1991.
*Longman Dictionary of Contemporary English.* 4th ed. with Writing Assistant. Harlow: Pearson, 2005.
Marks, Mike. "Untitled Cartoon." www.querbilder.de/comix/197/197.html (13 August 2007).
McCloud, Scott. *Understanding Comics: The Invisible Art.* New York: HarperCollins, 1994.
Medienpädagogischer Forschungsverbund Südwest. *KIM-Studie 2005. Kinder + Medien, Computer + Internet. Basisuntersuchung zum Medienumgang 6- bis 13-jähriger in Deutschland.* Stuttgart: MPFS, 2006. http://www.mpfs.de/fileadmin/Studien/KIM05.pdf (15 July 2007).
Mietzel, Gerd. *Pädagogische Psychologie des Lernens und Lehrens.* 6th ed. Göttingen: Hogrefe, 2001.
Müller, Florian H. "Studierende motivieren." *Förderung von Kompetenzen in der Hochschullehre. Theoretische Konzepte und ihre Implementation in der Praxis*, edited by Birgit Hawelka, Marianne Hammerl and Hans Gruber. Kröning: Asanger, 2007, 31–43.
Palmer, F.R. *Semantics.* 2nd ed. Cambridge: Cambridge University Press, 1981.
Peirce, Charles S. "Logic as Semiotic: The Theory of Signs." *Philosophical Writings of Peirce*, edited by Justus Buchler. New York: Dover, 1955, 98–119.
Reinfried, Marcus. "Visuelle Medien." *Handbuch Fremdsprachenunterricht*, edited by Karl-Richard Bausch, Herbert Christ, and Hans-Jürgen Krumm.Tübingen: Francke, 2003, 416–20.
Rojahn, Jobst-Christian, and Ulrich Schneider: "Gedichtinterpretation 1: William Wordsworth, 'I wandered lonely as a cloud.'" *Einführung in das Studium der englischen Literatur*, edited by Arno Löffler et al. 5th ed. Heidelberg: Quelle und Meyer, 1995, 29–45.
Stangl, Werner. "Die Entwicklung von Emotionen." http://arbeitsblaetter.stangl-taller.at/EMOTION/EmotionEntwicklung.shtml (13 August 2007).
Watterson, Bill. *Calvin and Hobbes.* London: Sphere Books, 1987.
Welke, Manfred. *Die Sprache der Comics.* 3rd ed. Frankfurt am Main: Dipa, 1972.

# About the Contributors

**Mark Berninger** teaches in the English Department at Johannes Gutenberg–Universität Mainz. His Ph.D. dissertation became a book, *Neue Formen des Geschichtsdramas in Großbritannien und Irland seit 1970* (*New Forms of History Play in Great Britain and Ireland Since 1970*). He is currently working on a new book on the impact of John Milton on later writers with a special focus on present-day references to *Paradise Lost*.

**Holger Briel** received his M.A. in Germanic languages from the University of Michigan, Ann Arbor, in 1985, and his Ph.D. in comparative literatures and cultural studies from the University of Massachusetts, Amherst, in 1991. He has published widely on subjects such as the pedagogy of cultural studies, media of mass communication, and new media.

**Georg Drennig** graduated with an M.Phil. from the University of Vienna, after writing his diploma thesis on *American Anxieties About Urbanity and the Batman Narratives*. He works as an English teacher in a middle school project for adolescent immigrants, teaches at the Department of Communications Science at the University of Vienna, and is currently working on a dissertation titled "The Globalization of the Local: Icons of Place in Time of the Pacific North-West in the 1990s."

**Jochen Ecke** studied English, French and film at Johannes Gutenberg–Universität Mainz, and graduated with a master's thesis on concepts of time and place in the later works of Alan Moore. In addition to his studies, he has directed a number of short films and commercials and has served as German translator for numerous comic books — works by Greg Rucka, Rod Espinosa and Ted Naifeh, among others.

**Jonas Engelmann** studied comparative literature, philosophy and politics in Mainz. His M.A. thesis dealt with *Auschwitz in the Works of Paul Auster and Hubert Fichte*. He is currently working on a Ph.D. dissertation about "Perspectives of Graphic Narration — The Aesthetics of Contemporary Independent-Comics," which is supported by a scholarship of the Hans Böckler Stiftung. He has published numerous articles on literature, comic and film and is editor of the popular culture magazine *testcard*.

**Paul Ferstl** is a lecturer in comparative literature at the University of Vienna. He studied comparative literature and German at the University of Vienna and the Université Libre de Bruxelles, worked as a research assistant and is currently writing a Ph.D.

dissertation dealing with interactions between literature and comics. His other research interests include the historical novel and the history of literary censorship in Austria.

**Mario Gomes** received his Ph.D. in cultural and literary studies at the universities of Bonn and Florence, Italy, in 2006 for a dissertation titled "Mind-Reading: A Poetological Model for the Interior Monologue." He is co-author of the experimental comic/design project *Maffia Dialogues*, together with the Italian designers Marco Ugolini and Alberto Vallesi (Florence, Italy).

**Gideon Haberkorn** graduated from Mainz University in 2004, and is now pursuing a Ph.D. in British studies, focusing on fantasy literature and the narrative construction of reality. He has also done work on children's literature and puppet theater, and he is a member of the International Association for the Fantastic in the Arts. He is completing his practical teachers' training, and makes frequent use of Bill Watterson's *Calvin and Hobbes* cartoons in both his Philosophy and English classes.

**Michel Hardy-Vallée** recently completed an M.A. thesis in English at McGill University on graphic novels: "Where Do the Pictures Fit in the *Overall* Picture? Graphic Novels as Literature." Founder of the bilingual *Hotel Critical Review/Revue Critique* multidisciplinary journal, he lives and works in Montreal, Quebec. A writer and photographer, his other research interests include bandes dessinée in Québec, photography, aesthetics, cognitive science, and philosophy of art.

**Dan A. Hassler-Forest** received his M.A. degree in film and television studies in 1999 from the University of Amsterdam, where he has been teaching since 2004. His academic work ranges from workgroups on genre to lectures for perspectives on games. Since 2005, he has also been teaching first-year lectures and seminars in the English literature department.

**Anne Hoyer** studied English and German at Humboldt-University of Berlin. She has also pursued Celtic studies in Berlin as well as English literature at Queen's University of Belfast, Northern Ireland. Her Ph.D. dissertation is "The Scottishness of *Oor Wullie*" (Ruprecht Karls–University of Heidelberg). She is currently working as a lecturer in linguistics at the University of Marburg. Anne Hoyer has published on the Scottish comic *Oor Wullie*. Current projects involve culturally specific aspects of the German comic *Karl* as well as Scottish names in *Oor Wullie*.

**Karin Kukkonen** completed her studies with a master's thesis on Alan Moore's *Watchmen* and now has embarked on a dissertation project on Bill Willingham's comic series *Fables*. She lives in Finland and Germany and teaches at the University of Mainz.

**Ben Little** is an associate lecturer in the media department at Middlesex University, where he is also completing his Ph.D. dissertation on Anglo-American comic books and the politics of the 1980s, "Politics in Pictures: The Influence of the 'British Invasion' on American Comics." When someone originally suggested that he should try writing something on comic books and semiotics, little did he suspect that comics would take over the next five years of his life.

**Paul M. Malone** is an associate professor of German in the Department of Germanic and Slavic Studies at the University of Waterloo, Canada. He is the author of *Franz Kafka's* The Trial: *Four Stage Adaptations* (Frankfurt: Peter Lang, 2003), and has also published on German drama, film, theater/performance theory, and virtual reality computer technology.

**Suchitra Mathur** teaches English language and literature at the Indian Institute of Technology, Kanpur, India. Postcolonial and feminist theories provide the theoretical framework for her teaching as well as her research, both of which have recently expanded to include Indian popular culture as represented by detective fiction, comic books, and Bollywood cinema.

**Anja Müller-Wood** is a professor of English literature and Anglophone cultures at Johannes Gutenberg–Universität Mainz (Germany). Her fields of research are early modern English culture and literature and 20th-century and contemporary Anglophone literatures. Her new monograph *The Theatre of Civilized Excess: New Perspectives on Jacobean Tragedy* was published last year by Rodopi, and she is currently working on a book about 20th-century and contemporary Anglophone confessional fiction from a biocultural perspective.

**Meral Özçınar** is a lecturer in film studies in the Faculty of Fine Arts at Canakkale 18 Mart University, Turkey. She is also a director of documentary films and a screenplay writer. Her research interests include philosophy and psychoanalysis with a special focus on theories of national identity, discourse, and narration. In addition, she works on a documentary film project about comics in the context of these fields.

**Jan Peuckert** studied management studies at Humboldt University, Berlin, between 1999 and 2005, and participated in an Erasmus student exchange to ISCTE, Lisbon, in 2001/ 2002. In 2001, he collaborated with Mario Gomes on the comic strip *Na Boca do Peixe*, published in *Os Fazedores de Letras*, Lisbon. He has been a research fellow in the Faculty of Economics and Management, Institute of Technology and Management, and chair of Innovation Economics of the University of Technology, Berlin (TU), since 2006.

**Andreas Rauscher** is an assistant lecturer in the Department for Film Studies at the Johannes Gutenberg–University of Mainz. His Ph.D. dissertation dealt with "The *Star Trek* Phenomenon," and as author and co-editor he has published books on the *Simpsons*, the *James Bond* series, and superhero films. He has written numerous articles on film and media studies and is currently working on a postdoctoral research project on the interdisciplinary perspectives of video game studies.

**Christina Sanchez** is currently working at the University of Augsburg, Germany. Before that, she studied English and French at the universities of Erlangen-Nuremberg, Reading, and Rennes. Her doctoral dissertation, which dealt with the consociation and dissociation of the English and German vocabulary, was supported by a scholarship from the German Studienstiftung des deutschen Volkes. She has been working as a freelance author for several years for dictionary publisher Longman/Langenscheidt and has also published widely in the field of language learning.

**Sandra Martina Schwab** teaches English literature at Johannes Gutenberg–University, Mainz, where she is currently working on her Ph.D. dissertation on dragon slaying and gender roles. Her research interests include folk literature, popular literature, in particular fantasy and romance, as well as life and society in early 19th-century

Britain. Among her recent publications are contributions to *The Greenwood Encyclopedia of Science Fiction and Fantasy* and to *The Encyclopedia of Popular Fiction*, forthcoming from Facts on File.

**Dirk Vanderbeke,** who has taught at the University of Wisconsin–Milwaukee, the University of Frankfurt/Main, Widener University in Chester, Pennsylvania, and at the University of Greifswald, holds a doctorate in English Literature from the University of Frankfurt/Main and is now chair of English literature at the University of Jena. His doctoral dissertation, "Worüber man nicht sprechen kann" (Whereof One Cannot Speak), dealt with aspects of the unrepresentable in philosophy, science and literature. His postdoctoral research projects included a study on "Theoretische Welten und literärische Transformationen" (Theoretical Worlds and Literary Transformations), which examines the recent debate about "science and literature" and science's role(s) in contemporary literature. He has also published on a variety of topics, for example, Joyce, Pynchon, science fiction, self-similarity and vampires.

**Dinah Zank** was born in 1980 in Ludwigshafen/Rhein, Germany. She is pursuing a master's degree in Japanese studies and East Asian art history at Ruprecht Karls–University in Heidelberg. Her research interests range from the aesthetics of Japanese girls' comics and contemporary Japanese art to the narrative court paintings of the Muromachi period. She is currently working as a guest curator and scientific researcher at German Film Museum and Museum für Angewandte Kunst in Frankfurt am Main, where she has co-organized the exhibition "Anime! High Art — Pop Culture."

# Index

À bout de souffle (film) 271
À la rechercher du temps perdu 62, 64
À l'ombre des jeunes filles en fleurs 64
ABC Warriors 147
Abu Ghraib 77
Action (magazine) 143–147, 150
Adaptation 3, 8, 23–26, 30–32, 60–63, 66–68, 171, 184, 255, 265, 266, 267
Adorno, Theodor 34
Advancer Tina 203
The Airtight Garage 258
Akira 191, 202, 225, 228
Alberti, Leon Battista 196, 197, 199
Album format 90, 92
Alice's Adventures in Wonderland 129, 130, 216
Alien from the Darkness 203
Alienation 76
Alienation effect 65
Allegory 28, 39, 146
Allen, Woody 263
Ally Sloper 238
Amar Chitra Katha 176, 177, 182
The Amazing Spider-Man (comics serial) 22, 266
Americanization 178, 179, 188, 250
Angoulême 275
Angus Óg 113
Angry Tessie 166
Animal Scroll 189
Anime 191, 198, 199, 201–203, 226
Anthropology 240
Anti-hero 25, 127–138
Anti-semitism 63
Apitz and Kunkel 99–107
Appadurai, Arjun 232
Arkham Asylum 130
Arkın, Cuneyt 171

L'Ascension du haut mal 47–49, 51–54, 57
Aslan, Mehmet 171
Asterix 102, 224–226, 238, 275
Astro Boy 189, 191, 226
Atatürk, Mustafa Kemal 167
Authenticity 46, 56, 58, 73, 80, 228, 231, 232
Autobiography 45–47, 51, 55, 56, 58, 91, 92
Azzarello, Brian 135, 136

B, David 46–58, 258
Babel 51
Babylon 5 22
Bacchus 105
Bachchan, Amitabh 177, 178
Bahadur (character) 176–178
Bakhtin, Mikhail 155, 158
Ballad 71, 72
The Ballad of Halo Jones 141, 145, 147, 148
Bana, Eric 30, 269
Banzai! 227, 229, 251
Barefoot Gen 45, 225
Barnes, Peter 262
Barthes, Roland 120, 123, 154, 200
Batman (character) 21, 37, 38, 41- 43, 127, 157, 181, 265, 272
Batman (comics serial) 18, 129–132, 135, 137
Batman (film) 25, 36, 266
Batman & Robin (film) 36, 131, 132
Batman Begins (film) 31, 34–42, 265
Batman Forever (film) 36
Batman Returns (film) 25, 266
Batman: The Killing Joke 35
Batman: Year One 35–37
Battle (magazine) 147

*Battle Angel Alita* 226
Battle of the Thermopylae 15, 16
*Battle Royale* 207
*Battleship Potëmkin* (film) 124
Baudelaire, Charles Pierre 87
Bava, Mario 13–16
*Bayçetin* 165
Bayeux Tapestry 70
*Baytekin* 164–166
*The Beano* 108, 113
The Beatles 141
Beatty, Warren 267
*Beck* 227
Becker, Boris 100
Bell, Allan 112
Belting, Hans 194
Benjamin, Walter 52, 53
Berger, John 208
Bergman, Ingmar 263
Berry, Halle 28
*Berserk* 227
Besson, Luc 207
*Beyblade* 227
Bhabha, Homi 181
Bilal, Enki 31, 205, 256, 272
Biography 72
*The Birds* (film) 267
*The Black Beach* 229
*Blade* (film) 26, 36
*The Blair Witch Project* (film) 73
*Blankets* 45, 256
*Bleach* 227
Bleed 121
Blockbuster 25, 28, 30, 35, 36, 73, 265
*Bloody Circus* 228
Bloom, Harold 35
*La Blue Girl* 203
Bolland, Brian 35, 142
*Bombaby* 181–182
Bond, James (character) 105, 154, 156
*Bone* 240
*Das Boot* 102
Bordwell, David 266
Borg, Björn 100
Bovary, Emma (character) 64
Bowman, Rob 25, 31
Brando, Marlon 105
Branson, Richard 175
Brassens, Georges 92, 93
Brecht, Bertold 124
Brentano, Clemens 104, 106
British Invasion 92, 140, 153, 159
Broadside 70–72
*The Broons* 109, 110, 112

Brösel 225
*Brought to Light* 74
Brown, Chester 90, 91
Brueghel the Elder, Pieter 70
*Bubbles from the Brunnens of Nassau* 105
Buckingham, Mark 151
Buddha 38, 198
*Buffy the Vampire Slayer* 22
Burak, Sezgin 171
Burikko 216
Burns, Robert 110
*Burst Angel* 227
Burton, Tim 24, 36, 266
Busch, Wilhelm 70, 89, 223
Buschová, Lenka 230, 231
Bush, George W. 35, 43, 74
*Bussi Bär* 275

*Calvin and Hobbes* 275, 279
Camera angle 24, 170, 221, 271
Camp 25, 31, 36
Campbell, Eddie 141
Canon 251, 256
*Captain America* 23
Captain America (character) 33, 154, 163
Caravaggio, Michelangelo Merisi da 105
*Card Captor Sakura* 218, 220, 226
Caricature 10, 102, 238
Carlsen Verlag 223–234
*Carrie* (1976) 27
Carrol, Lewis 129, 130, 216
Cartoon 10, 26, 28, 33, 75, 76, 79, 135, 176, 178, 191, 206, 274, 276, 277, 278, 280
*Cat's Cradle* 131
*Catwalk* 230, 231
Censorship 143, 145, 165, 167, 198, 201–204, 215, 224
Cervantes 197
CGI 23–25, 31, 265, 267
Chahine, Youssef 34
*La Charité de Giotto* 64
*Charley's War* 147
*Chasing Amy* 22
*Le Cheval blême* 51
*Chobits* 219
Choudhry, Chacha 176
Christian Solar Verlag 229
Churchill, Sir Winston 67
*City of Glass* (graphic novel) 61, 65
*Civil War* 26
CLAMP 218, 219
Claremont, Chris 21, 28, 29

Classicism 238
*Classics Illustrated* 60–63, 68
*Clerks* 22
Close reading 260
Close-up 19, 94
Clowes, Daniel 90
*Coçuk sesi* 166
Cognitive strategies 247
Colossus (character) 26
*Comic Party* 227
Comic Salon Erlangen 275
Comics Code 140, 142, 190
Comics in education 245
Comics literacy 235, 248
Comics studies 235
Coming-of-age 27
Coming-out 28
Conan Doyle, Arthur 104
Connelly, Jennifer 30, 269
Connery, Sean 105
Consumerism 179, 184
Content 242
Continuity editing 268, 272
Convention 88
*Cool Devices* 220, 221
Cotrim, João Paulo 118–126
Counter-culture 190, 216
*Cowboy Bebop* 226
Cox, Brian 27
Crawford, Robert 113
*Crewman 3* 229
*Crime and Punishment* 61
*Croc* 90
*Cromartie High School* 227
*The Crucible* 28
Cruikshank, George 63
Crumb, Robert 53, 142, 190, 225
Cultural Studies 240
Cyberpunk 199
Cyclops (character) 26

Dada 53, 199
Dafoe, Willem 23
*Daisuki* 227, 251
*The Dandy* 108
*Danger: Diabolik* 13, 14
*Danse Macabre* 70
Dare, Dan (character) 145
*Daredevil* 22
*The Dark Knight Returns* 22, 29, 35, 36, 151, 153, 157, 163, 268
*Darkman* (film) 24
*David* 105
Davidson, Bruce 27

Davidson, Peter 109
DC Comics 21, 22, 90, 142, 227
DC Thompson 108, 109
*Dead Poets Society* (film) 263
*DearS* 227
*Death Note* 207, 227
*Death Proof* (film) 202
DeFalco, Tom 143
Defamiliarization effect 241
Definition for comics 242
Delisle, Guy 90
Del Toro, Guillermo 24
Derrick (character) 105
Derrida, Jacques 121
*Detective Comics* 130
Devi (character) 175
Dialogue 2, 15, 55, 62, 64, 66, 173
Diamond Comics 176
Dick, Philip Kindred 146
*Dick Tracy* 267
Dickens, Charles 62, 63
Diderot, Denis 123
Diegesis 122
Dillon, Steve 142
Discourse 242
Disease 47, 51, 53, 55–57
Disney 60, 74, 192, 224
Ditko, Steve 21
*Dr. Jekyll and Mr. Hyde* 30, 266
*Dr. Slump* 226
*Dr. Strangelove or: How I Learned to Stop Worrying and Love the Bomb* 131
*Dogma* 73
Doillon, Jacques 207
Dôjinshi 188, 215, 228, 229
Donaldson, Dave 110
Donner, Richard 25, 26, 36, 266
Dostoyevsky, Fyodor 61
Doucet, Julie 46, 52–58, 90
*Dragic Master* 229
*Dragon Ball* 226, 228
Drawn+Quarterly 90
*Du côté de chez Swann* 64
*Dubliners* 87
Dunst, Kirsten 24
*Dünyayı Kurtaran Adam* 171
*DuO* 230
Dyptich 124
Dystopia 79, 80
*Dystopia: Love at Last Sight* 230

*E-Manga* 228
*Eagle* (magazine) 142, 145
Eastwood, Clint 27

Eco, Umberto 57, 58, 105, 172, 238, 242
Editing 30, 41
Education 60, 63, 72
Egmont Ehapa 223–234
Egmont Manga & Anime 223–234
*Eightball* 90
*1812 Overture* 42
Eisenhower, Gen. Dwight D. 67
Eisenstein, Sergei 124
Eisner, Will 11, 20, 45, 62, 63, 68, 122
*Elektra* (film) 31
Elektra complex 213
Elizabethan drama 253, 254, 255, 262
Elliott, Sam 30
Ellis, Warren 142, 151, 153, 156–161
Empowerment 185
Enlightenment 192
Ennis, Garth 132, 135, 137, 142
*Die Entdeckung der Currywurst* 62, 65, 66, 68
Epilepsy 46, 47, 50, 51, 53–56, 58
*Epileptic* 258
Escapism 168, 217, 222, 246
Ethnicity 128, 130, 131, 233
Europeanness 128
*The Evil Dead* (film) 24
Expression 242

*Fables* 151, 238
Fado 116, 120
*Fagin the Jew* 62, 63
*Fahrenheit 451* 80
Fandom 188, 227
*The Fantastic Four* (film series) 21, 23, 30, 31, 265
*Faust II* 61
Faustian pact 32
Fawkes, Guy 42
Feest Verlag 226
Feiffer, Jules 61, 62
*Fell* 151
Fellini, Federico 7, 8, 20
Feminism 55, 191
Fernandes, José Carlos 118
Fforde, Jasper 263
*Firefly* 22
*Fist of the North Star* 227
*Fix und Foxi* 224, 226
*The Fixer* 76, 78
The Flash (character) 21
*Flash Gordon* 164, 165
Flashback 19
Flaubert, Gustave 64
*Fluide Glacial* 191

Flusser, Vilém 2, 199, 200
Flying Robert (character) *see* Struwwelpeter
Ford, Harrison 105
Foreign language training 249
Formal devices 94
Formalism 86
Foster, Harold 89
Foucault, Michel 49, 50, 204
Fournier, Pierre 90
Fragmentation 49, 76
Frame narrative 65, 66
Franco, James 24
Franco-Belgian school 188, 200
*The Frank Book* 258
Frankenheimer, John 270
Frankenstein (character) 266
*Frankenstein* (film) 22
Frankfurt School 34
Franquin 91
*Freaky Angel* 230, 231
Free indirect speech 66, 67
Freeze frame 272
Freud, Sigmund 18, 212, 214
*From Hell* 12
*Fruits Basket* 226
Fry, Stephen 41
Frye, Northrop 238
*The Fugitive* (TV series) 30
*Full Metal Panic* 227
Fumetti 7, 13
Fundamentalism 179
*Fushigi Yugi* 226
Fuzokuga paintings 198

Gaiman, Neil 142, 153, 154, 253, 254, 255, 257, 258, 259
*Gasoline Alley* 45
Gaze 79
*Gemma Bovery* 62, 64
Gender 55, 145, 220–221, 230
*Genshiken* 207
Ghandi, Indira 183
Ghandi, Rajiv 179
*Ghost in the Shell* 226
*Ghost Rider* (2007) 31
*GI Joe* 38
Gibbons, Dave 35, 141, 151, 268
Gibson, Ian 141, 142, 145, 147–149
Gibson, William 146
*The Giddy Limit* 113
Giotto 199
*Girl* (magazine) 142
Girl power 217

Global 185, 195, 207, 208
Globalization 176, 179, 184, 185, 195, 207, 208, 250
Glocal 185
*God Loves, Man Kills* 28, 29
Godard, Jean-Luc 271
Godbout, Réal 90
*The Godfather* (film) 105
Goethe, Johann Wolfgang von 61, 103
Golden Age 151, 266
Gombrich, Sir Ernst 10
Good, Edmond 89
Goscinny, René 224
Gotham Comics 175, 184
*Gothic Sports* 230, 231
Gotlib, Marcel 95, 191
*Grand Prix* 270
Grant, Alan 141, 146
Graphic novel 1, 22, 90, 92, 95, 137
*Gravitation* 226
*Great Teacher Onizuka* 226
*Green Arrow* 22
Grimm, Jacob 216
Grimm, Wilhelm 216
*Grindhouse* (2007) 202
Groensteen, Thierry 11, 12, 15, 17, 20, 189, 205, 238, 239
Ground Zero 33
Guevara, Che 225
*Gundam* 226
Gupta, Sanjay 180
Gutenberg, Johannes 196
Gutters 122, 241, 271

Hage, Annika 230, 231
Hanuman 175
*Hara-Kiri* 90
Harrison, Ken H. 109
Head, Sir Francis Bond 105
*Heavy Metal* (magazine) 140
Heidegger, Martin 208
*Heidi* (anime) 106
Heine, Heinrich 104, 106
Heinrichs, Rick 19
*Hellblazer* 128, 135, 238
*Hellboy* (film) 24, 31
*Hello Kitty* 211
*Hellsing* 227
Hentai 205
Hergé 91, 224
Hermeneutics 240
Herzog, Felix 246
Heuet, Stéphane 62–64
Hilton, Paris 22, 159

Hinduism 180
Hippocrates 50
Historiography 71
Hitch, Bryan 151
Hitchcock, Alfred 7, 267
Hoffman, Michael 263
Hoffmann, Heinrich 104
Hogarth, William 70
Hokusai, Katsushika 203
Holler, F. James 246
Holmes, Sherlock (character) 104
Holocaust 73–74
Homosexuality 28, 188, 205, 230
Horrocks, Dylan 90
Horror 27
The Hulk (character) 21, 23, 154, 269
*The Hulk* (film) 13, 17, 19, 24, 30, 266, 267, 268, 270, 271
Hulton Press 142
Huxley, Aldous 146
Hybridity 199, 250

Iceman (character) 27–29
*Ichigo 100%* 227
Icon 277
Iconic turn 199
Iconography 183, 195, 198, 221
Identity 46, 111, 112, 117, 133, 147, 164, 167, 172, 182, 183, 185
Ideology 164, 165, 167–171, 182, 224
Illustration 57, 63, 64, 68
Imdahl, Max 193
*Immortal* (film) 31, 272
Imperialism 169
*In the Shadow of No Towers* 74, 75
*The Incredible Hulk* (film) 31
Independent comics 45
India 175–186
Indiana Jones (character) 105
Indrajal Comics 176
*Injukyoshi* 203
Inoue, Yasushi 207
Interdisciplinary education 249
Intermediality 255
Intertextuality 189, 254
*Inu Yasha* 226, 229
Iraq War 43
Irishness 130, 131
Irony 67, 217
*Iscel* 230, 231
Ishinomori, Shôtarô 225
Iwamoto, Yoshiharu 213
Iwamoto-Seebeck, Junko 228

*Jackie Brown* 270
Jackman, Hugh 26, 28
Janssen, Famke 27, 28
Jaxon 142
*Jibun-Jishin* 230
*Jimmy Corrigan* 258
*Jimmy das Gummipferd* 224
*Jôgaku zasshi* 213
Johnson, Mark Steven 31
Josetu 198
Journalism 3, 70–76, 79, 80
*Jubilee* 262
*Judge Dredd* (film) 25
Jump cuts 271
Jung, Carl Gustav 212–214
The Justice League 21
Juxtaposition 121

*Kabuki* 240
Kafka, Franz 62, 65
Kakalios, James 246
Kakuyu 189
Kaps, Joachim 227
Kapoor, Anil 178
Kapur, Shekar 177
*Kara Murat* 168–171
*Karaoğlan* 168, 170–172
Karasik, Paul 62, 65
*Karl* (comics series) 100–107
Kauka, Rolf 224
Kawaii 211, 212, 215
Kawaii-kei 215, 217–219, 221, 222
Kelman, James 113
*KERA Magazine* 216
Khalistan movement 183
*Kickback* 7, 8
*Kill Bill Vol. 1 and 2* (2003/2004) 202
Kindchenschema 111
King, Frank 45
King, Martin Luther 27
King, Stephen 27
*King of the Bandit Jing* 227
*Kingdom Come* 159, 161, 163, 238
*Kinova* 168
Kirby, Jack 162
Kitsch 250
*Das Kleine Arschloch* 225
Kline, Kevin 263
Koge, Donbo 221
Kohlsaat, Roland 224
Komiketto convention 215
Kominsky, Aline 191
*Kommissar Rex* 105
*Krazy Kat* 95

Kreitz, Isabel 62, 65–68
*Krrish* 175, 184
Kubrick, Stanley 131, 132
Kunkel, Eberhard 99–107
Kunkel, Patrick 99–107
*Das Kunstwerk im Zeitalter seiner technischen Reproduzierbarkeit* 53
Kuper, Peter 62, 65
Kurtzman, Harvey 95

Labs, Robert 229, 231, 232
Lacan, Jacques 193, 197, 208
Language learning 249
*Laocöon* 9, 124, 238
Lee, Ang 13, 17, 30, 31, 266, 267, 268, 269, 270, 271, 272
Lee, Spike 33
Lee, Stan 21, 22, 31
LeGuin, Ursula 146
Leonard, Tom 113
Lessing, Gotthold Ephraim 9, 10, 20, 124
Lester, Richard 25, 266
*Lève ta jambe mon poisson est mort* 55
Lewis, Albert Kanter 60
Lichberg, Heinz von 212
Lichtenstein, Roy 256
Lieber, Steve 18
*The Life and Opinions of Tristram Shandy* 62, 65
Linguistics 239, 278
Literacy 88
Literariness 86, 88
*Livewire Graphics* 60
Lloyd, David 7, 40, 145
Local 189, 194, 207, 208, 232
Lolita (concept) 211–222
*Lolita* (novel) 212, 213
Lolita complex 212–214
*Lone Wolf and Cub* 227
*Lord Haw Haw* 143
*Lords and Ladies* 263
Lorenz, Konrad 111
*Love Hina* 226
Low, Robert Duncan 109
*Lustige Taschenbücher* 191
Lutes, Jason 90

*Mad Magazine* 90
*The Madame Paul Affair* 55
Madness 50
Magneto (character) 27–29
Maguire, Tobey 23, 24
Mainstream 36, 45, 192, 266, 271
*Maison Ikkoku* 226

Malcolm X 27
*Malkoçoğlu* 168, 170, 171
Manara, Milo 205
*Mandrake* 176
Manga 140, 187–210, 211–234, 240, 246, 251, 256
*Manga Fieber* 228
*Manga Power* 227
*Manga-Talente* 228
*Manga Twister* 227
Mangascape 232
*MangasZene* 228
Marks, Mike 278
Marlowe, Christopher 259
*Marnie* 7
Marsden, James 26
Maruyama, Eri 233
Marvel Comics 21–26, 30, 31, 90, 143, 157, 191, 200, 225–227, 266
Marvel UK 142
Marx, Sascha Nils 229, 231
Masareel, Frans 70
Masculinity 134
Master narrative 46
Mathieu, Marc-Antoine 79
Matsuda, Seiko 215
Matt, Joe 91
Matte paintings 23
*Maus* 74, 86, 246, 256
*Max and Moritz* 223
Max und Moritz Prize 275
Mazzuchelli, David 62, 65
McCarthy, Joseph 27, 143
McCloud, Scott 70–79, 121, 201, 250, 257, 266, 270, 277
McDonald, Bruce 270
McDonaldization 176
McDuck, Scrooge (character) 106
McKean, Dave 31, 130, 142, 272
McKellen, Sir Ian 27, 28
McManus, Steve 144
McTeigue, James 34
*McTickles* 113
Media literacy 247, 248
Memory 51, 52, 54, 75
*Meng and Ecker* 143
Merleau-Ponty, Maurice 192–194, 208
Metadrama 255, 259, 261
Metafiction 103, 104, 262
Metapanel 122
Metaphor 14, 41, 49, 64–66, 74–76
Metonymy 49, 56
Michelangelo 105
*Mickey Mouse* (comics serial) 226, 256

*A Midsummer Night's Dream* 253–264
*Midsummer Night's Sex Comedy* 263
Mignola, Mike 31
Millais, Sir John Everett 213, 214
Millar, Mark 151
Miller, Arthur 28
Miller, Frank 13, 15, 16, 22, 25, 29, 31, 35, 37, 140, 151, 153, 241, 265, 268, 272
Mills, Pat 143, 146, 147
Mimesis 126
Mind map 257
Minimal pair 278
*Mirror Mask* (2005) 272
*Mise-en-page* 12, 15, 17–19
*Mise-en-scène* 15, 18, 24, 30
*Mr. India* 177, 178
Mitsukazu, Mihahara 216
Moe 218–220
Moebius 205, 238, 256, 258
*Mon-Star Attack* 230
Montgomery, Field Marshal Bernard 67
Moore, Alan 12, 13, 19, 25, 35, 40, 74, 141–143, 145, 147–149, 151, 153–157, 205, 241, 268, 272
Moore, Roger 105
Morris, Marcus 142
Morrison, Grant 130, 142, 153, 160, 161, 162
Morton, Tom 110
*Mother Courage* 124
*Moulin Rouge — La Goulue* 105
Movie novel 165
Mutant 27–30
*My New York Diary* 52–57
Mythology 180–183, 199, 238

Nabokov, Vladimir 212–214, 221
NACAE 245, 262
*Nadesico* 227
*Naglayas Herz* 229
Nagraj (character) 175–186
Nakazawa, Keiji 45, 225
*The Name of the Rose* 105
Narration 9, 10, 12, 16, 46, 47, 51, 62, 65, 66, 77, 78
Narrative 2, 8, 10, 17, 22, 34–37, 39, 58, 61, 62, 64, 65, 70, 74–76, 80, 119, 168, 170–173, 176, 190, 242, 246, 254, 259
Narratology 239, 242, 255
*Naruto* 226
Nast, Thomas 129
*National Lampoon* 90
National socialism 223, 224

Nationalism 165, 167–169, 172, 173, 176, 179, 181–185
Neill, Vic 113
*Nemesis the Warlock* 147
*Neon Genesis Evangelion* 226
New Journalism 73, 74, 78
New media literacy 251, 255
*New Treasure Island* 189
*Nextwave* 157–161
Nguyen, Nam 233
*Das Nibelungenlied* 104
*Nick Knatterton* 224
Nietzsche, Friedrich 156
Nightcrawler (character) 26, 29
*A Nightmare on Elm Street* (film) 27
*Nihon Keizai Nyûmon* 225
9/11 (event) 3, 33–35, 37–39, 43, 74–75, 159, 161
*09'11"01— September 11* (film) 33–34
Ninja 38
Nolan, Christopher 31, 34, 265
Nolte, Nick 30
Nonfiction 45
Noomin, Diane 191
Norrington, Stephen 26

Objectivity 76
Oda, Eiichiro 229
*Oh! My Goddess* 226
Oldman, Gary 41
*Oliver Twist* 62, 63
Omniscient narrator 269
*One Piece* 226, 229
O'Neill, Kevin 142
*Oor Wullie* 108–115
*Optic Nerve* 90
*Orcus Star* 230, 231
Orientalism 181, 188
Orwell, George 146
Otaku culture 215, 222
The Other 37, 38, 131–133, 137, 173, 188, 193, 199, 200
Othering 37, 137
Otherness 27, 127, 128, 132, 133, 135–137, 190
Otomo, Katsuhiro 191, 202, 225
Ozu, Yasujiro 207

Packard, Stephan 124, 240
Pai, Anant 176
*Palestine* 76, 77, 258
Palimpsest 194
Panini Verlag 226–234
Panofsky, Erwin 195

Paper cinema 165
Paquin, Anna 27
*Paradise Kiss* 227
Paratext 63, 65
Park, Judith 230–233
Parody 103, 104, 150, 220, 221, 230
La Pastèque 90
Pastiche 150
Patriarchy 173
*Paul à la campagne* 90
*Paul Has a Summer Job?* 92, 93
*Paul in the Métro* 91
*Paul Moves Out* 94, 96, 97
*Peace Maker Kurogane* 227
Pearl Harbor 33
Pedophilia 214
Peeters, Frederik 47
Peirce, Charles Sanders 277
*Pekos Bill* 167, 168
*Penthouse* 191
*Perfect Girl* 217
*Persepolis* 45
Perspective 221
Pfeiffer, Michelle 263
*The Phantom* 176
The Phantom (character) 179
Phoneme 278
Phonetics 278
Phonology 278
Photography 72, 73, 75, 76, 80, 199, 215, 243
Physiognomy 127, 129
Pictorial quotation 104
*Pin Up* 275
*Pilules bleues* 47
*PIP International* 191
*Pita Ten* 221
Plaka, Christina 230
Planet Manga 227
*Planetary* 153, 156–158
Play-within-the-play 255, 259
Plot device 181
Plot structure 221
Point of view 19, 30, 62, 76
*Pokémon* 226
*Pollyanna* 165
Polyphony 155, 163
Polysemy 279
Pop art 36, 214
Popular culture 22, 27, 28, 34, 35, 40, 168, 173, 177, 181, 185, 251
Pornography 204, 205, 212, 215, 220
Post-feminism 216
Postmodernism 46, 73, 158, 199, 208, 254

Pragmatics 276
Pratchett, Terry 106, 263
*Preacher* 128, 132, 134–137
Pre-Raphaelites 213
Pre-reading activity 254, 255
Prince Valiant (character) 89
*Promethea* 240
Propaganda 16, 33, 40, 172
Proust, Marcel 62, 64
*Prussian Blue* 230
Psychology 237
Psychosemiotics 240
*Pulp Fiction* (1994) 201
*The Punisher* (2004) 30
Pyro 27, 29

Rabagliati, Michel 90–94, 96, 97
Rabelais, François 158
Racism 169
Raimi, Sam 23, 24, 31, 265, 267, 270, 272
Raj Comics 175, 178
*Ranma 1/2* 226
Ratner, Brett 22, 25, 29
Rea, Stephen 41
Reader response criticism 240
Reagan, Ronald 141, 150
*Real Bout Highschool* 227
Realism 13, 54, 66, 73, 74, 76
*Red Dragon* (film) 29
*The Red Mask* 168
Red Rider (character) 89
Reformation 196
*Remember Pearl Harbor* (film) 33
Renaissance 196
Rentrop Verlag 225
Revisionary superhero narrative 35
Rhetorics 239
Riefenstahl, Leni 156
*Rising Stars of Manga* 228
Rite of passage 38
*Rob Roy* 112
*Robin* (magazine) 142
Rocha, Miguel 118–126
Rococo 218
Rodriguez, Robert 31, 265
Rogue (character) 27, 29
Role models 230
Romanticism 213
Romita, John 21
Ronin 219
Rorikon 211–222
*Rosencrantz and Guildenstern Are Dead* 263

Rosie, George 108
Rossetti, Dante Gabriel 214
Rowohlt Verlag 225
Rowson, Martin 62, 65, 68
*Rubrique-à-brac* 95
*Rush Hour* (series) 29
Russell, Bertrand 225

Sabu 176
Saccades 1, 11
Sacco, Joe 70, 76–79, 90, 258
Sadu (character) 175
*Safe Area Gorazde* 76, 78
*Saga of the Swamp Thing* 142
Said, Edward 37
*Sailor Moon* 207, 226
Salazar, António de Oliveira 116, 118, 120, 123
*Salazar — Now, in the Hour of His Death* 118, 120, 122–126
*The Sandman* 153, 154, 253–264
Satire 74
Satrapi, Marjane 45
Savoy 143
Schamus, Gareb 18
*Der Schimmelreiter* 104
Schmidt, Manfred 224
Schodt, Frederic 201
*School Rumble* 227
Schumacher, Joel 25, 36
Schwarzenegger, Arnold 132
Scott, Sir Walter 112, 262
Secret identity 177–179
Seebeck, Jürgen 228, 231
*The Seduction of the Innocent* 246
Seleque, John P. 246
Self-reflexivity 46
Semiotics 238, 239, 277
Sequel 63, 122
Sequence 121–122, 190
*Sgt. Frog* 227
Serial narrative 24, 188
*Sesame Street* 106
Seth 90–91
Sexuality 55, 198, 202–204, 207, 246
*Shahenshah* 178
Shakespeare, William 253–264
Shelley, Percy Bysshe 155
Shelton, Gilbert 142, 190
*Shinkan Special* 228
Shintoism 198, 203
Shklovsky, Viktor 241
Shôjo bunka 214, 217
*Shôjo kurabu* 213

Shôjo manga 214, 215, 218, 220, 226, 227, 231, 251
*Shônen kurabu* 214
Shônen manga 226, 227, 229, 251
Shuster, Joe 89, 156
Siegel, Jerry 156
Sienkiewicz, Bill 74
Sign 238
*Sigurd* 224
*Silent Möbius* 227
Silver Age 21, 36, 153, 266
Sim, Dave 240
Simulacrum 232
Simmonds, Posy 62–64, 68
*A Simple Plan* (1998) 24
Simpson, Jessica 159
*The Simpsons* 227
*Sin City* (film) 22, 31, 265, 272
Singer, Bryan 23, 24, 26, 28, 29, 31
Singh, Fauladi 176, 177
Situation comedy 24
*Slaine* 147
Slapstick 24
Slow-motion 270
*A Small Killing* 12, 13, 19
Small press 240
Smith, Jeff 240
Smith, Kevin 22
Snyder, Zack 13, 15–17
*Something Rotten* 263
*Sommarnattens Leende* (1955) 263
Space 12–13
*Spawn* (1997) 25
Speed lines 66
*Speed Racer* 191, 201
Spider-Man (character) 21–26, 33, 153, 154, 176, 178, 179, 181, 184, 185
*Spider-Man* (film series) 23, 24, 30, 31, 36, 265, 267, 270, 272
*Spider-Man: India* 175, 184
Spiegelman, Art 53, 61, 74–76, 246
*The Spirit* (2008) 31
*Spirou* 89, 92
Spitzweg, Carl 105
"Spleen" 87
Split-screen technique 17, 18, 30, 267, 269, 270, 271
Spyri, Johanna 106
Stallone, Sylvester 105
*Star Trek* 27, 179
*Star Wars* 171
Stephenson, Neal 146
Stereotype 63, 114, 127, 130–132, 134, 135, 137, 181, 275

Stevenson, Robert Louis 189
Stewart, Patrick 27, 28
Stone, Oliver 34, 43
Stoppard, Tom 263
Storm (character) 26
Storm, Theodor 104
Story 242
Story, Tim 31, 265
Storyline 62–63, 66
Straczynski, J. Michael 22
*Strangers in Paradise* 238
Strauss, Johann 171
Structuralist 86, 242
*Der Struwwelpeter* 104
Subculture 212, 216, 222, 227, 246
Subjectivity 46, 80
Suicide, Richard 90
*Super Gordon* 166
Superhero 22, 26, 31, 33–36, 38, 39, 42, 43, 47, 90, 153–163, 175–186, 191, 192, 240, 241, 250, 265, 270, 272
Superman (character) 21, 28, 89, 151, 154, 179, 185
*Superman* (comics serial) 176, 226, 256, 266
*Superman* (film series) 25, 26, 36, 266
Supremo (character) 177
The Surreal 47, 51, 57
Surrealism 74, 199
Surrealistic images 66
Suspension of disbelief 242
*Swift* (magazine) 142
Symbol 40, 47, 49, 54, 111, 119, 218, 277
Symbolism 213, 221
Synechdoche 93

Takabatake, Kashô 213
Takahashi, Rumiko 229
Takemoto, Novala 216
Takeuchu, Naoko 226
Talbot, Bryan 142
*Tales of Genji* 216
*Tankôbon* 219
Tappert, Horst 105
Tarantino, Quentin 201, 270
Target audience 275
*Tarkan* 165, 168, 170, 171
*Tarzan* 238
Tchaikovsky, Pyotr Ilich 42
Television 22, 23, 30, 36, 40, 75, 184
*The Tempest* 259
Templesmith, Ben 151
*Tenchi Muyo* 226
*Tenjo Tenge* 227

Tenniel, John 129
Tentacle sex 202, 203, 205, 220
Terrorism 35–38, 40–42, 162, 183
Tezuka, Osamu 189
Thatcher, Margaret 141, 144, 147, 149, 150
Theme 87, 94
The Thing (character) 154
*36 Views of Mount Fuji* 189
Thompson, Craig 45
Thompson, Kristin 266
*300* 13, 15, 19
Tijuana Bibles 70
Time 2, 9, 119, 121–122, 126
Timm, Uwe 62, 65
*Tintin* 89, 92, 111, 224, 238
*To the Heart of the Storm* 45
Todorov, Tzvetan 242
Tokyopop 219, 220, 227–234
*Tomb Raider* 229
Tomine, Adrian 90
*Tommiks Texas* 168
Tomoko, Hayakawa 217
Töpffer, Rodolphe 10, 70
Topic 94
Tör, Vedat Nedim 167
Toriyama, Akira 226, 229
Toulouse-Lautrec, Henri de 105
*The Tracey Fragments* (2006) 270
Transgression 51
Translation 191, 232, 279
Trauma 3, 21, 34–39, 41, 48, 51, 74, 80, 172, 213
Travesty 259
*Treasure Island* 189
Trembles, Rick 90
*The Triumph of Death* 70
Turan, Abdullah 169
Turan, Rami 169
Turkey 164–174
Turning point 66
*25th Hour* (film) 33
*Twisted Sisters* 191
*2000AD* 140–152
*Tykho Moon* (film) 31

*U-Comix* 191
Uderzo, Albert 224
*The Ultimates* 151
Underground 24, 45, 53, 90, 140, 190, 225
*Understanding Comics* 250, 257, 266, 277
*United 93* (2006) 34
Universal Pictures 30
*Urotsukidoji – Legend of the Overfiend* 202

Utatane, Hiroyuki 220
*Uzay* 166

*V for Vendetta* (film) 31, 34–36, 40–41
*V for Vendetta* (graphic novel) 40
Valium, Henriette 90
Varley, Lynn 13, 15
Velontrova, Luisa 233
Vertigo 160
Vess, Charles 253–258
Victorian age 216, 218, 259
Video games 23, 229
*Vimanarama* 160
Violence 201, 207, 246
Virgin Comics 175, 184
Visual art(s) 9, 10, 23, 61, 169
Visuality 24, 30–32, 46, 53–55, 61, 63, 64, 71, 73, 75, 77–80, 96, 119, 169, 170, 183, 184, 185, 190, 199, 201, 204, 206, 208, 231, 246–248, 265, 270, 274, 276
VIZ Communications 227
Völker, Alexandra 230, 231
Vonnegut, Kurt 131
Voss, Stefan 229
Voyance 194
Vu, Nhung 233

Wagner, John 141, 143
Waid, Mark 159
Ware, Chris 90, 91, 258
*Warrior* (magazine) 142
*Watchmen* 12, 35, 151, 153–157, 268
Watkins, Dudley Dexter 109, 111
*Waverley* 112
Wayne, John 105
*We* 146
*Wee Jimmy* 113
Weir, Peter 263
Welsh, Irvine 113
Welz, Larry 190
*Werner* 225
Werner, Nina 230
Wertham, Fredric 88, 128, 167, 246
Western 168
Westernization 173
Wetzel, Gina 230, 231
Whale, James 22
Whedon, Joss 22
Willingham, Bill 151
*Wimmen's Commix* 191
*Witches Abroad* 106
Wittgenstein, Ludwig 193
*The Wizard of Oz* 106
Wolverine (character) 26, 29

Wonder Woman 21, 154
Woodring, Jim 258
*World Trade Center* (film) 34, 43
World War I 147
World War II 33, 89, 135, 160, 167, 214, 224
*Wyrd Sisters* 263

The X-Men (characters) 21, 22, 27, 28
*X-Men* (film series) 28, 31, 36
*X-Men 2* (film) 27, 28
*X-Men 3—The Last Stand* (film) 22, 25, 26, 29, 30
*X2* see *X-Men 2*
Xie, Simone 233

*Y Square* 230, 231
Yalat, Suaz 172

Yamato, Waki 213
Yang, Tian 233
*The Yellow Kid* 238
Yildirim, Reyhan 233
*Yonen Buzz* 230
*Young Magazine* 219
Youth culture 222, 249, 250, 251
*Yu-Gi-Oh!* 226
Yuen, Corey 28

Zamyatin, Yevgeny 146
Zarate, Oscar 12
Zedong, Mao 225
Zhou, Ying 233
Zimmermann, Detta 230, 231

www.ingramcontent.com/pod-product-compliance
Lightning Source LLC
Chambersburg PA
CBHW051209300426
44116CB00006B/496